TRAVELS

IN

BELOOCHISTAN

AND

SINDE

TRAVELS

IN

BELOOCHISTAN

AND

SINDE;

ACCOMPANIED BY

A GEOGRAPHICAL AND HISTORICAL ACCOUNT

OF

THOSE COUNTRIES,

WITH A MAP.

BY LIEUTENANT HENRY POTTINGER

GYAN

Published by

GYAN

Gyan Publishing House
5, Ansari Road
Daryaganj, New Delhi-110002
Phone: 011-47034999, 9811692060
E-mail: books@gyanbooks.com

Distribution Network
gyanbooks.com
India, USA, Canada, UK, Australia

ISBN: 978-81-212-5979-8 (PB)
First Published, 1816

2nd Impression 2024

Printed at: Gyan Press, Delhi.

TRAVELS IN BELOOCHISTAN AND SINDE
AUTHOR: LIEUTENANT HENRY POTTINGER

TRAVELS

IN

BELOOCHISTAN

AND

SINDE

TRAVELS

IN

BELOOCHISTAN

AND

SINDE;

ACCOMPANIED BY

A GEOGRAPHICAL AND HISTORICAL ACCOUNT

OF

THOSE COUNTRIES,

WITH A MAP.

BY LIEUTENANT HENRY POTTINGER,

OF THE HONORABLE EAST INDIA COMPANY'S SERVICE;

ASSISTANT TO THE RESIDENT AT THE COURT OF HIS HIGHNESS THE PEISHWA;

AND LATE ASSISTANT AND SURVEYOR WITH THE MISSIONS

TO SINDE AND PERSIA.

LONDON:

PRINTED FOR LONGMAN, HURST, REES, ORME, AND BROWN,

PATERNOSTER-ROW.

1816.

TO

THE RIGHT HONORABLE

THE EARL OF MOIRA,

GOVERNOR-GENERAL AND COMMANDER-IN-CHIEF OF

BRITISH INDIA.

A NOBLEMAN EQUALLY DISTINGUISHED BY

HIS EXALTED STATION AND RANK,

HIS NUMEROUS VIRTUES AND TALENTS,

AND HIS ANXIOUS DESIRE TO PROMOTE THE ACQUIREMENT

OF USEFUL KNOWLEDGE,

THIS WORK

IS, BY PERMISSION,

MOST RESPECTFULLY DEDICATED,

AS A SMALL AND VERY INADEQUATE TOKEN

OF THE

PRIVATE GRATITUDE AND PUBLIC ESTEEM

OF

HIS LORDSHIP'S

MUCH OBLIGED AND FAITHFUL

HUMBLE SERVANT,

THE AUTHOR.

CONTENTS.

INTRODUCTION.

CHAP. I.

CHAP. II.

CHAP. III.

CHAP. IV.

CHAP. V.

CHAP. VI.

CHAP. VII.

CHAP. VIII.

CHAP. IX.

CHAP. X.

CHAP. XI.

CHAP. XII.

CHAP. XIII.

CHAP. XIV.

CHAP. XV.

CHAP. XVI.

CHAP. XVII.

PART II.

CHAP. I.

CHAP. II.

CHAP. III.

CHAP. IV.

CHAP. V.

CHAP. VI.

CHAP. VII.

CHAP. VIII.

CHAP. IX.

CHAP. X.

APPENDIX.

PREFACE.

THE general outlines of the subsequent pages were originally compiled in an official Report of a journey performed in 1810, and submitted to the Right Honourable the Governor-general in Council, for the information of the Supreme British Government of India, under whose immediate auspices the service was undertaken. I have since been enabled to add many particulars of a geographical and statistical nature to the contents of that Report; but, as the use *for which it was in the first instance drawn up,* necessarily *excluded* the detailed insertion of the anecdotes and relations that are comprised in this volume, it has, on a revision, appeared to me advisable to separate them from the former in the shape of a diary; and, accordingly, I have studied to include in the First Part of it such incidents as I thought curious or amusing, without subjecting myself to being charged with prolixity; while the Second Part contains the sum of my inquiries on the geography and statistics of Beloochistan and Sinde. The line has, however, been difficult to draw, and to some of my readers, on a transient perusal, a few of the descriptions in the narrative will probably appear trifling; but, at the same time, I conceive they may be deemed very interesting as of countries utterly unknown to Europeans, of whose people, governments and customs no records are extant since the time of Alexander the Great.

This last consideration, seconded by the solicitations of several esteemed friends, has alone induced me to appear before the public as an author; but, in adopting that resolution, as I disclaim all attempt at learned research or classical precision in the composition of my pages; I trust, in an equal degree, to the indulgence of the readers of this volume for any part of it that may be found unsatisfactory in matter, or deficient in style. The disguise in which I chiefly travelled, and the avowed indifference that that circumstance obliged me to assume, on the generality of subjects, together with the utter impossibility of taking detailed notes, will account for some omissions in the Second Part, that I have not been able to ascertain to my satisfaction since my return to India. It is also proper to observe, that a few of the geographical and statistical facts inserted in my account of Beloochistan, have already appeared in print in a summary shape in the valuable geographical memoir of the Persian Empire, published last year by Lieutenant Macdonald Kinneir, who had, for that purpose, access to the official documents forwarded to the East India House from Bengal; but as I have been enabled, by personal observation and very recent inquiry, not only to confirm their authenticity, but considerably enlarge them, I consequently omit no portion of them, and have merely thought it requisite to advert to that work in order to account for the coincidence that will appear with it in some places of this, both in language and matter.

Conscious as I am of the field for classical disquisition and conjecture, which I have journeyed over, I must here observe, that such topics are in direct opposition to the plan on which I have ventured to publish my travels; and also demand a much more intimate knowledge of the ancient state of the countries in question than I possess, and therefore, I have avoided entering into digressions upon them at any length, or adducing comparisons, unless they struck me to be so obvious as to require little comment.

I have now to perform the gratifying, though melancholy duty, of acknowledging the use I have made in this volume of the original Notes of my lamented friend and fellow traveller, the late Captain Charles Christie, of the Bombay Native Infantry, a man eminently gifted with all the feelings that could adorn a gentleman, a soldier, a scholar, a relation, or a friend. I have likewise to avow my thanks to Captain William Maxfield, of the Bombay Marine, for his ready acquiescence in my availing myself of his official communications on the province of Sinde. To another gentleman, whose name I have taken an opportunity of stating in the body of the work, I feel under such manifold obligations for his advice and opinions in the course of the compilation of it, that I shall not attempt to express them. To Captain Robert Close, first assistant to the resident at Poonah, I cannot omit to offer my thanks for the various kind suggestions he has favoured me with, on subjects also included in this volume. In conclusion, I have to add, that I am indebted to the perusal of a report on the province of Sinde, drawn up by Henry Ellis, Esq., M. P. (first assistant to the envoy to that Court in 1809,) for some particulars relative to the revenues and population of the country at that period.

NOTICE REGARDING THE MAP.

WITH respect to the construction of the map a very few words will suffice. The journey which I performed in 1810 furnished me with the grounds of my recent inquiries on Beloochistan, and the circumstance of my having accompanied the envoy to the court of Sinde in 1810, with the basis of those on that province. The routes of Captains Grant and Christie, as well as my own, are laid down from original papers, except that the positions at which they commenced and terminated having been, before or since, ascertained by means of observations, I have adopted their actual latitudes and longitudes. The native routes have been collected and compared with the most scrupulous care. Each province was, in the first instance, exclusively the object of my inquiry, and when I had satisfied myself on it, or was unable to obtain further information, I proceeded to another, and eventually embodied the whole. Of some of them I have projected six or seven different maps, and the method I finally resorted to to prove their correctness was, to explain the points of the compass to natives of particular districts, shew them any stationary town or village, and desire to be informed, where other towns of the same district lay. Whenever two of my informants disagreed, and I had an opportunity of doing so, I confronted them, and if they could not demonstrate on which part the error lay, I suspended my judgment until I could find other people who were acquainted with the disputed point. On some important places I have had the combined testimony of upwards of one hundred natives, the medium of which I have adhered to, and I have shewn my map to a man who had been in the habit of travelling in Sinde, and the province of Kutch Gundava, who, after he had had the situation of Hyderabad, the capital of the former province, explained to him, pointed out every place that was mentioned with astonishing precision. The river Indus has engaged my most particular attention, and I venture to pronounce it to be altogether as free from error as any thing of the kind can possibly be without actual survey. A portion of it has been ascertained by the latter method, by Captain Maxfield, of the Bombay Marine, and as I found my native accounts to correspond with what he had fixed, and I had myself seen; it was a satisfactory testimony towards the general reliance to be placed on it all. My geographical and historical account of the Persian province of Kirman is partly derived from Persian manuscripts, partly from oral inquiries, and partly from my own route through it.

PART THE FIRST.

NARRATIVE

OF

A JOURNEY

THROUGH

BELOOCHISTAN, AND A PART OF PERSIA,

PARTLY PERFORMED IN THE DISGUISE OF A MOOSULMAN PILGRIM,

CONTAINING

ANECDOTES AND DESCRIPTIONS

ILLUSTRATIVE OF THE MANNERS AND HABITS OF THE NATIVES,

WITH THEIR DIVISIONS INTO TRIBES, &c. &c.

INTRODUCTION.

FRENCH VIEWS ON INDIA. — EMBASSY TO PERSIA. — EMISSARIES. — BRIGADIER-GENERAL MALCOLM AND SIR HARFORD JONES DEPUTED TO TEHERAN. — THE LATTER WHY SENT. — GENERAL MALCOLM'S INSTRUCTIONS. — RECAL OF HIS EMBASSY. — RE-APPOINTMENT. — OBJECT IN VIEW. — CAPTAIN CHRISTIE AND THE AUTHOR VOLUNTEER THEIR SERVICES. — ACCEPTED. — INSTRUCTIONS AND ARRANGEMENTS. — OBSTACLES CONSIDERED AND ANTICIPATED. — ACCREDITED AS AGENTS OF A NATIVE HORSE DEALER. — HOW PROVIDED.

IN the course of the years 1807 and 1808, the long professed hostile schemes of Buonaparte became so conspicuously active and decided, with regard to British India, that our Governments, both at home and abroad, judged it indispensably necessary, to take steps to counteract those efforts. At the close of the former year, an embassador from France had been received with distinguished marks of friendship and attention, at the Persian court; and the emissaries of that nation were diligently employed in the acquisition of all such local information, as could, in any way, tend to secure the ultimate success of the object in view.

In the month of February 1808, Brigadier-General Malcolm was accordingly deputed as envoy to the Persian monarch, by the Right Honourable the Governor-General of India *; and about the same period, Sir Harford Jones was dispatched from England, in a similar character, furnished with credentials, bearing the sanction of His Majesty's name; a measure adopted, to afford him, in his nego-

* The Earl of Minto.

tiations with the ruler of the Persian empire, a weight and dignity to which the representative of a secondary government, however distinguished and exalted, could not be supposed to have pretensions.

The instructions with which General Malcolm was provided by the Bengal Government, pointed out to him, in general terms, the advantages to be anticipated, from making every possible exertion to ascertain the nature and resources of those countries, through which an invading European army might advance towards Hindoostan; and likewise sanctioned his employing, in the capacity of political assistants, or surveyors, any number of officers he should deem requisite, to give full effect to this suggestion.

Subsequent events, to dwell upon which would be entirely irrelevant to the subject of this Narrative, induced the Supreme Government to recal Sir John Malcolm, and postpone his mission until the latter end of the year 1809; when he arrived, a second time, at Bombay, on his way to the Persian capital. Captain Charles Christie, of the 5th regiment Bombay Native Infantry, and I were then just returned from Sinde, whither we had accompanied the Envoy on the part of the Governor-General; and on being made acquainted with the proposed plan, of exploring the regions between India and Persia, we volunteered to attempt the tour which is detailed in the following pages.

Our services having been accepted, and the authority of the Government of Bombay obtained for their being thus appropriated, I was directed by General Malcolm to place myself under the orders of Captain Christie, who received his instruction from the General: these instructions were of that indefinite tenor, which the very nature of the service we were about to proceed upon, demanded. They called our attention to such leading points as were most likely to merit the notice of Government, and meet the intention of that enlightened policy that had sanctioned the original measure; but, at the same time, they fully authorized us to select, with respect to our progress, mode of travelling, ultimate destination, and, in fact, all minor points, such a line of conduct as the circumstances we were placed in might render advisable; and were only peremptory in reminding us, that we were to regard our personal safety, beyond every other consideration.

It had been generally remarked, that a very principal obstacle to the accomplishment of similar undertakings, to that on which Captain Christie and myself were bent, had originated at the very commencement of them, owing to the great difficulty attendant upon an advance from the sea coast, where most Asiatics are known to be more suspicious of, and uncivil to European strangers, than at some distance inland. An arrangement, therefore, to effect our first outset from the port at which we might land, was considered of the last importance to us; and we were fortunate enough to succeed in making one, to which no possible objection could be discovered.

A Hindoo merchant, of great respectability and wealth, called Soondurjee Sewjee, who had been for many years preceding, the contractor for supplying the governments of Madras and Bombay with horses, to mount the cavalry of those two Presidencies, offered, (on being consulted as to the best mode for us to proceed) to furnish us with letters and bills, accredited as his agents, and dispatched by him to Kelat, the capital of Beloochistan, to purchase horses; from which city he observed, that we could follow such route as local knowledge might point out to us; and that, even in the extreme case of being forced to fly, we could take a different road towards the sea coast, from that which we travelled in going, and thereby secure, almost beyond a doubt, seeing a great portion of the country.

The bills and letters for us were, therefore, prepared; and a Hindoo Goomashtuh, or agent, of Soondurjee, named Peetumberdass, was appointed to accompany us as far as Kelat, for the purpose of giving a greater air of plausibility to our avowed characters. Captain Christie and myself, also selected two Hindoostanee men, who were bound to secrecy by promises of large presents, and whose fidelity and honesty, in the result, proved most exemplary. We were also, each furnished with a considerable sum of money, in gold Venetians, intended to use as a dernier resort, in case of the utmost necessity: these we carried in belts, tied round our waists, underneath our clothes; and, in addition to this supply, Captain Christie was empowered to draw bills on the government of Bombay, in favor of Soondurjee Sewjee, to any amount he might find necessary; so that nothing was omitted in our equipment, which could enable us to surmount opposition, and extricate ourselves from difficulties, or dangers. The month of December 1810, elapsed in these preparations; and I commence my Narrative from the day we quitted the Presidency of Bombay.

CHAPTER I.

DEPARTURE FROM BOMBAY. — PARTY. — DISGUISE. — TOUCH AT POREBUNDER. — MOTIVE. — TOWN AND TRADE. — GUZERATTE. — SAIL FROM POREBUNDER. — DEWS-COAST OF SINDE. — RIVER INDUS. — APPEARANCE OF THE WATER. — PORT OF ALEXANDER. — ARRIVAL AT SONMEANY. — RECEPTION. — OCCURRENCES THERE. — TRADE. — HINDOOS. — DESCRIPTION. — RIVER. — BAR. — WATER. — HOW PROCURED. — HOUSES. — LEAVE SONMEANY. — BEZUNJA BELOOCHES. — VILLAGE OF SHEIK KA RAJ. — INTERMEDIATE COUNTRY. — OOTUL VILLAGE. — COUNTRY. — RIVULETS. — THE AUTHOR AND HIS COMPANION DISCOVERED. — CONSEQUENCES EVADED. — WAREARA. — WELLS. — BELA. — COUNTRY. — BURIAL GROUND. — TOMBS. — HOLIDAY. — HORSE-RACING. — CAMELS. — SWIFTNESS. — MESSAGE TO AND FROM THE JAM OR CHIEF. — LETTER FROM SINDE. — OBJECT. — EVASION OF ITS CONSEQUENCES. — VISIT TO THE JAM. — RECEPTION. — CONVERSATION. — CHIEF'S IDEAS. — INVITES US TO STAY AT BELA. — DECLINE IT. — ORDERS FOR ADVANCE TO KELAT. — CHIEF'S APPEARANCE. — LANGUAGE. — DRESS. — DURBAR. — LETTER FROM MUSKAT. — CUSTOM. — BELA TOWN. — SCITE AND EXTENT. — POPULATION. — VISIT FROM MERCHANTS. — CAPTAIN CHRISTIE'S DECEPTION TOWARDS THEM. — ITS CONSEQUENCES. — PRESENTS. — JAM DURYA KHAN. — CONVERSATION. — MOUNTAIN GOATS. — BRAHOOES. — JAM'S RETINUE. — ATTEMPT TO DISCOVER US. — LETTERS. — RANA SETT.

LATE in the evening of the *2d January* 1810, Captain Christie and myself embarked on board a small native boat, in Bombay harbour, that had been hired for the purpose of conveying us to the port of Sonmeany, and instantly got under weigh; at day-light next morning, we found that our party, exclusive of the boatmen, consisted of two Hindoostanee servants, a Goomashtuh, or agent of Soondurjee, and his attendant, beside several Uffghan horse-dealers, on their return to their own country; to whom we had granted passages, thinking such acquaintances might be useful on landing.

It was quite dark when we embarked; and as we had a fresh breeze, and got well out to sea during the night, we were less apprehensive of being recognised by our fellow voyagers; however, we succeeded so well in disguising ourselves, by partly changing the European for the native dress, that although the Uffghans concluded, from our complexions, that we were Europeans, they did not, in the least, suspect our real characters. We found two or three of them intelligent, civil men, who gave us information, which, at that time, was highly interesting to us, and subsequently guided and assisted us very materially in forming our plans.

On the *7th of January*, we made the high land of Joonagur, on the coast of Guzeratte; and the following day anchored at Porebunder. Our real motive for touching at this place, was to have a personal conference with Soondurjee, who was employed there, on the part of the Bombay Government, in some political arrangements with the Rajah. We gave out, that we had been obliged to put in from a want of water; and as soon as we had cast anchor, Captain Christie and myself went on shore, where we remained the two following days, at the residence of Captain Maxfield, of the Honourable Company's Marine (then acting Custom Master). We here, also, contrived to elude the inquisitive vigilance of the Uffghans, who believed that we had passed our time at the house occupied by Soondurjee.

Porebunder is built on a creek of the sea, on the south-west coast of Guzeratte. It is a large and populous town; and the inhabitants carry on a brisk trade with Bombay, Sinde, and Malabar. The surrounding country bears the level feature usual throughout the whole of that province, if we except one range of mountains, distant from the town twelve or fourteen miles.

We sailed from Porebunder on the *10th of January*, and stretched away to the north-west, with a fresh easterly wind, attended, at night, with extreme cold, and dews so heavy as to wet every thing like rain. At noon on the 15th, we had the satisfaction of seeing the coast of Sinde, and found ourselves close in with it; the land is low, and flat; but we were certain, even before we saw it, of our proximity to it, from the extraordinary, and, to a person unacquainted with the cause, alarming appearance which the sea presented, owing to the great body of water that is disembogued by the River Indus, causing a very confused rippling, which, added to the discoloured sea, impresses an idea of a bank with a few inches of water upon it; though, on sounding, we found there were several fathoms. At 8 *p.m.* of the same day, we passed between Cape Mowaree (Monze) and Churna (Chilney) Island, keeping in the mid channel, which is not more than a quarter of a mile across, but deep, and free from danger: the island, by moon-light, and likewise the opposite shore, appeared quite barren, and the former has neither fresh water, or verdure on it.

The Bay of Sonmeany, which we now entered, is formed by Cape Monze and Chilney Island, on the one side, and Cape Urboo (Arabah) on the other; it is a very noble sheet of water, said to be free from rocks or shoals, and is capable of affording anchorage to the largest fleet: it is celebrated as the rendezvous of that of Nearchus, which lay under shelter of the island and mainland, for a considerable period. The description given by Dr. Vincent, from Arrian, of the Port of Alexander *, so exactly corresponds with its actual state, that it is a high testimony of the correctness of the Greek historian.

On the *16th of January*, at 1 *p.m.* we came to anchor on the bar of the Poorally River; the village of Sonmeany bearing north-east, distant about two miles; here we waited until three o'clock, at which hour, the tide flowing, we again got under weigh; and at five, anchored close to the village. We sent our Hindoo Goomashtuh on shore, who shortly returned with a canoe, for our baggage, accompanied by another agent of Soondurjee; whom we were rejoiced to meet at this place, as he had been in Beloochistan, the preceding season, to purchase horses, and was therefore well qualified to afford us information. We landed, by his advice, late in the evening, and were conducted to the house of a man called Rana Sett, the Ijarudar, or

* It was so named by Nearchus.

renter of the customs, whom we found with four or five Hindoo merchants, seated before a large fire: we were introduced to him as Europeans in the service of Soondurjee; he received us with civility, and, after common complimentary forms, observed, that anxious as he was to forward our master's interests, he was sensible he could not do so in a more effectual manner than by befriending us; and that we might accordingly command his utmost exertions; we thanked him for his kindness, and after sitting a few minutes, were ushered into a small hut, though one of the best in the village, which had been appropriated for our residence; here we supped on wheaten cakes and milk, sent to us by the Ijarudar, and lay down to sleep, happy to feel ourselves under a covering, however homely, a luxury we had not enjoyed on board the boat, which had neither cabin, or awning, to screen us from the sun or dews.

17th January. This morning we completely metamorphosed ourselves, by having our heads shaved, and adopting the entire native costume; after which, Rana Sett came to our hut, and Captain Christie requested him to accompany us to Bela, (the principal town in the country, and residence of the chief) to which he assented; he likewise proffered his services, in forwarding us thence to Kelat, the capital of the whole of Beloochistan, and was otherwise pointedly civil; before he left us, we shewed him a sample of the different articles which we had brought from Bombay as presents, and asked his opinion regarding them; he said the chintzes would be greatly prized, and that the few trifles we had of cutlery and glass ware, would also answer the purpose for which we had been charged with them by Soondurjee; though, had they been of better workmanship, they would have been still more acceptable to those to whom we were likely to offer them: some Scotch Plaid, which we had been advised to take, he did not approve of; as being too like their own Kumlees, or country blankets, but we afterwards found this idea to be erroneous, and that it was more admired than any thing else in our possession. When he rose to go away, he told us that he had sent a man to the Jungul, the evening before, to bring camels for ourselves and baggage; that he expected them in the course of the night, and would propose our moving next morning towards Bela.

This day, being the Moosulman festival of the Eed-ool-Qoorban, or Sacrifice, we treated all our Uffghan fellow voyagers to a dinner, at which they gormandized most voraciously. I did not perceive any feasting or rejoicing among the Mahommedan inhabitants of the place; who I fancy were too poor to afford it. One of the Uffghans, called Neknam, begged in the afternoon to be allowed to enter into our service, a request we thought fit to comply with, as he was an intelligent civil fellow, and had traversed all Beloochistan in his profession of a horse-dealer.

18*th January*. We were detained at Sonmeany on the 18th, by the non-arrival of the camels, and amused ourselves by walking about the place. I was quite astonished to find so much trade going on, when compared with the miserable appearance of the village, and its population. The commerce is entirely monopolized by the Hindoos, whose indefatigable industry is conspicuous wherever they are to be met with; and on my expressing my surprize to one of them at the bustle and active employment so apparent about the custom house, and Bunder, he assured me that the trade had been fourfold what it then was, until the latter end of the year 1808, when Sonmeany was ransacked and burnt to the ground, by the Juwassmee Arab pirates, which calamity it had not recovered.

The village of Sonmeany is advantageously situated on the southern bank of the Poorally river, and now contains about two hundred and fifty huts; it is completely defenceless, and on the side towards Bela, overlooked by hillocks of sand. The bar at the mouth of the river has only two fathoms on it at low water, but boats lie close to the village in six and seven: the inhabitants generally subsist by fishing, and with the exception of a few Hindoos are wretchedly poor: they procure their fresh water by digging a foot or two deep in the sand above high water mark; but it must be drawn off as it accumulates, otherwise it quickly becomes brackish; nor will the same hole answer a second time, until filled and dug afresh. The better kind of habitations at Sonmeany are formed of wooden frames, built up with bricks of unburnt clay, and the inferior huts are made of the boughs of the tamarisk tree, wattled together, and plaistered over with mud: the roofs are generally ill thatched, with a species of coarse grass, and made in a conical shape. I shall have occasion in the Second Part of this volume to speak of the general nature of the trade, revenue, and productions of the province of Lus, of which Sonmeany is the only sea-port, and I therefore refrain from entering into a more detailed account of them at present, and proceed with my narrative.

19*th January*. This morning after breakfast the Uffghans brought a Kandahar merchant to expostulate with us on the risk we ran by going the direct route from Bela to Kelat, and to recommend us to proceed by that which he had come, through Sinde. They could not however persuade us to do so, although the merchant used every argument, and declared that the very first tribe of Belooches we should meet with, in our advance, were the Bezunjas, "who (said he) "care not for the king, the khan, God, or the prophet, but murder and "plunder every person and thing they can lay hands on." We evaded as far as possible giving our adviser an explicit refusal, and in consequence he became so importunate that at length we told him we had no option, having been ordered by Soondurjee to go to Bela in the first instance; on hearing which, he expressed his hopes that we should not suffer for our temerity, and took leave. The baggage had been sent off at day-light this morning, to Lyaree, the second town in the province; and at two *p. m.*, we followed it; by half past four *p. m.* we had travelled eight miles over a salt marsh, varied with tamarisk and other Jungul, and in many places perfectly white with incrustations of salt: here we had the mortification to find our baggage waiting for us, and as the camels which carried it were out feeding, we were forced to dismount, and join several other travellers, amongst whom were our Uffghans, under the shade of some low bushes.

While our servants were baking bread, the Uffghans came in a body, and again urged us to select the Sinde route to Kelat; but we silenced them at once, by declaring, that we were resolved on visiting

Bela, even with the certainty, instead of the probability, of being obliged to return from thence: on this declaration, Neknam, our new servant, observed, that as he had a little property with him, and we were so obstinately bent on what he feared would be our ruin, he must separate from us, and take the road to the Lukh, or pass over the mountains into Sinde, which branches off near this halting place; "how-" ever, (added he,) we shall, please God, meet at Kelat, provided "you escape from those highwaymen, the Bezunjas; and I will "now, if you wish it, leave one or two of my companions with you, "who are trust-worthy men, and will sacrifice their blood in your "service;" to this latter proposition, we unfortunately, as it afterwards proved, assented; and two of them accordingly volunteering to accompany us, after supper, we bade the others adieu, and moved on seven or eight miles to the small village of Shaik ka Raj, where we unceremoniously took possession of an empty stable that we discovered by accident, the inhabitants being all fast asleep; this was the first place in which we had seen any symptoms of habitations since quitting Sonmeany, the intermediate country being one continued salt marsh: the direction of our route to-day northerly, and the distance I estimate at fifteen miles and a half.

20th January. A Hindoo Buneea or dealer, on his return from Bela to Sonmeany, came to pay his respects to us, as he passed this morning, and from him we received the very welcome intelligence, that the road between the former town and Kelat, was passable; a fact, which the reiterated assurances of the Uffghans, in declaring it not to be so, on account of the Bezunja Belooches, had latterly led us to doubt. We remounted our camels about one *p. m.* and, at five arrived at Ootul, a well built, clean village, containing four hundred houses: the road was in general very tolerable, the country uncultivated and perfectly flat, and in some spots covered with an impenetrable Jungul, among which I observed Babool trees *, of an extraordinary large size; we passed two small rivulets, the Wulta and Sanganee: the former

* Farnesian Mimosa.

is only a branch of the Poorally, into which it re-empties itself, after making a short circuit; the Sanganee was almost quite dry, where we crossed it, and the bed of it about twelve yards wide from bank to bank: the direction of the road north, distance nine miles. Water at Ootul is in very deep wells, and excellent; the people of the village appeared very contented and happy; they have immense flocks of sheep and goats, beside herds of black cattle and camels.

The Jemadar, or chief man of the village, came to us, before we had alighted from the camels, with a goat, as a present; but we declined taking it on any other terms than making him an equal return: we afterwards ascertained that this attention, on the Jemadar's part, originated in Captain Christie and myself being recognised by a man who had been a water-carrier to the mission to Sinde (to which we were both attached) the preceding year, and this discovery he instantly made public; however, we contrived to avoid any unpleasant consequences, that might have arisen from it, by admitting the fact, and affirming that we had since entered into Soondurjee's employment; a fabrication that was received without a question as to its probability.

21*st January.* We left Ootul about noon, and a little past six in the evening halted at a miserable village called *Waréara*, with not more than a dozen of houses, or rather sheds, in one of which, belonging to a dyer, we put up for the night: the distance of this march was eighteen miles, and the direction something to the eastward of north: the country barren, flat, and sandy: we saw two wells, the waters of which we tasted, and found them both brackish, as well as being in very small quantities.

22*d January.* This day, at four o'clock, we reached Bela, distant from our last halting place ten miles and a half: the country was much diversified, being, in some parts, a thick jungul; in others, sterile and bare; and in the vicinity of villages, three or four of which we saw, in a high state of cultivation.

About half way, we rode through the burial ground, in which the relations of the Jam, or chief of the country are interred: two of the tombs are built with low cupolas of free-stone, brought from the adjacent mountains, and they, and likewise many of the graves, are ornamented with white and black pebbles, arranged in different short quotations from the Koran, and encircled with wreaths of the like materials, which has a fanciful and pleasing effect, though so very simple.

As we approached the town of Bela, we found that it was a holiday, and the Jam had gone out to amuse himself with horse-racing, which is a favourite pastime among these people; on such occasions, the whole of the inhabitants, who can procure one or other, mount themselves on camels, or horses, and gallop over the country. The swift pace at which the former animals go, when urged to a gallop, and managed with dexterity, is almost incredible, and struck me with amazement on first beholding it, having been accustomed to contemplate the camel races, about which I had heard so many extraordinary stories, as a mere joke.

The Jam returned in the evening, and we ordered Toolsia (Soondurjee's agent, whom we met at Sonmeany) to go and announce to him our arrival, and ask his permission to stay a few days: he received our messenger with politeness, and not only sanctioned our sojourn at Bela, but promised to render us any assistance in his power towards our farther progress inland; this was an object, at once gained to us, of the very first importance, and gave us the greater satisfaction, as we had anticipated his making objections to our advance.

Our friend, the Ijarudar of Sonmeany, had got to Bela before us by pursuing a different route, and had prepared his own house for our reception, which was very private and comfortable, having the advantage of a wall and gateway in front, and though only consisting of one large hall, with a verandah and two closets, was much more than we could venture to occupy, in our humble character of Soondurjee's servants.

23d January. This forenoon, Toolsia acquainted us that Rana Sett had just read to him a long letter he had received from Kurachee, in Sinde, expostulating with him on the impolicy of being accessary to the admission of the agents of the British government into the territories of his master the Jam, and recommending our being forcibly put on board a boat and sent back to Bombay, together with all the people, of whatever description or *caste* they might be, who had accompanied us. The writer * of this letter added, that notwithstanding any mercantile intentions we professed, there could be no doubt of our real ones being, alone, to explore the country, on which the Honourable Company had hostile views: that an envoy had been sent at a great expence for the same purpose, the year preceding, to Sinde, but that the Umeers had taken steps to repel any attempts that might be made by the English: to these assertions Toolsia simply replied by shewing Rana Sett the letters of credit and recommendation with which Captain Christie and myself were furnished, as Soondurjee's agents, at which he appeared perfectly satisfied; but, as a further precaution, we directed Toolsia to take a proper opportunity of pointing out to the Ijarudar that the motive which had impelled his correspondent to pen the letter in question, no doubt proceeded from a dread that, under the auspices of the British government, (whose servant Soondurjee our employer was,) the Bunder or port of Sonmeany would soon usurp a share of, if not all, that commerce which now flowed through Kurachee, in Sinde.

About half past one o'clock, we were sent for to pay our respects to the Jam: we found him seated in his Durbar, or hall of audience, surrounded by nearly one hundred and fifty persons, the greater number of whom curiosity had drawn together, as his attendants formed a very small part of them; he received us very courteously, and stood up on our entering, and also on taking leave: in the course of conversation he put many curious though pointed questions to us,

* Duréadna Sett, a Hindoo merchant, who had derived many benefits from his connection with the Honourable Company's governments and agents.

relative to the religion, customs, and *castes* of the English; and whether the French were a similar people in their usages: he observed he had often heard, from those of his subjects who had been in India, of our eternal wars with that nation, and also of our superiority at sea, which he asked if we still retained: he likewise enquired the name of the King of England, the method of organization and extent of his navy and army, the distance of his capital from Constantinople, the form of government, &c. &c. &c.

To all these queries we afforded him the most explanatory answers we could at the moment; but the same simplicity which had dictated them, rendered it totally impossible for us to make him perfectly comprehend the different points he had spoken on: he was astonished beyond expression at many of our descriptions, and appealed to the two Hindoos, who had attended us to the levee, for a corroboration of them; they assured him that we had by no means exaggerated in any thing, we had related, that had ever come under their notice; but he shook his head with an air of incredulity, and observed, "You tell me of a vessel that will carry one hundred guns, and one "thousand men on board of her; it is morally impossible! Where "are the latter to get food and water? The King has scarcely so "many guns in his Tope Khanu, or arsenal; and the crews of two "such ships would over-run the whole of my country." We reiterated our assurances of the truth of all we had told him regarding the navy of England, and briefly stated its effects in the battle of Trafalgar; to this he replied, "As you say it has been so, I am "bound to believe it, but, had the holy Prophet foretold it, the "Noomrees (the people of Lus) would have demanded proof of "it from him."

He at length demanded our views and wishes: we informed him, at some length, that we were in the service of Soondurjee, a Hindoo merchant of Bombay, who had dispatched us to purchase horses for the market of India; and concluded, by saying, that we trusted to his kindness, to arrange for our proceeding on to Kelat: he instantly ordered his Deewan, or manager, to procure the requisite guides and servants for us, and expedite our departure, "though," said he, turning to us, "you had better remain with me for a month, "or six weeks, to avoid the cold, which is now so great at Kelat, "as to be likely to kill you all." We replied that our native country was exceedingly cold, and that we were, therefore, inured to it, and prepared for what we should experience by ascending the mountains immediately. "True," said he, "but you ought to have "a little consideration for those who are to go with you; however, "as your business does not appear to admit of delay, you may make "your preparations; and I will furnish you with letters to some of "the chiefs, through whose countries you must pass: a messenger "shall likewise be dispatched, this day, to bring Ruhmut Khan, the "head of the Bezunja tribe of Belooches, who shall himself conduct "you through his country, in which the greatest danger from rob-"bers is to be apprehended." He then signified his desire that we should take leave, which we did, much gratified by a reception so very friendly and favourable to our designs.

The Jam evinced himself, during this visit, to be a shrewd man, desirous of information, and has a very fine countenance; he conversed with tolerable fluency, in Persian, and, when he did not clearly understand our explanations, inquired the meaning of them from one of our Hindoos, in the Sindee language. He was seated on a white cloth Gaddee, or pillow, without any jewels or ornaments; and was very plainly dressed in an Ulkhaliq of red Keemkhab *, with a white turband of considerable dimensions, but not comparable in circumference, to those worn by the Sindees in general: his sword and shield lay before him on the carpet; his son, and two brothers, sat near him; and there was an appearance of poverty throughout the whole party, which they did not seem to be in any

---

* An Ulkhaliq is a double breasted dress, made with long sleeves, and to sit to the form as low as the hips, and having skirts reaching down to the calf of the leg; it is tied across the chest on the left side. Keemkhab is a species of silk, with gold or silver sprigs, or flowers worked on it.

way ashamed of, or solicitous to disguise. The Durbar, in which we were received, was a large open room, raised a few feet from the ground, the flat mud roof of it supported by a few common crooked sticks, in the rough and unpolished state they had been cut from the jungul: there was not the slightest semblance of state, or even order, in any thing; no Chobdars (mace bearers) or Sepoys; and those who sat round the Jam, offered their remarks and opinions on the conversation, without the smallest demur, though, at the same time, every one present treated that chief himself with such reverence and attention, as testified how much he was respected and liked by them.

While we were in the Durbar, an Arab delivered a letter, which was read aloud, according to a custom that prevails all over these countries; it related to a vessel belonging to the Imaum of Muskat, that had been cast away some time since, on the coast near Sonmeany, and from whose wreck a few trifling articles had been recovered. The Imaum requested they might be delivered to his people, to which effect orders were immediately proclaimed in an audible tone in the public Durbar by the Deewan. I observed that the letter, which was in Persian, was penned in a very respectful style, and without any assumption, on the part of the Imaum, about which the Jam appeared to be very particular, as he had it carefully interpreted by his Moonshee, into the Judgalee language, which is the colloquial dialect of this country.

We walked through the Bazar, on our way home from the Durbar, and found it very clean and neat; the streets are narrow, but from the elevated situation of the town, and its rocky site, they must always be dry, even in the wettest weather, as the rain cannot lodge for a moment. Bela is built on the northern bank of the Pooralee river; about one-third of the town, in the north-west quarter, is encompassed by a tolerably good mud wall; the remainder is totally unprotected against attack, either by horse or foot; it contains above two thousand houses, of which two hundred and fifty, or three hundred, may belong to Hindoos, who enjoy great security and protection in their mercantile speculations, under the mild and equitable government of the Jam.

When we returned to the house in which we resided, we were visited by several merchants from Mooltan and Shikarpoor *, with whom we had a great deal of chat on different subjects connected with trade; and after treating them with Beetel, or Areca nut, and cloves, which is the practice here, sent them away, deeply impressed with a favourable notion of our commercial skill and abilities. It was with the utmost difficulty I could refrain from laughing heartily at this meeting, when my esteemed fellow-traveller, Captain Christie, entered into a long and particular dissertation on the description of goods most fitted for the Bombay, or rather Indian market, to which our visitors listened with the greatest avidity and belief; even our own Hindoos began to doubt the evidence of their senses; and when the merchants departed, were quite amazed to find that Captain Christie had been, all the time, explaining a subject regarding which he might be said to be, in fact, entirely ignorant: this deception, trifling though it may seem, was attended with the most advantageous consequences to us afterwards; and, subsequent to its being practised, it would have been almost impossible to persuade the Bela merchants that we had assumed any character foreign to our station in life.

24th January. The Jam's Deewan, or manager, came to us early this morning, with his master's compliments, and inquiries after our healths: we were much vexed to find that he treated us with this kind of respect, as it betrayed a suspicion of the professions we had made to him the preceding day, of our being the servants of Soondurgee; however, to obviate its bad effects as far as possible, we gave a very submissive answer in return. About two hours after the Deewan had

* Mooltan is a large trading city, the capital of the province of that name in the Punjab. Shikarpoor lies east of Kelat, on the western side of the Indus, and is equally distinguished for its commerce.

left us, we sent the Jam a present*, with which he was amazingly gratified.

In the afternoon we were still further confirmed in our fears of being known, by a visit from Jam Durya Khan, the eldest of the Jam's two brothers, who insisted on our sitting down with him, and chatting for two hours: he is a well looking middle aged man, mild and polite in his manners, when compared with those of the generality of his countrymen, but dresses very shabbily; a circumstance not to be wondered at, as we heard afterwards that he had only a miserable pittance to subsist on, equal to fifteen hundred rupees (180l. sterling) per annum; a fact evincing the frugal simplicity in which these people live, and particularly exemplified in the instance of this chief, who is the third person, as to rank, in the country; and considered the head Sirdar or general of the army, when it is collected: he has then a small additional allowance, beside the use of two horses from the Jam's own stud: he gave us, unasked, a detail of the sources of revenue, and the nature of the government of his brother's country, contrasting the latter with what he had heard us describe of ours, at the Durbar, in a manner that proved he was by no means deficient in good sense or discrimination. We discovered by his discourse that he was a keen sportsman, and spent a great portion of his leisure hours in field diversions, to follow which he said he made several trips to the mountains every month, during the cold weather, and that he had frequently killed with his own gun, in an excursion of two days, twenty or thirty mountain goats (Boozé Kohee): these animals are very difficult of approach, and frequent the most dangerous and in-

* Consisting of the following articles:

One piece of Chinese silk.
One ditto European chintz.
Eight Coffee Cups and Saucers.
Eight China Bowls.
Eight cut glass Tumblers.
One piece of Indian silk.
Six common Knives.
Two pair of common Scissars.
One pound of Gunpowder.
One small Telescope.
A pair of Horse Pistols.

accessible precipices. Their flesh is greatly prized for its flavour and delicacy; and that circumstance, united with the labour that it requires to come near them, induced our visitor to quote the numbers of them he had killed, as a proof of his expertness as a sportsman. The Jam and all his family, are uniformly partial to the same kind of recreation; and so strict are the regulations regarding the preservation of every species of game, for the use of the chiefs, that particular districts in the mountains are set apart for that express purpose; and if a lion or tiger, or any other large animal, worthy of being hunted by them, appears in any part of the country, however distant from Bela, information thereof is immediately sent to the Jam, who sets off to destroy it. When he left us, our visitor expressed his hopes that an incident of this nature might occur while we staid at Bela, as in that event, he would mount us on two of his own riding camels, and let us accompany him to see the sport. We were very much gratified by this visit, which gave us a greater insight into the customs and habits of the people of Lus, than we could possibly have acquired by any other means, during our short stay in that province.

A party of Brahooes, or mountain Belooches, came into Bela this evening, with a string of sixty or seventy camels, laden with wheat, which they had brought from Bunkar, a small village, six or seven days' journey on the road to Kelat. We sent to the Suraé, and had one or two of them called to our house to make inquiries, who told us that unless we had a valuable Kaffilah*, there was not much to dread from the Bezunjas, who, they added, though the terror of the country, would allow us to pass without molestation on paying a small duty: they however advised, in case we had property, that we should go by the Sinde route; but that not being so, we were still further strengthened by this intelligence in our determination to proceed direct.

25th January. We purchased three or four camels to-day at a very

---

* A Caravan.

moderate rate, and were otherwise employed in making preparations for our journey, having had a message from the Jam's Deewan to acquaint us, that he expected the Bezunja chief to arrive every moment, and that we should leave Bela immediately after: to this we were very glad to give our cordial assent and approbation. About four o'clock in the evening, the Jam rode past our residence, and called us out, to ask how we were: he was mounted on a handsome northern horse, the trappings of which were ornamented with coloured silk, and was accompanied by twenty or thirty armed men, some of whom rode horses, and others camels: his son was on one of the latter, a very fine animal, which he guided with great cleverness and apparent ease, by two silken cords tied through holes made in the cartilaginous part of its nostrils on each side. The attendants who rode camels, formed a regular column of two and two a-breast, and the horsemen kept on the flanks; their arms were swords, shields, and Toofungs, or matchlocks.

26th January. This forenoon the Jam sent for our Hindoo Toolsia, and after some desultory conversation, said to him: "I am now "going to speak to you on a subject which I have not hitherto hinted "at, nor ever shall mention to any other person, not even to my own "son. I do not think that the two Englishmen here are merchants; "it is neither my wish or aim to enquire into their plans; but if they "are officers I ought, when they visited me, to have considered them "as my equals, and treated them accordingly. I therefore request "you will now inform me who they really are; you may depend on "the strictest secrecy, and if they belong to the British government "it will give me additional pleasure to serve them." The Hindoo saw immediately into the drift of the Jam's curiosity, which he did not satisfy; but adhered to our original tale of being Soondurjee's servants. The Jam next inquired what wages we had, and whether it would be possible to get, through our interest, two small guns, or wall pieces from Bombay. Toolsia replied, he would mention the chief's wishes to us, and then came away. We directed him to say, that we could not venture to make any promises, but that on our return to India we should endeavour to have them sent.

In the course of the evening the Deewan brought four or five letters of recommendation to the different chiefs, on our route to the southward of Kelat, which had been written by the Jam's orders, and were read to us. Rana Sett returned to Sonmeany this night; and when he came to take leave of us we presented him with a piece of chintz, a spying glass, and some other trifling articles. This man had been exceedingly civil, and we should have been pleased to have made him a better return for the services he had done us, but our character would not permit it. A few moments before he left us we had a most satisfactory evidence of his belief in our avowed intentions. When Toolsia purposely accused him of having dispatched an agent to Bunkar, a village on the Kelat road to buy horses, he confessed the fact, but in palliation of what he imagined would have given us great offence, protested he wanted a very inferior kind, and that at all events, his agent had positive instructions not to go further to the northward than Bunkar. We were vexed afterwards to learn, that he had recalled him in consequence of the supposed interference with our views.

CHAPTER II.

DEPARTURE FROM BELA. — COUNTRY. — GOOR OR RAW SUGAR. — MILLS. — BEZUNJAS. — RETURN TO BELA. — SEE THE JAM. — HIS GUESTS. — MOVE ON. — NIGHT SCENE. — REFLECTIONS. — AMUSEMENTS. — SYSTEM OF PLUNDER. — CONTRAST BETWEEN THE BELOOCHES AND THEIR NEIGHBOURS. — PROVINCE OF LUS. — POPULATION. — MANNERS AND CUSTOMS. — NAMES. — PECULIARITIES. — STATURE. — FIGURE. — DRESS OF MEN AND WOMEN. — FOOD. — ANIMALS. — LANGUAGE. — RESEMBLANCE OF THE PEOPLE TO HINDOOS. — NARRATIVE RESUMED. — DEMAND AND ALTERCATION. — ROUTE. — SEPARATE FROM THE BEZUNJAS. — HALT. — FRAUD OF A CAMEL DRIVER. — DETERMINE TO PROCEED EXPRESS TO KELAT. — MOTIVE. — BEZUNJAS DISAPPOINT US. — ADVANCE WITHOUT THEM. — INSTRUCTIONS. — POORALLY RIVER. — ITS COURSE. — MOUNTAIN ROAD. — PROVINCE OF JHALAWAN. — NARROW DEFILE. — HALT. — EXTREME COLD. — BARAN LUKH OR RAINY PASS. — DESCRIPTION OF IT. — COUNTRY VERY PICTURESQUE. — REFLECTIONS. — RIVER OORNACH. — GOATHERD. — PURCHASE A SHEEP. — TOORKUBUR. — SUPPER. — THE NAME OF THE PLACE. — ROUTE CONTINUED. — PLAINS. — WUDD TOWN. — DO NOT VISIT IT. — WHY. — POPULAR BELIEF. — A BRAHOOE KHEIL OR SOCIETY. — MANNERS AND OCCUPATIONS OF THOSE PEOPLE. — WOMEN APPEAR IN PUBLIC. — OBLIGING DISPOSITION. — GHEDANS OR TENTS. — FORMATION. — COMFORT. — SMOKE. — ADVANTAGES ON ACCOUNT OF THE COLD. — LEAVE THE BRAHOOES. — PRESENTS. — ROUTE. — COUNTRY. — BAD ROAD. — TOWN OF KHOZDAR. — SURPRIZE OF THE INHABITANTS. — HALT A DAY. — CAUSE. — VISITORS. — KANDAHAR MERCHANT. — HORSE-DEALERS. — MOOSULMANS. — FAKEER. — PRECAUTIONS AND RESULT OF THEM. — TOWN DESCRIBED. — VALLEY. — GARDENS. — FRUITS. — CHIEF'S NAME AND TRIBE. — HIS DEPUTY. — MESSAGE FROM HIM. — ANSWER. — INHABITANTS. — HINDOOS. — BRAHMINS. — PAGODA. — — DEBAUCHED HABITS. — CONSEQUENCES. — BAZAR. — MILLS. — BUNKAR VILLAGE. — ROUTE. — CHIEF. — SIZE. — ICE. — TEDIOUS MARCH. — COUNTRY BARREN. — ROAD BAD. — VILLAGE OF SOHERAB. — EXTREME COLD. — HOSPITALITY OF A BRAHOOE. — VALLEY. — SNOW. — LOFTY PEAK. — ROUTE TO RODENJO. — SURAE'. — ANTIMONY. — VILLAGE OF RODENJO. — DESOLATE COUNTRY. — REFLECTIONS. — CURIOUS TRADITION REGARDING THE NAME OF THIS VILLAGE.

JANUARY *20th.* We waited until three P.M., when finding there was no appearance of Ruhmut Khan, the Bezunja chief, we left Bela, and proceeded four miles and a half to a garden, belonging to the Jam, where we halted for the night, under the shade of a remarkably large tamarind tree. We were, as well as our attendants, who now consisted of six men, mounted on camels: but as Captain Christie and myself were still novices in the management of those creatures, we took a person up before us for that purpose. This part of the country is finely cultivated, and abounds with running streams; half way from Bela to the garden there is an extensive manufactory of goor, or raw sugar: the mill for expressing the juice from the canes is turned by a stream from the neighbouring mountains, and is to a degree simple in its construction: the water-wheel sets in motion two horizontal cogged rollers, and the canes being pruned of leaves, the ends are inserted between them. They gradually draw in the canes as they are pressed, and the refuse of the stalks comes out at the opposite side: the juice falls into a trough below, and from that runs into a cistern. It is afterwards boiled in flat copper pans, and the goor is then packed in bags, made from the palmyra leaf, and thus sent to the sea coast for exportation. It is also given to camels, and much used by the natives for culinary purposes. Two men and a boy are able to conduct the whole process, and the sediment of the boilers forms the best and strongest manure.

29th January. Whilst we were in the act of loading the camels this morning, the long expected Ruhmut Khan arrived at the garden, accompanied by fifteen or twenty followers: he peremptorily refused either to permit us to go through his country, unless escorted by himself, (observing that his reputation was concerned in our safety,) or to proceed with us, until he had talked to the Jam: we had, therefore, most unwillingly to unload the camels, and return with the Bezunja to Bela, where we dismounted at eleven o'clock. As we rode along we chatted with our new acquaintance, and found him possessed of all that ingenuous hospitality and predatory ferocity which are so curiously blended in the Belooche character; he repeatedly swore by his beard, that had we attempted to have advanced through his country, without his leave, he would have annihilated our whole party; and the next moment asked us, with great earnestness, to pass a week at his village, an invitation we should gladly have availed ourselves of, had circumstances admitted it: we told him that it had been our intention to have proceeded onward, and that we had hoped to have done so without molestation, or even observation. He affected to laugh heartily at what he termed our ignorance; though we were subsequently convinced we might have done as we proposed, and that the Jam had been guilty of a most foolish mistake, though from the best motive, in sending for this savage. "How could you," said he, "for one moment suppose "such a scheme practicable? Do you imagine you are always to be "among the Noomrees of Lus? No! You must be Belooches, and "look to me for protection. So far from your doing so, a hare "could not pass through Ruhmut Khan's country if he chose to "prevent it; but having once given his word for your safety, you "need not fear any thing mortal; farther, it rests with the Almighty "and his Prophet." We assured him that we were perfectly willing to trust to his honour, and had not the most distant doubt with regard to his abilities and means to protect us.

We saw the Jam in the course of the day, who explained our intentions to Ruhmut Khan, and informed him that he had received sixty rupees from us, for him, in consideration of our having a free passage and protection through his country. The Bezunja frankly observed, that as we were the agents of a merchant of such consequence as Soondurjee, he ought undoubtedly to pay more for our advance. The Jam rejoined, that he had made what he deemed a very fair agreement for both parties; and added, (to us,) that he would settle matters as soon as we left the Durbar; at the same time he invited us to remain at Bela that night as his guests, to do which we were reluctantly obliged to assent: we then came away, it being very evident, from the Jam's manner, that he did not choose to have any further discussion with the Bezunjas whilst we were present, owing, I fancy, to the blunt and unceremonious style in which not only their chief, but the lowest of his attendants, made their remarks and demands. Soon after we got back to our old lodgings, the Jam's servants brought us a sheep and four fowls, with a quantity of rice, clarified butter, and vegetables, sufficient to have dined thirty men. In the evening we had a message from Ruhmut Khan, to acquaint us that he would be ready to move next morning, and was to escort us to Khozdar, a village half way to Kelat.

30th January. Captain Christie and I returned to our baggage at the Jam's garden very early, but Ruhmut Khan and his followers had so much business in the city, (as they styled Bela,) that they did not join us until the afternoon, when we mounted our camels and proceeded four miles north by east, principally through the dry bed of the Poorally river, which here occupies the whole intermediate tract between the mountains, and is stated, in the rains, to form a torrent many miles in breadth.

During our stay at the Jam's garden this forenoon, we ascertained from some of Ruhmut Khan's people, that one of his party was a petty Surdar of the same tribe (the Bezunjas) called Buhadoor Khan, and that there was also a brother of the former chief, whom they honoured by the appellation of Moolla, a word signifying, in general, a priest, but expressive, among the Belooches and many other Asiatics, of a person who can read the Koran. They were all dressed in the same manner as their chiefs, with a loose white cotton shirt, which came below their knees, a pair of trowsers, of blue or striped cotton, and a small round cap, which sat close to the head; the only distinction I perceived, was in their horses and accoutrements; and when Ruhmut Khan visited the Jam he tied a Loongee * round his waist, an article of dress to which none of his attendants aspired. We halted on a high spot in the bed of the river, and the Belooches having quickly collected an immense pile of wood, we sat round a blazing fire the greater part of the night, while three or four Sookrees, or wandering musicians, who had come with the Bezunjas, en-

---

* Longees are long pieces of cloth, made of silk, or silk and cotton, used as sashes or turbands. Some of them, the manufacture of Sinde, are very beautiful and rich.

tertained us by singing the exploits of their different chiefs, accompanying their songs with the most frantic and unmeaning gestures; some of the songs and music were, however, soft and harmonious enough, except when the audience chimed in with the performers, which was, for my taste, too often the case.

A clearer picture of the savage life of the Bezunjas, and many other Beloochc tribes, cannot well be pourtrayed than by this scene: all outward distinction and respect for chiefs were at that moment thrown aside; at intervals they, as well as their people, in the height of their enthusiasm, snatched the Setars* or musical instruments from the hands of the Sookrees, and sung, in "descant wild," their favourite airs, gradually working themselves, by ridiculous and violent action, into a state of absolute phrenzy: the din then became universal and quite stunning, and the auditory continued to applaud and join in chorus with the singers until they were so completely exhausted that they could exert themselves no longer; the instruments were then laid hold of by others, and thus they were regularly passed round the circle.

31*st January.* At daylight this morning, Ruhmut Khan and his gang repaired in a body to a field of sugar canes, about two miles from our halting place, of which they brought away as much as they could possibly carry, while the terrified owner looked on, not even venturing to expostulate with the plunderers. Had I not been before struck with it, this circumstance alone shewed me the wide difference of character between the people of Lus and Beloochistan, which is rendered extraordinary, if we reflect on their proximity to each other and daily intercourse.

As our next march was the last we made in the former province, I shall, in a few words, give a summary sketch of its inhabitants, agreeable to the opinion I formed of them. The population of Lus may, according to several statements I received, amount to twenty

---

* Setar, a three stringed instrument, from seh, three, and tar, wire.

five thousand souls, of which nearly one-third are wandering families, who change their places of residence as convenience or inclination prompts: they are all of one tribe, though known by the four different appellations of Noomree, Judgall, Jokhya, and Jeth, which latter is the most commonly used term, and literally signifies a husbandman: the habits of these people are indolent in the extreme, and they are fond of smoking Bhung (cannabis sativa) and other intoxicating drugs, and loitering away their time in idle amusements. Although very well inclined to be civil to strangers, it is difficult to appreciate that quality in them, as their curiosity is so great, that they will not hesitate to walk into your most private apartments, and will even feel and examine the clothes on your back: another peculiarity of manner amongst them is, that they never, or at least very seldom, ask any questions. I have seen a Noomree come, uninvited, into our house at Bela, and after sitting two hours in a room crowded with people, go out without having uttered one syllable. The men have good features, and are about the middle size, strong and athletic. The women are ordinary, and pay no attention to cleanliness in their persons or garments. The dress of the former consists of a loose pyrahun, or shirt, a pair of trowsers, and a small cap, which often distinguishes those of one district from another. The women wear the same, except that their shifts are much longer, coming down to the ancles; and some of them have a small silk or cotton jacket under it. The food of the population of Lus is principally rice and other grains, of which they grow large quantities, seasoned with a little dried fish, or ghee; the better classes, both Moosulmans and Hindoos, also sometimes add flesh meat, a luxury which the great bulk of the people cannot afford. They have numerous and very large flocks of sheep and goats, beside excellent camels and black cattle; but their horses are scarce, beside being of diminutive size and vicious temper. The language of Lus is almost similar to that of Sinde: it is called Judgalee, or Jethgalee, a name evidently derived from that of the tribe. I may close this hasty sketch of the Noomrees by adding, that their appearance and manners struck both Captain Christie and myself, as greatly resembling those of Hindoos: there is an apathy and want of energy indicated by their countenances that I have never observed in any other Moosulman country; and which particularly distinguishes them from their neighbours in Sinde, Mukran, and Beloochistan.

To return from this digression. As soon as the Belooches had breakfasted, we proposed to move on, when, to our utter surprize, Buhadoor Khan and Ruhmut's brother, the Moollah, made a demand for the trouble they had been put to by us, and likewise for permitting us to advance: we briefly told them that the Jam had arranged with Ruhmut Khan, through whose territory, as the head of the Bezunjas, the road lay; and that, if they persisted in requiring any further remuneration, we should return to Bela, and take the route to Kelat by Kedge, the capital of the neighbouring province of Mukran: this threat had the intended effect of silencing their demands; and, after a violent altercation among themselves regarding what share of the sixty rupees, that Ruhmut Khan had pocketed, the two new claimants were to receive, we set off and travelled sixteen miles, nearly due north, over the hills composing the bank, or through the bed, of the Poorally river. The country was wild, barren, and covered with stones, and the river bed overgrown with impervious jungul of Guz (tamarisk), babool (Farnesian mimosa), &c. We separated, during the march, from Ruhmut and his party; and, at three *p. m.* halted to wait for him; at the same time, the owner of the camels, which we had hired at Bela, asked leave to go to his village in the mountains, about three miles off, promising faithfully to return in the evening; the result, however, proved that he had no such intentions. In consideration of the tedious pace at which we found our two loaded camels travelled this day, and the number of people who we thought it probable would accompany Ruhmut Khan, and might prevent our taking notes on, or bearings of the route; we determined, on his joining us, to take the riding camels and proceed to Kelat with all possible dispatch, entrusting the baggage to the care of one of our Hindoostanee servants, and a few of the Belooches.

1st February. We remained at our halting ground, in expectation of the arrival of the Bezunjas, until ten o'clock, and then mounted our camels, leaving instructions for Ruhmut Khan himself to follow us, and his men to stay with and guard the baggage. Our road led directly out of the bed of the Poorally river, which here runs away to the eastward, into a narrow water-course, along which we travelled north fifteen miles, and then breakfasted: this road affords abundance of excellent water, which issues in clear rivulets from the rocks; it is called the "Kohen-wat" or mountain road; and, from the entrance of it commences the province of Jhalawan, the most southern of Beloochistan Proper; it was, generally, wide enough for two camels to travel abreast, though, in one place, the path was so confined that we were obliged to dismount to get those animals through, the mountains rising for many hundred feet on each side, and overshadowing the road beneath. In the afternoon we moved on fourteen miles further, and slept round a large fire made from logs of wood, plenty of which are floated down here by inundations from the mountains. The night was piercingly cold, and, for the first time since landing at Sonmeany, we felt the hardships of a want of beds and warm cloathing.

2d February. We left Kanajee (the name of our halting place) at eight o'clock this morning, and having proceeded fourteen miles, arrived at the bottom of the pass called Baran Lukh, or the rainy pass, over which we walked: we were about an hour and a half ascending to the top of it, where the path, for one hundred yards or upwards, is very narrow, and would almost seem to have been excavated through the solid rock. From this elevated point we had an extremely fine view of the circumjacent country, composed of an irregular mass of barren and rocky mountains, among which reside a few Brahooe shepherds in small kheils or societies. Nothing could be more sublime or majestic than this scenery: the solemn stillness of the place, the varied forms which caught the eye among the rugged and stupendous mountains, piled, as it were, on each other like the waves of an agitated sea, gave the whole an indescribable effect, which impressed the mind with feelings of admiration and awe. There was no descent whatever from the summit of the pass, and we continued our journey along a stony plain, for a few miles, and then stopped for the purpose of allowing our camels to browse for an hour in the bed of the mountain-river Oornach, which had a small and refreshing stream of water in it. A Brahooe goatherd, who was tending a large flock of sheep and goats, accidentally joined us here; and from him we got some milk, and also purchased a sheep, for which we gave a rupee. We moved on five miles further, in the evening, to a place called Toorkubur, where we spent the night as we had done the preceding one, with the agreeable addition of having a supper of roasted mutton. I admired the dexterity with which our camel-keepers killed the sheep, and cutting the meat in small morsels, stuck them on the iron ramrods of their matchlocks, and thus cooked a most excellent Kubab, or roast. This spot is said to owe its name* to a celebrated Deeve, or demigod, called Toor, whose grave is marked by a neighbouring eminence, and of whose exploits the most fabulous accounts are related.

3d February. We left Toorkubur at seven this morning, and travelled twenty-four miles in the course of the day: our route principally lay over two plains, or more correctly speaking, vallies, neither being above twelve or fourteen miles in length or breadth, which had been lately cultivated to a considerable extent, by some of the wandering mountaineers, and were now overgrown and strewed with dry grass and stubble: the largest of these plains is that of Wudd, so called from a town or village of the same name, which is situated among the mountains, about six miles to the eastward of the road. We had a recommendatory letter from the Jam to Wulee Mohummud Khan, chief of Wudd, who is the head of the Brahooe tribe of Mingull, the first, in point of numbers, in Beloochistan; but having understood

* Toorkubur, from Toor and Kubur, a grave.

at Bela that he was absent, we did not think it adviseable to go to the village, and, therefore, dispatched one of our guides to deliver the letter to his Deewan or manager, with instructions to forward it to his master. The town of Wudd is, I understand, very small and ill built; the chief of it has in vain endeavoured to found another in the valley, respecting which the natives entertain a belief that it is haunted at particular seasons, and the people who were with us, positively affirmed, that Hindoos and others had several times attempted to settle there, but, that without a single exception, they all died, or were driven away within one year.

A little before sun-set we took up our lodging for the night close to the Ghedans or tents of three or four Brahooe shepherds, one of whom supplied us with abundance of milk, firewood, and water; this little Kheil or society had selected a most romantic and retired spot, immediately under a stupendous range of mountains, for their abode; their manners were mild, simple, and prepossessing, and the only cares they seemed to have, in this peaceful retreat, were to protect their flocks from the nightly depredations of wolves and hyenas, to tend them while grazing during the day, and to milk them morning and evening; at all of which, both sexes were equally alert and skilful. The flocks were just brought home as we dismounted, and it was surprising to see with what quickness and regularity they were all milked and pent up; at this every soul assisted, from the father of the family to the infant that could just walk; the ewes were milked into separate pails from the goats, as the butter made from them is not considered so likely to keep when clarified, though, when fresh, it is preferred by the Brahooes as being stronger: when the household avocations were over, the women and children came and sat round our fire, and chatted without the least reserve; their demeanour, as well as that of the men, evinced a truly hospitable desire to oblige, uninfluenced by the hope of reward, and few, who have not been situated as we were at that moment, can fully appreciate the gratification of such treatment as we met with from these wild and uncivilized shepherds. Having given one of the daughters of our host some flour to bake bread for us, it furnished me with a plea for looking into the Ghedan or tent to inquire, or rather look, whether it was ready or not: I was much struck with the cleanliness and comfort that prevailed in this extraordinary dwelling, which was merely composed of a few thin sticks, bent so as to form an arched roof, and covered with a kind of coarse, black blankets; the one I entered, was scarcely high enough to admit of my standing upright in it, the length of it appeared to me to be about ten or twelve yards, and the breadth as many feet, and it was most comfortably spread with coarse carpets, that I found were made by the Brahooe women; the fire was at one end, and caused the only inconvenience, from the want of a vent for the smoke, which escaped by the door; this, however, had the effect of rendering the Ghedan much warmer than it otherwise would have been, which, to these poor people, who are thinly clad, and more exposed to the vicissitudes of weather than any others whom I have ever met with, either in Europe or Asia, must be a great object.

4th February. We quitted our hospitable Brahooes this morning, having previously rewarded them for their kindness with a present of some coarse white cloth and tobacco, articles which they prized much more than money; and after marching upwards of thirty-five miles through a barren, mountainous country, the road extremely bad, and intersected by numerous deep and difficult ravines, arrived at the town of Khozdar at three *p. m.* The appearance of travellers at this season of the year excited great conjecture, and the inhabitants of the town viewed us with suspicion and surprize. We passed through the Bazar to the house of a Hindoo, to whom we had letters of recommendation, and after considerable detention, while a consultation was held whether we should be received or not, succeeded in procuring a vacant hovel, in which we put up for the night, and were shortly enabled to get some food for ourselves and cattle.

5th February. We halted at Khozdar this day, to replenish our supplies and give the camels a little rest; among others, we had a visit from a respectable merchant of Kandahar, who was here purchasing sheep for the market of that city, although the distance to drive them cannot be less than five hundred miles; he said he had intruded himself on us, to inquire after an uncle of his, who went to Hindoostan some years before, and had not been since heard of; and as he was (he added) in our line *, he thought it possible we might know something of him; he sat with us nearly two hours, and went away fully satisfied that we were real Moosulmans, in which opinion we did not consider it prudent to undeceive him. In the afternoon, a Hindoo Fakeer came to us, who declared, that he had performed a wandering pilgrimage all over Persia, Khorasan, Seistan, Kashmeer, Bokhara, &c. &c., on any of which regions he volunteered to give us such information as we wanted; we asked him a very few questions, fearing we might excite his suspicions of our real characters, but by his answers to those, he proved his boasted knowledge to be very superficial, and that, although he might have seen much, he had observed little.

Our stay here to-day gave us an opportunity of seeing the town; it is small, not having above five hundred houses, built in a valley encompassed by mountains, and surrounded by a low mud wall, also enclosing two or three gardens, which produce, in due season, grapes, figs, apricots, almonds, apples, &c.; but when we were there, the trees were leafless, and every thing bespoke the depth of winter. Khozdar is the usual summer residence of Meer Moorad Ally, of the tribe of Kumburanee, and a brother-in-law of Muhmood Khan, chief of Kelat; he was absent at Kutch Gundava †, but his Naeb, or deputy, a miserable looking old man, came to see us, and apologised on the score of indisposition, for not having done so the evening before; we acquainted him that we were the bearers of a letter from the Jam of Lus to his master; but as there was a probability of our eventually meeting him, we meant to take it on with us. The inhabitants of Khozdar are chiefly Hindoos from Mooltan and Shi-

* Horse-dealers.

† A country to the eastward, under the mountains. Vide Map.

karpoor *, and such is their influence in the place, that the keys of the town gate are entrusted in the hands of their senior Brahmin every night, of which class there are several, who officiate at a Pagoda that the community have here dedicated to Kalee, the goddess of fate: they seem to be a most dissolute debauched set, and at the season in which we were there, did nothing but smoke, chew Bhung †, and sit over the fire, which destructive vices give them all the symptoms and diseases of premature old age; the bazar is well supplied by means of them, and they have likewise two water mills, that are turned by a stream running through the valley.

6th February. From Khozdar to Bunkar, the distance ten or eleven miles, the road good, leading, with a considerable ascent, through the vallies of Khozdar and Baghwan, by which latter name the village is also often distinguished; like the former, it belongs to Meer Moorad Ally Kumburanee, but is neither so large or populous; and the whole of its inhabitants, save two Brahooe families, had emigrated to Kutch Gundava.

7th February. Our Mushks ‡ of water were frozen into a mass of ice this morning; and our people could not venture out before eight o'clock, at which hour we mounted, and after a tedious and most fatiguing march of nearly fifty miles, through a bleak and desert country, with a bad road, alternately over and between mountains, we arrived at the village of Soherab or Sooriab, situated in a plain of the same name, at nine o'clock at night: it became so piercingly cold after sunset, that we were obliged to dismount and lead the camels, which were nearly exhausted from famine and toil, when we got to the village, where a Mingull Brahooe kindled a large fire, and gave up his house to us, himself and family going into a neighbour's. The valley of Soherab is very extensive, being from

* Two large trading cities lying north-east and east of Kelat. Vide narrative of the 23d of January. (note.)

† Cannabis Sativa.

‡ Leathern bags, for carrying water, used by travellers all over the east.

thirty to forty miles in length, and from ten to twenty in breadth: it is watered by a stream, supplied by different springs in the mountains; and there are three or four villages in it, belonging to the brothers of Meer Moorad Ally of Bunkar, who have each a house here, at which they reside some part of the summer for sporting purposes: the mountains on the eastern side of this plain are exceedingly lofty, and the summits of them were white with snow; a snowy peak also appeared, during the latter part of our march to day, which we subsequently ascertained, lies upwards of seventy-five miles in a direct northerly line from Kelat, and must have been, at the most moderate computation, when we first descried it, at least one hundred and fifty miles from us.

8th February. From Soherab to Rodenjo, a stage of twenty-six miles, almost entirely over the plain of Soherab, which we finally quitted three miles from the latter halting place, half way there is a Suraé *, called Soormusing, or the Stone of Antimony, a name which it derives from the vast quantities of that mineral to be collected in the vicinity; this Suraé is a Munzil or stage for laden camels, and very fine water may be procured near it. The village of Rodenjo consists of a few miserable huts, and the people have no water except in wells, and that is neither good or plentiful: the contiguous country is bare and desolate, and nothing, I should conceive, but its being the first and only baiting place between Kelat and Soherab, and thereby having a considerable consumption of grain and other articles, could induce rational beings to fix their abode in so miserable a spot, when, by removing a few hours journey, they could enjoy the benefits of a fertile well watered district.

This place is named Rodenjo from a curious tradition, firmly believed by all the natives, of two merchants having accidentally met here on an extreme cold winter's night, the camels of one of them being laden with madder, and of the other with indigo, which two dyes are severally called in the Belooche language, Roden and Jo; the mer-

* Suraé, an inn, whence Karwansurae a Caravansery.

chant whose camels bore the latter, exchanged some of that valuable article to a great disadvantage, for a quantity of the former, with which he made a fire, and thereby preserved his life; while his more parsimonious fellow-sufferer. would not apply the smallest particle of his remaining merchandize to the same purpose, and perished from cold.

CHAPTER III.

ARRIVAL AT KELAT. — INTERMEDIATE COUNTRY. — WATER. — CITY GUARDS. — HINDOO AGENT. — HIRE A HOUSE. — VISIT FROM HINDOOS. — THEIR OBSERVATIONS. — SUSPICIONS OF THE AUTHOR AND HIS COMPANION. — SINDIAN ENMITY. — CLOTHS. — NECESSARIES. — VISITORS. — CURIOSITY. — COLD. — HINDOOSTANEE MEN, HOW BEAR IT. — PEOPLE OF LUS. — CONTRAST BETWEEN THEM AND THE KELAT MEN. — FIREWOOD. — SNOW. — AUTHOR'S FEELINGS. — MESSAGE. — DAROGHA, OR MANAGER. — BAUBLE MERCHANTS. — TRADE. — ATTEMPT TO DISCOVER THE AUTHOR AND HIS COMPANION. — ASSERTION. — DENIAL. — OPPORTUNE REMARK AND CONJECTURE. — BAUBLES WELL INFORMED IN COMPARISON WITH OTHERS. — WANT OF WORLDLY KNOWLEDGE. — ILLUSTRATED BY TWO ANECDOTES. — AUTHOR'S REFLECTIONS. — APPEARANCE, DRESS, AND MANNERS OF THE BAUBIES. — PRESENT OF FRUIT. — HOW DRIED. UNUSUALLY COLD DAY. — INTENSE FROST. — GHILJYE MERCHANT. — KAFILAH. — EXPLANATION OF THAT TERM. — LETTERS TO BOMBAY. — OFFER. — DECLINED. — THE AUTHOR AND HIS COMPANION PASS FOR OOZBECK TARTARS. — A VISIT TO THE CITY. — FASHIONS. — AUTHOR'S COMPLETE DISGUISE. — PROOF OF IT BY AN INCIDENT. — THE CITY OF KELAT. — WHY SO CALLED. — SITUATION. — PLAN. — FORTIFICATIONS. — AUTHOR'S OPINION OF THEM. — KHAN'S PALACE. — VIEW. — OUTWARD APPEARANCE. — CITADEL. — DEFENSIBLE. — TOOPUNGCHEES OR MATCH-LOCK-MEN. — GUARD. — CITY GATES. — NUMBER. — DISTINGUISHED. — HOW. — HOUSES. — SUBURBS. — HOW BUILT. — STREETS. — PATHWAY. KENNEL. — NUISANCES. — AUTHOR'S REMARK. — REPLY. — VERY INAPPLICABLE. — BAZAR WELL SUPPLIED. — WATER. — EXTRAORDINARY SPRING. — ITS QUALITIES. — WATER MILLS. — HOW ERECTED. — DESCRIBED. — PRECAUTION. — WHY REQUISITE. — GARDENS. — PLANTED. — PRODUCE. — POPULATION OF KELAT. — CLASSES. — NAMES. — INTRICATE SUBJECT. — EXPLAINED IN THE SUCCEEDING CHAPTER.

FEBRUARY 9th. We arrived at the city of Kelat this afternoon, after a march of twenty-five miles from Rodenjo; the intermediate country being very hilly, and here and there large patches of jungul; the route was about north north-west, and fresh water to be had in many places. When we had passed through the suburbs, which are pretty extensive; and reached the southern gate of the city; the Toofungchees or matchlock-men on guard inquired our business, and whence we had come. We briefly informed them, and desired to be shewn to the house of the Hindoo Shaloomull (Soondurjee's agent at Kelat), to whom we had letters of credit and recommendation; one of them accordingly directed us to his shop in the Bazar, where our Hindoo produced our letters, and demanded a place to put up in. Shaloomull and his son advised our renting a house outside the city walls, because the air and climate were there more salubrious than those of the narrow streets. With this proposal we gladly concurred, it being attended with the additional advantage of privacy, which was a thing, of all others, we were most anxious for at that time: the son, therefore, accompanied us; and after getting out of the fort and suburbs, and crossing a small brook that runs through the valley, we came to a house situated in a garden, which our conductor, having previously conversed with the owner, informed us was the one that his father proposed as our residence, and "which" added he, "is particularly well-suited for you horse-dealers, from "having a walled yard attached to it, large enough to contain sixty "or seventy horses."

Shortly after we had taken possession of our new house, which was a tolerably good one, built of mud on a frame of wood, like those of Bela, we were visited by all the better class of Hindoos, who were introduced to us by Shaloomull: to many of them we had letters of recommendation, that we now delivered, and the receivers expressed their willingness to shew us every attention: they informed us that we had arrived at a most untimely season, as the Khan, with his family, and the whole of the principal inhabitants of Kelat, had gone down to Kutch Gundava, to avoid the severity of the winter; "however," said they, "if you remain two months here, as the spring "opens they will all return; the merchants will likewise arrive about "that time from Kandahar, and you may then procure whatever "number of horses you are empowered to purchase." We told them that our plan was such, and that we had only come up so early to ensure the first choice of the market. Among the Hindoos, one old man (the agent of Seit Dureeadna, our Kurachee enemy) was excessively troublesome and inquisitive regarding our ultimate movements and intentions; he expressed, in unequivocal terms, his doubts of our professions, as well as his surprize, that we had not brought letters to him; and it was very evident to Captain Christie and myself, from the tenor of his discourse, that he had had previous intimation of our intended advance, with directions to watch our motions *; however, we got rid of the supposed spy and the whole party as soon as possible, under the pretence of having something to eat. Late in the evening Shaloomull again came out to us, to know if we had any commands for him; and as we had brought no clothes of any description with us save those on our backs, we gave him instructions to have some made, agreeable to the most approved fashion of the day; and likewise for a few other necessaries which were absolutely requisite during our halt here. When he departed we spread our kumlees † on the floor and slept soundly, happy to be respited for a short time from our fatigue.

10th February. This forenoon we had numberless visitors, who were prompted by curiosity to venture out of the city to see us, although the air was so piercing, that we were obliged to have a large fire burning in the centre of the room the whole day, and keep pretty near it; we, however, felt the cold much more than we should otherwise have

* The anxious solicitude which the Umeers of Sinde displayed, in the first instance, through the medium of Dureeadna; and, ultimately, by their avowed agents, as will appear in another part of this narrative, to frustrate our plans, and compel us to abandon our object by quitting the country with precipitation, is easily accounted for by that jealous suspicion and disguised, though inveterate enmity and dread, which are the leading, and indeed it may be said, the only impulse of all their actions towards the British government of India and its officers; and of which it fortunately happened that Captain Christie and I were fully aware, from being eye witnesses of their conduct regarding the mission from the supreme government of India to them the preceding year.

† A coarse kind of blankets.

done from a want of clothing; and the men who had come with us from Lus were rendered by it so utterly incapable of making the least exertion, or being in any way useful to us, that it made us resolve on sending them back and hiring others. I was rather surprised to find that those from Bombay stood the cold better, although Bela has a much more inclement winter than that part of Hindoostan.

Our shivering party, including ourselves, formed a wonderful contrast to our sturdy landlord and his brother, who set off a little after daylight in the morning to the adjacent mountains to cut fire-wood, with which they returned late in the evening, bringing us a present of a bag of snow, having heard us speak of it as novel; it was the first I had seen, except at a distance on our route up, for nearly seven years, and brought my native green isle, if possible, more forcibly to my remembrance, with all its tender ties and dearest hopes: the feelings attach an inseparable idea of home to any thing, however unimportant, which we have been accustomed to behold in our more juvenile days. At that time, removed as I was from even the pleasures of a social intercourse with the civilized world, this sentiment operated with still greater force; and I contemplated the snow with a mixed sensation of satisfaction and regret. Our landlord laughed heartily at the expression of our thanks for the treat he had brought us: "why," said he, with the utmost simplicity, "should you place such a value on a little snow; if you will accompany me one day to the mountains, you may see a whole country covered with it." I was, of course, silent, for it would have been useless, as well as impossible, to have explained my feelings at the moment to the person who addressed me.

11*th February*. We had a complimentary message from the Darogha or manager of Meer Mustapha Khan (the brother of the Khan of Kelat), regretting that indisposition precluded him from personally shewing us any civility; but, at the same time, requesting that we would not hesitate to command his services, in case he could be of use to us. We sent a reply, thanking him for his politeness, and promising to wait upon him the first time we went to the city. Our visitors to-day were quite as numerous as the preceding one, and we were vastly entertained with many parts of the conversation we had with them; they were in general Uffghans, of the tribe called *Baubee*, who are settled at Kelat for purposes of traffic. They were anxious to obtain information regarding the trade of Bombay; and our Hindoo, being fortunately acquainted with the rates of that market, was enabled to satisfy their curiosity.

Amongst them, a very well dressed man, called Fyz Mohummud, said he had been on intimate terms with an English gentleman who was formerly resident at Kurachee in Sinde. It was evident that he had only introduced this observation from a wish to ascertain whether we were really Englishmen or not, and if so, what our intentions might be; but we feigned total ignorance on the subject, and I simply answered, that I had heard from Soondurjee that the English had once had a Kothee or factory in Sinde. At length they came to the point by one of them declaring to his companions, in Pushtoo *, that he had himself seen us both, the year before, with the envoy to Sinde. We understood enough of that language to collect the meaning of his words; and, indeed, the look of astonishment with which some of the others, who had not been apprized of the plot laid to discover who we were, viewed us, would have been a sufficient interpretation of them; we, therefore, strenuously denied the charge, and were supported in our denial by the Jam's men who happened to be present, and who turned the idea into the ridicule which they devoutly thought it deserved. The Puttan, however, seemed far from inclined to withdraw his declaration, and was proceeding to describe minutely the time and place in which he was, as Captain Christie recollected, very correct, when Fyz Mohummud most opportunely observed, that there were many vicissitudes in life, and that we were all predestined to changes of fortune. I suspect from this

* The language spoken by the Uffghans.

remark, that he believed our attempt to refute the assertion that had been made, arose more from an unwillingness to acknowledge our reduced circumstances and station in life, than any other cause. Whatever was his motive, we were very thankful to him, as it had the effect of silencing the whole party, and obviated any further discussion regarding us.

These Baubees, though better informed than the generality of people I met with, either at Kelat, or in any other part of Beloochistan, did not appear to me to have the slightest conception of the most common forms of life or society, out of their own immediate sphere of observation: if we spoke to them of Kandahar, Kutch Gundava, or any place that they had several times visited, they were intelligent and ready to communicate; but when any thing or place which they had not actually seen became the topic of discourse, they were as little able to take a part in it as an infant of a year old; this seems to be very much the case with all the natives of those parts of Asia which I have traversed, and I am convinced from daily experience, that unless they have an object in view, they never think of making foreign observations and inquiries. To this rule, doubtless, exceptions may be found, but I fancy very few. The Hindoo, it is true, will tell you the readiest market for his goods; and the Moosulman horse-dealer, I also admit, knows where to go to purchase the best and cheapest cattle; but in these instances their avarice was concerned, and it induced them to inform themselves. I have been here led to make these reflections, which some will, perhaps, deem inapplicable, by recalling two questions that were put to us, by the very person who had spoken of his intimacy with the Resident in Sinde, and who might, from that circumstance alone, have been supposed to know a little better: he very gravely inquired if I knew whether the Firingee, *i. e.* European governor of Bombay, was a Hindoo or a Moosulman? and a few minutes after he made use of the word "Company," and wished to be informed how old she was. At first I could not conceive his aim; but he soon explained it, by saying he had always understood that the "Company" was an old woman, with an immense deal of money. This absurd supposition obliged me to explain to him, as far as I could venture to do, and farther, perhaps, than he could comprehend, the nature of the Sirkar, or government, that Europeans called the Company. To which he merely observed, that he had no doubt but I was right, as he had latterly been reflecting on the extraordinary age which the old woman must have attained since the factory in Sinde, upwards of half a century before, was called the Company's Kothee.

The appearance of the Baubee merchants is rather prepossessing; all of that class whom we saw were stout well made men, with good features, and their manners rather polite and refined than otherwise; their dress, at this season (winter), consists of a Pyrahun or shirt made of white cloth or coloured silk, a chintz Ulkaliq or tunic *, quilted with cotton; a pair of blue silk or cotton trowsers, very long and wide, and the better classes wear variegated worsted socks; their turbands are moderately large, being formed of a common sized Loongee, or silk cloth, under which they have a cap that covers the whole skull: over all, when they go out of doors, they wear a Posteen, or cloak made from sheep skins, with the woolly side inward, an appendage of dress which gives an incredible deal of warmth: they likewise usually carry in their hands, or tied over their shoulders, a spare Loongee. In summer they discard all the warm parts of their dress, wearing Pyrahuns or shirts of thin calico, a tunic of very light chintz, and, in lieu of the turband, many of them adopt a quilted cap. In the evening we had a present of some dried apricots from one of our Uffghan acquaintances, which we found excellent, when they had been steeped three or four hours in cold water; they are preserved simply by the stones being taken out, and the fruit then laid in the sun.

12th, *13th*, and *14th February*. The former was the coldest day

* Vide Narrative of the 23d January (note).

that had been felt at Kelat this winter, and we were indebted to that circumstance for a quiet forenoon, as it prevented idlers from coming out of the city to our house; we, therefore, took the opportunity to write some letters to Bombay. The frost was so intense, that as I was washing my hands on the sunny side of our house, at twelve o'clock in the day, the water was frozen instantaneously as it fell on the ground. Towards evening it had all the appearance of a heavy fall of snow, the air was thick and foggy, but it cleared off about nine *p. m.* and froze hard during the night.

On the 13*th* a Ghiljyee * merchant from Heraut called upon us; he had come down with a Kaffilah † of forty-two camels, laden with asafœtida, and wished us to give him letters to Soondurjee at Bombay, as he hoped that his good offices might assist him in the sale of his goods. He was very thankful for our immediate acquiescence with his request, and even carried his gratitude so far, that he proposed to dispatch one of our people with his merchandize, and he himself would go back to Kandahar and bring us whatever number of horses we required: this was, however, an obligation which we were by no means inclined, for many reasons, to place ourselves under to him, and we politely declined it. On departing, he said he would often visit us during his short sojourn at Kelat; and, accordingly, the next day, 14*th*, he again came, and chatted with us for two hours. We had perceived in all our communications with this man, that he believed us to be Moosulmans; and before he left us to-day, he asked us our *caste* and country. Having previously prepared an answer, Captain Christie replied, without the least hesitation, that we were descended from an Oozbuck family that had been settled in Hindoostan for some generations. He was quite satisfied

* The Ghiljyees are a class of the Uffghans.

† A Kaffilah and Karwan (or, according to European orthography, caravan), are usually synonymous. I believe a distinction does exist, at least the Belooches and their neighbours consider a number of travellers, with their property, to be a Karwan; but, on the other hand, where all the goods belong to one merchant, they speak of a Kaffilah.

of the truth of this, and only remarked that our colour was thus satisfactorily accounted for. *

15*th February.* The tailor having brought home our new clothes, we visited the city to-day, and, after strolling all over it, sat two hours at Shaloomull's shop in the Bazar. We were so metamorphosed in our Kelat habiliments, which were made after the fashion of the Baubee merchants; and I had practised with so much effect their peculiar mode of tossing about the loose Loongee, which is frequently carried in the hand, that an Uffghan came running up to me in the street, and asked, in the Pushtoo language, when I meant to return to Kandahar? To which our conductor replied, that I had not determined; and the inquirer turned away without discovering his mistake. This city, which is the capital of the whole of Beloochistan, and thence called Kelat, or the city, by distinction, that word having that signification in the Beloochie dialect, is situated on an elevated site, on the western side of a well cultivated plain or valley, about eight miles long, and two or three broad; a greater part of which is laid out in gardens and other inclosures. The town is built in an oblong square, and three sides of it are encompassed by a mud wall, eighteen or twenty feet high, flanked, at intervals of two hundred and fifty paces, by bastions which, as well as the wall itself, are pierced with numberless loop-holes for matchlock-men; but there are no cannon mounted at present, nor would the works, according to my judgment, be strong enough to bear them in their present ruinous condition. The defence of the fourth side of the city is formed by the western face of the hill, on which it is partly built, being cut away perpendicularly; on the summit of this eminence stands the palace of Muhmood Khan, chief of Kelat, and now nominal Beglerbeg of Beloochistan, commanding a distinct view of the town and adjacent country. I had not an opportunity of seeing the inside of the palace; but, viewed from the outside, it appears an irregular heap

* Many of the Tartars are as fair as Europeans.

of common mud buildings, with flat roofs forming terraces, that are protected by low parapet walls, pierced in the same manner as those of the fort, with loop-holes.

That quarter of the hill on which the Khan's residence is erected, has been enclosed by a mud wall, with bastions: it is still kept in better repair than any other portion of the fortifications; and on the whole, I conceive this citadel, with very little trouble, might be rendered more capable of defence than any other place I saw in Beloochistan. The entrance to it is on the south-western side, and there is constantly a guard of Toofungchees, or Matchlockmen here, and at the city gates, which are three in number, and distinguished by the names, Khanee, Kandaharee, and Belaee: the two latter are plainly so, from the roads to Kandahar, and Bela passing through them, and the other is a compliment to the Khan. The houses, inside the walls are upwards of two thousand five hundred, and the suburbs may exceed one half that amount. They are built of half-burnt brick, on wooden frames, and plaistered over with mud, or Chunam*; generally speaking, the streets are broader than those of native towns, and most of them have a raised pathway on either side for foot passengers, and an uncovered kennel in the centre, which latter is a great nuisance from the quantity of filth and dirt thrown into it, and the stagnant rain water that lodges there, as there does not exist any strictly enforced regulations for keeping it clean. Another obvious obstacle to the comfort and cleanliness of the city arises from the upper stories of the houses frequently stretching across the streets, and thereby rendering the part beneath them gloomy and wet. This is intended as an attempt, though barbarous in the extreme, to imitate the covered Bazars of Persia and Kabool, for on my remarking to a man who accompanied us through the town, the great inconvenience of it, he replied, "You must not judge of our Bazars until you have seen those "of Kandahar and Heerat; there they have whole streets covered "over, and yet no one ever thinks of finding fault with them." I

* Mortar.

was not, at that time sufficiently acquainted with the nature of the Bazars he alluded to, to ridicule the comparison as it deserved; and the Belooche fancied he had quite reconciled me to my objections by his sapient observation.

The Bazar of Kelat is extensive and well furnished with every kind of goods; flesh meat, vegetables, and the necessaries of life are procurable daily, and at a moderate rate. The town is supplied with delicious water from a spring in the face of a hill on the opposite side of the plain, whence it meanders nearly through the centre of it, having the town and suburbs on one side, and on the other the gardens. The stream from this fountain is so abundant that it turns several water-mills before it runs a quarter of a mile: its source is in a natural cavern in the rock, into which I walked ten or twelve yards; here the stream which is from two to three feet deep, clear as chrystal, and very rapid, divides itself into four or five branches, and the recesses from which they flow become so low and contracted that I could not penetrate farther. I do not recollect either to have seen or heard of a more luxuriant spring than this, and a remarkable fact attending it, is that the waters of it, at their immediate issue from the smaller channels possess a considerable degree of tepidity until after sun-rise, when they suddenly become exceedingly cold, and remain so during the day.

The water-mills turned by this stream, are on the same principle with all others I saw in Beloochistan, and are built immediately under a bank; or where there is no natural fall, an excavation is made to obtain one. The wheel is vertical, and its action is accelerated or retarded by depressing or raising it according to the weight of the water: this precaution is very requisite, as the rivulets are often swoln to a great height by the rain or melting of the snow, and the millers are then compelled to raise the wheel on a level with the water, which would otherwise turn it with too great velocity. Some of the mills have a second channel to discharge this exuberant supply, but the above is the most common method of remedying the inconvenience. The greater half of the gardens in the valley of Kelat, were planted by the father of the present chief, and are perhaps not yet arrived at that perfection which they may yet attain. They produce in plenty the various sorts of fruit so common in oriental climates; but as this is a topic, the consideration of which, agreeable to the plan I have laid down, more properly belongs to another place, I shall defer it for a future opportunity.

The inhabitants of Kelat may be said to be composed of four classes; namely, Belooches or Brahooés, Hindoos, Uffghans, and Dehwars; and as an explanation of their divisions into tribes, particularly the former, is a subject requiring considerable detail, I shall dedicate the subsequent chapter to the observations I have been enabled to make upon them.

CHAPTER IV.

BELOOCHES. — THE NAME OF THE WHOLE POPULATION. — OBSCURE ORIGIN AND HISTORY. — FICTION. — GREAT CLASSES. — BELOOCHES AND BRAHOOES. — TRIBES. — SUBDIVISIONS. — DESIGNATIONS. — WHENCE. — DISTINCTION BETWEEN THEM. — LANGUAGE OF THE BELOOCHES. — RESEMBLANCE TO PERSIAN. — PRONUNCIATION. — GROUNDS OF THE AUTHOR'S OPINION. — BRAHOEEKEE, OR LANGUAGE OF THE BRAHOOES. — DISSIMILARITY TO THE PERSIAN. — HINDUWEE. — PUNJABEE. — CONTOUR OF THE PEOPLE WIDELY DIFFERENT. — EXCEPTIONS SOMETIMES EXIST. — WHEN. — PRECAUTIONARY REMARK. — PRINCIPAL BELOOCHE TRIBES. — NAMES. — NHAROOES. — WHERE SETTLED. — RINDS AND MUGHSEES. — EMIGRANTS. — SUBDIVISIONS OF ALL THREE. — CHIEFS. — HILL TRIBES. — NHAROOES. — PARTICULAR DESCRIPTION OF THEM. — HARDY. — BRAVE. — SAVAGE. — ABHOR PRIVATE THEFT. — PREDATORY. — SENTIMENTS ON THAT POINT. — CHUPAOS. — WHAT. — UNDER THE ORDERS OF THEIR CHIEFS. — HOW CONDUCTED. — FOOD. — WATER. — PLAN USUALLY PURSUED. — ATTACK. — AMAZING RATE OF TRAVELLING. — MAKE A CIRCUIT. — OBJECT. — GREAT PERIL OF THE CHUPAOS. — LIKELY CONCLUSION TO BE DRAWN. — INACCURATE. — PROOFS. — RINDS AND MUGHSEE BELOOCHE CLASSES. — LESS PREDATORY. — CAUSE UNCERTAIN. — AUTHOR'S CONJECTURE. — REASON FOR IT. — APOLOGY FOR THE NHAROOES. — COMPARISON BETWEEN THE THREE CLASSES. — RINDS AND MUGHSEES NOT SO HARDY AS THE NHAROOES. — CLIMATE, THE OPERATIVE CAUSE. — SURMISE. — COLOUR. — RESEMBLANCE OF THE RINDS AND MUGHSEES TO EACH OTHER. — NOT APPLICABLE TO THE NHAROOES. — SKETCH OF ALL THREE CLASSES CONTINUED. — RELIGION. — ENMITY TOWARDS THE SHEEAS. — AUTHOR'S OPINION. — REMARKABLE HOSPITALITY. — PILFERING, HOW LOOKED UPON. — FIDELITY. — OBEDIENCE. — MOTIVE FOR THE LATTER. — DOMESTIC HABITS. — PASTORAL GHEDANS OR TENTS. — TOOMUNS OR VILLAGES. — KHEILS OR SOCIETIES. — THE LATTER DISCRIMINATED BY PREFIXES. — LIKELY TO MISLEAD BY BEING CHANGED. — EXEMPLIFIED BY AN ANECDOTE. — EXCEPTION TO LIVING IN GHEDANS. — HUTS. — RECEPTION OF GUESTS. — DETAIL OF THAT CEREMONY. — INDOLENCE OF THE BELOOCHES. — SMOKING. — GAMBLING. — PERNICIOUS HABITS. — NO DRUNKARDS. — FOOD. — FLESH-MEAT. — CAMELS' FLESH. — GAME. — VEGETABLES. — ASAFŒTIDA. — HOW EATEN. — USUAL NUMBER OF WIVES — OFTEN EXCEEDED. — INSTANCES. — WOMEN TREATED WITH RESPECT — ALLOWED TO APPEAR. — NOT UNIVERSAL. — SLAVES. — HOW PROCURED. — KINDNESS TOWARDS THEM. — TREATMENT WHEN FIRST TAKEN. — SOON RECONCILED. — PROVED BY AN ANECDOTE. — DRESS. — SHIRTS. — TROWSERS — CAP. — CHIEFS' DRESSES. — POOREST CLASSES. — WOMEN'S DRESS. — PER-

SONS IMMODESTLY EXPOSED. — HAIR OF YOUNG WOMEN. — HOW FASTENED. — OLD WOMEN. — MUFFLED UP WHEN OUT OF DOORS. — NOT SO WITHIN. — PROOF. — SOLDIERS' ARMS. — INCONVENIENCE. — NOT CONSIDERED. — MANNER OF FIGHTING. — WEAPONS. — WHENCE BROUGHT. — HOME MANUFACTURE. — AMUSEMENTS. — SHOOTING. — HUNTING. — COURSING. — FIRING AT MARKS. — CUDGELLING. — WRESTLING. — SWORDS. — SPEARS. — EXPERTNESS. — NEZUH BAZEE OR SPEAR PLAY. — HOW PERFORMED. — DANGEROUS. — EXERTION NECESSARY. — FUNERAL CEREMONIES. — SIMILAR TO ALL MOOSULMANS'. — FATIHU KHANEE OR PRAYER READING. — CONTRASTED WITH WAKES. — MARRIAGE CEREMONIES. — PRELIMINARY STEP. — SANG OR PROMISE. — ITS NATURE. — OFFERINGS. — BETROTHED COUPLE. — CONDUCT TOWARDS EACH OTHER. — CEREMONY. — SUBSEQUENT CONDUCT OF THE BRIDEGROOM. — CONSUMMATION. — DOWRY. — AUTHOR'S OPINION. — REFLECTIONS. — MORAL CHARACTER. — FEMALE HONOR. — JEWISH RELIGION. — LAWS. — INSTANCES OF THEM. — DANGEROUS EFFECTS RARE. — BRAHOOE CLASS. — TRIBES. — KHEILS. — WANDERING PEOPLE. — HARDY. — EXTERNAL APPEARANCES CONTRASTED WITH THE BELOOCHES. — OCCUPATIONS. — MANUFACTURES. — FOOD. — VORACIOUS APPETITES. — FLESH-MEAT. — THE REASON THEY ASSIGN FOR INDULGING. — MEAT HOW PRESERVED. — VERY PALATABLE. — PRECAUTION IN STORING IT. — BRAHOOES FAITHFUL. — HOSPITABLE — INDUSTRIOUS. — AUTHOR'S CONTRAST OF THEIR CHARACTER — GREAT BRAVERY. — AUTHORITY OF THEIR CHIEFS. — UNCOUTH MANNERS. — NOT UNPLEASING. — GRATEFUL. — AMUSEMENTS. — MARKSMEN. — SWORDS. — NO SPEARS. — MEN'S DRESS. — DOMESTIC OCCUPATIONS. — WOMEN NOT SECLUDED. — WOMEN'S APPAREL. — RELIGION. — MARRIAGE. — INTERMENT. — GREAT SIMPLICITY. — LIST OF BRAHOOE TRIBES. — CHIEFS. — NUMBERS. — COMPLICATED SUBJECT. — ANALYSIS OF VARIOUS NAMES. — FREQUENTLY CHANGED. — INTERMARRIAGES. — PECULIAR DIVISION OF ONE TRIBE. — PUNCTILIO OF THE RIND BELOOCHES AND BRAHOOES. — HINDOOS. — TOLERATED. — THEIR FEARS OF THE GOVERNMENT. — NUMBERS. — OPULENCE. — GLOOMY. — THE CAUSE. — AUTHOR'S REFLECTIONS. — PAGODA. — DHURUM PYSA. — WHAT. — BRAHMINS. — EAT FLESH-MEAT. — NOT STRICT. — INSTANCES. — DRESS OF HINDOOS — APPEARANCE. — ACCOUNTS — DIALECT. — BABBEES. — ALREADY SPOKEN OF. — TRIBE OF NOOTI. — COUNTRY. — OCCUPATIONS. — MERCHANTS. — GUZERATTE. — DEHWARS OR DEHQANS — WHO. — ORIGIN UNCERTAIN. — DIALECT. — SURMISE. — INCORRECT. — PURSUITS. — VARIOUS ACTS OF VASSALAGE THEY PERFORM. — IMMUNITIES THEY ENJOY. — MANNERS. — NOT ALLOWED TO MARRY WITH OTHER TRIBES. — RELIGION. — DOMESTIC LIFE — TREATMENT OF THEIR WOMEN. — TAUJIKS. — WHO. — CONCLUSION. — ADDITIONAL CLASSES. — DISCUSSION DEFERRED.

THE Beloochies, who form the great bulk, or perhaps, very strictly speaking, the whole of the population throughout Beloochistan, are a people whose origin is so obscure, and whose history, like that of all other barbarous tribes, is so blended with romantic fiction and tales of wonder, that I have found it exceedingly difficult to reduce either the one or the other to any credible form. They are divided into two great classes, severally known by the appellations of Belooche and Brahooé, and these two are again subdivided into such an infinite number of tribes, who take their names from the most trivial circumstances, that it is morally impossible to account for them: the chief under whom they serve, the district or country to which they belong, or the tradition whence they derive their descent, are the most common designations they assume. Between these two superior classes, the leading distinctions that I observed were in their languages and appearance; and unquestionably they constitute the greatest that can exist between men of the same colour and inhabiting the same nation. The Belooche or Beloocheekee (so the language of the Belooches is called), partakes considerably of the idiom of modern Persian, and at least one half its words are borrowed from that language, but greatly disguised under a corrupt and unaccountable pronunciation: the similarity of sound is, however, so very striking, that during my journey amongst these people, I latterly understood from my knowledge of Persian, almost every sentence that I heard spoken in Beloochee. The Brahoočkee is, on the contrary, so dissimilar in its sound and formation, that I never recollect to have remarked in it a single expression in any way approaching the idiom of Persian. It contains an extensive portion of ancient Hinduwee words, a circumstance which will be explained in the historical account of this class, and as it strikes the ear, bears a strong resemblance to Punjaubee, the dialect spoken in that part of India called the Punjaub.*

The contour of the people of these two classes is as unlike in most instances as their languages, provided they be the descendants of a regular succession of ancestors of either; but the frequent inter-

* I here speak alone of the sound, as I am equally unacquainted with either of the languages I venture to compare.

marriages which take place among them, have tended to such a degree to blend together the peculiar characteristics of both, that in many families, and even whole tribes, they have ceased to exist; and, therefore, the offspring of such unions form a third class, who may, perhaps, often differ to a trifling extent in appearance, from their progenitors, although they are incorporated into one or other of the classes. I conceive it here necessary to state again, what I have done at the commencement of this chapter, in order to prevent confusion, that the aggregate population is exclusively known by the name of Belooches, which adheres to one of the two classes it diverges into; but as they must be considered separately, I shall henceforward always distinguish each as Belooches or Brahooés.

The Belooches, from the most accurate information I could acquire on this perplexing subject, branch, in the first instance, from the original class of that name, into three principal tribes, called Nharooés, Rinds, and Mughsees. The former, the Nharooés, principally inhabit that portion of Beloochistan which lies to the westward of the desert, and there are likewise Kheils, or societies, of them at Nooshky, a village north-west of Kelat, and in Seistan: the other two tribes, the Rinds and Mughsees, are settled in Kutch Gundava, a low country to the eastward, at the base of the mountains, to which fertile plain they have emigrated at different periods, from the province of Mukran, and have become incorporated with the Jeths, or cultivators of the soil, as the subjects of the Khans of Kelat; a few of them likewise reside in the hills to the north-eastward of Kutch Gundava, and on the skirts of the desert north of Kelat. *

The subdivisions of the Nharooé tribe are about eight or ten, and those of the Rinds and Mughsees each amount to many more than double that number. I annex a list of such of all three as I posi-

* For all the geographical points mentioned in this paragraph, I must refer my readers to the Map. I am sensible of the advantages of detailed explanation as I advance, but in a narrative of this kind it would be endless to subjoin notes on every place that is spoken of in the course of it.

tively ascertained, with the names of some of their Sirdars or leaders; and I am likewise enabled to add the avowed strength of a few of them in fighting men; but I am myself of opinion that it is much exaggerated:

Nharooé Belooche Tribes.

Names.	Numbers.	Chiefs.
1. Rukhshanees	700	Mihrab Khan.
2. Sajadees	450	Meer Shah Suwar.
3. Khasogees	150	
4. Koords or Shuhedees	4500	Oolfut Khan.
5. Meengs or Minds	300	Shah Suwar Khan.
6. Urbabees	6000	Shah Mihrab Khan.
7. Mulikahs	250	Eesa Khan.

To the first of these the head of the class belongs, and the whole are, in consequence of that, as frequently distinguished in common conversation by that appellation as that of Nharooé. The authority, however, which Mihrab Khan enjoys is merely titular.

Rind Belooche Tribes.

Names.	Numbers.	Chiefs.
1. Rindanees	8000	Sirdar Khan.
2. Goolumboolks	700	
3. Poghs	300	Meer Saheb.
4. Jullumbaneés	800	
5. Deenareés	700	Fyzoollah Khan.
6. Poozhes	600	
7. Kulooés	700	
8. Jutooés	75	
9. Doombukeés		
10. Booledés	900	Meer Syfoodeen.

Rind Belooche Tribes — continued.

	Names.	Numbers.	Chiefs.
11.	Doankeés	80	
12.	Kharaneés	1000	Meer Abbass.
13.	Omranees	4000	Sabit Khan.
14.	Kosas	150	Shumsher Khan.
15.	Changyas	100	Meer Buhadoor.
16.	Nousherwanees	700	Sikundur Khan.
17.	Bugothees		
18.	Mureés		
19.	Goorchanees	3000	Futtuh Khan.
20.	Muzarees	2500	
21.	Direeshks	500	
22.	Lugharees	5000	Jumal Khan.
23.	Loords	1000	Mohummud Khan.
24.	Chachreés	1500	
25.	Moundustreés	1500	Lushkur Khan.

Mughsee Belooche Tribes.

	Names.	Numbers.	Chiefs.
1.	Mughsees	8000	Jaffer Khan.
2.	Ubruhs	3000	Qaem Khan.
3.	Lashareés	20,000	Gholam Mohummud Khan.
4.	Matyheés	1000	Ally Mohummud.
5.	Boordeés	200	Jullall Khan.
6.	Oonurs		Dooreea Khan.
7.	Nareés	500	
8.	Jutkeés	4000	
9.	Kullunduraneés	700	Noor Khan.
10.	Moosaneés	6000	Kureem Khan.
11.	Kukraneés		
12.	Jukraneés		

Mughsee Belooche Tribes — continued.

Names.	Numbers.	Chiefs.
13. Eesobaneés		
14. Jukrahs		
15. Jullaneés.		
16. Toorbundzýees		

Of the Rind Belooches, the nine tribes last enumerated are those that dwell in the hilly regions to the north-eastward of Kutch Gundava, and there might be, perhaps, a few others added to that class, and likewise to the Mughsees, of whom I shall hereafter speak in my account of the province of Sinde.

The Nharooés are commonly a tall, handsome, active race of men, not possessing great physical strength, but adapted and inured to changes of climate and season; and accustomed to undergo every species of fatigue. They are fearless of death, and, in battle, said to fight with great gallantry, only requiring a leader to direct them to the proper point for a display of their impetuous valour. Bound by no laws, and restrained by no feelings of humanity, the Nharooés are the most savage and predatory class of Belooches; and, while they deem private theft dishonourable and disgraceful in the extreme, they contemplate the plunder and devastation of a country with such opposite sentiments, that they consider it an exploit deserving of the highest commendation; and, steeled by that feeling, they will individually recount the assistance they have rendered on such occasions, the numbers of men, women and children they have made captives and carried away or murdered, the villages they have burned and plundered, and the flocks they have slaughtered when unable to drive them off.

The lawless incursions, during which these outrages and cruelties are committed, are here called *Chupaos;* and as they are almost always conducted under the immediate superintendance and orders of the chiefs, they form a very considerable source of profit to them.

The depredators are usually mounted on camels, and furnished, according to the distance they have to go, with food, consisting of dates, sour cheese, and bread; they also carry water in a small leathern bag, if requisite, which is often the case in the midst of their deserts. When all is prepared they set off, and march incessantly till within a few miles of the point whence the Chupao is to commence, and then halt in a jungul or some unfrequented spot, in order to give their camels rest. On the approach of night, they mount again; and, as soon as the inhabitants have retired to repose, they begin their attack by burning, destroying, and carrying off whatever comes in their way. They never think of resting for one moment during the Chupao, but ride on, over the territory on which it is made, at the rate of eighty or ninety miles a day, until they have loaded their camels with as much pillage as they can possibly remove; and, as they are very expert in the management of those animals, each man, on an average, will have charge of ten or twelve: if practicable, they make a circuit, which enables them to return by a different route from the one they came: this is attended with the advantage of affording a double prospect of plunder, and also misleads those who pursue the robbers, a step generally taken, though with little effect, when a sufficient body of men can be collected for that purpose.

From this description of Chupaos, which was given me by several different Belooches who had been upon them, they are evidently services of great peril and danger. Many of the marauders, who are separated from their companions in the night and left behind, are seized, mutilated, and murdered in the most cruel manner by the exasperated inhabitants; others are killed in the skirmishes which take place, and some die from fatigue and want of rest. It might, therefore, be supposed to require a certainty of great gain, as an inducement to the Belooches to risk their lives in such desperate undertakings; but so entirely is this reversed, that the Chupaos are often unsuccessful, from the natives of the devoted districts having previous information, and taking means to repel them; and again, some that succeed in a partial manner, barely repay them for the camels that die during or after it from over-work. At times, however, the robbers reap the reward of their intrepidity, and Mihrab Khan Rukhshance told me that he himself once shared, from a Chupao into the Persian province of Laristan, slaves and other spoil to the amount of six thousand rupees *, a large sum in the estimation of a savage.

The Rinds and Mughsees are less predal in their habits and mode of life than the Nharooés; but whether that proceeds from an innate detestation of such outrages, or a dread of the Khan of Kelat, I am unable to pronounce with certainty. I should, however, be inclined to suspect the latter cause as operating more forcibly than the former; for we find that the Muzareés, Direeshks, and other Rind tribes, who live in the hills, and are in a great measure out of the immediate precincts of the Khan's authority, infest the roads and commit the most atrocious robberies and murders on travellers, a practice more to be reprobated than even that pursued by the Nharooés; in extenuation of whom I may observe, that as they never enter into any engagements, they always deem themselves in a state of warfare with the surrounding nations, and the Chupaos I have described, form their system of carrying on hostilities. The Rinds and Mughseés resemble the Nharooés in size and stature; and like them, have good features and expressive countenances, but are not capable of bearing an equal portion of hardships and labour. The climate of the country, in which they chiefly now reside, seems to have enervated and deprived them of that energy of mind and body which doubtless once appertained to them in their native mountains of Mukran, and which is still to be traced in the tribes already mentioned as inhabiting the hills. They are darker in colour than the Nharooés, a circumstance also to be attributed to the heat of the climate of Kutch Gundavee. The men of these two classes, or any of the tribes emanating from them, whom I met with, either during

* 750l. Sterling.

my journey or since my return to India, did not strike me as differing from each other in manners or appearance, and a stranger might readily have supposed they were all of the same class, which is not the case with the Nharooé and its different ramifications; but as I shall have an opportunity, in the course of my narrative, of exemplifying the distinctions I perceived amongst them, I now proceed to finish the sketch of the Belooche character, by describing those points in which they all appeared to me to correspond.

With regard to religion, they are, with a very few exceptions to the westward, Soonee Moosulmans, and inveterate in their hatred and enmity against the Sheeas *, under which persuasion, I am convinced, it would be more dangerous to appear in Beloochistan, than even as a Christian.

The hospitality of a Belooche is proverbial, and I found it equally conspicuous in every part of the country which I visited. Among them pilfering is considered a most despicable act; and when they once offer, or promise to afford protection to a person who may require or solicit it, they will die before they fail in their trust. They obey their chiefs with alacrity and willingness, but this obedience seemed to me rather to result from a confidence placed on the propriety of what they are ordered to perform, and a wish to uphold the respectability of their tribes, which depends much on that of the Surdars or chiefs, than from any feelings of deference and respect that they entertain towards the latter; for I observed, that in many instances, even under their immediate eye, they acted as if they held themselves scarcely amenable to their authority. In their domestic habits, the Belooches are almost all pastoral; they usually reside in "Ghedans," or tents, made of black felt, or coarse blanket, stretched over a frame of wicker-work, formed from the

* The Soonnees are those Moosulmans who contend that the lawful succession to Mohummud rested in the four Imams, Aboobukur, Omar, Othman, and Ali, while the Sheeas as strenuously contend that Ali alone, as the nephew and son-in-law of the Prophet, had that right.

branches of the Guz (Tamarisk) bush: an assemblage of these Ghedans constitute a Toomun, or village, and the inhabitants of it a Kheil, or society, of which, from the nature of their formation, it is clear there may be an unlimited number in one tribe; and I know half a dozen of instances where they exceed twenty or thirty: they are commonly discriminated by a titular prefix, such as Umeerée, Daodée, Surdaree, &c. to the word Kheil, as the Umeerée Kheil, the noble society, Daodée Kheil, David's society, &c. &c. This complicated subdivision of the tribes into Kheils, is likely to confuse a casual observer, and more especially from their changing, as they often do, their distinguishing titles with their places of residence. For example, when I was at Nooshky, on the borders of the desert, there was a Kheil of Mingull Brahooés, (a people whose country is to the southward of Kelat,) encamped about two miles off; and, on my asking one of them his tribe, he replied, Mingull, and his Kheil, Nooshkyée, or the society of Nooshky. It is right to add, that some of the Belooches, particularly the Nharooé clans, prefer mud houses to tents, and even live in forts; nor is it uncommon, in the western parts of Beloochistan, to find one half the Kheil residing in Ghedans, and the other in huts; I believe that the preference which is shewn to the latter, is on account of the cold.

Their reception of guests is simple, yet impressive. When a visitor arrives at a Toomun, a carpet is spread in front of the door of the Mihman Khanu, or house for guests, of which there is one in every town or village in Beloochistan; the Sirdar, or head of the Kheil, immediately appears, and he and the stranger having embraced, and mutually kissed hands, the followers of the latter successively approach, and the Sirdar gives them his hand, which they press to their foreheads and lips. So far the reception is conducted in profound silence, and the parties now sit down, on which the chief addresses the stranger, and asks him, four several times, how he does, to which the other answers in the usual complimentary terms; he then inquires in the same manner for his family and friends, and even for the health of his followers who are present, to whom the visitor turns, as if to appeal for information; they all nod assent to being in good health; and the ceremony concludes, by the new-comer making an equal number of inquiries for the welfare of the family, Kheil or society, followers, and friends of the Sirdar. By nature the Belooches are extremely indolent, and, unless occupied by some favourite amusement, they will spend whole days in lounging from one Ghedan to another, smoking and gambling; many of them are addicted to the pernicious custom of chewing opium and Bhung*, but I neither met with, or heard of a single instance of habitual ebriety, from spirituous liquors or wine; in fact that species of the vice of drunkenness seems to be unknown amongst them. Their various foods are wheaten and barley cakes, rice, dates, cheese, sweet and sour milk, which last they infinitely prefer; soup made from dholl, or peas, and seasoned with red pepper, and other heating herbs, and flesh-meat whenever they can procure it, including that of young camels, and every kind of game: of vegetables they prize onions, garlic, and the leaves and stalk of the asafœtida plant, which they roast or stew in butter, raw or clarified. They usually limit themselves to one or two wives, and their chiefs four; but this totally depends on choice. I saw men of the lowest station, who had seven or eight living, and Mihrab Khan, chief of the Rukhshanees, had just espoused his sixteenth when I was at his capital. They treat their women with attention and respect, and are not so scrupulous about their being seen by strangers as most other Moosulmans, although they by no means allow them to appear in public at all times.

The Belooches keep great numbers of slaves of both sexes, the fruits of their Chupaos, whom they treat with a kindness and liberality that is quite gratifying to see. When first taken, they look upon themselves as the most unfortunate beings in existence, and, to say the truth, the treatment they then experience, is of the

* Cannabis Sativa.

harshest and most discouraging description; they are blindfolded and tied on camels, and in that manner transported, to prevent the possibility of their knowing how to return; the women's hair, and men's beards, are also shaved off, and the roots entirely destroyed by a preparation of quicklime, to deter them from any wish to revisit their native soil; but they shortly get reconciled to their fate, and become very faithful servants. I shall relate an anecdote, which will best exemplify the footing on which they live with their masters. Captain Christie, speaking on this subject, expressed his surprize to, Eidel Khan Rukhshanee, the Sirdar of Nooshky, that the numerous slaves which he had, should work so diligently, without any person to look after them. "Why not," said he, "they are clothed, fed, and treated like the other mem-"bers of my family, and if they do not labour, they are well aware "that bread will be scarce, and they must then suffer as well as our-"selves; it is their interest to have plenty, because they know what-"ever may fall to my lot, they get a share of it." Captain Christie assented to the justness of these observations, but added, that he should have thought them likely to run away. "Nothing of the "kind," replied the old Sirdar, "they are too wise to attempt it: "in the first place, they don't know the way to their own country; "but even admitting they did, why should they wish to return? "They are much happier here, and have less worldly cares; were "they at home, they must toil full as hard as they now do; beside "which, they would have to think of their clothes, their houses, and "their food; situated as they now are, they look to me for "all those necessaries; and, in short, that you may judge yourself "of their feelings, I need only inform you, that the severest punish-"ment we can inflict on one of them, is to turn him about his "business."

The common dress of the Belooches is a coarse white or blue calico shirt, open about fourteen inches down the front, buttoning round the neck, and reaching below the knee; their trowsers are made of the same cloth, or a striped kind of stuff called Soosee, and puckered round the ancles: on their heads they seldom wear any thing except a small silk or cotton quilted cap, which is made to sit to the shape of the skull, and over this, when in full dress, they add a turband, either checked or blue, and a Kummurbund or sash, of the same colour round their waists. The chiefs and their relatives likewise appear in winter with an Ulkhaliq, or tunic, of chintz, lined and stuffed with cotton; and the poorer classes, when out of doors, wrap themselves up in a surtout made of a peculiar kind of cloth, manufactured from a mixture of goat's hair and sheep's wool. The women's attire is very similar to that of the men, their shifts are usually cotton cloth, dyed red or brown, very long, quite down to the heels, open in front below the bosom, and as they wear nothing under them, their persons are considerably exposed; their trowsers are preposterously wide, and made of silk, or a fabrication from that and cotton mixed. The young women, both married and unmarried, have a very ingenious method of fastening their hair up, by dividing it into different locks, twisting them round the head, and inserting all the ends in a knot on the crown; it looks very tidy, and at a short distance I repeatedly mistook it for a cap. The old women tie handkerchiefs round their heads, flowered with worsted or silk. When they go abroad, both young and old muffle up their faces so as not to be seen, but in their houses they are not, as I have already stated, at all particular; and when I was at the village of Nooshky, I was frequently in the Sirdar's Ghedan, when his whole family was present.

A Belooche soldier, when armed cap-a-pee, makes a very formidable display. He carries a matchlock, sword, spear, dagger, and shield, besides a multiplicity of powder flasks, priming horns, and pouches; the latter crammed with balls, slugs, flints, tinder boxes, and other warlike apparatus, which, on active service, must encumber him beyond conception; they do not, however, seem to mind it, and a warrior's prowess is often estimated by the weight of his accoutrements. They are all capital marksmen, and on that account in battle, avoid as much as possible, coming to close combat; but when they have no alternative, they either throw away their fire-arms, or sling them by the side of the camel, or horse on which they are mounted. The best and most prized warlike weapons they have, are of foreign manufacture. Matchlocks, swords, and daggers, they get from Persia, Khorasan, and Hindoostan: shields from the latter country; and for spears they are generally indebted to their neighbours the Sindians. At Kelat there is an armoury for matchlocks, swords, and spears, belonging exclusively to the Khan, but the workmanship I saw from it was bad and clumsy.

The amusements of the Belooches are such, as we should expect to find among a wild and uncivilized people: they are enthusiastically fond of every species of field sports; and much of their time is passed in shooting, hunting, and coursing, for which latter purpose, they bestow a vast deal of attention on the training of their greyhounds: a good one is valued at two or three camels, or even more, and I was informed that the Khan of Kelat has been known to pay to the value of four hundred rupees * for one dog. Firing at marks, cudgelling, wrestling, practising with swords, and throwing the spear, are likewise, all favourite diversions with them; and neighbouring Kheils cope with each other at these exercises: the four latter they understand scientifically, and at the former, some of them are so incredibly expert, that I am assured they can invariably hit a target, not more than six inches square, off a horse at full gallop; and I can positively affirm, that the different guides I had during my journey killed, at the distance of fifty or sixty yards, every small bird, such as larks, sparrows, &c. they fired at, with a single ball; nor did they appear to consider this as any signal proof of their dexterity as marksmen. Before I close this enumeration of their diversions, I may describe a very hazardous, though popular one among all classes, which they perform on horseback, and call Nezuh Bazee, or spear play. A wooden stake of moderate thickness is driven into the ground, and a horseman at full speed, pierces it with the point of his

* *50l. Sterling.*

spear in such a manner, as to force it out of the earth, and carry it along with him; the difficulty and danger in accomplishing this feat, is evidently augmented or decreased, according to the depth that the stake is in the ground; but in its easiest form, it requires a violent and dexterous exertion of the arm and wrist, combined with the most critical management of the horse and spear at the same instant.

The funeral and marriage ceremonies of the Belooches, being such as are prescribed and regulated by the Koran, unless in some minor points in the latter, are therefore so similar to those of all other moosulmans, that they require from me very little observation. When a patient is supposed to be in imminent danger, a Moollah, or priest, is called to explain and read the Koran to him, which he continues at intervals to do, until the sick person either gets better or dies; in the latter event, people are immediately sent for to mourn; and food is prepared at the house of the deceased three successive days and nights, for such friends as choose to be present at the Fatihu Khanee, or reading of prayers for the dead. To do this, is likewise the duty of the Moollah; and whether the deceased was in affluent or indigent circumstances, his relations are always very anxious to see a number of guests on the occasion; and will distress themselves greatly, to entertain those who attend. It appeared to me from the verbal account I had of this custom, that it exactly corresponds with the nocturnal watchings of the dead known in Great Britain by the name of wakes; the night is passed in the same revelry and joviality, and although there is no intoxication, yet between gossiping and eating, the Belooches do not fail to make merry, and a Fatihu Khanee* would seem to a stranger to be any thing else than a mournful ceremony for the dead. With regard to their marriages, there are no peculiarities, and consequently, the few remarks I have to make upon them are equally uninteresting with the preceding subject. When a young man wishes to espouse the daughter of a particular

* Fatihu Khanee, literally prayer reading, from Fatihu, a prayer, and the Persian verb Khandun, to read.

Belooche, he commonly deputes his brother, or some other very near relation to her father, to break the matter to him, and propose an alliance; should the match meet with the father's approbation, he gives his consent, and the preliminaries respecting the interchange of presents are immediately concerted between the two parties; this reciprocal contract is called the Sang or promise, and although sometimes made amongst* the highest classes before the betrothed couple have seen each other, it is considered of so sacred a nature, that it cannot be violated under any circumstances whatever; and should a person thus affianced die, his brother is bound by the rules of honour and propriety to marry the girl. The offering on the part of the lover generally consists of camels, sheep, goats, or other live stock, and is sent to the house of his intended father-in-law, a few days after the conclusion of the Sang, together with a prepared entertainment sufficiently large to include the whole Kheil, provided the young man's condition in life will admit of his going to that expence. It happens not unfrequently, that the Sang is entered into before the girl is marriageable, and in such case, the betrothed couple are permitted to see each other at her father's house, where the lover visits on the footing of one of the family; the girl is, however, on no account allowed to go to the house of her intended husband's parents, nor is there any familiarity or even verbal intercourse * sanctioned between them, except in the presence of others. As soon as the girl arrives at a proper age to take upon herself the duties of a wife, the Uroos or marriage ceremony is performed by a Moollah, in presence of the friends of both the bride and bridegroom; the latter once more feasts the Kheil, in the most sumptuous style he can afford; and remains as his father-in-law's guest for some days after consummation; his mother-

* Among the Uffghans, the mother of a betrothed girl is sometimes known to connive at the lovers giving vent to their mutual passions before the nuptials are celebrated. This commerce is called Namzud-bazee, words expressive of giving a name, as the girl is then considered by the mother as virtually espoused. The Belooches hold the practice in great abhorrence, and I believe the father of the girl equally does so, even though an Uffghan.

in-law then allows him to depart with his wife *, and on taking leave he is presented with her dowry, as fixed by the Sang, which includes, beside a greater or lesser proportion of similar stock to that given in the first instance by the young man, a quantity of cloth, carpets, and other household furniture, regulated according to the means which the girl's parents possess of endowing her.

In the course of my investigation of the foregoing point, and others connected with it, I discovered among the Beloochies many customs of the law of Moses, so much so, that their moral institutes relating to marriage, seem to be exclusively derived from that sacred law-giver, and they are so remarkably scrupulous in their observance of them, and correct in their general sentiments on those points, that it is very seldom an instance of conjugal infidelity occurs. Whether this coincidence may be the effect of chance, by the adoption of customs and rules among themselves, or whether it may be attributed to a more remote cause, is a question which my scanty acquaintance with the origin of these people, renders me unable to solve; tradition, both oral and written †, assigns to them descent from the Israelites, as a branch of the Uffghans, but they strenuously deny any connection with either, as an unfounded assertion; however the truth may be, the Belooches of the present day have certainly no traces left of the mien or manners of Jews; still that does not entirely annul the possibility of their being descended from such; for admitting it as an ascertained fact that they were, we may readily suppose that frequent alliances with the Arab, and other invaders of these countries, would have changed their appearance, though they might still have preserved some of their ancient laws, of which the following are instances that are not, to the best of my knowledge, so expressly prescribed by the Koran as they seem to hold them. In

* The mother of the bride must see the proofs of consummation. A similar custom is observed by the Armenians, but to a much more indelicate degree. It is clearly of Jewish origin.

† Vide 2d volume of the Asiatic Researches, page 74. 5th Edition.

the event of the death of a young woman's husband, his brother is bound to marry her, and the issue of that union inherit the property of the deceased: should there be no brother, the widow is at liberty to select a second husband for herself, she being from the hour she is married, removed out of the influence of her father's authority, or that of any of her other relations. The elopement of a married woman from her husband, or a betrothed virgin from her father's house being accounted equally contrary to their honour and duty, in whichever case it may occur, the death of the woman and the person with whom she elopes is the only complete expiation they acknowledge for it: they are both, however, said to be crimes unknown in Beloochistan proper: a man may put away a wife whom he has married believing her to be a virgin, provided he can prove to the contrary *; but it is very rare that an instance occurs of this law being resorted to: the difficulty in satisfactorily proving the charge, and the deadly feuds it would give rise to between families, restrain any attempts at unfounded accusation.

The Brahooe or second great class of the natives of Beloochistan now remains to be spoken of, but as I have been obliged to characterize it in most instances, while contrasting the Belooches and that people, I have but a few brief particulars to add regarding them. They are, as the Belooches, divided into an indefinite number of tribes and Kheils, and are a still more unsettled wandering nation, always residing in one part of the country during the summer, and emigrating to another for the winter season: they likewise change their immediate places of abode many times every year in quest of pasturage for their flocks, a practice which is rare amongst the Belooches. In activity, strength, and hardiness few people surpass the Brahooés; they are alike inured to the cold of the mountainous regions of Beloochistan, and the heat of the low plain of Kutch Gundava. They differ so much from the Belooches in external appearance, that it is

* Deuteronomy, Chapter XXII. verses 13, 14, 15, &c.

impossible to mistake a man of one class for a member of the other. The Brahooés instead of the tall figure, long visage, and raised features of their fellow-countrymen, have short thick bones, with round faces, and flat lineaments; in fact, I may assert, that I have not seen any other Asiatics to whom they bear any resemblance, for numbers of them have brown hair and beards. In husbandry and other domestic occupations, they are laborious hard workers, and those who reside in the vicinity of the plains to the southward of Kelat, till large tracts of land, and dispose of the produce for exportation to the Hindoos of Kelat, Bela, and Khozdar; this and the sale of the cheese and Ghee, made from the flocks, with a few coarse blankets, carpets, and felts, form the only traffic the Brahooés enter into. Their food is the same as the Belooches, except that they prefer flesh-meat to every thing else, and devour it in a half dressed state, without bread, salt, or vegetables; they are famous for having most voracious appetites, and their flocks of sheep and goats, being very numerous and prolific, enable them to indulge their inclination for meat by consuming a greater quantity. They affirm, perhaps with truth, that in the cold mountains which they inhabit, it would be impossible to survive during the winter without a certain portion of animal food, which they deem not only nutritious, but to have the same heating properties that are attributed to spirituous liquors in Europe, and to serve for this consumption they accordingly cure a supply of meat the latter end of Autumn, by drying it in the sun and then smoking it over a fire of green wood: the meat thus prepared has by no means a disagreeable flavour, and its taste may be very aptly compared to that of the reindeers' tongues exported from Russia; it will keep for several months, and when they store it up for the cold weather, the only precaution they conceive requisite is to place it so, that one piece shall not touch another.

The Brahooés are equally faithful in an adherence to their promises, and equally hospitable with the Belooches, and on the whole I greatly prefer their general character. From what I have already said on it, it is evident that they are a more quiet and industrious class, and their habits are decidedly averse from that system of rapine and violence pursued by the other; nor can we fairly ascribe this to any sentiment save a good one, for in personal bravery and endurance of privations and hardships, the Brahooés are esteemed superior to the inhabitants of all the neighbouring countries: their chiefs exercise a much more despotic authority in the various tribes and Kheils, than among the Beloochés, and the people are equally tenacious of their respectability, though they obey them from a different feeling: in manner they are mild and inoffensive, though very uncivilized and uncouth; but as the latter is evidently the effect of a want of worldly knowledge and guile, their awkward attempts to be civil please, because we see that they are incited to make them by a natural propensity to oblige, unaccompanied by any interested motive. They are free from the worst traits of the Belooches, which are comprised in being avaricious, revengeful, and cruel, and they seldom look for any reward for their favours or services: their gratitude is lasting, and fidelity such, that even the Belooche chiefs retain them as their most confidential and trust-worthy servants.

The amusements of this class are so correspondent with those already described of the Belooches, that I need not particularize them: in general the Brahooés pride themselves on being better marksmen than the Belooches, who admit the fact, and ascribe it to their having more practice, for none of them ever quit their Ghedans, even to go a few hundred yards, without a matchlock: they are likewise good swords-men, but never use spears, considering them a useless cumbersome weapon. A Brahooé always dresses in the same style, and whether it be summer or winter, freezing hard, or under a vertical sun, his whole cloaths are comprised in a loose white shirt, a pair of trowsers of the same texture, and a felt cap; the shepherds sometimes wear a covering of white felt, made so as to wrap round the body, and come to a peak above the crown of the head; this habit will keep off a vast deal of rain or snow, and is exclusively used for that purpose. The domestic life of the Brahooés is simple in the extreme; the men tend the flocks, till the ground, and do other out-door labour, in which they are, if needful, assisted by the women; but commonly the duties of the latter are to attend to the household affairs, such as milking, making butter, cheese, and Ghee, and they also weave and work carpets, felts, and coarse white cloth. They are not, as I have previously remarked*, secluded from the society of the men, but all live and eat together. Their dress consists of a long shift and pair of trowsers, both of cotton cloth, and after they arrive at the age of puberty they wear over the former a kind of stays, made to lace behind, the fronts of which are decorated with ridiculous devices of birds or animals worked in coloured worsted. In religion the Brahooés are all Soonnitte Moosulmans, and their external forms of religion, marriage and interment, are practised according to the tenets of that sect. I have therefore no remarks to add upon them, for there seems to be nothing peculiar or observable in their attention to them, unless I may note that the same simplicity that is so apparent in the common occurrences of their lives, equally pervades their manners with respect to these more important considerations.

Before I proceed to offer a few cursory remarks on the remaining classes of the inhabitants of Kelat, namely Hindoos, Babees, and Dehwars, I shall finish this section by annexing the names of some of the Brahooé tribes, from which specimen the diversity of the whole will be appreciated, and the consequent perplexity, if not impossibility of making satisfactory inquiries will be more readily understood.

Brahooé Tribes.

Names.	Numbers in fighting men.	Chiefs.
1. Kumburanees	1000	Muhmood Khan.
2. Zuhreé	8000	Qadir Buksh.
3. Mingull	10500	Wulee Mohumud Khan.
4. Soomlareé	4000	

* Vide Narrative 3d February.

Brahooé Tribes — continued.

	Names.	Numbers in fighting men.	Chiefs.
5.	Goorgunanee	300	
6.	Imam Hoosseinee	2000	Sheik Lohar.
7.	Koolche Bhugwa	500	
8.	Muhmoodaneé	500	
9.	Mooruha	1000	
10.	Kooreé	150	
11.	Burjaeé	1000	
12.	Rikeé	700	
13.	Punduraneé	3000	
14.	Rysutko	100	
15.	Sherwareé	8000	
16.	Rysanee	1500	Moola Mahomed.
17.	Neechareé	2000	
18.	Bezunja	1000	Ruhmut Khan.
19.	Shŏŏjaōōdeeneé.	1000	
20.	Momasineé	1500	
21.	Harooneé	200	
22.	Rodaneé	600	
23.	Sasoolee	200	
24.	Kuroo Chukoo	500	
25.	Bujaeé	700	
26.	Koorda	200	
27.	Nagrée	2000	
28.	Kejun Booladee	7000	
29.	Nusseer Rodanée	3000	
30.	Chotwa	700	
31.	Khidraneé	5000	
32.	Meerwareé	7000	
33.	*Kuludaeé*	300	
34.	Guloosooreé	700	
35.	Kolatcheé	250	

Brahooé Tribes — continued.

Names.	Numbers in fighting men.	Chiefs.
36. Laugeé	3000	
37. Kuree	1500	
38. Muhmood Shaheés	3500	
39. Debukeé	4000	
40. Rysaneé	800	
41. Kysareé	1000	Meer Kysar.
42. Mooreé	300	
43. Gudjagay	200	
44. Jyaneé	60	
45. Moosoowaneé	1000	
46. Sarawaneé	10000	
47. Surfuraneé	2500	
48. Poorjuhaeé	200	
49. Koochka	300	
50. Bhooldra	300	
51. Bhooka	300	
52 Rideé	1700	
53. Eeseeraneé		
54. Mihranee		
55. Jumalzyeé		
56. Gwarraneé		
57. Samozyeé		
58. Poatyeé		
59. Chungozyeé		
60. Dodyeé		
61. Jaikho		
62. Rodenzyeé		
63. Hussuneé		
64. Chumrozyeé		
65. Mŏŏrŏŏeé		
66. Bumbukzyeé		

Brahooé Tribes — continued.

Names.	Numbers of fighting men.	Chiefs.
67. Rahzyeé		
68. Shadunzyeé		
69. Shahozyeé		
70. Kuntinzyeé		
71. Rumuzanzyeé		
72. Sherzyee		
73. Goolzyee		
74. Bungoolzyeé, &c. &c. &c.		

Were it answering any purpose I could at least enumerate twice as many more, but the foregoing list includes the principal ones in point of numbers, and will suffice to prove the multiplicity of the Brahooé tribes, to say nothing of the absolutely innumerable Kheils into which they are subdivided: many of the preceding names are to be accounted for, while others have no rational meaning whatever. The Kumburaneés are so called from Kumbur, the founder of the government, and the ancestor of Muhmood Khan, the chief of all Beloochistan. The Zuhrees and Punduranees inhabit the districts bearing those names; the appellation of Goorgunanees is, I believe, derived from the word Goorg, the Persian for a wolf; the Sherwarees and Sherzyees in the same manner from Sher, a lion; the Haroonees and Kysarees from Haroon Khan and Meer Kysar, hereditary titles adopted by their leaders; the Muhmoodanees from Muhmood Khan, the present Khan of Kelat: the Jumalzyees, Chungozyees, Shadunzyees, and Goolzyees, from the terms, Jumal, Chungo, Shadun, and Gool, severally meaning, beautiful, good, happy, and rose, which joined to the affix, zyee, a tribe or horde, forms the beautiful tribe, &c.; and to conclude, the Dodyees being formed of two tribes united, take their designation from Do two, and Dyee, a nurse, the signification being literally two nurses. To these examples numerous others might be added, which an oriental scholar will easily recognise. In their continual migrations from one part of the country to another, the names of inferior tribes I am led to imagine, are often changed: I venture to make this conjecture from having more than once asked Brahooés questions regarding tribes, that I was certain had inhabited the next district to theirs some years before, but of whom they avowed entire ignorance, or said they must have then had another designation.

The Brahooés all intermarry with each other, except the Kumburanees, regarding whom there is a peculiarity which does not attach to any of the other tribes; that of being divided into three distinct gradations of rank, marked by the appellations Ahmedzyees, Khanees, and Kumburanees. At the time I was at Kelat in 1810, the former consisted of only seven persons, viz. Muhmood Khan, his son, two brothers, a sister, his aunt, and cousin; the Khanees are of the secondary rank of chiefs, such as Meer Moorad Allee of Khozdar, and his brothers: there are between twenty and thirty of this degree; the word Kumburanee includes, when they are thus particularized, all the remainder of the tribe, but in common it is applicable to the whole body. The Kumburaneés receive wives from, but do not marry their daughters into other tribes. Some of the Brahooés and Rind Belooches stand on the same punctilio with each other, but for this I could never hear any competent reason assigned, and I conclude it originates in their own imaginary pre-eminence.

The Hindoos who reside at Kelat are principally mercantile speculators from the cities of Mooltan and Shikarpoor*, and are much respected both by the government and people in general: nor is any molestation offered to them in the free exercise of their religion. They do not, however, venture to bring their wives or female relations to this city, an unanswerable proof of their not themselves, having that entire confidence in the good faith of the government, which its toleration, and the encouragement it holds forth to them to colonize here might seem to authorize. Their numbers are very considerable, as

* Vide Note on these cities in Narrative of the 23d of January.

they occupy between four and five hundred of the best houses within the city walls, and many of them are likewise extremely opulent, but notwithstanding all their wealth, and its concomitant benefits and comforts, it is easily perceived that the Hindoos of Kelat are a very miserable race of beings: their usual practice is to visit their native place once in the course of three or four years, and sometimes oftener; but the life of sad privation which they lead in the interim, debarred of the society of their wives and families, renders them gloomy, discontented and sickly, and a more lamentable evidence of the venality and thirst of gain inherent in the Hindoo character cannot be adduced, than in these men, whom we see, even after they have acquired what would be to them a vast independence, voluntarily sacrificing every rational blessing and earthly happiness at the shrine of lucre. I have already said that their religion is tolerated at Kelat, and accordingly they have a pagoda and several Brahmins attached to it, who are maintained by voluntary contributions, and a duty which the Hindoos, by an ancient grant, are permitted to levy on goods entering the city; this is called Dhurum pysa or religious money, and its extent and origin shall be hereafter mentioned. The Hindoos here are by no means strict in their observance of the Brahminical laws, and I was astonished to find, that both the Brahmins and their disciples eat every kind of flesh-meat except beef, even though killed by a Moosulman: they likewise drink water out of leathern bags, and some of them wear caps made of Bokhara skins, all of which are breaches of, and in direct opposition to the strict religion they profess. Their dress is an Ulkhaliq or tunic, made of chintz, tied on the right side of the breast, a fashion by which that part of the costume of all Hindoos is distinguished from the Moosulman's who fasten theirs on the left; a pair of long tight pantaloons which come down to the feet, and a large turband, coloured or white, according to the fancy of the wearer; they differ little in appearance one from another, having sallow complexions with dark black hair and beards, the latter of which they are accustomed to let grow; their language is that dialect of the Hinduwee, spoken in the Punjab provinces, and they keep their accounts in the same.

I have in a preceding place* inserted a few desultory observations on the Babees, whom I conceive to form a third class of the permanent inhabitants of Kelat, but as they are not natives of Beloochistan, and moreover are a tribe of no note whatever among their countrymen, little further need be said of them; they are an industrious pastoral set of people, the majority of whom dwell in the dominions of the king of Kabool, and in the Douranee country †, where they pasture their flocks and reside in tents; some of them are also, as has already been shewn, great merchants, and to follow their commercial avocations they quit their native wilds, and settle in cities or towns: of this last description are those at Kelat, and I have reason to believe there are many similarly situated in the northern parts of the provnce of Guzeratte.

The Dehwars, or Dehkans, which words are synonymous, and signify villagers, are the fourth and last class of those whom I have described as constituting the population of the city of Kelat; they are, like the others, not confined to it alone, and are to be recognized in different districts of the country, under various names, which are ordinarily those of the places they inhabit: thus those of Mustoong, Teree, and Pringuwadh (villages north of Kelat), are not styled Dehwars, but Mustoongees, Teereechees, and Pringuwadhthees. Of their origin I have been unable to discover any certain traces; their colloquial language is common, pure Persian, from which fact many assert that they are the descendants of those people, who remained behind on Nadir Shah quitting Beloochistan in 1747; but on the other hand, this is in a great measure confuted by our finding that

* Vide Narrative 11th February.

† The Douranee are the first class of Uffghans. Ahmed Shah Abdalli was a Douranee, and the succession to the throne remains undisputed in his family; they are subdivided into Oolooses or tribes, and the territory they inhabit is very extensive: Kandahar is the capital of the Douranee country, beside which there are other cities of inferior note. For a detailed history of this nation as well as the whole of the Uffghans, I refer my readers to the work just published by the Honourable M. Elphinstone, late Envoy to the Court of Kabool from the supreme government of India, and now resident at Poonah, a gentleman whose ability and erudition eminently qualified him for the task he has so well accomplished, and to whom I am equally indebted for his friendship and communications.

a tribe answering to their description, was known in that country long previous to the invasion of Hindoostan by that monarch. Their pursuits are agricultural, and those who reside in or near Kelat, are bound to serve the Khan without pay; to provide water, fuel, grass, and grain, for his guests, their retinue, and cattle; to attend the Khan himself on his hunting excursions in the neighbourhood, and to furnish Kasids, or couriers, on all occasions when required on the public service. In return for this vassalage, they enjoy various immunities, of which the most advantageous and desirable are, holding their lands free of rent or taxes, paying no tolls upon the produce on bringing it to market, being exempt from military service out of the immediate district of Kelat, and having the privilege of grazing their flocks on any part of it, except it be cultivated or enclosed. In manners and appearance the Dehwars are distinct from all the other natives of Beloochistan; quiet and harmless in disposition, they seem happy to give a tacit acknowledgement to the superiority that both Belooches and Brahooes, with whom they are not allowed to intermarry, arrogate to themselves over them, as though it were to prevent the possibility of disputes on that head. They reside in villages, as their name imports, consequently never migrate, but cultivate the soil in the vicinity of them, disposing of the products to the pastoral tribes and Hindoos. Those who are removed to a distance from the capital, pay a small portion also to the chiefs under whose authority, or rather protection they dwell. In stature and figure the Dehwars are below mediocrity, nor are they in other respects at all a comely race, their blunt features, high cheek bones, and bluff cheeks, rather render them the reverse; but notwithstanding their want of good looks, there is an artless, honest, and good-humoured expression in their countenances, which is perhaps full as pleasing. They are civil and obliging to strangers, but devoid of that spirit of hospitality for which the Belooches and Brahooes are so justly famed. Although they furnish no quota of troops when the Khan goes to battle, yet they are accounted so faithful and trustworthy, that a detachment of them is always on guard over his palace at Kelat, and likewise at the city gates. They are Soonnee Moosulmans, and in religion and domestic habit so exactly coincide with the particulars already given of the Brahooes, that it would be useless to treat more in detail of those points. They ridicule the seclusion of women, adopted in most Mohummudan countries, as a barbarous and unfeeling custom; and their sentiments on this head, and their treatment of females shew them to be more enlightened than any of the followers of the Arabian prophet I have ever conversed with. Among the Uffghans there is a very extensive tribe, also well known in many parts of Asia, denominated Taujiks, whose characteristics are described as corresponding so minutely with those of the Dehwars, that I can see no doubt of the ancestors of both having sprung from the same stock. The Taujiks are reputed inoffensive, industrious, and observant of their promises or agreements, devoted to husbandry and pasturage, and having their abode in villages of mud houses, that are by them called Dehs, and not Toomuns, which last is the usual term in Uffghanistan.

Having now brought to a conclusion my own immediate observations, together with the result of my inquiries on the various inhabitants of Kelat, I shall resume my Narrative, premising that there are two or three additional classes, such as the Jeths of Kutch Gundava, the Mukranees, or natives of Mukran, and the Sindians, or people of Sinde, who shall all be discussed when I come to speak of those provinces.

CHAP. V.

NARRATIVE RESUMED. — VISITORS. — MEDICINE. — DAROGHA OF MUHMOOD KHAN. — LETTER. — PRESENT. — SECOND TRIP TO THE CITY. — MOTIVE. — ACQUAINTANCES. — VISIT FROM A MOOLLAH OF KIRMAN. — CONVERSATION. — DISCOURAGING ACCOUNT OF HIS JOURNEY. — HOPES. — MOOLLAH'S PROPOSAL. — ACCEPTED. — BAGGAGE ARRIVES. — CAUSES OF DETENTION. — PROCEEDINGS OF THE BEZUNJA BELOOCHES. — THREATS. — HOW RESISTED. — ULTIMATE CONDUCT AND BOAST. — STEPS TAKEN BY THE UMEERS OF SINDE TO DISCOVER THE AUTHOR AND HIS COMPANION. — DESCRIBED IN A LETTER. — DETERMINATION IN CONSEQUENCE. — PREPARE TO QUIT KELAT. — DESIGNS OF OUR UFFGHAN SERVANTS. — HOW EVADED. — LUDICROUS SCENE ABOUT OUR MEDICINES. — MISTAKES MADE BY THOSE WHO WERE TO TAKE THEM. — NOT FATAL. — HOONDEES OR NATIVE BILLS. — ROUTE DISCOVERED. — RESOLUTION MADE IN CONSEQUENCE. — NOOSHKY. — HIRE BRAHOOE CAMEL DRIVERS. — DILATORY CONDUCT OF THE HINDOOS. — OBJECT. — SUCCEED. — REFLECTION ON THEIR DEALINGS. — AFFECTING STORY OF A YOUNG MAN. — HIS FATHER MURDERED. — ALLEGED CAUSE. — GREAT MEDICAL FAME OF THE AUTHOR AND HIS COMPANION. — REQUESTED TO VISIT THE FAMILY OF ONE OF THE MINISTERS. — ACCEDE. — MOOLLAH'S EXHORTATION. — AMUSING ACCOUNT OF CAPTAIN CHRISTIE'S RECEPTION IN THE SERAGLIO, AND THE TERMINATION OF HIS VISIT. — THE DAROGHA OF THE MINISTER COMES FOR MEDICINE. — HIS RODOMONTADE. — LITTLE ATTENDED TO. — ROBBERY IN THE CITY. — STEPS TAKEN. — THIEVES CAUGHT AND PUNISHED. — HOW. — OBSERVATION ON IT. — OBLIGED TO VISIT THE KHAN'S DAROGHA. — HINDOOS FIX ON A DAY FOR LEAVING KELAT. — UFFGHAN'S INTERFERENCE. — INQUISITIVENESS OF THE DAROGHA. — PROBABLE CAUSE, AND ADVANTAGE. — DEPUTATION FROM KABOOL TO MUHMOOD KHAN. — ANSWER. — SURMISE. — FRIENDLY OFFER OF THE MINISTER'S LADY. — ACCEPTED.

FEBRUARY 16*th*, 17*th*, 18*th*, 19*th*, 20*th*, and 21*st*. I include these several days under one head, to obviate the necessity of writing a regular journal of each, as they passed without any thing so novel or interesting as to demand particular notice. We had, as usual, a concourse of visitors, some of whom were very pressing to obtain medicine from us; but for the present we evaded their importunities, on the plea of our baggage not being arrived; an excuse we had cause to regret having made, from the trouble it afterwards occasioned us. On the 16th we had a visit from a most civil and respectable man, a Darogha or overseer of Muhmood Khan, who had arrived two days before from Kutch Gundava, for the purpose of procuring and carrying down to that place some articles that were needed by the Khan, who was preparing to celebrate his marriage with one of the daughters of Meer Moorad Allee of Bunker: he told us, that having accidentally learned that two agents of Soondurjee (with whose brother he had been long intimately acquainted), were come up from Bombay, he thought it right to pay his respects and tender his services to us: we expressed our due sense of this civility, and added, that we should trouble him to be the bearer of an Ureezuh * to his master from us, in which it was our intention to solicit his sanction to our sojourning at Kelat or elsewhere in his dominions, for some time. The Darogha replied, that it would give him much pleasure to take charge of it, and that he would also avail himself of the first favourable moment to state our views to the Khan, who he was confident would not hesitate in acceding to our request. On the 18th he again waited on us to get our letter, and Captain Christie then informed him, that we had been entrusted by Soondurjee with a small present for the Khan, and proposed sending it down to the Kutch Gundava, when our baggage joined us; but this he advised us against, and said the most proper time to offer it would be on the Khan's return to Kelat.

Our stay at this city had already been protracted much longer than we had calculated upon, but the unforeseen delay in the arrival of the servant, whom we had left with our things at Kohunwat, and for whose safety we began to have serious apprehensions, prevented our

* Ureezuh, a petition, here means a letter from an inferior to a superior.

forming any decisive arrangements for quitting it; we became, however, each succeeding day more anxious to obtain information on the nature and geography of those countries through which our projected route was to lead us, and finding that the Hindoo who accompanied us from Bombay, was both injudicious and abrupt in making inquiries on topics of that sort, we ourselves went to the city a second time on the 20th, for the purpose of doing so. Among the tribe of merchants, travellers, fakeers, and fortune-hunters, to whom we were introduced this day, was a Moollah, or priest from Kirman, the capital of the province of that name in Persia. He had come to Kelat in quest of a sister, who had been carried away during a Chupao*, by the Nharooes of Bunpoor, and purchased as a slave by the family of Sooltan Sahib, a confidential agent and adviser of Muhmood Khan. We invited this man to visit us at our house, in order to interrogate him relative to his journey from Persia, accordingly he made his appearance the following morning (the 21st), when we ascertained that he had travelled from Kirman to Kelat by Bunpoor and Kej †, of which places and their inhabitants he gave us a succinct account; but on our hinting at a proposition to him to return as a guide and companion to us, that we might purchase horses in the Kirman market, he swore by Mohummud and the King's beard ‡, that nothing human could persuade him to venture back by the same route. " In it," said he, " a person has two alternatives, " and he who must choose either of them, the Lord and the Prophet have pity upon him! the one is to wander in an uninhabited " waste, where neither water or food are to be had; the other, to " be among those dogs the Nharooes, where you are to expect to be " annihilated every breath you draw." He added, (with a fervent prayer and hope that the Almighty might confound the whole race)

* See an account of those incursions in the preceding chapter.

† Bunpoor has been spoken of as the residence of the chief of the Nharooes. Kej is the capital of Mukran. Vide Map and 2d Part.

‡ This is a very common oath amongst the Persians.

that they had seized his horse, and plundered him of every article he was possessed of, not even sparing the clothes he wore. This recital was rather discouraging to us, but we consoled ourselves with recollecting the notorious disposition of all Persians to exaggerate, on occasions where their own personal exertions or safety are called into question, and therefore trusted, in the event of our ultimately attempting that route, that we should not find circumstances so decidedly adverse as the Moollah represented. We asked him no further questions, fearing to excite his suspicions, and when we had conversed on indifferent topics for half an hour, he returned to the city, having previously volunteered to bring some Persian books another day, and read to us, a proposal we most willingly agreed to, as it helped to pass the forenoons, which were very dull and lagged sadly, from our having no means of amusing or employing ourselves.

22d February. This afternoon at three *p. m.* we had the gratification to receive our baggage, and the Hindoostanee servant who had the principal charge of it, gave a miserable picture of the sufferings and distress of the party from cold and bad camels; they had succeeded with vast trouble in advancing, (even at the tedious rate they did) owing to the people of Khozdar dreading the severity of the winter season at Kelat so much, that they could hardly be persuaded to bring their cattle. This servant related, that after our departure they waited two days at the Kohunwat, during which period, neither Ruhmut Khan, or the owner of the hired camels whom we had allowed to go to his home, appeared, so that there could exist no question, but that the latter had received his clue from the Bezunjas: the morning of the third day Ruhmut came with eight armed men, and instantly demanded where we were; he was exceedingly irritated and disappointed, on being told we were gone on without him, and asked half a dozen of times, whether we were merchants or thieves, to elope in so infamous a manner: in the evening he was joined by his brother Buhadoor Khan and the camel driver, the last of whom made some frivolous excuse for his long absence. Nothing could exceed the rage of the two petty chiefs, when they found we had escaped from their clutches; one instant they were for pursuing and making us, as they said, repent the disrespect we had shewn for their authority, the next, they vowed the severest vengeance upon us as we returned, but at length their deliberations ended in agreeing to examine our baggage, on which they protested the Soong or impost would be at least one thousand rupees. Our man acquainted them that its whole value would not amount to one half that sum; but that as to their Soong, under any circumstances, he recognized no right they had to levy it, and had no orders from us on the subject. "Perhaps," said Ruhmut, interrupting him, "you "are not aware that we Bezunjas plundered and murdered the "Moghul merchant in this identical spot *." "You must not," replied our Hindoostanee man, "think to treat us in the same "style, or suppose that we four or five armed men will so tamely "resign our lives and master's property, as the pusillanimous "Moghul." The Bezunjas seeing him resolute, protested they had no idea of using any coercive measures, and begged our people to take off their swords and make themselves easy, as they would guard the baggage throughout the night: to this the servant rejoined, that it was customary with him and his fellow-travellers to be always Kumurbustu † (prepared) during a journey. At last, finding our people immoveable, and having nothing to eat, the Bezunjas resolved to go back to their homes, and entreated to have four rupees worth of white cloth, which was given to them; their leader (Ruhmut) then said, that there was no occasion for his convoying the baggage, as the road was perfectly secure without him, and that though they had lacs of rupees, no one would dare to molest them when they had

* This is a fact. They attacked a Moghul merchant, who made no resistance, and put him to death with his whole party: the Khan of Kelat was so incensed at this outrage, that he sent for Ruhmut Khan's father to meet him, half way to Kelat, and killed him with forty of his tribe.

† The word Kumurbustu conveys a meaning for which our language affords no exact expression. It signifies in this instance, determined in mind as well as armed. It is derived from Kumur, the waist, and Bustun, to tie up.

his permission to pass; after this bravado, he and his myrmidons mounted their horses and camels and rode off, and our people proceeded on their journey next morning at day-break.

On reaching Khozdar, they found that Meer Moorad Allee had written to his Naeb or deputy at that town, to send us down to Kutch Gundava, where all the horses in the country were then collected; this plan, whether formed to befriend us or otherwise, was anticipated by our having travelled so expeditiously; it however proved fortunate in the end, as his Naeb deputed a man to attend the baggage to Kelat, who was very useful at Soherab, where the Darogha of the village insisted on every thing paying custom, and was otherwise disposed to interfere, when Meer Moorad Allee's man produced that chief's letter, directing our being treated with every attention and hospitality, which silenced the tax-gatherer in a moment.

A Kasid or messenger had overtaken our servants at Khozdar with a letter from Soondurjee's agent at Bela; from it we learned that four or five days subsequent to our quitting Sonmeany six men came there from Kurachee in Sinde for the purpose of discovering who we were; that on hearing we had left it for the interior, two of them went back to Kurachee and the others followed us to Bela, whence we had likewise fortunately set out previous to their arrival; they therefore waited on the Jam, and in public Durbar desired in the name of the Umeers of Sinde to know who we were, and on what business we had proceeded to Kelat. The Jam briefly acquainted them that he had not thought it necessary to inquire either our names or views, but that he had heard from rumour that we were the agents of Soondurjee, and gone to Kelat on his business. Much chagrined at this unsatisfactory account of us, the Sindians went off to Hydcrabad * to lay their information before the Umeers. On a perusal of this letter it no longer remained dubious that they would persevere in their efforts to have us seized and forcibly sent or ordered out of the country; and though we were

* The capital of Sinde.

apprized of the want of cordiality between Muhmood Khan and those chiefs, yet it was impossible to foresee what steps he might be induced to take by their misrepresentations: it therefore seemed highly advisable for us to quit Kelat with the least possible delay, and in order to account for this sudden resolution, and the preparations necessary to give it effect, we gave out that Soondurjee had written to us to go to Kandahar and Heerat*, and return with what horses we could procure at those places on the opening of the spring.

To augment our various perplexities at this moment, we heard that the two Uffghans had been constantly squabbling with our people, and that at Khozdar they had even publickly avowed, we were not merchants but spies, who were deputed expressly to see and examine the country; that we meant to go to Kabool or Peshawur† to see the king, and eventually to Persia. The Darogha of Meer Moorad Allee, who was present when these affirmations were made, mentioned them to our Hindoostanee servant, and advised him to caution us against these vagabonds, who we afterwards discovered had made a compact, to insist upon our giving them a camel each, as a bribe for their silence. This villainy was sufficient to point out the absolute necessity of parting with them, but it also shewed that it must be done with prudence, and Captain Christie therefore merely warned them, that he was aware of the infamous falsehoods they had been guilty of asserting, and reminded them that if they expected any reward from Soondurjee, they must be more circumspect in their disclosures in future. They of course denied the whole charge, but promised in other respects to abide by our instructions. In the afternoon the Kirmanee Moollah brought the Persian poem of Yoosoof and Zulee Kha‡, and read to us for a couple of hours: our landlord who was a Dehwar, and consequently understood Persian, with several of our neighbours joined

* The capital of Khorasan. Vide Map.

† Cities in the Uffghan dominions at which the court is usually held.

‡ The Loves of Joseph and Potiphar's wife.

the group, and were highly gratified by the Moollah's performance; he read extremely well, and seemed quite enraptured with his subject.

23d February. It was noised throughout the city this morning, that our baggage had at length reached us, and by breakfast time we were overwhelmed with applications for medicine, which continued without intermission till the evening: the askers would take no excuse, and to a by-stander it would have afforded a most ludicrous spectacle, to have seen Captain Christie and myself encircled by crowds, who fancied themselves afflicted with every disease that issued from Pandora's box, all of which, and their diagnostics they were describing at the same moment, and that too in a jargon which neither of us could clearly understand: we presently reduced them to some order, and being not only willing to oblige, but anxious to acquire friends by doing so, we dispensed the medicines with a liberal hand according to the best of our judgments, trusting, in no small degree, to the effect of our nostrums on the imagination. Some of our patients committed the most absurd mistakes, the consequence of not comprehending our directions, or not choosing to conform to them: one man began to drink a bottle of eye water, and returned to tell us that it had operated as an emetic, others swallowed what we had given them as external applications, fortunately without any bad effect; but the most serious blunder was that of a miller who lived close to us, and who took at one dose a very large quantity of aperient medicine, which nearly killed him; he had been told to divide it into seven or eight parts, but hoping to derive the same benefit by adopting a less tedious mode, he confessed he had, knowing our injunctions, mixed and drunk it off.

24th February. We ordered our Hindoo this day to have Hoondees, or native bills of exchange, prepared in our favour on Soondurjee's correspondent at Heerat in Khorasan, and likewise the cities of Kirman and Yezd, in Persia; but he found it impossible to get them on either of the latter places. His inquiries, however, led to a discovery, that ultimately proved of the highest importance to us regarding the routes through Seistan *, into which track we resolved to penetrate; and, as all the roads thither appeared, agreeable to the most exact intelligence we could gain, to unite at a village called Nooshky, sixty or seventy miles north-west of Kelat, our first plan was to go there, and thence advance as might be expedient. The men whom the Jam at Bela had provided us with, declared that they wished to take their discharges and return to their native town: this resolution exactly tallied with the scheme we had long formed, of sending them back before we finally quitted Kelat; and, agreeable to their request, they were all paid off, and a letter transmitted by them to the Jam: we hired four Brahooes as camel-drivers instead of them.

25th, 26th, 27th, and *28th February.* The dilatoriness of the Hindoos who were to draw out our bills on Heerat, and the manifold obstacles they threw in the way of our getting them elsewhere, doubtless with the design, in which they at length succeeded, of charging us extravagant exchange and brokerage, kept us in a continual state of suspence and indetermination for the last three or four days; once, they even declared that we could not procure them on any terms, unless we agreed to stay at Kelat until Shaloomull wrote to Shikarpoor †, and received an answer. As this would have occupied three weeks, Captain Christie peremptorily refused to comply, and after much altercation and subterfuge on the part of the Hindoos, we were forced to put up with the gross imposition of paying five and a half per cent commission, exclusive of the regular exchange of the day. We were much chagrined at this, but looked upon the loss of some hundred rupees as very secondary to getting clear of Kelat. Such conduct is quite in unison with the commercial ideas and dealings of all Hindoos; they would never dream of construing this

* A province of ancient Persia, now independent.

† A town on the frontiers of Sinde within the Uffghan territories, famous for its commerce and Hindoo population.

transaction in any other way than a fair and unexceptionable mode of realizing a sum of money by the pressing wants of another persón. Soondurjee's agents, believing it to be on his account, of course exerted themselves to make the most advantageous agreement, but the other party saw our impatience and took care to profit by it.

On the *26th*, a decent old man came and begged, with tears in his eyes, that we would accompany him into the city to pay a medical visit to a sick person, whom we found in a most emaciated, weak state. We prescribed a little medicine for him, but it was of no avail, as he died four or five days afterwards; we were, however, glad to hear that we were not censured as the cause of his demise, which was generally supposed to have been occasioned by a slow kind of poison, that one of his five step-mothers had administered to him. On first visiting him, we had been surprised to see him, though immured in a miserable low hovel, very elegantly apparelled, and attended by a number of servants, and on enquiry he proved to be the son of Rohoollah Beg, a Babee merchant of immense wealth, who had been put to death about a fortnight before, at Kutch Gundava, by Meer Mustapha Khan, the brother of the Khan of Kelat. The melancholy state of this young man, in whose manners and address there was something superior, excited our curiosity as well as commiseration, and urged us to investigate the particulars of his father's case. We were told, that Meer Mustapha Khan having long suspected him of carrying on a treasonable correspondence with Futteh Khan, the minister of Shah Muhmood (at that time one of the competitors for the throne of Kabool), had gone one night to his house at Kutch Gundava, and, assisted by four servants, literally cut him in pieces. This atrocious and cowardly act, for the Babee was an old defenceless man, caused a very considerable ferment and murmur among all classes of the people, as the execution (if such it may be called) of a man of so much consequence, was an unparalleled event. The Meer too had instantly dispatched a messenger to Kelat, directing the detention of Rohoollah Beg's sons, and the seizure of all his property, which order gave good reason to many for averring, that the opulence of the unfortunate man was his only crime. However that might have been, it was strictly obeyed; his dwelling and warehouses were taken possession of by the Darogha of the Meer, and an inventory made and transmitted to that chief of the valuable articles they contained, which were said to have exceeded thirty lacs of rupees*; two sons were imprisoned, and the third, being then dangerously ill, was allowed as a great favour to reside in the hut where we attended him, under a guard of matchlock-men.

The Kirmanee Moollah was now a daily visitor, and one whom we were always glad to see and welcome, being a very conversable intelligent companion. On the *27th* he was accompanied by five very smart boys, the sons of Sooltan Saheb, one of the Khan's Wukeels †. The eldest of them presented us with a small box of delicious grapes, packed in layers of cotton; and previous to their going away, he told us that he had been desired by his mother, who had heard of our fame as doctors, to request that we would see his two sisters, who had been indisposed for some time. After a little importunity, which we thought it as well to allow him to make, to enhance our acquiescence, Captain Christie consented to wait on the family the next day, and it was stipulated that the Moollah should come, and conduct him to the house. He accordingly made his appearance very early on the *28th*, and we then perceived, that he was more desirous than ourselves for the enhancement of our medical skill, trusting through our mediation, to obtain the enfranchisement of his sister, who, I have already stated, was a slave in the house. "Take your book under your arm," said he to Captain Christie "and "feel the lady's pulse, and then observe, that it will cost a vast deal "of money to procure the necessary medicines. You must likewise "recollect, on no account to grant them any prescriptions until you "have bargained, what sum you are to receive on the daughters being "restored to health. Their father is possessed of incalculable wealth,

* 375,000l. Sterling.

† Wukeel, in Beloochistan, is a person who transacts every kind of business for another.

" and if you demand it, they will be happy to give you two or three " hundred rupees for each cure." After this exhortation, Captain Christie and the Moollah set off, and as the scene was admirable which ensued, I cannot do it greater justice, than by giving the particulars of it in the words of my late friend, as extracted from his journal:

" On our arrival at the house," writes Captain Christie, " we were " kept waiting in the court-yard a few minutes; I was then welcomed " by the Darogha or steward, and invited up into the Haram; on " entering the apartment, the lady of Sooltan Saheb rose up to " receive me; she was a tall thin figure, dressed in a loose brown " shift, open in front, coming down to the heels. I seated myself " by her on the Numud (felt), and the slave girls ranged themselves " opposite. After many apologies, she submitted the case of her " eldest daughter, about fifteen years of age, troubled with cutaneous " disorders; she stretched her hand out from under a cloth that I " might feel her pulse, but I could not obtain a sight of her face; " her figure, as far as I could judge when she raised the cloth to " put forth her arm, was small but elegant. It appeared to me that " her disease originated in eating dates and other saccharine and " heating food, and I prescribed accordingly: they considered it a " hardship that I stinted her allowance of meat, which to a Brahooé " lady was a great deprivation. The next case brought before me " was another daughter, a beautiful girl of twelve years of age, that " had weak eyes, and it excited a little mirth among them when I " innocently asked to see them; however, they instantly consented, " and she unveiled as lovely a face and form as ever was beheld: all " she required was a little eye-wash, and I agreed to send it to her. " I had taken my watch out of my pocket whilst feeling the eldest " daughter's pulse, to give a greater air of science to my acts, and " unguardedly trusted it into the hands of the Darogha, a fat Mool- " tanee Hindoo *, who, with all the impertinent stupidity inherent

* A native of the city of Mooltan.

" in his cast, opened it, and the first notice I had of my misfortune " was the watch running down. I looked up. Ah! said I, Koo-" rumsak! (rascal) you know not the mischief you have done. He " laughed, although confused, and told me to set it right by the skill I " possessed. Stop Lallakoo *, said the old lady, as I was rising to " quit the house in a passion, I have a son fourteen years old, and " wish you to give him medicines to strengthen him; he is now " about to be married, but he is thin and puny, I want you to pre-" scribe for him that he may acquire bone and muscle, in fact, to " make a man of him, you know what I mean; here the slave girls " tittered: of course (she continued, first addressing herself to them " and then to me) the physician is my brother, why should I disguise " any thing from him? But it grows late, and I have caused you " much trouble. I took my leave, glad to escape from such trouble-" some cases, but at the lower gate I was attacked by all the slave " girls, one wanted medicine for her eyes, another longed for a " child, a third had got the Bad, or wind †; however, I came off " without waiting to hear one half of their complaints, and hastening " down the Bazar, mingled among the Uffghans, where the slave " girls (two or three of whom still followed) soon lost sight of me."

About an hour after Captain Christie came home, a Darogha of Sooltan Saheb followed to receive the medicines, which were given to him: he talked in a very bombastic style of his master's power and authority, and assured us that his interest was so great, that if we succeeded in making him our friend, there was no impediment or obstruction to our mercantile views that it would not be in his power to remove, and that he had only to request the Khan to remit the duties on our goods, to have it immediately complied with. We professed our satisfaction at the probability of our being instrumental to the reco-

* An expression of endearment, synonymous with darling, pet, &c.

† This is a very common explanation of a disease amongst Asiatics: whenever they are at a loss, they say they have got the Bad or wind. It usually means rheumatism.

very of the two daughters, whom Captain Christie had seen, though the truth was, that our wish to be so was not in any way augmented by the rodomontade of the Darogha, and our departure from Kelat was so certainly to be taken before Sooltan Saheb could in any way befriend us, that we had no longer any inducement on that score.

1*st* and 2*d March*. There was a grand hubbub and uproar in the city on the morning of the 1*st*, owing to the house of the late Roohoollah Beg having been broken into the preceding night, and plundered of shawls and other valuable merchandize, to the amount of forty-five thousand rupees. It was clear from the precautions they had observed, that the depredators were no strangers, and as a part of the stolen goods must have been removed on camels, and the fort gates were shut all night, there was a proclamation issued by the Khan's Naeb, or deputy, prohibiting any person, on pain of confinement, from travelling for the space of three days on any of the roads within twenty miles of Kelat. Four men, however, who turned out to be the thieves, were apprehended the succeeding night in attempting to lower some of the booty over the works, where they had camels ready to remove it. The Naeb reported the transaction to the Khan, and in the interim, by his own orders, they were most severely flogged, their beards were singed off, and they were tied back to back on two camels, and thus conveyed through the streets, with a kettle drum beating in front of them, exposed to the insults and indignation of the populace, who did not confine themselves to mud, eggs, and such other harmless missile weapons, but pelted them so soundly with stones, billets of firewood, and brickbats, that they were carried back to prison deplorably mauled. Their case, it seemed, was much aggravated by their being dependants of Meer Mustapha Khan, who had always treated them with marked kindness and confidence; but exclusive of this, the natural detestation of the Belooches to any species of private robbery was alone sufficient to secure them the chastisement they experienced.

A person who dropt in on the 2*d*, apparently as a casual visitor, reminded us of a promise we had made a day or two subsequent to our arrival at Kelat, of calling upon the Darogha of Meer Mustapha Khan, who we learned, though still indisposed, had been daily expecting us, and was highly affronted at our want of respect towards him. We attempted to excuse our neglect on the plea of not wishing to intrude; but the Darogha's servant, for such our remembrancer proved, was not so easily satisfied, and we had to yield an assent to his proposition of paying our respects to his master the following morning. We had resolved on quitting Kelat on the *4th* instant, and packed the flour and dates for our journey into the Koorzeens*; but in the afternoon of the *2d* all our Hindoo acquaintances came in a body and protested that we should not go until the *6th*, which being the first day of the new moon was looked upon as a very lucky hour. The two Uffghans were present during this visit, and discovering that we shortly meant to be off, they spoke to Captain Christie, and were very solicitous to be made acquainted with our plans; however, that officer managed to persuade them that we should not, at all events, move for ten days, or perhaps more. They next began to advise our going direct to Kandahar, and thence to Heerat, observing that our travelling by an unfrequented route like that of Seistan, would excite suspicion, and eventually come to the ears of the king of Kabool, or his minister, who would take measures to stop us at Furrah†: we were much too well apprized of the villainy and sinister intentions of these fellows to pay any regard to their counsel, though we made a feint of doing so, and said we would ponder well ere we decided on any particular road.

3d March. We saw the Darogha of Mustapha Khan, who was more polite than we anticipated, after what had occurred yesterday: he said he was ready to procure us any thing we might stand in need of, asked numberless questions about our future intentions, whether we pur-

* A kind of saddlebags, either for horses or camels, made of coarse carpet, and laced in the centre.

† A town of Khorasan, half way between Kandahar and Heerat. Vide map.

posed to go on to the northern countries, or remain at Kelat? What number and description of horses we required? If we were trading for ourselves, or by whom employed? Our replies to all which he noted down as we made them on a piece of paper, and in fact from his whole conduct to us, there could not be a doubt but that he had lately been instructed by the Khan or his brother to ascertain who we were. We left him seemingly quite convinced of our pretensions as horse-dealers, and had it been likely we should stay much longer in Muhmood Khan's territories, the Darogha's report of us to that chief might have had a very favourable result, in enabling us to carry on the disguise we had assumed, with still less probability than before of a discovery. Among the other news of the day, he mentioned that a party of fifty horsemen had passed through Kelat the preceding evening, on their way from Kandahar to Kutch Gundava, to claim, on behalf of the minister of the King of Kabool, the release of the family, and restoration of the effects of the late Roohoollah Beg. This interference tends to establish Meer Mustapha Khan's avowed reasons for putting the Babee merchant to death, as well founded; and it must be added, in justice to that chief, that he has ever been reputed a very just governor. We afterwards heard that this mission did not succeed, as Mustapha Khan returned a verbal answer to the minister's furman *, informing him in the coarsest language, that he was an ignorant brute, for even fancying that he would be weak enough to pay any attention to his commands, and recommending him not to depute any of his people again on such errands, if he had any regard to their being treated with common politeness. In the evening we received a message from the lady of Sooltan Saheb, desiring that we would send any valuable property we might have with us to her house, where it should be taken the utmost care of, as it was dangerous to keep it outside on account of the thieves: we

* A Furman means a royal mandate, but was here applied in derision to the minister's epistle.

thanked her for this offer, and although in truth we had nothing of any value, we pretended to take advantage of it, and dispatched our Hindoo with a bundle of old clothes, not worth five shillings; this artifice succeeded admirably in persuading the whole of that family, beside many others who had been sceptical, of our intention to revisit Kelat.

CHAPTER VI.

HINDOOS ATTEND WITH LETTERS. — QUIT KELAT. — UFFGHANS' RAGE AND DISAPPOINTMENT. — THREATEN TO INFORM. — HOW PACIFIED. — PARTY. — HOW MOUNTED. — VILLAGE OF GHURRUK. — RAIN. — ROUTE. — KANDAHAR ROAD. — WELL. — LUKHS OR DEFILES. — ONE VERY DANGEROUS. — WATER. — DREADFUL COLD NIGHT. — BARREN COUNTRY. — DIFFICULT PASS. — MINUTELY DESCRIBED. — DESERT. — AUTHOR'S FEELINGS ON SEEING IT. — DESCEND THE PASS. — RIVER KYSUR. — HALT ON ITS BANK. — BABOOL TREE. — DESERT GRASS. — CAMEL THORN. — FROST. — TOOMUN OF NOOSHKY. — RECEPTION THERE. — UNPLEASANT PREDICAMENT. — SEASONABLE ADVICE. — MIHMAN KHANU. — IMMEDIATE CHANGE IN THE PEOPLE'S MANNER. — DINNER. — THE CHIEF COMES. — CONVERSATION AND PROPOSITION. — DECISION. — ALTERED. — CAUSE OF THIS. — OPINION. — AGREEMENT FOR GUIDES. — REMARKABLE ANECDOTE OF THE HOSPITALITY OF THE BELOOCHES. — ANNOYANCE FROM VISITORS. — MOHUMMUDAN CREED. — SIRDAR OR CHIEF. — TEA. — BELOOCHE COURT OF JUSTICE. — THE TRIAL DESCRIBED. — ITS ORIGIN. — JUDGMENT. — BRAHOOE. — ASAFŒTIDA. — LUDICROUS SCUFFLE. — COMPLAINT. — HOW REDRESSED. — ACCOUNT OF THE ASAFŒTIDA PLANT. — DRUG OF THAT NAME. — HOW COLLECTED. — WHENCE BROUGHT. — DOUBTS OF A FURTHER PROGRESS IN THE ROUTE SELECTED. — INQUIRIES. — DISCOVERY OF ANOTHER ROAD. — THE AUTHOR AND HIS COMPANION DETERMINE TO SEPARATE. — CONTRARY TO INSTRUCTIONS. — REASONS FOR OVERLOOKING THEM. — MODE ADOPTED TO ACCOUNT FOR THIS SEPARATION. — EFFECTUAL. — ANXIETY TO SET OFF. — KILLED TWO SMALL GOATS. — CONSIDERED EXTRAVAGANCE. — HINDOO'S PRESENT. — SURPRIZE. — THE TOOMUN QUITE OFFENSIVE FROM ASAFŒTIDA.

MARCH 4th, 5th, and 6th. Nothing new transpired the two former days. On the 6th after breakfast, the Hindoos brought the letters and bills, which they had sealed at an auspicious moment, and presented them to Captain Christie, with divers prayers and invocations to the Deity *. We ordered the camels immediately, to

* The Hindoos at Kelat have fallen into many of the absurd practices of the Moosulmans, and even exceed them. Nothing is done without calculation of stars and events, and they account for every mishap by some neglect of this (as they fancy it) duty.

the utter amazement of the Uffghans, who accused us of duplicity and of having deserted them; in the end they became quite furious, and swore that they would advertise the Khan's Naeb, or deputy, of our flight as they termed it, who would send horsemen to overtake and fetch us back. Captain Christie fearing they might really put this threat into execution, ordered our Hindoo to give each of them a present, at the same time privately intimating to him to defer doing so for a few days: this appeased their wrath, and subsequently they went on to Kandahar without giving further trouble. Our party was composed of the two Hindoostanee servants, and four Brahooe camel drivers, beside Captain Christie and myself; we had five camels, one being spare in case of accident, and two of us rode on each of the others, having double saddles made for the purpose. The route to-day was between bare hills with mountains at no great distance on either side, the road good, with abundance of fine water and some low jungul. We intended to have gone further, but the afternoon setting in with an appearance of rain, we struck off the path a little to the right, and put up at the small village of Ghurruk, seven miles north north-west of Kelat; this place and a portion of ground adjoining, belongs to Syyud Moorad, a dependent of Muhmood Khan, along with whom he was absent at Kutch Gundava: we got a vacant house from one of his relations, and reposed comfortably under the gratifying reflection of having once more commenced our journey.

7th March. We quitted Ghurruk at seven o'clock this morning, the night had been exceedingly cold and rainy, and the camels from being exposed to it travelled badly all day, notwithstanding which we performed a distance of twenty-eight miles, and halted at sun-set in the bed of a mountain water-course; near us was a pool of rainwater, and plenty of fire-wood to be had for gathering it. Four miles from Ghurruk we crossed the direct road from Kelat to Kandahar, and ten miles further on had our breakfast of dates and bread, at a well where we met with a number of Brahooes who were transporting wheat to Nooshky on asses. The country we passed through to-day was mountainous and barren; we ascended two Lukhs or defiles, one of them peculiarly hazardous, the rugged path not exceeding two feet in width, and on the left hand an abyss at least a quarter of a mile deep. We chiefly marched to the northward of west, but the road was so very intricate, that it was with vast trouble we kept any account of the different directions; the only spots at which we found water, were the well twelve miles from Ghurruk, and our halting place in the evening.

8th March. We passed a miserable night from the cold, which was so intense, that unprovided as we were with warm clothing or beds, it was impossible to sleep, and we were not equal to making the least attempt to move until nine *a. m.* when the sun-beams got pretty warm, and literally speaking, renovated us; we then mounted, and by five *p. m.* had proceeded thirty-one miles; the intermediate country being if possible, more bleak and barren than yesterday, and the path equally winding; we had several Lukhs or passes to surmount, the last of which I conceive worthy of a minute detail, as it would almost seem from its situation on the edge of the desert, to have been intended by nature as an insurmountable barrier to these elevated regions, and is beyond all comparison the most difficult defile I have ever seen in any country. It is separated on the south-east side or that towards Kelat, from the other mountains, by a deep and narrow ravine, the sides of which are solid black rock and very nearly perpendicular; emerging from this gulph by a rugged path, we ascended the south-east face of the pass, from the top of which the desert burst on our view, extending as far as the eye could trace, with the semblance of a smooth ocean from the reflection of the sun on the sand; the emotions of my fellow-traveller and myself were at this instant of the most enviable nature; in the prospect before us we already saw half our hopes realized, and all our doubts regarding this far-famed desert laid at rest; we congratulated ourselves on the accomplishment of the object for which we had quitted India, even to this extent, and contemplated that circumstance with feelings which inspired and stimulated us with new life to prosecute our undertaking. On descending the north-western side of the Lukh, to do which took us nearly five hours, it being eleven miles long and extremely steep; we entered the bed of a water-course between the mountains, and on a level with their base, which led us out into the desert by innumerable mazes. The last half mile of our route was through the bed of the river Kysur, which at this season affords the easiest, though by much the longest road to Kelat. This river is said to be deep and rapid during wet weather, and in the hot months of May, June, and July, often quite dry; when we crossed it, the stream was from two to three feet deep, and six or seven yards wide. We halted on the opposite bank for the night, finding that we could not get to Nooshky before it became dark. The only plants we saw to-day were some scraggy bushes of a species of the Babool tree *, and in the river beds great quantities of the Lye †. I should also add, that one of the mountains over which we passed, was literally studded with bulbous roots similar to those of tulips, that were just beginning to bud, and our Brahooes assured me that their fragrance in another month, would be perceptible to a great distance. The grass called by the natives "Khushé-"put," or desert grass, also abounds in this part of the country; the Brahooes collect it at the proper time as winter food for their goats and sheep; it grows in bunches or tufts with thick coarse stalks, leaves long and sawed at the edges, and is very sweet and nutritious. The Shinz ‡, called by the Persians Kharé Shootoor or camel thorn, is likewise to be seen here, but not in such plenty as in the lower countries.

9th March. There was a hard frost last night, yet it was comparatively warm to the preceding one. We got to the Toomun or village of Nooshky about nine *a. m.*, after travelling six miles west by south over the desert, which is diversified with hillocks of sand, and

* Farnesian Mimosa.

† The Tamarisk.

‡ Hedysarum Alhagi.

some detached hills stretching out two or three miles from the great chain of mountains, that here runs away south-westerly. On our arrival we were instantly surrounded by the whole population of the Toomun, attracted by so novel an occurrence as the appearance of strangers. We sent for a Hindoo of the name of Sookaram, to whom we had a letter of recommendation; and when he came, ordered him to get some flour and dates ready to complete our stock, as we should proceed on without delay: he smiled at what he thought our temerity, and represented the risk there was of our being murdered and plundered on the road; at the same time he added, that a Karwan or caravan had set out the day before for Gurmsyl *, and we had better, if resolved on going, take a guide and endeavour to overtake it. We desired him to hire one quickly, and while he was absent, dismounted and sat down in the desert to eat our breakfast. The Hindoo presently brought an old man who asked forty rupees to conduct us to Gurmsyl, which we refused as a preposterous sum; we were therefore at a stand. Sookaram looked more helpless than ourselves, and could render us no assistance. The Sirdar or chief of the Toomun was from home, and the Belooches, who were crowded about us, began to be rude and troublesome. In this dilemma we were cogitating what we ought to do, when a man, whom from his dress we took to be a Persian, advised our going to the Mihman Khanu, or house for guests. "There," said he, "you will be safe "and unmolested, and when the Sirdar comes back in the evening, "he will furnish you with a guide." We adopted this plan, and the change of conduct in the people was instantaneous, for, though still curious to discover what we were, they became attentive to our wants and comforts, spread a carpet, brought pillows from the Sirdar's house for us to rest upon, and, in short, from the moment we entered the Mihman Khanu, appeared to respect us as the guests of their chief, and entitled to all the Belooche rights of hospitality; nor was this

* A district of that name north-west of Nooshky, and distant about 75 miles.

confined to ourselves and people, for a man was also produced to tend our camels out to graze.

The Mihman Khanu was a Ghedan of wicker-work, the roof covered with black Kummul or blanket, excessively cool and refreshing to us, who had been sitting for three hours in the red sand exposed to a noontide sun. We laid aside our arms and lay down to sleep, having no longer any fears either on account of our property or persons. About sunset they sent to us, from the Sirdar's, a tray of hot bread with a wooden bowl full of Dholl or pea-soup, and shortly after we had dined, the chief himself came to visit us. When the usual ceremonials of embracing were gone through, he began by expressing his surprise at our not having brought letters to him from Kelat or Kutch Gundava, which latter province he concluded, as a matter of course, we had visited; declaring it would be out of his power, as he valued the Khan's friendship, to assist us in escaping (for he had no doubt we were followed by some person), and hinting at our being the sons of Rohoollah Beg the Babee merchant; "however," continued he, "you may make yourselves easy, as I shall feel it my "duty to protect you so long as you chuse to remain with me." We assured him that he was entirely wrong in his surmises regarding us; that had we known it would be required, we could have obtained a passport from the Khan himself; that we were poor men of no condition whatever, descended from an Oozbuck Tartar family that had settled for some generations in Hindoostan, and were then in the employment of a Hindoo, who had dispatched us to Heerat for horses. He did not press the subject farther, but after some desultory discourse, on rising to retire, he observed, "I shall send you a message by the "Hindoo Sookaram who is our joint acquaintance, you must give "him an explicit answer, and your business may then be arranged "according to your wishes." In the course of ten minutes Sookaram returned, when we found that the Sirdar's message was much to the same import, as his interrogatories and remarks whilst with us; we reiterated our former statement, and asked the Hindoo how he could possibly doubt it, when he called to recollection, that he had received advices by us to the same effect from his Kelat correspondents. He allowed we were right, said that he had made use of the same reasoning to convince the Sirdar, and that he had been empowered to offer us two guides, simply to shew the road, and that we were to trust to Providence for our safety; or otherwise, that the Sirdar would, for a trifling remuneration, depute his own son and twelve matchlockmen for our convoy to Dooshak the capital of Seistan *, which was one half the way to Heerat, our avowed destination. We promised to reflect on these propositions, and let the Sirdar know our intentions next morning, on which Sookaram went to his own home.

10th March. We decided in the course of the night on taking the two men, principally because there could be no plea for procrastination in their being got ready, and Captain Christie went out a little after daylight to apprize the Sirdar, who was examining our camels in front of the Ghedan, of this determination. He seemed to receive it without any disappointment, and said that they should be ordered immediately; but that we were to bear in mind, that he was in no wise accountable for our safety, on which point he should not enlarge, as we must have had sufficient warning of our danger. We were induced to hope that these alarms were only counterfeit, to enable the chief to make a good bargain with us, and therefore were inclined to adhere to our resolution. At this instant, the same man who had advised our coming to the Mihman Khanu the day before, and who we now found was a Seistanee Hindoo of the name of Bŏŏdhŏŏ, accidentally joined us, and hearing what was passing, he said to Captain Christie, " You had better have a care how you venture with two guides. I am acquainted with all these countries; " if the Sirdar will allow his son to accompany you, do not hesitate, " but close the agreement; the expence will be a trifle compared " with the loss of your property, and possibly your lives, if you go " unprotected." Some other Hindoos now offered the same advice,

* Captain Christie afterwards passed through Dooshak. Vide Map.

and when we maturely reflected, that our even being plundered would have entirely ruined our plans, we thought it adviseable to attend to it. We conceived it, however, equally indispensable to remove the erroneous impression that the whole of the Kheil had imbibed, about our having valuable property with us; accordingly we determined to send back to Kelat every article of dress, and reduce our baggage to the cloaths we were then wearing, and a bag of dates and flour. We signified both these intentions to the Sirdar and people around him, but he protested that the latter was rendered quite unnecessary, by his son's attending us, as he would be a safeguard for whatever we might choose to take. It was then fixed that the son and twelve Toofungchees or matchlockmen should escort us to Dooshak, and that we were immediately to write by a Kasid or courier to Kelat, for the cash that was to be paid to them for this trouble, the amount of which was to be settled by the Hindoos.

When we had closed this bargain, and the Sirdar had pledged himself to make preparations for our speedy departure, we returned into the Mihman Khanu, and had a breakfast of bread and milk which came from the Sirdar's Ghedan. An event occurred this morning, which will shew how inherent the spirit of hospitality is in these people. One of our Hindoostanee servants had begun to bake some cakes, when he was discovered by the Belooches, who called out, "What! "are you going to disgrace our Toomun? Cannot Eidel Khan * find "food for his guests?" The man explained to them, that it was his mistake from not knowing their customs, on which they were quite pleased, but told him, that though they lived in a desert and were a poor set, they had once entertained Nusseer Khan† and his army for five days so profusely, that he ever afterwards called them the Dil Kooshas, or open-hearted i.e. generous.

* The Sirdar's name.

† The father of the present Khan of Kelat: this is a fact. He had been to Mushed in Khorasan, to assist the King of Kabool against the Persians, and came home through Seistan and the desert.

All the forenoon we were hemmed in by a crowd of idle Belooches, who teazed us a good deal by their unconscionably long visits and impertinent questions. We had been prepared to undergo a tolerable ordeal of this annoyance, but it far exceeded any thing we had feared. Some of them stayed four and five hours at a stretch, smoking, chatting, and singing all the while. They were headed by a forward fellow called Jooma Khan, who we soon learned, was the Sirdar's eldest son and our intended chief guide. He and his associates were particularly anxious to find out, whether we were of the Soonnee or Sheea sect of Moosulmans*: they suspected from our fair appearance, that we were Ujumees†, and at length very coolly asked us to repeat the Mohumudan Kulimu or creed, which we did agreeable to the former persuasion, knowing them to be followers of its tenets. In the evening the old Sirdar himself walked over to sit with us, and as a little of the tea we had brought from Bombay still remained, we made a cup for him; he seemed gratified by this attention, and was a regular and very welcome visitor afterwards, for he not only kept the others in due order, but was possessed of a great deal of information and anecdote, and was always ready to answer the queries we put to him.

11*th March.* We were greatly entertained to-day, by seeing the Sirdar hold a court of justice relative to a robbery or seizure that had been made in the night. The complainants were Mingull Brahooés belonging to the Toomun of Buhadoor Khan, which was about three miles off. The defendants were Belooches of Nooshky: the parties pleaded against each other, and as they could not lay claim to the honor of doing so with elegance, they mutually seemed determined, that the superabundance of their oratory should make amends for the quality, and the uproar was general for full three hours: each told his own story agreeable to his ideas, and all were speaking in the same breath, so that he who strained his lungs most, had the best prospect

* The two great sects of Moosulmans. Vide note on the religion of the Belooches, in the 4th chapter.

† Persians, who are all Sheeas.

of gaining attention. The Sirdar listened to them with all imaginable patience and good humour, and when they were absolutely wearied with talking, he delivered his sentiments and judgment in due form, and the meeting broke up.

From what I could learn of it, the trial appeared to be a trivial concern about the right of pasturage on a neighbouring hill, from which the Belooches tried to exclude the Brahooés by expostulation, and at length resorted to the unwarrantable expedient of seizing their flocks: the latter however got the victory, as the decision was in favour of their having at least an equal right with the former. In stating this opinion, which was received without a murmur, the Sirdar told his Kheil to recollect, that the Brahooés had originally settled near Nooshky with the sanction of the Khan and himself, and that they were consequently entitled to enjoy every privilege. I observed that a relation of the Mingull chief attended with his people, and that Eidel Khan addressed himself several times to him, during the investigation. These courts are always held in the Mihman Khanu, when it is unoccupied, but as we were in possession, the carpets and Numuds (felts) were spread before the door, and the whole party sat down in the sun without any scruple.

In the midst of the proceedings, a luckless wight, a mountaineer made his appearance with two asses laden with asafœtida plants that he had gathered and brought in for sale, and the people were so eager to purchase, that they ran in a body and overwhelmed him and his merchandize in the sand, where there was a vigorous scuffle and scramble kept up for half an hour: every soul present joined in it except the Sirdar and the Mingull chief, both of whom, like Captain Christie and myself, enjoyed a hearty laugh at the tumult: the poor fellow who was so unceremoniously handled, extricated himself and his animals as quickly as possible, and shortly after came to prefer a complaint to the Sirdar, for the treatment he had met with; it was asserted on all hands, that the Hindoos (who wanted it to retail again) were the first to commence the attack on the panniers, and that they had also secured the greatest portion of the spoil; they were therefore ordered to satisfy the Brahooé, which they did with some tobacco and sugar.

Both Beloöches and Hindoos are very partial to the asafœtida plant, and esteem it a great treat: they roast or stew the stem, and boil or more commonly fry the head and leaves with Ghee*. This plant grows spontaneously on the mountains in the northern parts of Beloochistan, whence the shepherds bring it to market. When ripe, the efflorescence or head has much the appearance of a cauliflower, being of a light straw colour: the stem is from one to two and a half feet long, three or four inches thick, and the leaves resemble those of the Indian large beet root: the drug known in Europe by the same name, of which amazing quantities are yearly imported into Hindoostan, is called by the Belooches, and I believe Persians, Sheeri Heeng, or the milk of asafœtida: it is extracted from the stalk close to the root, and sometimes from the root itself, about the time the plant is ripening, which is indicated by the leaves losing their natural dark green colour, and becoming a light yellow: at this juncture, the stem is cut off about six inches above the earth, the ground is cleared away about it, and an incision, about an inch long, made immediately where the roots ramify. The asafœtida from one stalk usually equals one pound, and sometimes more: it may be gathered in three days after the stalk is lopped, and the root produces the succeeding spring.†

12th, *13th*, *14th*, and *15th March*. From various consultations we had with the Sirdar in the course of the last four days, there ap-

* Boiled or clarified butter.

† None of the asafœtida which comes to India is the produce of Beloochistan, as that country does not even afford enough for home consumption. The mountains in the neighbourhood of Heerat, in Khorasan, are plentifully stocked with this plant. Captain Christie, in a paragraph of the memoir of his journey now before me, speaks of the hills between which his road lay as abounding with the asafœtida plant, and also enumerates that drug as one of the staple commodities of Heerat. I have understood, that if an incision to draw off the gum be not made at a proper period, the stem will burst, and the Sheer or milk (which hardens to the consistence we see it by exposure to the air) exudes, but by this effort of nature the quantity is greatly lessened. Good asafœtida ought to be of a pale yellow colour and quite dry; the gatherers often mix it with Ghee to increase its weight.

peared to be considerable doubts of the practicability of our further progress in this direction: we had therefore been very sedulous in our inquiries towards gaining a knowledge of the routes in the more southern divisions of Beloochistan and Mukran. On the evening of the 14*th*, the Sirdar's son and his nephew (Moorad Khan) chanced to be with us, when the discourse, as usual, turned on our journey: they both added their voice to Eidel Khan's, in strongly advising our taking any other road than that by Seistan. "Why don't you," said Moorad, "either go by Kedge* and Bunpoor to Kirman? or from this "place to Surhud†, and thence through Nurmansheer‡ to that city, "from which you can at all times get to Heerat? if you select either "of these methods, I will myself be your guide to the frontiers of the "Shah's§ dominions." The idea of accomplishing two routes immediately offered itself, and when our visitors departed, Captain Christie and I talked the matter over, and came to the resolution of separating, and taking different courses across the desert. In this resolution, though contrary to the strict meaning of the instructions that had been furnished us on leaving India, we felt justified, on due consideration of the unquestionable advantages that would result from a greater acquisition of geographical and statistical knowledge of the regions we were then exploring, than could be looked for by our advancing together; accordingly the next day, when the Seistanee Hindoo, Boodhoo (whom we found to be an active fellow and had therefore employed him in lieu of Sookaram) came, we were prepared to mention our plans to him, in case we could do so without his supposing they were preconcerted: he most opportunely prefaced his conversation by entreating us to abandon every idea of the Seistan route. "I have been "talking," said he, "to Eidel Khan, and he enumerates so many "dangers and obstacles, that I am very fearful you will lose your lives,

* The capital of the province of Mukran.

† A village on the western boundary of Beloochistan.

‡ The south-eastern district of the Persian province of Kirman.

§ The kings (of Persia)

" or be way-laid and pillaged." He then proposed to give us letters on his agents at Kandahar, the road from which city to Heerat we were aware was frequented by travellers, but at the same time, it was the last we should have fixed upon: we evaded however an explicit refusal, by saying that as Soondurjee's servants, we dare not judge for ourselves, and then hinted at the possibility of our having orders by the Kasid from Kelat, to proceed by the way of Surhud and Nurmansheer to Kirman: this surmise, as we had anticipated, he soon made public throughout the Toomun, and it eventually served as an excellent excuse for carrying our project into execution.

We had now been five days at Nooshky, and were most anxiously awaiting our Kasid's arrival, hoping to set off immediately after. Our host's hospitality did not diminish in the least; every morning more bread, sour milk, and cheese were sent, than our whole party could consume: his slaves attended with water to wash, and the same routine was observed again in the evening: twice we purchased and killed small goats, sending a leg to the Sirdar, and a part of the remainder to the different Hindoos; but we discovered that this would not answer, as they accounted it profuse extravagance, although they cost but one rupee each. In return for our present of a slice of meat Boodhoo brought us, one evening at dinner time, what he prized as a much greater delicacy, and on which he expatiated with all the zest and rapture of a professed epicure; this was a tender young asafœtida plant stewed in rancid butter, and our polite friend could hardly be persuaded that we were serious, when we declared that we could not relish the gout of the dainty he had prepared for us; indeed the smell was not tolerable, for the green plant is even more rank and nauseous than the drug itself; a fact our olfactories attested, as they were abundantly regaled for two or three days subsequent to the supply being brought from the Brahooé, of which every soul in the Toomun had a share, so that the people were not only offensively strong, but the very air was impregnated with the effluvia.

CHAPTER VII.

MESSENGER ARRIVES FROM KELAT. — CAPTAIN CHRISTIE PREPARES TO DEPART. — FURNISHES THE AUTHOR WITH INSTRUCTIONS. — UNLUCKY DAY. — CONVERSATION UPON IT. — UNSATISFACTORY RESULT. — SIRDAR'S WARNING ABOUT HIS NEPHEW. — ENTREATY. — ACCEDED TO. — TERMS. — DISAPPOINTMENT. — UPBRAID THE SIRDAR WITH FALSEHOOD. — HIS REPLY. — STRONG WIND. — SAND. — APPREHENSIONS OF FURTHER DETENTION. — — INCORRECT. — CAPTAIN CHRISTIE LEAVES THE AUTHOR AT NOOSHKY. — HIS PRESENT TO THE SIRDAR. — REASONS FOR MAKING IT. — WINDY, GLOOMY DAY. — SIRDAR'S ATTENTION. — HEAVY RAIN. — AUTHOR'S UNCOMFORTABLE SITUATION. — A SECOND MESSENGER FROM KELAT. — LETTERS. — INTELLIGENCE OF VAST IMPORTANCE TO THE AUTHOR. — SINDIANS AT KELAT. — DECLARATION. — PROCEEDINGS. — STEPS TAKEN TO AVERT THE CONSEQUENCES. — HIRE A GUIDE. — NARROW ESCAPE FROM DETECTION. — ANECDOTE. — WRITE TO THE HINDOO LEFT AT KELAT. — MESSAGE TO THE SIRDAR. — HIS ASTONISHMENT. — REBUKE. — HOW SILENCED. — OFFERS LETTERS.

MARCH 16*th*, 17*th*, 18*th*, and 19*th*. Our messenger returned from Kelat on the 16*th*, bringing a Hoondee, or Native Bill for the money we required, and a letter from the Hindoo whom we had left at that city. Captain Christie therefore went to the Sirdar, paid him the sum that had been agreed upon, and requested that he might be sent off immediately: he also announced to him that I had got an order to proceed by the southern road to Kirman in Persia, and was to stay at Nooshky, until a man should come to receive some superfluous necessaries we had with us: the old fellow talked of a lucky day for Captain Christie to commence his journey, with other nonsense likely to delay him, and on the 18*th* seemed so unconcerned with regard to, and dilatory in, his promised preparations, that, that officer told him we should positively return to Kelat if he did not name an early day for his quitting Nooshky. The Sirdar most artfully tried to excuse himself, on the pretence of it being very difficult to procure trustworthy and obedient men to accompany him, but at last he appointed the *20th* for his departure, and the evening before, I received the following instructions from Captain Christie:

" *Nooshky*, 19*th March*."

1st. " You will most probably arrive at Kirman by the Surhud " route in forty days, from thence you are to send a letter to me to " Heerat, under cover to Hurry Sing, our Hindoo agent there."

2d. " I expect to reach Heerat by Dooshak in thirty days, and if " so, shall be at Kirman in twenty more, unless prevented by unfore- " seen obstacles, but I will leave directions with Hurry Sing to write " to you, in case I should be gone before your Kasid (messenger) ar- " rives, and in the event of my finding it impracticable to pass Doo- " shak (of which you are aware there is some probability), I will endea- " vour to convey instructions to Hurry Sing to apprize you of this cir- " cumstance, and also to give you credit for all sums you may draw " upon him for."

3d. " If you cannot get to Kirman as above, try to the north- " ward with caution, and should you eventually ascertain it to be " impossible to advance in a westerly direction in that parallel, either " make for the sea-coast or Bunpoor, and thence to Kirman."

4th. " Should you be confined or in distress, you must strive by " every means to give me intimation of it, in order that I may " afford you every assistance in my power; this I will of course " equally apply to myself."

5th. " If I am cut off, which you will perhaps hear from Hurry " Sing or otherwise, you had better proceed by the safest route to " join General Malcolm. If that is not feasible, you must judge " for yourself whether to go back or to the sea-coast, recollecting to " regard your own safety above all other considerations."

6th. " Should I neither hear of, nor from you before the 1st of " June next, I shall conclude you have been obliged to go back or " are killed, and this you will also apply to me."

7th. "On reaching Kirman, go to the principal Hindoo there, so "that I may obtain from him instant information regarding you on "my arrival at that city."

(Signed) CHARLES CHRISTIE, Capt.

20th March. This morning Captain Christie was firmly bent on starting, and went to the Sirdar, who instantly said that he was ready to abide by his promise, but that the day, being the Hindoo festival of the Hooly, was exceedingly unlucky, and that no person in his senses would think of setting out on a journey on such an occasion. To this absurd discourse Captain Christie replied, that we could have no objections on that score, as we had been travelling for some months. "What you say is correct," rejoined the Sirdar, "but those who go with you from this place are not so circum- "stanced, and on their account you should select a propitious hour "to depart." Our assumed character of Moosulmans did not permit us to reprehend and ridicule this fresh source of detention, and concomitant uneasiness, as we could have wished, and Captain Christie was necessitated to yield an assent to remaining until the 21*st* instant, on which day afternoon, the Hooly would cease.

Before bed-time the Sirdar sent one of his slaves to desire that we would speak to him, and having led us a long way from the Toomun into the desart, he conjured us, as the greatest obligation we could confer upon him, not to employ in any way whatever his nephew Moorad Khan, whom he loaded with every epithet that was opprobrious and disgraceful. "As sure as you do," said he, "he "will mislead you, and then who is to call a vagabond like "him to account. Should I be accessary in any manner to de- "frauding you, I am always to be laid hold of, and made to answer "for my misconduct, which is not the case with that outcast ruf- "fian." We promised not to hire Moorad, or in short have any thing to say to him, unless through the medium of his uncle, who was greatly pleased at our ready concession, which I fancy he by no means anticipated: but we determined to adhere to it no longer than exactly suited our purpose. We conjectured that the Sirdar had partly fabricated the assertions he had used regarding the malpractices of his nephew, or at least that he had our benefit little in view by the disclosure of them, and that he merely wished to dissuade us from applying to any other person than himself, for guides or assistance.

20th and *21st March.* Our spirits and expectations were quite exhausted with the frequent disappointments we had experienced about quitting Nooshky, and there were so many rumours in circulation, all of which came to our ears with perhaps no trifling exaggeration, that we actually began to imagine, the Sirdar did not mean to provide Captain Christie with an escort. Under this impression the latter once more applied to him on the *21st*, to dispatch the party, upbraiding him with a breach of his word in deferring it longer, and declaring, that if we were obliged to put our threat of revisiting Kelat into execution, the Hindoo merchant by whom we were employed, would not fail to state the transaction to Muhmood Khan in such a light, as would draw upon the Kheil the severe reprehension of that chief and his brother. "It was only last night," continued Captain Christie, "that you judged it necessary to put "me on my guard against the perfidious promises of your nephew, "and what am I now to suppose, when you prove yourself capa- "ble of the same acts with which you charge him."

This rebuke staggered him so much, that he told Captain Christie he felt unequal to reply to it, that he had been nearly thirty years the head of the Kheil of Nooshky, and never till that period charged with dishonesty; he solemnly protested that his son had made an Istikharu, or calculation of future events the evening before, assisted by the two Moollahs or priests of the Toomun, and that they had found the omens so decidedly inauspicious for moving that day, that he himself had countermanded the preparations till the next morning, when they should set off, let what would, betide them. As a palliative to the reprimand, we informed him of the reports we had heard, on which he confessed that we had sufficient reason to be dissatisfied with our stay, and needed no additional cause to render it irksome.

A strong north-westerly wind, that had prevailed for the last three or four days, increased to a gale this forenoon, and raised the sand of the desart in clouds that obscured the sun at mid-day, the open-work sides of the Mihman Khanu admitted it in heaps, and covered us several inches thick. It moderated towards night, and while we were rejoicing at this respite, we were mortified by hearing that the camel which Jooma Khan, the Sirdar's son and Captain Christie's chief guide, was to ride, had gone astray in the desart, and that people were ordered out to seek for it. This we looked upon as a mere trick, and therefore went to sleep with the full expectation of another attempt being made to detain Captain Christie, in which however we were happily disappointed.

22d March. This morning I had the pleasure of seeing Captain Christie depart; before he mounted his camel, he made the Sirdar a small though most acceptable present, of a piece of Scotch plaid, half a piece of silk, a knife, and pair of scissars, of which he was very proud; he perhaps scarcely deserved this mark of attention, owing to the trouble he had caused us in getting away from Nooshky, but even when lingering under, and most exasperated by his evasions, we could not avoid the reflection, that it was only natural for an uncivilized and untaught barbarian to, avail himself of so opportune an occurrence as that of two-merchants, for such he rated us, visiting his Toomun, to obtain as much money from us as he could venture to exact, consistent with the hospitality of his tribe.

Jooma Khan's camel was not forthcoming when Captain Christie set off, but his father declared that if it was not found before noon, he should follow on horseback. He expressed his hope that Captain Christie would forgive any unpleasant circumstances that had arisen during his sojourn amongst the Rukshanees *, assuring him

* The name of the tribe.

that his son and the men that accompanied him, were entirely at his disposal, and in case of necessity, would prove that they were ready to sacrifice their lives for his safety; he concluded by offering up a prayer for that and his prosperity, and the cavalcade trotted off. In less than an hour, the camel that was said to have strayed was brought in, and Jooma Khan hastened away to overtake the party.

The day was unusually dark and gloomy, with a high oppressive wind and vivid lightning, which the Belooches said portended rain, but it subsided without that relief in the evening. The Sirdar then came to the Mihman Khanu to sit with me, and perceiving that I was much out of spirits at the loss of my esteemed and invaluable companion, he strove to cheer me, by declaring that he would take every care of me for the sake of my brother *, who had entrusted me to his charge; he also exerted himself whilst he staid, in the kindest, and I may add, the most effectual manner to entertain me, and I derived not merely great pleasure from his communications, but much information, which has been detailed under various heads in the foregoing pages.

23d March. The rain that the clouds yesterday had foretold, poured down in torrents to-day, attended by a tempest of wind and such volumes of sand, that it was impossible to distinguish objects at the distance of ten or fifteen yards; the roof of the Ghedan not being more proof against water than the sides were against sand, it rained through in every corner, and by the evening I was sitting in a bed of mud, and literally cased with a coat of mail of the same material.

The second Kasid returned from Kelat, with a man who was sent by our Hindoo to receive the overplus baggage, he was also the bearer of two letters, one written in the Persian and the other in the Shastree † character, which latter was in this part of the world, a

* While together we always passed for brothers.

† The Shastree is a kind of Nagree character. It is so called from some of the Shasturs or religious tracts being written in it.

complete cypher. The Persian letter contained neither news or any thing that could tend to a discovery of us, and when I had looked it over I handed it to the Sirdar, who had come in to hear the news, to convince him that I had no secrets; the other letter conveyed intelligence of the greatest moment to me, which was that two men dispatched by the Umeers of Sinde, had come to Kelat, avowedly intending to seize Captain Christie and myself, and carry us down to Hyderabad *, where they made no scruple in declaring we were to be bastinadoed. It further appeared, that they had gone to Muhmood Khan at Kutch Gundava, who in solution of their questions respecting us, told them that he had heard by means of a letter, of the arrival of two persons of our description at Kelat, though he did not understand from it that we were Europeans, which he was inclined to doubt, that at all events they might lay hold of us, provided they could discover and prove to his satisfaction, that we were spies of any nation; but on the other hand, that they were to beware of molesting us, if we were merchants or the agents of such, whatever our *caste* or country might be.

The Umeers' men told the Khan, that one of us at least, had been with the British Envoy † to Sinde the year before; that we were no more horse-dealers than they were, and had assumed that character, exclusively as a plea for surveying the country. These men had been twice to the house we occupied at Kelat, and denounced the vengeance of the Umeers against our Hindoo, unless he made a full disclosure; the Khan's injunctions, however, deterred them from taking any mode of compelling him to satisfy their inquiries, and finding him impenetrably secret, they remarked that we must eventually return to that city, as we had no other way of escaping out of the country; and that they should sit down quietly until we appeared.

* The capital of Sinde.

† Nicholas Hankey Smith, Esq., of the Honourable Company's civil service. Vide Chapter VIII. Part II.

Our Hindoo concluded his letter by saying, that he had used every precaution to prevent either of the Kasids or messengers from being seen by the Sindians, and believed he had succeeded; but that it was well known among the Hindoos at Kelat, with some of whom he had been obliged to negotiate bills, that we were still at Nooshky, where he surmised that the Umeers' men might arrest us with little difficulty, and therefore suggested our decamping with every possible haste.

On perusing this letter, I saw it was necessary to adopt prompt measures, and resolved on leaving Nooshky next morning. I gave Boodhoo, the Seistanee Hindoo, directions to prepare a quantity of flour and dates, and sending for Moorad Khan privately, agreed with him to be my guide to Surhud, on the western frontier of Beloochistan, for sixty rupees. My object in making this hasty arrangement was solely to accelerate my departure; had the expence been any consideration, it is probable the Sirdar would have given me, agreeable to his promises, guides at a cheaper rate; but I knew I should indubitably be detained in the event of trusting to him, and in my situation I felt that by allowing myself to be so, if only for eight and forty hours, I was running a very great risk.

I was nearly involved in another serious scrape to day, by an awkward circumstance. Captain Christie and I had made an agreement, to which we usually adhered, of never speaking to each other before strangers in any language except Hindoostanee, but it happened that Boodhoo the Seistanee Hindoo was present one day when we forgot our rule, and began to converse in English; he asked what dialect it was, and I replied without hesitation that it was Telinga *, thinking it as unlikely that he or any other person in the Toomun should be acquainted with that tongue, as with either Greek or Hebrew. Nothing more passed, and I had forgotten the matter entirely, but not so Boodhoo, for as I was eating my dinner, he came over to the Mihman

* The Telinga is the dialect spoken in Telingana and the northern Sirkars.

Khanu with a Fakeer, whom he said he had brought to chat with me in Telinga. I was puzzled how to act, as I knew not a syllable of that language; however, I put a bold face upon it, and when the Fakeer had seated himself, I turned towards him and rapidly addressed several queries to him in English: he certified his ignorance of what I had said by a significant smack* of the tongue and a shake of the head, and when I came to inquire into his peregrinations I found there was no occasion for having been under any alarm respecting his knowledge of Telinga, as he had not been farther southward in the peninsula of India than the city of Surat.

24th March. Finding it impossible to get away before the afternoon, I postponed the commencement of my journey till to-morrow, and employed myself in writing to the Hindoo at Kelat, to direct that he would take an early opportunity of closing his accounts at that city and returning to Bela, where he could remain without any chance of molestation, until he received further instructions from either Captain Christie or myself. About dusk I sent Futtuh Mohummud (my Hindoostanee man) to acquaint the Sirdar that I was to leave Nooshky next morning, and that I should be happy before I did so, personally to express my thanks to him for all the hospitable kindness I had received at his hands. He testified great surprize at this message, and told my servant that he would see me in half an hour at the Ghedan of Boodhoo the Hindoo. I accordingly went there, and had a very long conversation with him on different subjects; at length I introduced that of my intended departure. "Have you," said he, "already ceased to pay due attention to the good example which your brother afforded you by relying on me for his guides; and is it thus you attend to the cautions I gave you both about Moorad Khan? You are a very young man, and God send you may have no cause to rue your acquaintance with my nephew." He would have gone on for an hour in the same strain, but I slipped

* This is a very common and expressive negative in many parts of Asia.

twenty rupees into his hand, which I had ready for the express purpose of silencing him, telling him that as I was destitute of any thing worth his acceptance, I begged he would purchase a turband as a memorial of my gratitude with that sum. This had an instantaneous and wonderful effect in pacifying him, and before we parted he offered to give me letters to some chiefs whose territories I was likely to pass through.

CHAPTER VIII.

LETTERS. — THE AUTHOR SETS OFF FROM NOOSHKY. — GRATIFICATION. — PARTY. — ARMS. — GOOMBUZ OR CUPOLA IN THE DESERT. — CURIOUS TRADITION RESPECTING A CITY. — STONES ON THE SIDE OF THE PATH. — ROOSTUM'S HORSE. — LABOUR AND TROUBLE IT MUST HAVE TAKEN TO PLACE THEM. — COUNTRY. — KAREZ VILLAGE. — BRAHOOI TOOMUN. — NOOSHKY. — DISTRICT. — INHABITANTS. — SIRDAR. — HIS INCOME. — WHENCE DERIVED. — TOOMUN. — GHEDAN. — MINUTE DESCRIPTION. — HINDOO SHOPKEEPERS. — AWE THEY FEEL TOWARDS THE BELOOCHES. — BELOOCHE CHARACTER BRIEFLY STATED. — AUTHOR IS ATTACKED BY FEVER. — BALE RIVER. — ROUTE. — MARBLE. — ASAFŒTIDA PLANTS. — WATER. — WOOD. — ROUTE AND DISTANCE. — EXTRAORDINARY BUILDINGS DISCOVERED. — DESCRIBED. — TOMBS OR PLACES OF WORSHIP. — NATIVE OPINION ABOUT THEM. — PROBABLY CORRECT. — THUNDER STORM. — AUTHOR AND HIS FOLLOWERS SHELTERED FROM IT. — HIS APPREHENSIONS. — FORTUNATELY UNFOUNDED. — TOWN OF SARAWAN. — DESCRIBED. — BALL RIVER. — WELL. — BADOO RIVER. — SOLITARY SHEPHERD. — CHIEF OF SARAWAN. — REVENUES. — GREAT FERTILITY OF HIS DISTRICT. — TUKH OR PASS ON THE ROAD HENCE TO KELAT. — DISTRICTS PASSED THROUGH. — KHARAN DISTRICT. — LOCUSTS. — REMARKABLE INSTANCE OF THE SAGACITY OF THOSE INSECTS, AS ASSERTED BY THE NATIVES. — TOWN OF KHARAN. — ITS CHIEF. — TRIBES. — RESOURCES. — KHARAN CELEBRATED FOR CAMELS. — SHORT MARCH. — SANDY DESERT. — HIRE A SECOND GUIDE ACROSS IT.

MARCH 25th. The Sirdar came to the Mihman Khanu this morning at day break, accompanied by a Moollah, who wrote three letters that the former dictated to chiefs, of whom I shall hereafter have occasion to make mention. The man with the spare baggage and my letter set off on his return to Kelat immediately after breakfast, and I quitted Nooshky myself about ten o'clock, with as much unfeigned joy as I should have felt in escaping from a prison. My stay there had been protracted by a series of unpleasant delays for a period of sixteen days, though on first entering the Toomun I should have repined at the idea of being there as many hours. My party only consisted of five, exclusive of myself, and none of us were well armed, so that we had to trust more to our good fortune in not meeting with people inclined to plunder us, than to our means of repelling them.

Three miles from the Toomun we passed a Goombuz or cupola, which according to tradition stands near the site of an ancient town, whose inhabitants were so affluent that, as one means of disposing of their wealth, they mixed the Chunam or cement for the erection of all their houses and edifices with milk instead of water; which flagrant instance of unnecessary and ostentatious waste so incensed the Deity, that a curse was denounced on the place, and it gradually sunk into misery and decay. At present there is no other vestige of this fabulous city than this Goombuz, which has certainly a very singular appearance, being built in the desert a long way from the mountains, which here run off to the southward. I was not near enough to examine with precision the style of architecture (whether different from that of the present day in those countries) or the materials; but the former seemed to have nothing remarkable in it, and from Moorad's account the only thing observable with regard to the latter, is the amazing hardness of the Chunam, which he compared to marble. A short way in advance I observed some very large stones on the side of the path, at the distance of twenty or thirty yards from each other, and on asking the meaning of them, I was gravely assured, that they had been placed there by * Roostum, to commemorate the pace at which his favourite steed galloped. This solution, it is needless to add, I laughed at; but, for whatever purpose the stones in question may have been brought to the spot they are now at, it is clear that their transportation from the nearest mountain must have been attended with great trouble and cost;

* The Persian hero of the celebrated poem the Shah Namuh by Firdoosee.

many of them are several tons weight, and six or seven yards square.

We travelled sixteen miles to-day over a sandy flat country, and halted at sunset with mountains in front of us at three and a half miles; those bounding the desert, were generally during the route, eight or nine on our left, and sand-hills at intervals on our right. Half-way we passed a deserted village called Karez: there is a well of very good water close to it, whence we carried on a supply for the night. I saw numerous herds of camels, which animals are turned loose here to feed on the Guz* and Shinz†, with both of which the plain is well stocked. From our halting place in the evening we perceived the smoke rising from a Toomun of Guzhgee Brahooes, but as it would have been out of our way, we did not pay them a visit.

I was here on the confines of the district of Nooshky, with respect to which little remains to be added. I have already stated, that it is peopled by a branch of the Nharooé class of Belooches, named the Rukshaneés. The Sirdar or chief is Eidel Khan, a man about sixty years of age, possessing many qualifications that would have distinguished him in a higher sphere among his countrymen, but which are clouded by his excessive avarice. The only source of exclusive revenue that he seems to possess, is a water-mill turned by the river Kysur; and that must always be a very precarious one, as it often fails from a want of water. The Toomun of Nooshky comprises two hundred Ghedans, the formation of which has been repeatedly described. I was twice in the Sirdar's, which differed little from any of the others: the fire was in the middle of the floor, and on two sides of it, walls about six feet high are built to rest against; they were covered with carpets, and the whole was very neat and clean. Suspended from the roof were the matchlocks, swords, and shields belonging to the family. There are six Hindoo shopkeepers in the

* Tamarisk. † Hedysarum Alhagi.

Toomun, who have ventured to bring their wives and children here, although it is evident they stand in great awe of their protectors, for such they style the Belooche inhabitants, who, generally speaking, are idle, ignorant, unmannerly, and predatory; the latter quality they inherit in common with the whole race, and they are likewise much addicted to gambling. Hospitality and an adherence to such promises as relate to their personal bravery or fidelity, seem to be very justly their great boasts. When the crops fail at Nooshky, which is the case nine years out of ten, they depend on Gurmsyle and Kutch Gundava for grain, and in fact bring more or less every year from those places.

26th March. I moved this morning at six, though very unwell from a fever that had come on the night before, and after marching three miles over the plain, entered the hills by a stony path: we soon got among lofty mountains, a branch of the great range, and winding round the bases of them, or through rocky vallies for seventeen miles, came to a river bed nearly dry, called the Bale, in which, or along the banks of it, we advanced six miles further, and then having selected a spot where the camels might graze close to us, stopped for the night. Our road was very bad to-day, and in some places not more than two yards wide, the rocks rising like walls for many hundred feet on each side. I observed several blocks of white marble in the narrow water courses, and a profusion of the asafœtida plant growing on the precipices above us: the bed of the river Bale is very broad, and the bare desert that limits it, is elevated to a great height above the channel. The direction of my route to-day was south south-west, and the distance twenty-nine miles: very good water was to be had in two or three rivulets, beside that in the Bale, and logs of dried wood lay strewed about.

27th March. I was so weak from the effects of my fever, which had continued with great violence the whole of yesterday and throughout the night, that I could scarcely sit on my camel this morning, however to think of resting (with the journey I had before me) was out of the question, I therefore started about seven *a. m.*, taking one of the Brahoośs as a supporter, on the camel behind me. I travelled in the course of the day twenty-five miles south south-westerly, the path (where there was any trace of such) either lying in the bed of the river Bale, or along the elevated plain forming the banks of it, over which it frequently tended owing to its serpentine course: we had plenty of water in the river bed, and the jungul of * Babool, Lye†, and Taghuz‡ was often so thick, that the camels forced their way through with difficulty, even when we were dismounted.

About four miles from our halting place we, this evening, passed the remains of some very extraordinary tombs, built on the western bank of the river about four hundred yards from it: they were of a quadrangular shape, and had each been surrounded by a low wall of curious open freestone work, which conveyed to me at the moment, the idea of the meshes of a net stretched at one end into a conical shape: these walls enclosed an area of four or five square yards, and the entrances to them, as well as the buildings, fronted due east: there were several large mounds of earth and stones scattered over the desert to a considerable distance, which induced me to get off my camel, but as it was raining at the time, and I was but just able to walk, I did not stay to examine any of them minutely. I could discover no inscriptions, and it was in vain that I subsequently made strict inquiry with respect to these places, as I had not the good fortune to meet with any person who had seen them. All the satisfaction that my guide could give me was, that they were built in the time of the § Guebres, but that is the source, to which is ascribed every thing uncommon or inexplicable throughout this country, and ought not therefore to be implicitly credited; it is, however, probable that in this instance the

* Farnesian Mimosa.

† Tamarisk.

‡ The Taghuz is a species of the Tamarisk of which I have not seen any botanical description, nor met with the plant any where except in Beloochistan. It is in appearance very similar to the Lye, but the bark and leaves are a pale white, and covered with a kind of powder.

§ Infidels: so he styled the followers of Zoroaster.

conjecture was right: there was nothing whatever Mohummudan or Hindoo in the style, and if we remove the erection of them from those nations, it naturally rests with the Parsees* unless we choose to attribute it to a still earlier period. They were evidently very ancient, for notwithstanding the durable nature of the materials of which they were composed, they were every one mouldering and in a complete state of dilapidation. The most remarkable circumstance regarding them, if true, was pointed out to me by Moorad Khan, who informed me there was no stone of the same description (with that they were erected with) to be found in any part of the country, and added that it would be of no value, for the people of our days were incapable of executing such workmanship. I am still dubious whether these buildings were formerly sepulchres or places of worship; inside of each there was a raised mound covered with stone, which had, beyond a doubt, the appearance of a grave, but it is also possible that this was the altar for the sacred fire of the Atush Kudu †: their numbers speak, more than any other argument, to their having been cemeteries.

At midnight came on a violent thunder storm, which lasted for two hours, but very fortunately it had rained slightly when we came to our ground, and we had therefore taken up our quarters under the bank of the river, where some former flood had undermined it: our uncouth retreat sheltered us from the rain, and saved me from a wetting which I was ill fitted to bear at the time, but I could not compose myself to sleep, fearing that the river might overflow and sweep us all off: it faired however before the water had risen to any height

* Parsee is the modern name for these people, it is distinct from Persians who are Moosulmans.

† A fire-temple. The Guebres worship that element as an emblem of God. There are several Atush Kudus in India. At the city of Yezd in Persia, which is distinguished by the appellation of the Darŭl Ebadut, or Seat of Religion, the Guebres are permitted to have an Atush Kudu (which they assert has had the sacred fire in it since the days of Zoroaster) in their own compartment of the city, but for this indulgence they are indebted to the avarice, not the tolerance of the Persian Government, which taxes them at twenty-five rupees each man.

though it was beginning to tumble down with vast noise and force.*

28th March. I marched twenty-eight miles in a south south-westerly direction this day, chiefly over a bare plain. A little more than three miles from where we slept, the water in the bed of the Bale river runs off in a branch to the south-eastward, and supplies the town of Sarawan, which lay due east from me at that time, about three leagues off: travelling fifteen miles farther on the road, across a plain diversified with various kinds of underwood, and here and there a clump of large Babool trees, I came to a well of tolerable water in the dry bed of a rivulet, called the Badoo; here we heard from a solitary shepherd, who was tending a few half-starved goats, that there had been until the day before, a large Toomun of Nousherwanee Belooches in this neighbourhood, and that they had migrated to the mountains of Kharan, from a scarcity of water and forage for their cattle. Having filled our Mushks †, we advanced a little way, and took up our lodging in a thick patch of jungul.

The town of Sarawan which I saw in my progress of to-day is very small, not containing more than five hundred houses and huts, that are defended by a mud wall with bastions; it is placed in the centre of a bare and sterile district, about twenty miles from the Sarawanee mountains, whence it takes its name. The only inducement that the projector of this town could have had for selecting this situation, I should suppose to be, the unfailing and plentiful store of excellent water that is afforded to the inhabitants by the Bale; and it must be admitted that in a clime so obnoxious to drought, and its concomitant miseries of famine and dearth, as this part of Beloochistan, the advantages of a constant supply of that article are invaluable. The chief of Sarawan is Gool Mohummud Khan of the

* These floods are very common and exceedingly dangerous. I have seen a limpid brook four or five inches deep swell in the course of ten minutes to a rapid and impassable torrent, carrying every thing before it.

† Leathern bags for water.

tribe of Kumburanee; he pays no tribute to the Khan of Kelat, but furnishes the whole of his troops, amounting to two hundred men, at his own expence for the service of government. His revenues are trifling, and he receives them in produce rated according to the plentifulness of the season, which, notwithstanding the general barrenness of the soil, is sometimes so great in proportion to the consumers, that thirty or forty measures of wheat, of seven pounds and a half each, will sell for one rupee. When the harvest is unproductive, as was the case in the years 1808 — 9, and 10, the natives send their camels, of which they have immense numbers, to Gurmsyl, Kutch Gundava, and Sinde, and bring what grain they need from those countries.

There is a Lukh or pass over the mountains in the direct route from Sarawan to Kelat, but I understood it was so difficult of access, that laden camels seldom attempted it, preferring to go from the former town to Kharan* and thence to Kelat, which though a much longer, is a more easy road.

29th March. I had the satisfaction to find myself quite rid of my troublesome companion the fever, and left my ground in high spirits before sunrise. I marched upwards of thirty miles west-south-west, principally through the districts of Jalalan, Khurgoshkee, and Bhugut, which are inferior departments of Kharan, and exhibit a great deal of arable ground; much of it had lately been tilled, but the seed sown was mostly destroyed by a want of rain, and the portion that had been preserved by particular attention to irrigating it, and other artificial means, was devoured by a swarm of locusts, so that the unfortunate husbandmen had all decamped to the hills. It is a strange though unquestionable fact, that those destructive insects never penetrate to these districts unless in years of drought and famine; they then come as though it were to complete the devastation, and what is still more astonishing, they invariably appear from one quarter (the south-east) and return to the same; the

* Vide Narrative of the 29th March.

natives therefore affirm, that they are apprized of the existence of a desert, in which they would infallibly perish were they to make a further flight to the north-west. We passed one very deep well to-day, but the water was either dried up, or so low that we could not reach it with the rope we had for drawing; however, as we had still a part of yesterday's stock, we were not very anxious about it.

The town of Kharan lay about forty-five miles east-south-east from our halting place in the evening. It is said to be considerably larger than Sarawan, and is fortified in a similar manner. The district which bears the same name is extremely mountainous, and forms the north-western extremity of the province of Sarawan *. Its Sirdar, Abbas Khan Nousherwanee, was tributary to Muhmood Khan till within these last four years, when he declared himself exempt from controul in any shape whatever; he can call five or six hundred men of his own tribe into the field, and the Nousherwanees are considered excellent and hardy soldiers. The camels of Kharan are the most celebrated in all these regions for strength and activity, a circumstance that gives their masters in their predatory pursuits a decided superiority over their neighbours.

30th March. I was only enabled to accomplish a march of seventeen miles and a half to-day, owing to a halt which I made, for four hours, at a spot where I was fortunate enough to meet with a party of Puzh Brahooes, one of whom I prevailed upon for a trifling reward, to be my guide across the sandy desert that I was to enter the next morning; and with regard to which I was rather uneasy, as Moorad did not seem quite certain of the route, and confessed, when we had got another man, that he had never passed it so far to the northward. We replenished one of our water bags out of a pool of bad rain water that we happened to light upon, and slept in the desert, which had already began to assume a wavy appearance.

* Sarawan is one of the largest provinces of Beloochistan.

CHAPTER IX.

SET OUT EARLY. — WELL. — DESCRIBED. — WATER BRACKISH. — RED SANDY DESERT. — DIFFICULTIES. — WAVES. — CAMELS GO DOWN THEM ON THEIR KNEES. — NO VEGETATION. — MOUNTAINS DISCERNIBLE. — HALT BEHIND A SAND WAVE. — ATMOSPHERE OPPRESSIVE. — PROCEED OVER THE DESERT. — MOST EXTRAORDINARY PHENOMENON OBSERVED — DESCRIPTION. — NATIVE OPINION. — AUTHOR'S THEORY. — THE FLOATING SANDS DIFFERENT FROM THE SUHRAB OR "MIRAGE" — PROOF. — CORROBORATION BY A FAKEER — BOODOOR DRY RIVER — DESERTED VILLAGE OF REGAN. — WATER. — LEAVE REGAN. — HARD BLACK DESERT. — MOUNTAINS TO BE SEEN. — HALT. — VIOLENT TORNADO. — ITS CAUSE AND FREQUENCY. — UNPLEASANT. — ADVANTAGEOUS. — BĀDE' SUMOOM OR PESTILENTIAL WIND. — DREADFUL EFFECTS OF IT ON THE HUMAN FRAME. — ITS APPROACH UNFORESEEN. — SURMISE AND PRECAUTION. — THE LATTER SIMPLE. — MARCH AT NIGHT. — THE GUIDE LOSES THE PATH. — THE AUTHOR BY HIS COMPASS REGAINS THE DIRECTION, AND OBTAINS GREAT CREDIT FOR HIS WISDOM. — VERY LONG DAY'S JOURNEY. — OBLIGED TO HALT. — NO WATER OR PROVISIONS. — ARRIVAL AT THE VILLAGE OF KULLUGAN. — THE AUTHOR ASSUMES THE DISGUISE OF A RELIGIOUS MENDICANT. — CAUSE OF THIS. — RECEPTION. — TREACHEROUS CONDUCT OF A GUIDE. — EMBARRASSMENT. — HIRES ANOTHER GUIDE AND ESCORT. — LONG DISCUSSIONS WITH THE CHIEF AND PEOPLE. — INSTANCE OF THEIR GROSS IGNORANCE DESCRIBED IN AN ANECDOTE. — REFLECTIONS ON IT.

MARCH 31st. We were on our camels this morning by four o'clock, and moved five miles west by south to a well, where we filled every thing that would contain water preparatory to encountering the desert. This well was at least one hundred and fifty feet deep, nearly square, and not more than six feet in diameter: the sides of it, for two fathom below the surface, at which depth the strata became firm and hard, were propped by split date trees vertically placed, and held in that situation by the pressure of the ends of pieces of the same wood running horizontally across the pit. An aperture was left at one corner to admit a small bucket or copper vessel for drawing the water, which I was both surprized and disappointed, considering the deepness of the well, to find so brackish as to be barely palatable.

We quitted this well just as the sun rose, and proceeded the greater part of the way on foot, twenty-seven miles farther, over a desert of red sand, the particles of which were so light, that when taken in the hand they were scarcely more than palpable: the whole is thrown by winds into an irregular mass of waves principally running east and west, and varying in height from ten to twenty feet; most of these rise perpendicularly on the opposite side to that from which the prevailing wind blows (north-west), and might readily be fancied, at a distance, to resemble a new brick wall. The side facing the wind slopes off with a gradual declivity to the base (or near it) of the next windward wave. It again ascends in a straight line, in the same extraordinary manner as above described, so as to form a hollow or path between them. I kept as much in these paths as the direction I had to travel in would admit of, but had nevertheless exceeding difficulty and fatigue in urging the camels over the waves when it was requisite to do so, and more particularly where we had to clamber up the leeward or perpendicular face of them, in which attempt we were many times defeated, and reduced to go round until an easier place or turn in the wave offered. On the oblique or shelving side the camels got up pretty well, as their broad feet saved them from sinking deeper than we did ourselves, and the instant they found the top of the wave giving way from their weight, they most expertly dropt on their knees, and in that posture gently slid down with the sand, which was luckily so unconnected, that the leading camel usually caused a sufficient breach for the others to follow on foot. All symptoms of vegetation had ceased for the latter ten miles of my journey this day, except a few stunted bushes of the Taghuz * and a

Vide Narrative of the 27th, Note.

hardy little plant called by the Belooches Sirrikoh *, bearing a purple flower with a very powerful odoriferous smell. My guide appeared to be chiefly regulated in his movements by a chain of mountains that were at times just discernible to the southward. I did not halt until it was almost dark, being desirous of getting through the desert as quickly as in my power. We spent the night under shelter of one of the sand-waves, where the atmosphere was uncommonly hot and close.

1st April. I travelled to-day twenty miles across a desert of the same description as yesterday, and consequently the like impediments opposed me, which were trifling, however, compared with the distress suffered, not only by myself and people, but even the camels, from the floating particles of sand; a phenomenon which I am still at a loss to account for. When I first observed it, about ten *a. m.*, the desert seemed at the distance of half a mile or less, to have an elevated and flat surface from six to twelve inches higher than the summits of the waves. This vapour appeared to recede as we advanced, and once or twice completely encircled us, limiting the horizon to a very confined space, and conveying a most gloomy and unnatural sensation to the mind of the beholder: at the same moment we were imperceptibly covered with innumerable atoms of small sand, which getting into our eyes, mouths, and nostrils, caused excessive irritation attended with extreme thirst, that was increased in no small degree by the intense heat of the sun. On questioning my Brahooé guide who, though a perfectly wild savage, had more local knowledge than any other person of the party, he said that this annoyance was supposed by his countrymen and himself to originate in the solar beams causing the dust of the desert (as he emphatically styled it) to rise and float through the air; and, judging from experience, I should pronounce this idea to be partly correct, as I can aver that this sandy ocean was only visible during the hottest part of the day †. To prevent the

* Literally, mountain top. I have found no botanical name or description of it.

† The most simple theory that I can suggest for these moving sands, and which I offer with diffidence, is this. When the violent whirlwinds that prevail in the desert, terminate

supposition of my having been deceived in its reality, I may here add, that I have seen this phenomenon and the Suhrab, or watery illusion, so frequent in deserts, called by French travellers the *Mirage*, in opposite quarters at the same precise moment, and that they were to my sight perfectly distinct; the former having a cloudy and dim aspect, whilst the latter is luminous, and can only be mistaken for water: to corroborate what I have advanced, I may likewise state that I afterwards was joined by a Fakeer from Kabool, who had come through the desert from Seistan, and told me that he had witnessed the moving sands to a much greater degree than I had described (or was willing to give him credit for), as he talked of being forced to sit down in consequence of the density of the cloud which enveloped him.

To proceed with my journal. Sixteen miles from our last halting-place, we reached the eastern bank of a dry river called the Boodoor: it was at least five hundred yards in breadth, running in a south-south-east direction towards the coast; the bed of it in many places impervious from a thick jungul of different kinds of trees and brushwood, the haunt of wolves, jackalls, and other wild animals. We turned to the right and proceeded five miles north-westerly up the river bed to a spot where there had a few months before been a vil-

in gusts of wind, they usually expand over several square miles, raging with irresistible force, and bearing upwards an immense body of sand, which descends as the current of air that gave it action dies away, thus creating the appearance in question. It might perhaps be demanded, what should prevent the sand from altogether subsiding, when it has so far done so, as to rest apparently on the waves? To this I should answer, that all the grosser particles do settle, but the more minute become rarified to such a degree, by the heat excited by the burning sun on the red soil, that they remain as it were in an undecided and undulating state, until the returning temperature restores their specific gravity, and then by an undeviating law of nature they sink to the earth. It will be perceived that this coincides in some measure with the opinion of the native Brahooes, but conformable to their notion, it is evident that the floating sands would be apparent at all periods of excessive solar influence, which not being the case, it becomes necessary to find a primary cause for the phenomenon.

lage aptly called Regan *, whose inhabitants had gone to Gurmsyl (which district lies north-north-west of this place) owing to the scarcity. Here we halted on the western brink, and with much digging and difficulty procured two Mushks, or skins, of water. I imagine the direct course from the well we left yesterday morning to Regan, would have been about west; but our guide, fearing to lose himself, kept to the southward, where he could at intervals descry the mountains.

2d April. I set out from Regan just as the day began to dawn, and having made a westerly march of twenty-one miles, halted at three in the afternoon. The desert was not near so sandy, and in many places was composed of a hard black gravel without a trace of verdure, or even a bush to be seen. In the latter part of my route I could distinctly trace with my eye, a chain of lofty mountains stretching all round in front from south-west to north-west; and when we alighted off the camels, my guide shewed me the break in them through which we were to gain egress from this inhospitable waste.

I experienced this forenoon a violent tornado or gust of wind, accompanied by a torrent of rain which continued for half an hour, and was absorbed by the earth as it fell. It came on most unexpectedly, and had the guide not apprized me of its strength, we should probably have fared worse than we did, for it would have been an act of temerity to have tried to sit on the camels during its impetuous fury. Before it began, the sky was clear, save a few small clouds in the north-west quarter, and the only antecedent warning it afforded, was the oppressive sultriness of the air and a vast number of whirlwinds springing up on all sides †; the moment the Brahooé saw

* Sands. I have considered the Boodoor river, and its probable source, fully, in the second part of this work.

† These whirlwinds would perhaps be more correctly called by some other name, but as the wind issued from them I venture to adopt the term. They are vast columns of sand, which begin by a trifling agitation with a revolving motion on the surface of the desert, and gradually ascend and expand, until the tops of them are lost to the view, in which manner they move about with every breath of wind like a pillar of sand. I have

these whirlwinds disperse, which they did as if by magic, and a cloud of dust approaching, he advised us to dismount, and we had hardly time to do so and lodge ourselves snugly behind the camels, when the storm burst upon us with a furious blast of wind: the rain fell in the largest drops I ever remember to have seen, and the air was so completely darkened, that I was absolutely unable to discern any thing at the distance of even five yards. Moorad happened to place himself about so many paces in front of me, and when I looked up, during the height of the tempest, I saw nothing of him, and therefore concluded he had shifted his position, but when it was over I found him still in the same spot. These bursts are by no means rare, and though unpleasant at the instant, have their attendant advantages, as they cool and purify the atmosphere, which would otherwise be quite intolerable at any season, and is so notwithstanding their prevalence, throughout the hot months from June to September.

Within that period, the winds in this desert are often so scorching and destructive, as to kill any thing, either animal or vegetable, that may be exposed to them, and the route by which I travelled is then deemed impassable. This wind is distinguished every where in Beloochistan, by the different names of Julot or Julo, the flame, and Badé Sumoom, the pestilential wind. So powerfully searching is its nature, that it has been known to kill camels or other hardy animals, and its effects on the human frame were related to me by those who had been eye-witnesses of them, as the most dreadful that can be imagined; the muscles of the unhappy sufferer become rigid and contracted; the skin shrivels, an agonizing sensation, as if the flesh was on fire, pervades the whole frame, and in the last stage it cracks into deep gashes, producing hemorrhage, that quickly ends this misery. In some instances life is annihilated instantaneously, and in others the unfortunate victim lingers for hours, or perhaps days, in

seen thirty or forty of them at the same time of different dimensions, apparently from one to twenty yards in diameter. Those who have seen a water spout at sea may exactly conceive the same formed of sand on shore.

the excruciating tortures I have described. To render this terrible scourge still more baneful, its approach is seldom, if ever foreseen; and among all the Belooches with whom I have conversed regarding it, no one asserted more than that they had heard it was indicated by an unusual oppression in the air, and a degree of heat that affected the eyes; the precaution then adopted, is to cover themselves over, and lie prostrate on the earth. A curious fact is established by this custom, that any cloth, however thin, will obviate the deleterious effects of the Badé Sumoom on the human body.

3d April. As I had a very long march before me, I determined on starting in the middle of the night: the guide protested that he knew the way, and in fact, had he comprehended any thing of the course we were to take, he could not have contrived to make a mistake, as we were now completely clear of the sand, and the face of the desert had changed into a hard black gravel, without a bush, a stone, or the most trifling irregularity of surface, to interrupt our progress; notwithstanding which, before we had gone five hundred yards, I discovered by the heavens that we had already formed two or three complete circuits round the spot at which we had baited. I was now as much bewildered as any of my followers, and was on the point of calling a halt until day-break, when it recurred to me that I had the bearings of the pass into the mountains, and that by feeling the needle of my compass, I might ascertain the direction in which we were to move. I therefore forced the glass of it out, and holding the compass in my right hand, turned round till I brought the north point of the index to my thumb; the west being then exactly opposite to me, I marked some of the stars, and proposed to officiate as conductor. Moorad and the Brahooé both wished to dissuade me from what they believed to be a vain attempt, by vowing we should only get farther astray, but my Hindoostanee man was willing to trust himself to my guidance, and his example induced the others to accede to my proposition; we therefore advanced, and at dawn of day found ourselves in the direct line that the guide would have pursued at mid-day, and thirteen miles nearer the mountains. This trivial incident was looked upon by my companions, who were ignorant of the use of my compass *, to be little short of an act of divine inspiration, and a fortnight posterior to its occurring I was astonished to hear it cited by a man to whom Moorad had told the circumstances, as a wonderful proof of my wisdom.

We travelled without intermission till seven o'clock in the evening, and had then, by my computation, completed a distance of upwards of forty-eight miles. I should have continued onwards, but my people and camels too, were worn out with the fatigue of this and the two preceding days, and on communing, I stood the only advocate for exerting ourselves in an endeavour to gain the mountains ere we came to a stop. To augment our distress, the provisions fell short, and we had served out the last remains of water before we halted, so that we were compelled to watch away the night under the various hardships of fatigue, hunger, and thirst: the latter only incommoded me, but I consoled myself, and encouraged the despondent, with the reflection that early next morning we should be able to procure all that was necessary to our comforts.

4th April. Twelve miles from our halting place, partly over the gravelly desert, and partly among stony bare hills, I arrived at the village of Kullugan, situated in a narrow and most romantic valley of Mukran. My intention on quitting Nooshky, was to have gone to the town of Jalk about fourteen miles to the northward, but Moorad, who I now learned was married to a daughter of the Sirdar, prevailed upon me to come to this place. When I had got within half a mile of the village, he suggested that I should remain under the shade of some date trees, whilst he rode on to apprize the chief of my coming. I objected to this, as seeming to arrogate consequence to myself, but Moorad assured me that it was customary with strangers, and I afterwards invariably practised it in this part of the coun-

* Whenever any one saw my compass and enquired what it was, I answered, it was a Kiblah Nooma, i. e. a pointer out of the Kiblah (the tomb of Mahomed at Mecca, to which all Moosulmans turn when they pray), and that I used it in my devotions.

try. Moorad returned in a short space to tell me that Meer Khodadad (as he entitled the Sirdar) had desired I would instantly adopt the name and character of a Peerzaduh *, otherwise he could not be responsible for my safety even in his own house. "You are no "longer," added Moorad, "to consider yourself in the Khan's † "territories, or to calculate on the same good order and security that you saw existing there; we are now in Mukran, where "every individual is a robber by *caste*, and where they do not hesitate to plunder brothers and neighbours. Your's is the very worst "name that you can henceforward travel under, and it would be an "useless attempt to try to persuade the people, that a merchant's "servant was not possessed of property, or at least the means of "obtaining it." I could guess at no sinister motive that Moorad could harbour for inciting me to this scheme, and although I made due abatement for his amplification, I knew from what the old Sirdar at Nooshky had told me, that there was a good portion of truth in his statement. There was no time to parley, and I therefore obeyed Meer Khodadad's instructions, and immediately assumed the religious air and mien becoming my new appellation.

On entering the village I dismounted at the door of the mosque, where I was formally introduced by Moorad to his father-in-law, the Sirdar, and three or four Moollahs, or priests, as a Peerzaduh from Kelat, and then on my pilgrimage. The former began a long apology for being obliged to lodge me in the mosque, as the Mihman Khanu, or house for guests, was not in a habitable state; but said that he had ordered a vacant house to be swept out for me. I rejoined, that any place would answer for the short stay that I was to make at his village; and shortly after he, and the pack of idlers that had collected to hear the news, left me to repose for an hour or two. In the evening I was conducted to my new mansion, a miser-

* From Peer, a saint; and Zaduh, the offspring. It means a religious devotee, and is considered a most sacred appellation.

† Of Kelat.

able hovel, with two small rooms, and presently the Sirdar sent me a quantity of food for myself and people, which we were heartily glad to receive, having fasted for upwards of thirty hours. I had slight symptoms of a recurrence of fever at night, and happening to mention this to the Sirdar, he sent one of his slaves to Shampoe me *, from which operation I found great relief; the man continued to do so until I fell sound asleep; and I arose next morning quite refreshed and well.

5th April. After breakfast, which was provided by the Sirdar, and consisted, like dinner the evening before, of barley cakes and sour milk, I took Moorad aside, and briefly told him that my business would not admit of my tarrying at Kullugan longer than the next day, when I purposed setting out for Surhud; that I therefore wished him to procure for me the small stock of provisions that I required, for which I should be happy to pay an equitable price; and finally, that he would prepare himself to proceed along with me. He replied, that the famine, of which he doubted not I had seen proofs even in the few hours I had been in the place, had raised the value of food amazingly, and likewise rendered it difficult to be had, but that his father-in-law intended, on his account, to spare me a few dates, and a little barley-flour from his own household store. This communication with respect to the dearth, however disagreeable, was not my principal cause of vexation, for Moorad added, that he had been given to understand, that it would be exceedingly hazardous to think of advancing any farther, without some matchlockmen as a safe-guard; and that going to Surhud was totally out of the question, as the Belooches of that place † had, within the last three weeks, ransacked Kullugan, and of course the inhabitants of the

* The most common mode of Shampoing is to knead, as it were, the body all over; squeezing and stretching the joints at the same time. There are, however, many other ways of its being done. I have seen a man who, as soon as he lay down, had three or four people to come and pat every part of him (not even missing his face) until he went to sleep.

† The tribe of Koords.

two villages were implacable enemies. "You had better therefore," said he, "decide on taking the route of Bunpoor or Huftur *, and "for a trifling remuneration, Meer Khodadad will himself accom-"pany us." To this I answered that I had no money, and reminded Moorad of the assurance he had given me when I first hired him, that I should not be put to any additional expence for guides as far as Surhud. He acknowledged the fact, stating that he was not then aware of, and could not foresee the tumultuous state of the country, but that to evince his entire willingness to undergo any toil in my service, he was ready at that moment to attend me back to Nooshky; though with regard to prosecuting my journey, his opinion was, that unless I had some other protection, it was utterly impracticable, and what he would not countenance by his presence. I brought forward every argument that I could devise to change his resolution, but the vagabond had me in his power, and being certain that I neither would profit by his offer of returning, or had the means of compelling him to fulfil his original stipulation, he remained inflexible, and I was ultimately necessitated to conclude an agreement with him, to pay Meer Khodadad fifty rupees, in consideration of his convoying me with six armed men either to Huftur or Bunpoor, and that we were positively to depart the following day after twelve o'clock prayers. I instantly put the cash into his hands, and with a view of preventing any fresh demands, took care to shew him that I had only twenty-six rupees remaining, which I remarked was to provide food for myself and three men, exclusive of incidental charges for guides, during a journey of seven hundred miles that I had still to perform, before I could reach the city of Kirman, the scoundrel viewed this remnant of my funds with the utmost *sang froid*, and told me to trust to Providence for my support. I turned from him to hide the chagrin I felt at being so basely treated, and in a few minutes he sent his father-in-law to assure me, that so far as he was

* Towns which I afterwards visited.

concerned, he would adhere to the bargain, and that I might make myself confident of setting off at the appointed hour, a point on which I had laid particular stress, dreading a repetition of the delays I had such reason to remember at Nooshky.

At sunset we had our dinner as usual, and by the time I had swallowed a hasty meal, the house in which I lodged was crowded with people. Khodadad was one of the assembly, and I learned that he had been so thoughtful the evening before, as to direct that I might not be pestered with visitors, owing to my indisposition; an act of careful politeness that I had not known equalled since I landed at Sonmeany, and which I confess I had not anticipated at Kullugan. We had a great deal of conversation on various subjects that I could have wished to avoid, especially religion, a topic which the Sirdar took every method of introducing, with the evident design of discovering to what sect of Moosulmans I belonged. I soon discerned from his sentiments that he was a rigid Soonnee, and therefore adapted my discourse to his opinions, by which artifice I eluded all serious controversy, and what with the former instructions of Futtuh Mohummud (my Hindoostanee man) and his well-timed assistance in the course of the evening, managed not only to acquit myself without blunders, but to impress my auditors with such notions of my theological skill, that my voice on two or three occasions decided the point at issue.

About ten o'clock I spread my Kummul* in a corner, and stretched myself upon it, in the expectation that the assembly would follow my example and retire; but my attention was presently drawn to an argument that afforded me high amusement. This was between two of the villagers, one of whom most vehemently asserted that the sun and moon were actually the same luminary: his opponent urged, as far as I could understand, many incontestable proofs to the contrary, and at length losing all patience, called silence, to some others

* Country blanket.

who had intermeddled in the dispute, and exclaimed: "Let him be, "I will give him his answer." He then sneeringly demanded how he could reconcile with his position the sun and moon being visible at the same moment in opposite sides of the heavens: the other was posed a little, but either feeling unconvinced, or determined, as a point of honor, not to give in, he coolly rejoined that the latter was the reflection of the former. The debate would probably have continued some hours, had it not been suggested to refer to me: I feigned sleep, but found that I should have had to listen to a minute recapitulation of the whole matter, to escape which I acknowledged that I had overheard the discussion, and although far from a competent umpire, was inclined to disagree with the last speaker: this opinion was received as conclusive, and the assembly broke up. This anecdote furnishes a remarkable example of the ignorance of these people, and is hardly reconcileable with our ideas of the reasoning faculties bestowed on man, to suppose that beings possessing a knowledge and belief of their Maker, and acquainted, however rudely, with the common forms of life, should be capable of such gross absurdity.

CHAPTER X.

PRAYERS.—THE AUTHOR OBLIGED TO TAKE A PART IN THEM.—QUITS KULLUGAN.—GUIDE'S VILLAINY.—PARTY.—KULLUGAN VILLAGE.—SIZI.—PLAN OF BUILDING.—OBJECT CONTEMPLATED.—SUMMARY OBSERVATIONS ON THE STATE OF SOCIETY.—AUTHOR'S MEDICAL FAME.—HOW RAISED.—CONSEQUENCES.—HE IS BESET BY THE WOMEN OF THE VILLAGE.—IMPORTUNITIES.—HOW EVADED.—NARRATIVE CONTINUED.—WET NIGHT.—BAD ROAD.—DISTRICT OF KALPOORUKAN.—DIZUK.—TWO EXTRAORDINARY HILLS.—NAMES.—DESCRIPTION OF THEM.—NARROW ESCAPE FROM BEING ATTACKED.—VILLAGE OF GULL.—INVITATION.—REPAST.—THE AUTHOR IN A MOST AWKWARD PREDICAMENT.—REPEATS A PRAYER AND AVOIDS DETECTION.—DISTRICT OF DIZUK.—CHIEF'S NAME.—REVENUE.—SHAH MIHRAB KHAN.—RELIGIOUS CONTROVERSY.—REMARKABLE OBSERVATIONS OF A NATIVE, AND THE AUTHOR'S REFUTATION OF THEM.—ADVANCE ON THE JOURNEY.—DISTRICT AND TOWN OF SIBB.—VILLAGES OF KULLUGEE AND PAGTE.—ACCOUNT OF SHEIK MOORAD KHAN KOORD BELOOCHE.—NATURE OF THE SOIL.—INTRICATE ROAD.—FACE OF THE COUNTRY ENTIRELY CHANGED.—KOTHUL, OR PASS.—DESCRIPTION OF IT.—VILLAGES OF SHUROK AND MUGHSEE.—CHIEF OF THE LATTER ASSASSINATED.—PARTICULAR ACCOUNT OF THAT TRANSACTION.—CAUSE.—AUTHOR'S REFLECTIONS.—LOORIE'S.—THE GIPSIES OF THE EAST.—THEIR HABITS AND AMUSEMENTS.—RUMI AND KOORUH.—RELIGION OF THE LOORIES.—CURIOUS PROVERB.—DRESS.—VICES.—SENSUALITY.—INCESTUOUS COMMERCE.—CHUPAO, OR INROAD, OF KHAN JUHAN KHAN.—HIS PLUNDER.—THE AUTHOR DISCOVERS THAT HIS GUIDE REALLY BELIEVES HIM TO BE A RELIGIOUS DEVOTEE.—DISCUSSION ON RELIGION.—REASONING.—MEANS ADOPTED TO SILENCE THE GUIDE.—SUCCESS.—EXPLANATION.

APRIL 6th. Meer Khodadad was punctual to his declaration, and I left Kullugan as soon as noontide prayers were finished. I was very reluctantly compelled to go to the mosque and take a part in them, an act of duplicity I had hitherto evaded, and was still solicitous to do so; but the Sirdar came to my lodging and called to me, as a matter of course, to join him; for the truth was, he thought that I had stipulated for having prayers before we set out. I perceived there was no alternative, so I simply went through the motions of prostration, keeping my eye fixed on the Sirdar, and muttering to myself. When I was mounting my camel, Moorad came up to kiss my hand, and said that as his father-in-law was to escort me, there was no need for his going. I had anticipated this close to his villainous conduct, and did nothing to induce him to alter his determination, as I was rather pleased than otherwise, at leaving him behind. My guard had decreased to three men, or rather boys, exclusive of Meer Khodadad and a Fakeer from Kabool, who was thus far on his way to Mecca. We travelled about six miles a little to the southward of West, through a water-course between mountains, and passed two villages named Poora and Ybee. At four *p.m.* we halted in the most open spot we could find, to prevent the possibility of our being surprized during the night.

Kullugan contains about one hundred and fifty houses, many of which are two or three stories high, being thus erected to enable the owners, when attacked, to take refuge in the upper part; indeed, the majority of the inhabitants sleep above, ascending by a ladder through a trap-door, and drawing it up after them; so that should the robbers come at night, they cannot molest the family, nor get at their stock of grain and other provisions. The village is built on one side of a narrow grove of date trees, that extends to the southward upwards of a mile, the soil beneath it was planted with rice and other grains, a broad rivulet ran through the centre, on the borders of which grew numbers of lofty spreading trees with rich and luxuriant foliage; the mountains, at that season clothed with verdure, overhung the hamlet; and, on the whole, I thought it more embellished by nature with her various beauties, than any place I had ever seen. The impression it made upon me was rendered still stronger, by the sudden transition from that expanded and desolate waste I had just journied over to this sequestered and beautiful spot.

In the second part of this work, the province of Mukran is treated of in detail, and as these districts form a part of it, I shall be brief in my observations on them at present. Every village here has a Sirdar or chief, who appears to be elected to fill that station by the general suffrage of the people, and receives from them a voluntary grant of a small portion of the annual crops of grain and dates, in lieu of which he is bound to entertain such strangers as are deemed deserving of that attention; but in Mukran the genius of hospitality is far behind that of Beloochistan, and the occasions of its being exercised comparatively few. The natives of the districts from Kullugan to Hufter are called Mukranees, or people of Mukran. They are a small race of men, and though very hardy, and, as far as I could judge, brave, live in constant dread of their powerful neighbours the Belooches, with whom they admit themselves unable to cope. Their dress, occupations, and habits are much the same: their women are very ordinary, and I particularly remarked, that there was not one in the village of Kullugan (the only place in which I sojourned sufficiently long, to make any observations of that nature) who had not weak eyes, for which malady I gave two or three of the Sirdar's relations a little eye-water, made from alum and opium, that I happened to have with me. I was afterwards tormented by all the females in the village, not merely for relief in that one complaint, but divers others which the ladies had no scruples in minutely describing to the Peerzaduh, the only name they accosted me by. Several of them fervently prayed for the sake of Mohummud, and as I hoped to derive a blessing by my pilgrimage, that I would confer on them an amulet to remove barrenness; others complained of hysterics and vapours, and in fact their ailments were equal to the number of individuals, as each had a separate case to lay before me. At last, to escape from their importunities, I was constrained to avow my inability to instruct or prescribe in those matters.

7th April. After passing a very wet comfortless night, we were glad to rise off the cold ground before day-break, in hope of warming ourselves by the exercise of moving. I then discovered that a sad mischance had befallen me, in the loss of one of my shoes, which was carried away by a fox or some other animal; and unfortunately the road was so miserably bad, that it required us to dismount two or three times in every so many hundred paces; but notwithstanding this concatenation of obstacles, I marched, in the course of the day, twenty-six miles, alternately through deep water courses, over rocky ledges of mountains, or stony plains. The route was very circuitous, and a great part of it led across the small district of Kalpoorukan* which is subject to the chief of Dizuk, near whose largest town I halted in the plain at seven o'clock in the evening. There are two very extraordinary hills in this neighbourhood; one of them named Kohé Gubr, or the Guebre's mountain. I was not nearer to it than twelve or fourteen miles. It is very striking in its shape, rising in the form of a lofty cupola, and towering far above all the other mountains in its vicinity. On the summit of it, it is reported, are the remains of an Atush Kudu or fire temple, but I could meet with no person who had actually been at it. The other is a detached hill in the plain, styled Kohé Gwanka or the hill of echo, from its possessing the surprizing power of distinctly repeating any words spoken in a low tone of voice within fifty yards of its base. It was almost dusk when I passed about a quarter of a mile from it, but my people hallooed out, and it certainly reverberated whatever they said without the slightest deviation. I should conjecture from its appearance that it is hollow; and, since my return to India, I have heard from a native of those countries, that there are hieroglyphic characters on the Kohé Gubr. They are both, however, superstitiously held to be the residence of Deves or sprites, and many marvellous stories are recounted of the injury and witchcraft suffered by those who essayed, in former days (for now they are shunned by all classes) to ascend or explore them.

Whilst we stopped at sunset to allow Meer Khodadad leisure to say his prayers, at which he was regular three times in the day, eighteen armed men joined us. We had previously perceived them

* Kalpoorukan, I believe, signifies full of fairies or spirits.

hovering about, as if reconnoitring our strength, and when we came to commune together, they gave us to understand, that having descried our party about two o'clock in the afternoon, they concluded we were bent on plundering some of the villages in the district that night; and had therefore laid a plan to attack us in the twilight, when they correctly estimated, that we should have made no preparation for repelling them; but that, on seeing us dismount, they were induced to approach to ascertain our views. As they were stout looking men, nearly double our number, and much better armed, it is most probable several of us would have been killed or wounded, had not the halt we so providentially made, frustrated their scheme by leading to an eclaircissement. Khodadad informed them, that I was a Peerzaduh on a Huj or pilgrimage, on which, they professed increased satisfaction at the discovery of a mistake that might have caused me the slightest molestation; and I had to undergo the ceremony of embracing them all round; after which they staid but a few minutes and then left us, to return to their homes.

8th April. I reached the village of Gull, the first in the district of Dizuk, by seven *a. m.*, and had passed through it a few hundred paces, when a Moollah belonging to the mosque, who had heard of me from the villagers that were with us the evening before, sent a boy to entreat, that I would turn back and partake of some refreshment. I saw clearly that this politeness originated entirely in curiosity, and it would have been more satisfactory to me, not only for that reason, but because I anticipated religious discussions, to have evaded a compliance with the invitation; but having no good plea for doing so, and being urged to accept it by all my companions (who did not chuse to forfeit a good breakfast for what they considered my punctilio), I was obliged to return, and found four or five well-dressed respectable men sitting on carpets spread under a shady tree, with bread and butter-milk in wooden dishes before them. They all rose up to receive me, and when we had reciprocally kissed hands and embraced, I was placed on the right hand of the principal

Moollah, who uttered Bismillah * and we commenced our meal, at which the whole were fortunately so occupied, that they had little time to ask me questions. When we had done eating, a slave brought water to wash as before we sat down, and my left hand supporter, who spoke middling Persian, looked round and said to the group, "The Peerzaduh will repeat a Fatihu or prayer of thanks-"giving." This call upon me was as unexpected as unwelcome, and I was greatly perplexed for an instant; however, as I had acquired a trifling knowledge of the most common Mohummudan prayers, from the instruction of my Hindoostanee servant subsequent to quitting Bombay, I assumed a very grave air, stroked down my beard with all imaginable significance, and muttered a few sentences, managing to articulate rather distinctly, the words Ullah, Rusool, Shookr, &c. †; this succeeded admirably well, and we separated with the same forms with which we met.

I proceeded about nine miles further through the district of Dizuk, which is very fertile and populous, containing either seven or eight villages, each of which has a distinct name, but the natives usually designate them by the general term of Dizuk, a custom very prevalent all over Beloochistan, or, I might add, Asia, and very liable to mislead strangers. The principal chief is Neamut Oollah Khan, to whom I had a letter from the Sirdar of Nooshky, but I did not deliver it, because he would have detained me some hours, or perhaps the night. He receives one tenth of the whole produce, which is immense in wheat and dates, as they have a never failing supply of water from a brook that meanders down the vale, and the plantations of palm trees are numerous and extensive. Shah Mihrab Khan, who resides at Huftur, a town six days' journey hence, has a village here, which he himself afterwards told me, yielded him an income equal to

* Bismillah, "In the name of God." This invocation is used by pious Moosulmans on every occasion, however unimportant. Here it answers to our grace.

† Ullah, God; Rusool, the Prophet; Shookr, thanks: these words were the most likely to occur in a prayer of the kind I was called upon to give.

ten thousand rupees a year; and as Neamut Oollah Khan possesses seven of the same description, his revenues may be fairly estimated at sixty or seventy thousand rupees per annum.

During a halt we made this forenoon near a village called Surjo, where I was to purchase a pair of shoes, a crowd of people collected around us and commenced an attack, in due form, on religious matters. They took me for a Persian, and consequently stamped me as a Sheea, which sect they most vehemently hate; but I silenced them in a few minutes with the aid of my Hindoostanee man, who was ever my faithful supporter on these occasions. As I rose to depart, a man observed to me that I was certainly destined to go to heaven. "Your "looks," said he, "indicate that you had, in your native country, "wherewithal to subsist upon, and, therefore, voluntarily to abandon "those comforts and travel in this style, is a penance which will unquestionably give you great claims to future reward. Should I," added he, "go in the same way, I have no reason to look for similar "advantage, because I am as poor and miserable at home as I can "be elsewhere *." I protested that he then saw me in my true station in life, but he smiled at this; and, at last, fixing his eyes on my feet, he said that they alone confuted my declaration, and proved I had not been accustomed to such penury. I instantly went to my shoes and put them on, for notwithstanding I had persevered in exposing my feet to the sun, even till they were often blistered, I could never get them to assume the weather beaten colour of my hands and face. The man followed me until I mounted my camel and rode off, but I am confident, although the fairness of my skin attracted his observation, that he did not suspect me of being an European. †

* The doctrine contained in this speech is rather at variance with the equality held forth to all good Moosulmans by the Koran, but it is always encouraged, plainly with the aim of inducing men of property to go on pilgrimage, who thereby give *éclat* to the act, exclusive of the large presents they make to the shrines they visit.

† All Asiatics attach an idea of rank to fairness of colour. Why, I know not, unless it is that their chiefs are usually fairer than the commonalty; this may perhaps be owing to their being brought up with greater care, immured and sheltered from vicissitudes of climate and season; in their mature age they are also less liable to exposure.

9th April. We passed the night at the bottom of the w range of Dizuk hills, which we ascended this morning, and travelle over ten miles westerly, when we entered a very extensive plain composing the district of Sibb. A small town of that name lay about four miles south of my road, and two west of it there is a village called Kullugee, and another nearly north named Pogee. I did not visit any of these places, of which the Sirdar is Sheik Moorad Khan, a Koord Belooche, who has been invited by the primitive inhabitants to colonize here, with a few of his tribe, in order to defend the district, a task for which his bravery and resolution appear to have well qualified him. He has hitherto succeeded in maintaining his independence, though repeatedly attacked by the troops of Shah Mihrab, Khan of Puhra, who is confessedly by far the most potent chief in this side of the country. The district of Sibb is, generally speaking, barren, and would be entirely so, were it not for a broad water-course on the western side of it, in the bed of which there are large wheat fields, and groves of palm trees. When we had crossed the plain of Sibb a second ridge of low mountains presented itself, at the back of which we halted. The aggregate distance to-day was twenty-three miles, and the course nearly west. In some of the narrow ravines I observed the Lye or tamarisk bush, but no other shrubs or vegetation.

10th April. The path, during the whole of this day's journey, was very winding, and the face of the country surprizingly altered; indeed it was scarcely conceivable that so entire a change could have taken place within so limited a space: instead of the mountains and hills being, as those near Kullugan and Dizuk, clothed with verdure and shrubs to the summits, here they were a mere mass of black rock; and in lieu of the expanded flat districts of Kalpoorukan, Dizuk, and Sibb, the few level spots that I met with were intersected by low stony ridges and deep ravines, which made them both difficult and unpleasant to journey over. We had one Kothul *, or defile,

* Kothul is the Persian word for a pass or defile; Lukh, the Belooche.

ther remarkable for its great acclivity or length, but the natural strength of its situation seemed to me to be such, that it was tenable y a few men against any force. The passage is excavated for two hundred yards, to the depth of ten feet, out of the solid stone, and the ascent so abrupt, that stones hurled down would be attended with inevitable death to any one coming up. I reckon the extreme length of my march this day at twenty-eight miles, though in a straight line it was not half that distance from one halting place to the other. At the seventeenth and twenty-fifth miles are the two small villages of Shurok and Mughsee, both encompassed by a mud wall. I rode into the latter with the intention of remaining there that night, but hearing that a gang of Loorees had murdered the Sirdar a few days before, and that their leader was officiating in that capacity, by command of Shah Mihrab Khan, I did not deem it prudent to sojourn any length of time in the power of such blood thirsty ruffians, and therefore passed on and slept in the jungul.

Although I had long accustomed myself to regard the people of this part of Mukran as hardened in every species of inhumanity, I must confess I was confounded by the cool depravity evinced by an old man who was the head of the murderous gang, and who, after having minutely detailed to Khodadad and my camel drivers the particulars of the assassination, pointed with great apparent exultation to a very high house in the village, and said that the son of the unfortunate Sirdar had taken refuge there at the moment of the massacre of his father's family; and that they were momentarily expecting him to descend to be put to death: the hoary sinner (for he was really such) added, with the same merciless composure, that the youth might as well come down quickly and relieve them from the tedious task of starving him out, which was the only mode of expulsion they meant to pursue, lest they should damage the building and property in it. I ventured to ask, what Shah Mihrab Khan had thought of this outrage towards a man who had held the village in fief from him; and, to increase my astonishment, I was informed, that subsequent to the commission of the nefarious act, the Loorees had simply offered to acknowledge his authority and pay the customary fines, on which their proffered allegiance had been accepted, and their King, as they called him, formally invested in the Sirdaree or chiefship of Mughsee. Revenge alone had stimulated the gang to this atrocity: they had desired permission, prior to the seed-time, which had then elapsed about two months, to settle for a season in the neighbourhood of the village, in order to cultivate a small piece of ground, which application was harshly refused, and they were threatened with chastisement if seen, after a certain period, within the district. They disappeared, until the armed men that had been called together to expel them, had returned to their agricultural occupations *; and, one night, making a forced march from a spot at which they had been secreted in the mountains, they suddenly seized the Sirdar's house and butchered him and his whole household: the villagers made no attempt to save any of them, and spoke with the utmost indifference of the cruel fate impending over the son. In more peaceful climes than these, where the lives and properties of men are guarded by laws divine and human, the mind revolts at the bare idea of such wickedness, and it is scarcely credited that it exists; but in these regions the case is widely different: here, the most familiar topics of conversation are bloodshed and rapine, and habit has brought the natives to view crimes, at which human nature ought to shudder, not only with unconcerned apathy, but as subjects of amusing discussion.

The Loorees, who were the active people on this occasion, are a class of vagabonds who have no fixed habitations; and in many other respects their character bears a marked affinity to the gipsies of Europe. They speak a dialect peculiar to themselves, have a King to each troop, and are notorious for kidnapping and pilfering. Their favourite pastimes are drinking, dancing, and music, the instruments

* Here, and in many other parts of the country, the people quit the villages in spring, and go to any fertile valley or plain within a moderate distance, where they feed their flocks and cultivate a little grain, returning at the end of autumn.

of which they invariably carry along with the fraternity, which is likewise attended by half a dozen of bears and monkies, that are broke in to perform all manner of grotesque tricks. In each company there are always two or three members who profess an insight into the abstruse sciences of Ruml and Qooruā *, beside other modes of divining, which obtains them a ready admission into every society, among a people who believe so firmly in predestination.

The religion that the Loorees pretend to, is Mohummudanism, but they are avowedly indifferent about it, and never trouble their heads respecting the different points contested between the Soonnees and Sheeas, conforming to the opinions of each sect according to the convenience of the moment †. I had not an opportunity of conversing with any of them on these subjects, but, from inquiries since made, I understand they contemn many of the principles of the Koran as highly absurd. They say that man was born to live, to die, to rot, and be forgotten; and that during his existence, if he is happy, he has only to pray for a continuance of it; but, if the contrary, he is at liberty, not only to forego his devotions, but to put an end to his sufferings. When one of them happens to die, they bury every thing with him that could be exclusively considered his, such as his cloaths, sword, and matchlock, in order that that article of their belief relative to his being forgotten may be accomplished.

Both men and women dress in the most preposterous and fantastic way that they can devise, adorning themselves with feathers, skins,

* Ruml is an Arabic word signifying sand. The method of divination by it is scattering a quantity on a board over which certain ceremonies have been performed, and then reading the characters. The person thus officiating is called Rummal. Qooruā or Kooruh means a lot. It is practised in different ways, but most frequently by bones of a dead man cut in the shape of dice, and marked with hieroglyphic characters. These are thrown, by the person wishing to know his destiny, and the fortune-teller explains the result.

† I asked Qaem, Khan of Huftur, the next town to Mughsee, whether the Loorees I had seen at the latter place were Sheeas or Soonees, "Oh!" said he, laughing, "they "are either as it happens to suit them: here they are Soonees: in Persia they would be "Sheeas, and if they were among the Kharujees (outcasts), they are ready for that "religion."

berries, shells, and other baubles. They are impudent and immodest in demeanour, and addicted to every species of vice and gross sensuality; for, as they never marry, the females live promiscuously with the men. Nor are any bounds set to this incestuous commerce. They have seldom offspring, so that they prefer stealing girls, who are instructed by the force of example; but when any of the women do conceive, the issue is considered the joint property of the whole community, and at a certain age initiated accordingly.

In my route to-day, the spot was shewn to me where Khan Juhan Khan, a Seistanee chief, had encamped about two months before, when he made an inroad into these districts with seven or eight hundred banditti, and swept away every thing that he could lay his hands on. I should have conjectured that his booty could not have been great, and was surprized to learn that it amounted to some thousand sheep and goats, beside a few slaves and camels. Captain Christie was afterwards at the town at which Khan Juhan Khan resides in Seistan, and heard him spoken of as the terror of the neighbouring countries.

This evening, a little before sunset, Meer Khodadad desired I would come to prayers. I excused myself and sauntered away from the spot we had halted upon, whilst the Kabool Fakeer was bellowing out the Uzāān *, and as time was short, he could not follow to press me; but the moment their devotions were over, he came to me, where I was ruminating on the extraordinary scene I had witnessed at Mughsee, and after a short preamble, said, that he could not imagine the reason for my disinclination to join himself and his people at prayers. He remarked that Futtuh Mohummud was equally censurable with myself; and that, in every light, it was unpardonable in both of us who were going on pilgrimage, and on whom the per-

* The Uzāān is a word for which I know no English phrase: it signifies a warning or call preparatory to prayers. The person who makes it is called the Moouzzin, and in mosques it is done from the top of the highest minaret. The effect is very pleasing and solemn when (as is mostly the case) the Moouzzin has a clear and sonorous voice.

formance of religious duties was therefore doubly incumbent. It instantaneously occurred to me that Moorad Khan had imposed upon him, and me likewise at Kullugan, so far, that he fancied us to be pilgrims in *reality*; and when I got leisure to reflect on the manifold proofs he had given of this supposition, by his behaviour and discourse during the period he had been my guide, I wondered at my own stupidity in not having found it out sooner.

I was, however, very well pleased with the discovery, and did not think of undeceiving Khodadad, who continued his exhortation by observing that I ought to be more conversant with religion, and to know more of its obligations than himself; and yet, that he would not go a mile from his own house without constant regard to his orisons. I told him, in reply to this admonition, that there were certain conditions in which our holy and mighty prophet Mohummud had interdicted us from the worship of the Creator or himself, that in that state my companion, as I called Futtuh Mahomed, and myself then were, having worn the cloaths on our backs upwards of a month, and that he was surely aware that every good Moosulman was bound to cleanse his person as well as mind, prior to making his petitions to heaven.

I was in hopes that this reasoning, grounded on the highest authority that a Mohummudan acknowledges *, would have silenced him, but he resumed the discussion by reminding me, that the same command that I had just cited expressly declares that every allowance is to be made for travellers, "but God knows," said he, "with whom "my fate has destined me to travel, I cannot comprehend who you "are, whether Jews, Kafirs †, or accursed Sheeas." I took the prophet to witness we were none of these, nor any thing else than real Soonnite Moosulmans; and was about to advance, most dogmatically, further arguments to uphold the propriety of my objections, when one of my camel drivers appeared to tell us that the bread was baked, and we returned with him to get our dinner. When I related

* The Koran. † I fancy Kafirs included all Christians.

this adventure to Futtuh Mohummud, he was highly indignant at the idea of being taken for a Yahoodee or Jew; swore that Meer Khodadad was a fool, and unacquainted with the religion he pretended to teach others, and that he would prove this before the whole party next day; accordingly, he offered him a piece of bread and bade him eat just what was Hulal or lawful of it, and no more*: the Sirdar did not see the subtlety of the request; and having been well rebuked for interfering with others before he was perfect in his own duty, it was explained to him.

* Among the other ridiculous and trifling points that are prescribed by the Koran, a man is forbidden to swallow any thing that sticks between his teeth when eating. This was clearly meant to induce the followers of the Prophet to keep their mouths clean, but it is so perverted, or rather so closely adhered to, by some rigid Moosulmans, that they pick their teeth and wash their mouths between every mouthful of meat that they take.

CHAPTER XI.

BARREN AND UNINHABITED COUNTRY. — SURHUD BELOOCHES. — THAT VILLAGE PLUNDERED. — THE GUIDE'S BOMBAST AND THREATS. — RIVER BED. — THICK JUNGUL. — VARIOUS KINDS OF TREES. — PATH VERY INTRICATE. — VILLAGE OF ASMANABAD. — DESCRIPTION OF THE RIVER BED AND ITS APPEARANCE. — DISTURBED IN THE NIGHT BY WILD BEASTS. — THE VILLAGERS ALL ON THE ALERT. — ERRONEOUS OPINION THEY HAVE ABOUT HUNTING WILD HOGS. — A FAKEER LEAVES THE PARTY. — THE AUTHOR'S SATISFACTION. — TOWN OF HUITUR. — RECEPTION. — THE SIRDAR OR CHIEF. — THE AUTHOR SUSPECTED OF BEING A NATIVE PRINCE IN DISGUISE. — HE EVADES A DISCUSSION BY GIVING THE CHIEF A PISTOL. — GETS A LETTER. — TOWN OF PUHRA. — RECEPTION. — THE AUTHOR DISCOVERED TO BE A EUROPEAN. — NO BAD CONSEQUENCES ENSUE, OWING TO THE LIBERALITY OF THE CHIEF. — THE VEXATION AND DISAPPOINTMENT OF THE GUIDE. — HIS BEHAVIOUR. — HALT A DAY TO MAKE ARRANGEMENTS. — BELOOCHES VERY TROUBLESOME. — A GOOSAYEN ARRIVES. — HIS STORY AND PEREGRINATIONS. — THE AUTHOR PROPOSES TO HIM TO ACCOMPANY HIM. — THE CHIEF'S LEVEE. — WHERE HELD. — AN EVENING ASSEMBLY. — DISCUSSIONS AND CONVERSATION. — RUDE IDEAS OF THE CHIEF. — EXEMPLIFIED BY AN ANECDOTE. — AUTHOR'S APOLOGY FOR HIS PROLIXITY. — HIS REFLECTIONS ON THE SUBJECT.

APRIL 11*th*. I marched twenty-five miles to-day, through a barren and uninhabited tract, consisting of rocky hills and dry water-courses, in the bottoms of some of which there were various kinds of low brushwood that might serve for camels to browse on, and likewise a little water. The direction was quite as intricate, and tended still more to the southward than yesterday; and we were in the evening, as nearly as I could compute, south-south-west of our last halting place; and, in a straight line, about ten miles from it.

Between twelve and one o'clock, I met with three families of Surhud (Koord) Belooches, who were flying from that place, which they informed me had been ransacked and entirely desolated fifteen days preceding, by the nephews of Khan Juhan Khan, aided by some of the troops of that chief. I purchased a goat from these unlucky refugees (who were going to Sibb to enrol themselves under the banners of Sheikh Moorad Khan), for which they only asked half a rupee, but I having no less coin, they got a whole one. Meer Khodadad quite exulted at the discomfiture of the Surhudees, and fervently thanked God for having inflicted so signal a judgment on them, in return for their attack on Kullugan. He protested, with all possible bombast, that it had only relieved him from the task of rooting out the tribe for its unwarrantable Chupao, or inroad, into his district. It was clear, however, from what he had previously confessed, that nothing was farther from his intentions than putting this bravado into execution.

12*th April*. I set out this morning at five o'clock, and after proceeding a mile and a half west-south-west, over mountains, descended by a steep shelving bank into a river-bed, varying in breadth from two hundred yards to three quarters of a mile, overgrown with an impervious jungul of Lye, Taghuz, Babool, and Khurbo *, and affording abundance of water. The two latter trees, for here they grow to a vast size, were in flower, and their fragrance, assisted by that of numberless small wild shrubs, completely perfumed the air. The intricacy of the path, through this wilderness of sweets, was so very great, that I expected every moment we should lose it. We seldom moved more than fifteen or twenty yards in the same direction, until the last four miles of my route, where the river bed expanded into a hard flat, covered with bushes and stunted trees. I halted at sun-set in this plain, which is about seven miles across and bounded by hills, close to some cultivated ground and the ruins of a large village called Asmanabad, the population of which, except two or three families, had removed to Huftur and Puhra.

* Lye, Tamarisk, Taghuz, another species. Babool, Farnesian Mimosa. Khurbo, Oleander or almond flower.

The total of this day's journey, by my computation, was thirty-two miles, and the medium of our course the same as the preceding one. The river bed, as well as the plain at the southern extremity of it, bore all the traces of being visited by violent floods. Logs of wood, stones, and rubbish, were, in the serpentine mazes of the former, heaped together of extraordinary size, and I observed grass and weeds entangled in the upper branches of trees, twelve or fifteen feet from the earth, in such a form, that it was evident they had been lodged there by the subsidency of water. In the course of the night we were serenaded by the mingled howlings of wolves, hyenas, jackalls, and other animals, that kept a long way from us, but would no doubt have approached much nearer, had they not been intimidated by the hooting and shouting of the villagers, who were on the alert in expectation of the wild hogs paying their wheat fields an unwelcome visit. These voracious animals are very plentiful in this part of the country, and particularly partial to such junguls as I passed through in the forenoon, whence they sally forth in droves of thirty or forty, and will grub up some acres in a very short time. The natives, most erroneously, deem hunting them Huram or forbidden, so that they take no steps to destroy the breed, which is said to be multiplying incredibly fast, and will most likely continue to do so, until the people discover the absurd error they lie under. *

Our friend, the Kabool Fakeer, separated from us this day, to take the road to one of the sea-ports of Mukran, whence he meant to

---

* It is usually a received, though very erroneous, idea, that a Moosulman cannot touch pork; and many of our servants in India take advantage of their master's ignorance or good nature on this head, and refuse to remove a plate from table, off which it has been eaten. I should be sorry to interfere with any strict religious prejudices of any class, but I certainly never would retain a servant who declined doing so, as it only requires (even in the strictest sense) that he should wash his hands. When I was at Bussorah in 1811, I saw Arabs cut open a wild boar that one of the gentlemen had shot, take out the inside, cleanse and wash it, and afterwards carry the animal on their shoulders to the boat, while a parcel of low *caste*, ignorant Indians, looked on and refused to assist. These very men would have been happy to have had their descent from the Arabs believed ! !

embark for Muskat, and so on to Juddah and Mekka. I derived great satisfaction from his departure, as he had latterly been very meddling and troublesome on the subject of praying, and had even gone so far as to quote from the Koran a sentence, implying that it was lawful and meritorious to put any Moosulman to death who neglected, on any plea whatsoever, the observance of the rites prescribed by that divine book. As this charitable suggestion was decidedly levelled at me, I conceived it high time to interfere, so I handed my pistols out of the bag in which they usually hung by the camel's saddle, and warned him that he had better not make the attempt. This unexpected mode of opposing his cavils was so effectual, that he did not again venture to express his sentiments in public; but I believe he was privately the chief abettor of Meer Khodadad's religious zeal and harangues.

13th April. I arrived this morning, by six o'clock, at the town of Huftur, which lay four miles west by south, over a shrubby plain from Asmanabad. As soon as I had alighted at the Mihman Khanu, or guests' house, a Belooche came to spread carpets and ask my name and intentions. To which I replied that I was a Peerzaduh on my route to the holy city of Mushed *. When we had breakfasted, the Sirdar paid me a visit; he was only in dishabille, having on a muslin shirt, blue silk trowsers, and a shawl round his head, instead of a turband; but I thought his dress the most becoming I had seen, and his manners were prepossessing and dignified. He spoke the best Persian I had heard any native of Beloochistan do, and when we had chatted some time, he said he felt convinced that I had not avowed my real character in the message I sent him in the morning; and that he strongly suspected I was a Shahzadu, or prince, in disguise. He begged with great earnestness that I would acknow-

* The city of Mushed, in Khorasan, is a place of religious pilgrimage, from containing the tomb of the Imam Moosa Ally Reza. It is called, by way of distinction, Mushidé Mookuddus, or the sanctified Mushid, and has always, in the wars between the Persians and Uffghans (in which, from its situation, it has constantly been a subject of contention), been reduced by famine, it being considered impious either to bombard or storm it.

ledge the truth, and declared I should be treated with all due respect. Finding it impossible to satisfy him by asseverations, I produced my pistols by way of giving a turn to the conversation, and as he admired the workmanship, I desired his acceptance of one of them; he was very much gratified by this present, and had politeness enough not to resume the topic which he saw I wished to avoid.

Having received a small supply of provisions and a letter from Qaem Khan to his brother, the Sirdar of Puhra, I quitted Huftur at two *p. m.*, and reached the former town before six: the road very good, and measuring between eleven and twelve miles over a gravelly plain with clumps of palms interspersed on it: two very luxuriant brooks cross the path at the seventh and ninth miles.

I found Shah Mihrab Khan, the chief, with the bulk of the inhabitants, just going into the mosque, and was invited to participate in the prayers, which I declined. When they were over, the Khan stepped upon a terrace or mound elevated five or six feet above the other seats, at the door of the Mihman Khanu, on which mats had been spread, and began by inquiring where I had come from and the object of my journey. Khodadad stood spokesman and reiterated the reply he had heard me make to Qaem Khan in the forenoon, adding, that my wish was to be furnished with a guide and a small stock of provisions, and forwarded on towards Nurmansheer *. At this juncture I put the letter I had brought from Huftur into the Khan's hand, who called a Meerza, or writer, and directed him to read it aloud. The people all listened attentively, and when the man had got nearly through it, I was startled to find that Qaem Khan had expressed his suspicions of my alledged rank; though I must also do him the justice to observe, that I am conscious he did so from the most friendly motive, that of exciting his brother's interest regarding me.

During the momentary pause, created by this untoward surmise, all eyes were turned upon me, and a lad of ten or twelve years of

* The south-eastern district of Persia: subject to the government of Kirman.

age exclaimed, "If he did not himself say he is a Peerzaduh, I "would swear that this is the brother of Grant the Firingee (or "European *) who was at Bunpoor last year." I endeavoured to let the lad's remark pass unnoticed, but the confusion of my looks betrayed me, and the Khan immediately told me, in the most good humoured manner, if it was so, not to disguise the truth, as no person should offer me the least degree of insult or hindrance; upon which assurance, seeing there was no advantage in further prevarication, I admitted I was a European then in the service of a Hindoo, and thus far towards Kirman on his concerns.

It would be folly in me to attempt pourtraying the consternation and wrath of Meer Khodadad at this disclosure; to confirm the truth of which I added, that though not a brother, I was a near relation of the Grant that the boy alluded to. He viewed it as a complete paradox, and addressing himself alternately to Shah Mihrab Khan and the villagers, rehearsed the various polemical rencounters we had had since leaving Kullugan, the manner I had refuted his lectures and taken him to task, the testimony of his son-in-law Moorad Khan, with some instances he had related of my sanctity, all forming, in his opinion, a concatenation of proofs sufficient to falsify the avowal I had made. The Khan laughed heartily at the tale, but told the indignant speaker to recollect that he was not the only person who had been imposed upon, an allusion that I fancy referred to his brother; to which Khodadad peevishly replied, that he was aware of that, though he believed that no other person had been so long and intimate with me without finding me out. "I have," vociferated a bystander, in a voice which I soon distinguished to be one of my camel drivers, "I have been with him two months, and notwith-

* The late Captain Grant of the Bengal Native Infantry. This enterprising officer landed in 1809 at Gwuttur in Mukran, penetrated inland as high as the latitude of Bunpoor (within sixteen miles of Puhra), returned by a different route along the sea-coast to Bunder Abass, and thence came back by sea to Bombay. The inquiries he made during this arduous attempt were copious and correct. I knew he had been a great favourite with the chief of Bunpoor, which induced me to claim relationship with him.

"standing I knew he was neither Syyud or Peerzaduh*, yet, as I hope "good may betide me, I had as little conception as yourself that he "was a Firingee or European." His indignation now took an opposite course, and he execrated Moorad as an unprincipled scoundrel, who had been accessary to so flagitious an imposture. By this time it was nearly dark, and the confabulation terminated by the Khan retiring to his own house and my taking possession of a corner of the Mihman Khanu, where I had shortly a sumptuous supper of mutton soup, boulli, and wheaten cakes.

14th April. After breakfast I carried Shah Mihrab Khan an humble offering, consisting of a little fine gun-powder, a few pistol flints, a pen-knife, and a pair of scissars, entreating him to expedite my departure, and also to afford me a little flour, my stock of that article, and dates, being comprised in what Qaem Khan had given me at Huftur. He promised that a guide should be in readiness to set out with me the next morning, and commanded his Deewan or steward to let me have ten maunds (about fourteen pounds) of barley flour, observing that wheaten was not procurable. He then suggested my going the straight road from Puhra to Basman, by doing which I should have avoided Bunpoor, and shortened my journey two stages. I expressed my obligations for the kind consideration towards my benefit and ease, from which this suggestion arose; but told him, as was strictly the case, that having heard Captain Grant speak repeatedly of the liberality shewn to him by Mihrab Khan of Bunpoor, I preferred proceeding by that route, in order to visit him.

The Khan readily took this excuse, and said he left it optional with me; but the real truth was, that I reckoned on being out of food before I got across the desert into the Persian province of Nurmansheer, unless I could persuade the Bunpoor chief to extend his generosity towards me.

* The Syyuds are those Moosulmans who pretend to be descended from the Prophet. The meaning of a Peerzaduh I have already explained in a note on the Narrative of the *4th April.*

After this arrangement I returned to my lodging in the Mihman Khanu, and passed the remainder of the day in the midst of a concourse of idle obstreperous Belooches, who harrassed me with preposterous queries and remarks. A Goosayen * came in from Surhud in the afternoon, and relieved me from the task of entertaining the whole village, for half my auditors flocked round him, and insisted on being treated with the latest intelligence from that quarter, which he retailed, particularly the plunder of the village of Surhud by Khan Juhan Khan, with great pomposity and effect. When I got leisure, I inquired who my fellow-lodger was, and ascertained that he had commenced his peregrinations from the city of Mooltan, whence he had strayed through Kashmeer, Kabool, Kandahar, and Seistan, and had left the latter kingdom, with the intention of paying his devotions at the pagoda of Hinglatz, near Sonmeany in Lus, but had since altered his plan, and was then going through Persia to visit the celebrated Joālā Mookhee, or flaming mouth, on the borders of the Caspian sea †. As he appeared a chatty companion, with much less bigotry or nonsense than devotees of his description have in common, I offered to give him a seat on one of my camels to Kirman, which he willingly accepted; however the animal fell sick, and the disappointed Goosayen only got as far as Bunpoor.

The Khan held his customary levee after evening prayers, on the mound near the Mihman Khanu, at which the majority of the inhabitants attended; and I availed myself of so very favourable an opportunity of attaining local information, at which I was very successful. The shades of night first gave warning that it was time to disperse; and even then we were all so well pleased with each other's company, that a proposition made by one of the Moollahs,

* The Goosayens are a class of Hindoo Fakeers, or pilgrims.

† The Joālā Mookhee is at Badkoo or Baku, a sea-port of the Caspian. It seems to be caused by the vast quantities of Naptha found there.

See Kinneir's Geographical Memoir on the Persian Empire.

to meet after dinner in the Mihman Khanu, was warmly applauded on all sides. The Khan, with much affability, said that he should come, and we had an overflowing house, which did not break up till past midnight: his presence kept every person of the party at a proper distance, beside stimulating them to add to the good fellowship by a display of their amusive anecdotes and abilities, in both of which he himself excelled.

I accidentally discovered that he was totally uneducated, for happening to disclose that I had brought letters from Eidel Khan at Nooshky, to different chiefs, through whose districts I passed, but had not delivered them, he asked leave to see them, and on my reading the superscription, expressed his astonishment by asking me if I was a Moollah, that is, if I could read and write? I replied, I knew my own language tolerably well, and also understood a little Persian and Hindee. This answer led to his wishing to have explained the difference between English and Persian when written, and as I could not do so to his satisfaction by words, he sent for pen, ink, and paper, and dictated a long sheet of sentences, which he wound up with his own name and titles. He begged I would also put mine, my profession, the Christian year in which I had visited his capital, and the treatment I had experienced, whether good or bad. The paper was then put in charge of his Meerza or writer, to be kept until some other Firingee might make his appearance, whom he said he should call upon to interpret it, and judge of my disposition by the manner in which I spoke of him. I could not help feeling that he had adopted, with regard to me, a kinder and more courteous course than I had any right to anticipate, after the deception I had tried to put upon him, and I recorded my sentiments conformably.

I have been induced to dwell more circumstantially on the occurrences of this evening, than they may perhaps seem, on a cursory perusal, to merit; but have done so here, and likewise in various other places in this narrative, because it places, in my opinion, the genius and character, not only of the individual I am speaking of at the time, but his whole tribe in the most prominent point of view, and shews the grounds on which I have drawn the outline of the Belooches in a preceding place. Here we recognise a chief, whose income and domains, when placed in comparison with those of all the surrounding toparchs, are princely, associating with his meanest subjects, admitting them to a free and unceremonious avowal of their opinions, even in opposition to his own; and entertaining so contemptible an idea of literature, that he could not read or write. Asia alone may be said at this day to afford instances of such barbarism, but the coincidence of it with the habits and establishments of the savage nations that subverted the Roman empire, is singular and exact.

CHAPTER XII.

ARRIVAL AT BUNPOOR. — INTERMEDIATE COUNTRY. — BROOKS. — GUIDE RETURNS TO HIS HOME, AND IS DISMISSED WITH A CAMEL AS A PRESENT. — THE TOWNS OF HUFTUR AND PUHRA. — SIZE. — CHIEF'S TRIBE. — BRIEF HISTORICAL NOTICE OF IT. — ITS RISE. — MULIKUH BELOOCHES. — NEARLY EXTERMINATED. — BY WHOM. — URBABEES. — GENERAL APPEARANCE OF THAT PEOPLE. — NARRATIVE RESUMED. — RECEPTION AT BUNPOOR. — UNCOUTH MANNERS AND FIGURE OF THE CHIEF. — HIS STEEL STICK. — HIS RESPECT FOR A BRITISH OFFICER ILLUSTRATED BY AN ANECDOTE. — SCANTY SUPPER. — THE CHIEF'S AVARICE. — HIS CHARACTERISTIC ADVICE TO THE AUTHOR. — ENMITY AGAINST THE PERSIANS. — REMARK ON THAT SUBJECT. — AUTHOR'S QUERIES TO HIM. — ABUSIVE AND ENTERTAINING REPLY. — OPINION UPON IT. — HE REFUSES TO ASSIST THE AUTHOR. — DEMANDS HIS PISTOLS. — REFUSED. — NEGLECTS TO SEND ANY FOOD. — GOOSAYEN BEGS FOR HIMSELF AND THE AUTHOR'S FOLLOWERS. — AN AVOWED FRIEND. — HIS OBJECT. — THE AUTHOR OBLIGED TO GIVE UP HIS PISTOLS. — LEAVES BUNPOOR. — DESCRIPTION OF THAT PLACE. — TRADITION RESPECTING THE CITADEL. — OPINION OF ITS STRENGTH. — THE POPULATION OF BUNPOOR. — TRIBE. — CHIEF'S FAMILY. — SIXTEEN WIVES. — THE AUTHOR SEES THE YOUNGEST. — HER APPEARANCE HOW ACCOUNTED FOR. — THE AUTHOR'S CONJECTURES. — REVENUES OF THE CHIEF. — BROTHERS. — LANGUAGE SPOKEN HERE. — MARCH OF FORTY MILES. — WELL. — KASKEEN DRY RIVER. — AUTHOR'S EYES SUFFER FROM CONSTANT EXPOSURE TO THE SUN AND GLARE. — ARRIVAL AT THE VILLAGE OF BASMAN. — RECEPTION. — CHIEF'S ADVICE. — ATTENTION. — HALT FOR A DAY. — REMARKABLE HOT WELL. — DESCRIPTION OF IT AND ITS WATER. — VOLCANIC HILLS. — TRADITION. — THE CHIEF'S OBSERVATIONS. — THE NAME OF THE HILL. — SAL AMMONIAC AND SULPHUR FOUND THERE. — AUTHOR'S IMPATIENCE. — PERCEIVED BY THE CHIEF. — GUIDE COMES. — GREAT HOSPITALITY AND KINDNESS EXPERIENCED BY THE AUTHOR. — HIS GRATITUDE. — IMPRESSIVE THANKS OF HIS FOLLOWERS TO THE CHIEF.

APRIL 15*th*. I waited with great impatience until nigh ten o'clock this forenoon, when a person came to tell me that the Khan wished to speak to me at his own house. This summons I joyfully obeyed, and found that chief dictating the contents of two letters to his Meerza, or writer, which were entrusted to my charge as soon as finished. One of them was for Mihrab Khan, chief of Bunpoor, the other for Moorad Khan, Sirdar of Basman. The Khan then gave the guide the strictest injunctions to see that I was provided with a steady man at Bunpoor; and on no pretence to leave me until he had my permission. I again assured him of my gratitude for his attention, and, taking leave, mounted my camel at mid-day, and arrived at Bunpoor about half-past four o'clock, after travelling sixteen miles south-west-by-south, over a bushy flat with two or three small patches of cultivated ground. At two different places we rode a little way along the edge of a brook that I ascertained to be one of those I had crossed between Huftur and Puhra, and which supply this neighbourhood, not only for purposes of domestic use, but cultivation.

Meer Khodadad, whose wrath towards me had entirely evaporated in the course of the night, attended me the first mile from Puhra; and when I embraced him at parting, I bestowed upon him, as a token of my approbation, one of my three camels: it was a very fine animal when I quitted Nooshky, but had become miserably emaciated during the journey, and latterly retarded my progress, so that in fact I was ridding myself of a nuisance and making Khodadad a most acceptable present.

The towns of Huftur and Puhra are small, but very neat and well built; the former contains two hundred and fifty, and the latter four hundred houses, both being situated in groves of palm trees, whence a great source of revenue results to their owners. Shah Mihrab Khan is the most powerful chief in this quarter; his regular troops, or at least those that he can muster at a few days notice, are six thousand, and he is acknowledged to be the paramount authority from Dizuk to Basman. His brother (Qaem Khan) holds Huftur under him, as do all the Sirdars their respective territories, within a circuit of ninety or one hundred miles. In person he is remarkably handsome, and his address displays innate superiority and polish. His tribe is that branch of the Nharoes called the Urbabees, who are stated to have been of no note whatever, and had dwelt in obscurity in a sterile and elevated tract near Surhud, whence the progenitors of the present Khan emigrated with a body of followers to Dizuk, in which district they acquired a footing by a donation of soil from some of the Mukranee chiefs. The hereditary possessions of Shah Mihrab Khan consequently lay there, but on his marriage with a daughter of Syyud Khan, the father of the Bunpoor Sirdar, he collected an army, and aided by his father-in-law, seized on Huftur and Puhra. These led to other conquests, and his revenues are now computed at four lacs and a half of rupees * annually.

The original masters of the villages of Puhra, Huftur, Mughsee, &c. and the intermediate country, were the Mulikuh Belooches, who have been nearly exterminated during their struggles and contentions with the Urbabees, and those few that have escaped from the sword of their enemies fled to Nurmansheer, where the Persian government allotted them a territory and affords them protection.

The Urbabees are the fairest tribe of Belooches I met with, and there is a peculiar elevation in their countenances that pre-eminently distinguishes them among their countrymen. They are, without almost an exception, tall, handsome men, with great indications of activity. Their predatory character, on which they pride themselves, is sufficiently proved by their deeds, and has been previously touched upon. †

To resume my Narrative. The moment I dismounted at Bunpoor, I sent up the letter to Mihrab Khan, and in a few minutes a corpulent old gentleman, about sixty years of age, hobbled down, preceded by six or eight attendants. I should not have recognised him for the chief, had he been alone, as he was very meanly apparelled, in a common white shirt, a pair of blue cotton trowsers, and a small

* 56,250l. Sterling.

† Shah Mihrab Khan himself mentioned to me, with evident satisfaction and triumph, that he had been outlawed by the government of Kabool beside that of Persia. Possibly it flattered his vanity to be thought of so much importance, as he was the only instance of proscription by name in Beloochistan.

skull cap on the crown of his head; but what first and principally attracted my ears and eyes, was a polished steel staff that he carried in his hand, about four feet long and as many inches thick, covered with large rings of the same metal, with which he kept an incessant and loud jingle. As he approached I perceived, that being lame, he used the staff as a support, exclusive of the pleasure he apparently felt in making a noise with it, for even whilst chatting, he never desisted from shaking the rings from one end to the other, where there were large knobs to prevent their slipping off entirely.

I greeted him with a very respectful salutation, in return for which he told me three or four times, in a gruff voice, that I was welcome; and desired me to be seated on a bench at the Mihman Khanu door, on which he had placed himself. My guide, who was a most garrulous fellow, waited for no questions, but instantly rehearsed every incident that had taken place at Puhra, on which the Sirdar made a great number of inquiries respecting Captain Grant, of whom he spoke in terms of unqualified admiration and praise. One anecdote will evince the high opinion he cherished of that regretted officer. When I had been there half an hour, he ordered all the finest horses in his stud, which contains seventy or eighty, exclusive of brood mares, to be led out for me to see, and pointed out two very handsome colts that he proposed I should purchase. I pleaded my inability to do so from a want of cash. "How can you," asked he, "talk of "that as an obstacle. Go down to the sea-port towns and declare you "know, not to say you are related, to Grant, and you may have as "much money as you desire to borrow." He presently left me to say his even-tide prayers, and in the course of an hour sent a scanty meal for myself and three men.

16th April. Mihrab Khan came to the hovel in which I was lodged this morning before sunrise, when I presented him with a few flints, a flask of fine gunpowder, and a knife; he was much disappointed at this offering, which was very inadequate to the expectations he had formed on my appearance, and desired, in a peremptory tone, that I would let him see every thing I had with me. I replied, that I was quite ready to comply with any commands he might give me, but that he was to recollect, I was a servant travelling on another person's affairs, and save what I had tendered, had nothing in the world that I could with propriety offer him. This avowal was corroborated by one of his own relations, to whom I had explained my circumstances the night before; this man, however, unfortunately excepted a pair of common horse pistols, which Futteh Mahomed and one of my camel drivers usually carried in their girdles. The Khan asked to look at them, and when he had examined them for some minutes, observed that they were not equal in any respect to those he had got from Captain Grant. I again reminded him of the difference of our stations. that he was a merchant trading on his own capital, while I was only a menial of a Hindoo horse dealer.

He interrupted me, at this remark, by demanding why I ran such risks and wandered in such a miserable plight merely to enrich a rascally idolater. " Take a gun," added he, " and fight, rather than " slave in this disgraceful manner: it is a drudgery attended with " neither credit or advantage, and if you will hearken to my advice, " it is, to return without going to Kirman, and when you arrive in " India, pitch the Hindoo vagabond, by whom you are employed, " and his concerns, to the devil. Turn soldier and Chupao * the " country!" To this harangue, so completely characteristic of the deliverer of it, I answered, that although I highly applauded his counsel, it was out of my power at that moment to adopt it, but, that, if it pleased God I should get in safety to Kirman, I certainly purposed abandoning the Hindoo's service and my wandering life. The barbarian was not by any means convinced of the necessity which I alledged for prosecuting my journey, but as he saw I was resolved, he contented himself with very frankly telling me that, in his opinion the most hazardous and difficult portion of it yet remained to be gone through.

* Plunder.

When he had exhausted his rhetoric on this head, he began to interrogate me on the nature of the British government, the extent of its navy and army, the means by which such large bodies were paid, fed, and disciplined, and whether they were usually employed at home or abroad. Having explained these particulars as far as I supposed would be comprehensible, he begged to be informed why we Firingees, or Europeans, did not root out the Persians (whom he styled Kafir Sheeas), saying, "I have understood, both from Grant "and yourself, that the English government is eminently powerful; "and if that is really the case, it will find no difficulty in extermi-"nating that abominable race, for I myself can dispatch two hundred "horsemen and ravage a whole district, even bringing off their very "dogs." I answered, that those were subjects altogether out of my line or sphere in life, and what I never gave myself the trouble to think upon.

I was now desirous, in my turn, of ascertaining precisely the terms on which the Persians and Belooches, in general, stood with each other, as a clue by which to regulate my conduct on reaching Nurmansheer; and I therefore enquired if the intercourse was frequent between him and the government of Kirman, or if any species of trade was carried on between the two countries. "Intercourse!" rejoined he, laughing, "no! we have had none for these last two "years, nor is it likely to be again renewed: a few months anterior "to that period Shah Mihrab Khan, Qaem Khan, and myself, sent "our collective armies on a Chupao into Laristan *, and laid waste "that province; it was in our possession for nigh three months, and "when the troops came away, having immense flocks of camels, "they brought all the grain and dates; the consequence was, that "there were no revenues forthcoming, and the Hakim of Meenab † "was called to Kirman to be made answerable for the defalcation; "but when he represented the true statement of the business to the

* The south-eastern province of Persia.

† The capital of Laristan.

" Shahzaduh *, he was released from confinement, and two messen-
" gers were forthwith dispatched with threatening Furmans † to us:
" we were apprized of this, and wrote to Moorad Khan of Basman,
" to advise them not to advance nearer than that village, so there
" they staid until we transmitted them letters for the Prince, setting
" him and his threats at defiance, and telling him that he was an
" infamous blackguard."

This explanatory reply was so interlarded with opprobrious epithets and virulent abuse, that it was impossible to hear it without laughter; and to increase the effect, the old fellow worked himself quite into a rage, and pounded the ground as vehemently with his mace, as though he had been wreaking his vengeance on the bones of the Persians. He afterwards entered into a prolix enumeration of the various kinds of booty that had fallen to his share, the aggregate of which he valued at six thousand rupees, a sum that, though *ostensibly small, will be looked upon in quite a contrary light, if we* call to mind that there were the combined troops of three powerful chieftains serving on the Chupao; that it was made into a tract naturally sterile and thinly peopled; and that every individual, unless it were the Khanuzads, or household slaves of the leaders, received a dividend equivalent to his rank and achievements. The principal articles specified by him, were slaves of both sexes, camels, dates, wheat, carpets, matchlocks, and other weapons; horses they seldom get hold of, as the principal inhabitants, to whom they usually belong, mount them on the first alarm, to be prepared for flight.

When the Khan was going away, I hinted to him my extreme distress with respect to provisions, and hope that he would assist me; to this entreaty he roughly and brutishly answered, that so far from giving me any provisions to carry away, he was very doubtful whether he could feed me and my followers while I staid at Bunpoor. I rejoined, that if he would spare me the same quantity that we should

* A prince, from Shah, a king, and Zaeedun, to be born.

† Royal letters are so called.

consume by halting a day or two with him, I was ready to set off for Basman that very instant; he however left me, without taking any notice of this proposition; and about an hour after, I had a message from him, demanding the pistols he had seen. At first I positively refused to comply with this unauthorized demand, and bade the bearer of it tell his master that I was confident he would not have made it, had he reflected for an instant on the dangers of the road I had to travel, and knew that they were my only means of defence. This appeal to the feelings of the savage had no effect, and at length by the advice of Futtuh Mohummud, I sent him a single one, which was instantly returned, with the Khan's Sulam (compliments), and he must either have both or none. Matters thus rested the whole of the day, as I was resolved to hold out for a short time, to try what advantage might accrue from it. In the evening we had no dinner, which scurvy omission of the duties of hospitality I interpreted as a prelude to the old rascal's continued obstinacy, or perhaps ill treatment of me, and I lay down to sleep hungry and dispirited. The poor Goosayen, who had come with me from Puhra, and anticipated a share of my dinner, was determined not to take the disappointment so calmly; and he sallied forth to beg, returning in the course of half an hour, with his wallet crammed with scraps of bread and dates, of which he and my two Brahooes made a most comfortable supper.

17*th April.* Before it was clearly light this morning, a man came to me with great affectation of secresy, and said that his friendship for my relation Grant, with whom he had been on the most intimate terms, induced him to take that method of apprizing me, that the Khan had come to the determination of not furnishing me with a guide, and in short, not allowing me to leave the place, until I let him have the pair of pistols. I was exceedingly averse to being thus, in every sense of the word, forced to give them up, and offered my informant and avowed well-wisher a trifling reward, to be my conductor to Basman, but he denied any knowledge of the route, and likewise said that he might as well be banished, as he never dare return to

Bunpoor or its neighbourhood. I could not therefore expect he would make such a sacrifice for me; and on subsequent reflection I had no doubt but he was deputed by Mihrab Khan himself, to make the communication. I was thus left without any alternative, and sent him the pistols as soon as I knew he was risen, begging a guide might be ordered, who accordingly made his appearance in less than half an hour, and after I had got a letter for the Sirdar of Basman, which I took merely as a matter of form, I left Bunpoor with unfeigned regret that I had ever seen it. We travelled sixteen miles north north-west, over a bare stony plain without water or food for camels, and halted at sun-set.

The village of Bunpoor is small and ill-built: it has been at one time surrounded by a low mud wall, with small bastions at intervals, but the whole is now gone to decay, and as there are no date trees, or any symptoms of agriculture in the neighbourhood of the village, it bears a most desolate and impoverished appearance. The chief's house, or citadel, is erected on the summit of an extraordinary mound of earth, the popular tradition with respect to which is, that an immense army of Guebres passing this way, the commander in chief directed the horsemen to fill the bags from which they fed their horses, with mould on leaving the hills, and their numbers were so great, that when they deposited it in a pile, it formed the present hill. I went to the top of it the last thing I did before quitting Bunpoor, to receive Mihrab Khan's letter, and take leave of him, and should conceive the height to be at least one hundred yards, and the circumference of the base eight hundred. You enter into it by a low arch, to the extent of ten or twelve yards, from whence the ascent is by a flight of steps, made with rough blue stone: the first of these flights is built to a very surprizing depth through the mount, and turns backwards to gain the face of the hill, and the others are sunk in the mound to the depth of four or five feet, but open above. They all lead angularly to each other, and I should look upon this fortress as strong enough to defy any force that Persia can employ against it. If this mount is really artificial, it must have been raised with vast labour, as it lies fourteen miles from the mountains, nearer than which there is no pit or ravine whence so large a quantity of earth could have been taken. There is one well of very fine water half way up, which the natives ridiculously assert and believe to be a Fursukh * deep.

The people of Bunpoor are Rukhshanee Belooches, which is the leading tribe, though not the first either in numbers or wealth, amongst the Nharooés; they are a brawnier and swarthier race than their neighbours the Urbabees, with whom they live on the most amicable footing, and the chiefs of the two clans are doubly connected by marriage. Mihrab Khan of Bunpoor has a numerous family, and sixteen wives, the last of whom was present when I paid my respects to that chief in his castle. She was a very young girl, extremely fair, but without either figure or face to boast of. I afterwards understood from my guide, who was a cousin of the Khan, that she was of a Persian family; he made no scruple in letting me see her, and told me he did so from being aware of our customs, which he had heard from Captain Grant and myself, but I fancy I was as much indebted to the lady's innate curiosity, which had prompted her to appear, as to any other cause, for the gratification of seeing her.

The revenues of the chief of Bunpoor are usually farmed out, and the season I was there, he received in lieu of them, 26,000 rupees, 140 camels, 140 matchlocks, 140 sheep or goats, 140 measures of wheat, and the same of dates, each measure being one hundred and six pounds. The extent and boundaries of his territory will be found in the second part of this work. He has several brothers younger than himself, none of whom are ever allowed to enter his castle, nor are they apparently in easier circumstances than the rest of his subjects.

The language spoken at Bunpoor, is Persian and Beloochekee mixed.

* A Fursukh or Parasang is three miles and seven-eighths.

18th April. I travelled upwards of forty miles to-day, over a desolate flat country, in which distance we only found water at one well in the bed of a dry river called the Kaskeen, six miles from where we had slept, nor was it either good or plentiful: this well is about twenty-two miles from Bunpoor, and lies nearly due north. An inflammation that had begun in one of my eyes at Puhra, from continual exposure to the sun and glare, extended to them both to-day, and they were so weak that I could barely see five yards before me. I was therefore obliged to keep them muffled up from the excessive light and heat, and rode with an old black silk handkerchief tied over my turband, so as to cover my face, which prevented me from making any further observations.

19th April. After a north-westerly march of four miles, at seven o'clock I arrived at Basman, a small hamlet situated in a clump of palms close under mountains. I halted in the shade of some very fine spreading walnut trees, about one hundred yards from the village, whilst my guide rode on to advertise the Sirdar, Moorad Khan, of my approach; he accompanied him out to me, and I delivered the letters from Shah Mihrab Khan of Puhra, and Mihrab Khan of Bunpoor, at the same time verbally intimating my anxiety to be provided with a guide to Nurmansheer, as speedily as possible. While he was perusing the letters, his slaves brought out carpets, which they spread; and when we had sat down, he recapitulated, in a mild and persuasive accent, the substance of the warning I had had from the Bunpoor chief, respecting the risks I should run on the road, adding, that he was not aware of any person having attempted to cross the Dusht or desert, into Nurmansheer, for many months, and therefore, if I had an option, he strongly advised me to abandon my intention of proceeding any farther. I explained to him that I could not do so, and after a little further conversation, he started up, saying, "I will make your arrangements, you must be hungry, and I "have been sitting here without attending to your wants." In the course of half an hour I received a sheep alive, and a large bowl of hodge-podge, made of green barley, (husked by heating it over a fire, and rubbing it in a coarse cloth,) mixed with butter-milk. This mess is far from palatable, but I found it was not their food from choice, but absolute necessity and starvation; and during my sojourn here, I was eye-witness to people boiling and eating mulberry leaves and a kind of pulpy acid grass, to which camels are exceedingly partial, whence it is called by the Belooches Ootch Khoor, or camel food. My camel-drivers soon killed the sheep, and in despite of the bad flavour of the hodge-podge, we had a most sumptuous repast. In the evening, Moorad Khan came out, and chatted until dinner-time, when I had a second dish of the barley, and a similar bowl of mutton-broth sent to me.

20th April. My guide not being fully prepared, I halted this day at Basman, at the earnest request of the Sirdar, and about twelve o'clock, strolled out to a hot-well which had been mentioned to me at Bunpoor, and here also, as a wonderful curiosity. I found the well upwards of twelve yards in circumference, and two or three feet in depth; in the centre of it was a circular pipe built of red burnt brick, about eight inches in diameter, and within as many of being level with the water, which boiled out of it as thick as a man's thigh, with considerable violence, and so heated that I could not venture to put my hand into the ebullition. One side of the well had been gradually worn away by the incessant gushing of water over it, and thence a limpid brook flows past the village, and suffices the husbandmen for the irrigation of their grounds. I bathed in this stream about five yards from its source, and found the water pleasantly tepid, with a strong sulphureous smell and taste, which unfit it for culinary purposes; but the Belooches regard it as aperient in its effects, and an excellent specific in cutaneous disorders.

On my return home to the village, Moorad Khan pointed out to me a mountain about fifteen miles distant, where he said water oozed from various clefts in the rocks, hot enough to boil meat in a few minutes; and that he and many others were of opinion that the fountain I had been to look at, was connected with that hill by a subterraneous aqueduct; in support of which conjecture he avowed that heaps of pieces of, and even whole bricks, similar in shape and quality to those I observed the vent into the well to be made of, had been found in many places in the intermediate space. I inquired who was likely to have been at such incredible expence and pains as must have attended the construction of a conduit under ground, for such a length of way, and that too in a country so diversified with mountains, hills, and deep vales. He informed me that some foolish people attributed it to Deeves (sprites), or other supernatural agency, but that there was likewise a tradition amongst the tribes, that in former times a Guebre city had stood on or near the site of the present village of Basman, and that the inhabitants had formed the aqueduct for the enjoyment and benefit of the baths. " How-" ever," added he, " all this is very doubtful, and must ever re-" main so: we Belooches do not puzzle ourselves with such thoughts " and researches; we are contented to have heard that our fore-" fathers saw it in the same state that we now view it."

The mountain to which the Sirdar alluded, is here invariably spoken of by the name of the Kohé Noushadir, or hill of sal-ammoniac, which drug is said to be a native production of it, and found in the fissures of the rocks. I had not an opportunity of seeing any of this mineral, but Moorad Khan assured me that plenty of it, and also an incrustation of brimstone was to be gathered; and had I remained with him a second day, he would willingly have sent a man for a specimen of both. He told me that they were unacquainted with the uses to which sal-ammoniac might be applied, but that the sulphur, when pounded, was valued as the best and strongest ingredient of that sort for gunpowder.

My impatience to be again on the wing was so visible throughout the whole forenoon, that the chief himself remarked it, and about five *p. m.* he brought the guide to avouch his readiness to attend me the next morning. When I embraced Moorad Khan, and bade him adieu at dusk, I felt real vexation that I had no means of making him the smallest requital for his friendship and hospitality, both of which I shall ever remember with gratitude and thanks. The last virtue he possessed in an unbounded degree; and with regard to his kindness I may hazard the assertion, that he was the only person, of any class or description, that I met with from the hour I quitted Nooshky until the day I reached Sheeraz, who felt any sympathy for me, or took a real interest in my safety and welfare. Shah Mihrab Khan and others were undoubtedly as civil and attentive, as I had any right to anticipate, but Moorad Khan's manner was more expressive than his deeds; and even my two wild camel-drivers were so sensible of that being the case, that they exclaimed when he was leaving the place we had been sitting at in the evening, "We shall "not forget you, Moorad Khan. May your noble desires be accom-"plished, and your store increase! You have not much, but what "you do possess, you bestow with a willing hand and good grace *.

* I particularly recall this grateful effusion of my Brahooes, from a quibble in it, which the Persian scholar will readily perceive on the words Moorad Khan (the chief's name), and Mooradi Khanee (noble desires.) For the satisfaction of those unacquainted with that language, I may add, that Moorad signifies desire, wish, &c. and Khanee, noble, is derived by the Belooches, from Khan, a nobleman.

CHAPTER XIII.

LEAVE BASMAN. — THE AUTHOR DISMISSES HIS GUIDE. — MOTIVE. — HIRES ANOTHER. — ROUTE. — NATURE OF THE COUNTRY. — VILLAGE OF BASMAN. — THE LAST IN BELOOCHISTAN. — DESCRIPTION OF IT. — MANNER OF BUILDING. — THE SIRDAR OR CHIEF. — HIS TRIBE. — REVENUES. — MANNERS. — LANGUAGE. — PURSUITS. — BARREN ROUTE. — EXTREME HEAT. — SUFFERINGS OF THE AUTHOR AND HIS FOLLOWERS FROM THIRST. — HIS IDEAS ON THAT SUBJECT. — SENSATIONS ADDED TO BY THE SUHRAB OR "MIRAGE." — THE SUPPOSED CAUSE OF THAT PHENOMENON. — EXTRAORDINARY APPEARANCE OF IT ON A HILL. — MARCH AT NIGHT. — WELL CALLED GEHGAN. — SALT. — ARRIVAL AT REGAN IN THE PROVINCE OF NURMANSHEER. — FACE OF THE INTERMEDIATE COUNTRY GREATLY DIVERSIFIED. — HEAT EQUALLY GREAT AS THE PRECEDING DAY. — SNOWY MOUNTAINS. — THEIR EFFECT. — RECEPTION AT REGAN. — ALARM. — THE CHIEF'S OBLIGING CONDUCT. — HALT A DAY. — REGAN. — DESCRIPTION OF IT. — PRECAUTIONS USED BY THE PEOPLE. — THE CHIEF. — HIS FAMILY. — JUREED BAZEE. — HOW PLAYED.

APRIL 21*st*. Having filled our Mushks or skins, with water, I left Basman at sunrise, and when we had gone a few miles, gave my guide a rupee, and dismissed him. The object I had in view on this occasion, was once more to get rid of the appellation of a Firingee or European, from a conviction that it was the very worst I could travel under, as subjecting me to every species of fraud and extortion, beside the disagreeable, though inevitable penance of sitting to be gazed at like a shew, in every town or village that I entered. I had contemplated dropping it, as a matter of course, the moment I was out of Beloochistan, or at least the inhabited part of it, and that being the case from the commencement of my march this morning, I was vexed to learn that my conductor, although not a native of Basman, had, by some means or other, ascertained my nation, and would have consequently blazoned it all over Nurmansheer. My camel drivers at first protested that they also would go back with the guide, as we should inevitably be lost in the desert, but I shortly convinced them of the expediency of parting with him, and softened their apprehensions by adverting to the great probability of our meeting with some shepherds, one of whom we might persuade to accompany us; but even were we not so fortunate, I said, I trusted from my general idea of the direction of the route, to be enabled to find our way.

I had not, however, taken this step more than an hour, when one of my men espied a Belooche at some distance on a hill, whom we hailed, and when he had come sufficiently close to be spoken to, which he did with the utmost caution, I proposed to him, with a promise of a handsome reward, to guide me to Regan, the first town in Nurmansheer. He hesitated some time, and I believe would have declined the offer, but one of my camel drivers, with great presence of mind, assuming for himself and his companion the character of men from Bunpoor, told him that I was a Syyud * pilgrim, that I would pay him well; and, to crown the whole falsehood, that he might return with them. After a little further conference, he asked me to wait for a short time till he ran to his Ghedan. I did not at all admire this proposition, both on account of the time lost by it, and because I feared that he might have some sinister end in it, and would perhaps bring down eight or ten stout fellows to plunder us. In this suspicion, however, I did the shepherd great injustice, for which I most willingly make him this acknowledgement, as he was very punctual, and came back to the place at which we had dismounted in less time than I even expected. He was completely altered in his appearance, having scarcely a rag on his back, and I instantly remarked that he had not brought his Toofung, or matchlock, which was in his hand when we first descried him: this he subsequently confessed, he had left behind from the apprehensions

* The Syyuds are the descendants of the Prophet.

he had of our being pillaged. As soon as the new guide joined us we remounted, and were by my reckoning, upwards of forty miles north-north-west from Basman, when we halted at eleven o'clock at night. In this distance we met with water at the seventh mile in a small hole in a rock, but it was so strongly impregnated with iron as not to be drinkable. The country, the whole way, was barren and mountainous, except the latter six miles, where we had chiefly a stony plain, equally devoid of water or vegetation.

I have already said that the village of Basman was the last fixed inhabited place I was at in Beloochistan, out of which country I conceived myself to be at the end of this day's route, for although several Belooche tribes dwell still farther to the westward, it will be found that they are not the original inhabitants, but settled there within these very few years. I therefore propose, henceforward, to offer, in the progressive detail of my journey, any geographical and statistical remarks on the provinces of Persia, through which I passed, that my own observation or local knowledge qualifies me to make, it not being my intention to include any portion of that Kingdom, as it now exists, in the second part of this work.

The hamlet of Basman requires very trifling notice. It contains about one hundred and fifty houses, some of them two or three stories high, built of stones without cement or mortar, but so well let into each other as to be quite proof against rain, and they are plastered inside with mud: the whole are surrounded by a wall of the same materials. The Sirdar Moorad Khan is a Koord Belooche, a tribe inhabiting the mountains to the north-eastward: he married, about two years ago, a daughter of Mihrab Khan of Bunpoor, and received the Sirdarship of Basman as her dowry; he has not above fifty fighting men, and just sufficient income to subsist upon; his manners are mild; his address has all the Persian politeness and urbanity, and this was the first place I had come to, where Persian was the colloquial language. The Basman people are in general neither so large or tall as the Urbabees or Rukhshanees; their arms and pursuits are the same.

22d April. Between six in the morning, and the same hour in the evening, I travelled thirty-one miles over a desolate flat waste, in which there was neither water or vegetation of any kind, save a few stunted bushes of the Taghuz * that I observed in some of the dry water-courses, and here and there a stalk of the Shinz or camel thorn †. A westerly elongation of the range of mountains I crossed yesterday, was generally five or six miles to the southward of me; but in some instances projected northerly, almost close up to the road. The heat was greater and more oppressive than I had hitherto experienced since leaving India, and I, and my people also underwent more, from a want of water, as I was fearful of expending the little that remained of our Basman supply, to which I trusted as a *dernier resort.* The Suhrab, or water of the desert ‡, floated all round us, as though it were mocking our distress by its delusive representation of what we so eagerly thirsted for, the absence of which I can affirm with perfect confidence, from my individual experience, to be the most insupportable of all the wants of what are termed the absolute necessaries of life. A person may endure, with patience and hope, the pressure of fatigue or hunger, heat or cold, and even a total deprivation of natural rest for a considerable length of time; but to be scorched under a burning sun, to feel your throat so parched and dry that you respire with difficulty, to dread moving your tongue in your mouth from the apprehensions of suffocation which it causes, and not to have the means of allaying those dreadful sensations, are in my ideas the extreme pitch of a traveller's calamities. The Suhrab, of which I have just spoken, is said to be caused by the rarefaction of the atmosphere from extreme heat; and, which augments the delusion, it is most frequent in hollows where water might be expected to lodge. I have seen bushes and trees reflected in it, with as much accuracy as though it had been the face of a clear and still lake; and once, in the province of Kirman in Persia, it seemed

* A species of the tamarisk.

† The Hedysarum Alhagi.

‡ From Suhr, the desert; and Ab, water.

to rest like a sheet of water on the face of a hill, at the foot of which my road lay, exhibiting the summit, which did not overhang it in the least degree, by a kind of unaccountable refraction. This phenomenon is, however, very uncommon, and the Persians who were travelling with me attributed it to exhalations from saline particles, with which the hill abounded.

When Futtuh Mohummud, my faithful attendant, had baked * the bread, it was put to the vote, and unanimously carried, that we should divide the remainder of the water, which admitted of each of us, including the guide, having about one pint; and when we had supped on this frugal fare, we lay down to sleep.

23d April. The night being beautifully clear, with moonshine, I resolved to take advantage of that and the cool air, in hope of getting to Regan by the evening; accordingly, I only allowed a rest of two hours, and then started at one *a. m.* At the end of six miles we came to a Chushmuh, or spring, called Gehgan, of which the water was so salt that, thirsty as we were, we could scarcely relish it; however, having taken a hearty draught and filled up the Mushks or skins, we proceeded on twenty-two miles farther, and halted about ten o'clock in the morning at the edge of the jungul of Nurmansheer. From this place it is about fifteen miles to the town of Regan, where I arrived about five *p. m.*; having previously passed two small dismantled forts and a village called Mydan.

The face of the country was very much diversified throughout this day's march. From our last halting place to Gehgan, it was hilly ground, and thence to the jungul of Nurmansheer, a hard bare plain; then nine or ten miles of a continued thicket of low bushes, intermixed with trees; and the latter five or six miles, it assumed a more

* Our method of baking was the most summary I had ever heard of. A pile of dried sticks being collected, a quantity of sand, equal to half a bushel or so, was thrown on the top of it. It was then lighted, and by the time the sticks were consumed, the sand had become red hot. The dough, being made, was placed in the midst of the sand, and was ready to eat in ten minutes. In this process, the only care necessary is to cover the dough completely so as to exclude the air, otherwise the bread will burn.

fertile appearance, with many extensive tracts in cultivation, watered by abundant streams from the mountains, at one of which the guide filled his small hand Mushk with water and left us. He said he dare not go to Regan to return alone, so I gave him a couple of pounds of flour and three rupees, with which he was more than satisfied. The direction we travelled in also varied as much as the aspect of the soil, and our route lay between the south-west and north-west points of the compass.

I do not imagine, if I had had a thermometer to ascertain the fact, that I should have found the actual heat at all inferior to that of the preceding day; but we had plenty of water, such as it was, to quench our thirst; and another very singular circumstance that induced, at least to my imagination, an idea of coolness, and therefore made me suffer less from the temperature, was a range of lofty mountains about twenty-five miles to the southward of us, whose tops were covered with snow. Had the wind been blowing from them I could readily have admitted that my feelings were more than imaginary, but the air was still, or at most, just perceptible from an opposite quarter.

On reaching Regan, I rode straight up to the fort gate, where there were several people sitting, and children at play: the latter ran off shouting and terrified, and even the men's looks denoted mingled consternation and astonishment. Some of them thought us the forerunners of a Chupao, and none could divine how we had entered the country unperceived. Before I could dismount and offer an explanation, the news had spread over the whole place, and the chief, Abbas Allee Khan, immediately called for me to enquire whence I had come, and on what business. I informed him, in a few words, that I was the servant of a Hindoo merchant, travelling from Kelat to Kirman; and, while I was in the act of speaking, handed him a short letter that I had obtained from Moorad Khan of Basman, to attest my assertions, and recommend me, for a guide, or any other civilities, to such chiefs as I should happen to see. On perusing it, he said he was neither inclined to doubt my word or disoblige me, and that he would therefore not prevent my going on towards Kirman by the nearest road, though, in reality, his duty, agreeable to the orders of the Prince at that city, required that I should be sent by him to Rusheed Khan, the governor of the province (or district) of Nurmansheer, who resided at a town called Krook, that would have been thirty miles out of my way. He afterwards put some queries to me regarding how I had fared among the Belooches, and expressed his wonder that they had permitted me to advance unmolested. I told him that I believed my poverty was my passport, because, instead of having any thing to deprive me of, they had every thing to give me. He smiled at this conceit, and rejoined, that so long accustomed as I had been to guest-rites, he supposed I would also expect him to entertain me. I was about to reply in the negative, when he added, " and I will do so. You must " not think that the Shahsuwars * are the worst Belooches you have " seen." I departed to spend the night under some trees outside the fort, as they make it an invariable rule here, never to permit strangers to sleep within the walls; and, in the course of half an hour, a plentiful repast of barley bread and milk was brought to us.

24th April. I was induced to stay this day at Regan to give my people and camels a short cessation from the excessive fatigue they had latterly endured, under the additional evil of a very small allowance of food, for, from the time we left Basman, our stock afforded us but one meal a day; and the poor camels had literally eaten nothing, as I had, very unwillingly, been obliged to discontinue their portion of flour ever since we were at Huftur, and they had no time to browse. They had become thin and weak to the last degree, and we had consequently to walk on foot the greater part of the way between Basman and Regan, leading them behind us. †

* The name of his tribe.

† Camels will go at an astonishing rate, and for a great length of time, on a daily allowance of flour. It is generally not more than half ground, and mixed with water into

Regan is a very neat mud fort, or rather fortified village. It forms a square of about two hundred and fifty yards each face. The walls are high and kept in excellent repair, with bastions at the corners and in the centre. I should guess the walls to be five or six feet thick at the base, but they gradually taper away, and are not more than eighteen inches at the top; there is but one gate, which leads under the southern central bastion, and a guard is constantly kept there to prevent strangers from having ingress to the place, a precaution which exists throughout the whole of this province. The dwellings inside are encompassed by a second wall, to render them private as well as for purposes of defence. The space between this inner wall, which varies in height and solidity at the option of the owner of the house which it surrounds, and the fortifications, is perhaps thirty feet, and in it every description of cattle are kept at night. A path five or six feet broad is appropriated to the public use, and the remainder is portioned off into small pens and sheds, proportioned in size to the number of animals to be enclosed in them; the holder of each is bound to have it cleansed daily, a very necessary regulation, and one to which his own interest impels him to adhere on account of the manure thereby collected.

In addition to the fixed watchmen at the gateway, who are Toofungchees or matchlockmen, paid by the government; sentinels mount in all the bastions round the works as soon as it is dark, and keep a very vigilant look-out the whole night, frequently hallooing and shouting, to encourage each other, and warn any skulkers who may be outside, that they are on the alert. These nocturnal tours of duty being for the safety of the commonweal, are voluntarily performed by the inhabitants, who live in a continual state of alarm

---

balls of the size of a young infant's head, and thus stuffed down their throats; the Belooches often add opium and goor (vide Narrative of the *28th January*) to these boluses, and think the larger they can be crammed down they are the more efficacious. I allowed my camels, when at Kirman, fifteen pounds of flour a day each, which they swallowed down every evening, although they were eating clover and grass continually. This fact shews their wonderful endurance of hunger, in fasting for five or six days.

and apprehension, originating in their dread of the Belooches of Surhud, Bunpoor, and other districts to the eastward, who seldom fail to pay them, or some other part of the Persian dominions, a hostile visit once or twice a year. The chief of Regan, Abbas Allee Khan, is a Beloochee by birth, as are most of those who live under his authority; he has six sons, who are all exceedingly fine young men; they were very obliging and anxious to gratify me, for in the evening when we were chatting, they accidentally spoke of the Jureed Bazee*, and when I told them I had never seen it, two of them instantly ordered out their horses, and had a bout on the plain in front of the fort gate. They seemed to be masterly riders, and had their horses in admirable manage, but that is indispensable in this pastime, which I shall here concisely describe, premising that it is a very common one amongst all classes in Persia. The Jureed Bazee is of two kinds. One played by two men on horseback, with a spear shaft twelve or more feet long. The other by a single horseman, with a stick two or three feet in length. In the former, the two combatants alternately gallop after each other, throwing the Jureed or spear shaft, with full force; the aim of the thrower is to hit and unhorse his opponent, while he, by his dexterous agility, is not only to elude the blow, but to seize the weapon in the air, and attack in turn. The other game simply consists in putting your horse to his utmost speed and dashing one end of the short stick on the ground, so that it may bound upwards with a projectile tendency, and then catching it. This knack is soon acquired, and unattended by the slightest risk; but I repeatedly trembled, when I first saw, in the former sport, the Jureed flying with uncommon velocity towards one of the brothers, whom I thought it must inevitably bring to the ground. I believe, however, that I was the only person of that opinion, as the players enjoyed it very much, and the spectators expressed no sentiments save applause at their expertness.

* The Jureed Bazee, or spear-play, from Jureed, a spear, and Bazeedun, to play.

CHAPTER XIV.

THE AUTHOR LEAVES REGAN. — ARRIVES AT BOORJA. — INTERMEDIATE TRACT. — INSOLENCE OF THE CHIEF. — AUTHOR AVOWS HIMSELF AN ENGLISH MERCHANT. — RESULT OF THE DISPUTE. — TOWN OF NUHEEMABAD. — THE CHIEF. — ABSENT. – POLICY OF THE PERSIAN GOVERNMENT. — DESCRIPTION OF NUHEEMABAD. — HIRE THE SAME GUIDE. — HIS DISHONESTY. — JUMALEE TOWN. — MEET THE CHIEF OF NUHEEMABAD. — THE AUTHOR INTRODUCES HIMSELF. — OBJECT IN SO DOING. — CHIEF'S REMARKS. — GIVES A LETTER TO THE GOVERNOR OF THE CITY OF BUMM. — VILLAGE OF LOORABAD. — INTERVENING COUNTRY. — AUTHOR ARRIVES AT BUMM. — WAITS ON THE GOVERNOR. — GREATLY ANNOYED BY THE PEOPLE ON GUARD AT THE PALACE. — THE GOVERNOR APPEARS. — SURPRIZE AT THE AUTHOR'S DRESS. — DESCRIPTION OF IT. — HALL OF AUDIENCE. — GOVERNOR'S POLITE CONDUCT. — AGE. — NATIVE PLACE. — PREPARATIONS FOR THE JOURNEY. — DEPARTURE FROM BUMM. — WATER-MILL. — INSOLENCE OF A SYYUD. — PRONOUNCES THE AUTHOR TO BE AN UFFGHAN. — CAUSE FOR UNDECEIVING HIM. — CONVERSATION. — INSULTING. — MEANS TRIED TO SILENCE IT. — FORTUNATE QUERY PUT TO THE AUTHOR. — HOW ANSWERED. — RESULT. — PROVINCE OF NURMANSHEER. — BOUNDARIES. — KROOK THE CAPITAL. — SHORT HISTORICAL ACCOUNT OF THIS PROVINCE AND ITS INHABITANTS. — SOIL. — CLIMATE. — AUTHOR'S OPINION. — REVENUES. — PRODUCTIONS. — CITY OF BUMM. — VERY STRONG FORTRESS. — DESCRIBED. — CELEBRITY. — WHENCE DERIVED. — LOOTF. — ALLEE KHAN ZUND SEIZED HERE. — EXTENSIVE RUINS. — FORMER MAGNIFICENCE. — CELEBRATED FOUNTAIN. — ITS USE. — SITUATION OF BUMM FAVOURABLE FOR SUCH. — NARRATIVE RESUMED.

APRIL 28th. The moment the gate of the fort was opened this morning, a guide that I had asked for the night before, came out to join me, and I quitted Regan at six *a. m.* and travelled fourteen miles north north-west, through a level woody country. We stopped to eat our breakfast at some fields of barley, which the natives were busy cutting, a circumstance that rather surprized me at this early period, but I found the grain still more generally ripe as I advanced to the westward. As soon as the extreme heat had abated, I again moved on, and at seven in the evening halted at a very small circular fort, called Boorja (or the bastion), in which there is a village of fifty or sixty houses; the jungul was more impervious than in the fore-part of the day, and the path so winding, that I am certain we must have traversed three times the actual distance from Regan to this place. I computed our evening's march at fifteen miles, making the day's journey twenty-nine; there was plenty of water in running streams, and some of the scenery was beautiful in the extreme, the variety of trees, among which I could distinguish the Peepul, Neem, Tamarind, Babool, Mangoe, Walnut, wild almond, and Guz *, the latter of the largest size I had ever beheld, were in full foliage and bloom, and displayed a rich and surprizing contrast to the rugged and snow-topt mountains on our left hand.

I had scarcely alighted from my camel, when an ill-looking dirty scrub, who afterwards turned out to be the Kud Khoda, or chief of the place, made his appearance, and demanded in a most authoritative tone, who we were, and our object; to which I made him an answer in the same style, desiring to know by what right he had presumed to make any inquiry. At this period my guide, who had been into the village for a brand to kindle a fire, came up, and addressed my interrogator as the Kud Khoda or chief, telling him that I was the person he had spoken of; this observation irritated me still more, as I was convinced by it that the fellow knew all he had questioned me about, and had unwarrantably hastened out of the fort for the mere purpose of displaying his self-created consequence, by being insolent; however, he found himself, in the sequel, egregiously mistaken. " Yes," replied he to the guide, " I see it is; he does not exactly

* Peepul, Ficus religiosa. Neem, Melia azadirachta. Babool, Mimosa Arabica. Guz, Indian Tamarisk.

"appear to know his station; but I shall try whether he or I have "most power here, by dispatching him to Rusheed Khan to-morrow "morning; he will catechise him to some purpose." I should have laughed at the petulance of this blusterer, but, as he had the means of carrying his threat into execution, I deemed it wise to put a stop to any coercive attempt of that kind, and I thought it easiest done by menacing him in return. I therefore told him that I was an English merchant, and that he had better beware how he interfered with me. This declaration rather astounded him, but after a short pause, he turned to my Belooches, and rejoined, that they could not plead the same excuse for appearing in Nurmansheer, and please God they should, at all events, go to Krook. I had no longer patience to bear with such arrogance, and told him that he was an impudent scoundrel, that he dare not send me or any of my people to Rusheed Khan, and that he might be assured I should represent his conduct to the prince on my arrival at Kirman. The guide and some by-standers now interposed, and I imagine the fellow felt conscious that he had been too precipitate in his menaces, as he growled in a very low accent, that I ought to remember I was in the King's dominions, where strangers could not travel without accounting for their intentions. I made him no reply, and as it began to rain just after he had done speaking, he slunk off into the fort, leaving me master of the field.

26th April. I cautioned my guide to sleep near us, in order to preclude the possibility of delay on his account, and left Boorja this morning long ere any person had thoughts of moving abroad. At the end of ten miles north north-west, over a plain diversified with bushy and tilled ground, I arrived at the town of Nuheemabad. The Kud Khoda of this place is Kureem Khan, a Belooche of the Koord tribe, and brother of the principal chief of Surhud, Oolfut Khan, but having quarrelled with him and the other Sirdars of that country, he was dispossessed of his paternal inheritance, and fled to Nurmansheer, where the Kirman government granted him the depopulated fort and town of Nuheemabad, a system of donation that it has extensively practised for the last five or six years, and the reason of which is noticed in the general description of this province in a subsequent page. Kureem Khan exerted himself in persuading his countrymen to repair to his new possessions, and settle under his authority, in which he has so well succeeded, that Nuheemabad is now a good deal larger than Regan, very populous and flourishing. He was absent at Krook, and I was not therefore permitted to see the inside of the fort, but the outworks are kept in the nicest order, and look, from their neatness and smoothness, more like the walls of a house than a large fortification. It is built on the identical plan of Regan, except that being an oblong square, there are two bastions instead of one on each of the longer sides. After halting the whole day at Nuheemabad, in expectation of Kureem Khan's return, I hired the same guide who had come with me from Regan, to shew me the road to the city of Bumm. The fellow availed himself of this chance to make me pay most exorbitantly, and, in fact, I could have got a man for less at Regan, to have conducted me the whole way, but as I had been informed by my camel-drivers, that Kureem Khan had been once to Kelat, on a visit to Muhmood Khan, I intended to introduce myself to him on that score, and therefore made certain of his civilities.

27th April. Thirteen miles of a north north-westerly route, through a very fertile tract in the highest state of cultivation, intersected in every direction with running streams, brought us at nine o'clock this morning to Jumalee, a small town, around which two or three hundred people were rebuilding a dilapidated wall. We breakfasted under some very umbrageous walnut trees on the bank of a brook close to the town, and resumed our march at eleven *a. m.* but had not advanced above two miles, when we encountered Kureem Khan. I immediately rode up, and told him who I was, adding, that I had heard of his visit to Kelat from Muhmood Khan, and hoped, in proof of his friendship for that chief, he would direct me in the proper mode of obtaining a guide and passport from Bumm to Kirman. He desired I would return with him to Jumalee, where, after some unimportant discourse, and his consulting with two or three horsemen that were in company with him; he acquainted me that it would be absolutely requisite for me, in order to get the permission I wished, to wait upon Rusheed Khan at Krook, adding, that it was not more than six Fursukhs off (twenty-two miles). I reiterated an assurance that I had before made to him, that I had no sort of objection to doing so, except what arose from its being so much out of my way, and reasoned that as I was going to Kirman, and should pay my respects to the Prince, there could surely be no cause for putting myself and followers to such unnecessary fatigue. He deliberated for a moment, and without replying, called for pen, ink, and paper, and wrote a letter, which I concluded was for Rusheed Khan; however, when he had done, he reached it over to me, saying, "I have in this letter written your story to Lootf Allee "Khan, the governor of Bumm, who will act with you as he chooses, "but you must not neglect to repeat to him verbally, that it was "alone owing to your earnest request, that you were not sent by "me hence to Krook." I promised to conform to this injunction, and having bidden him good bye, mounted my camel, and rode fourteen miles west north-west to the small village of Loorabad, near which I halted at eight *p. m.*

The interjacent country, with the exception of the first half mile, was a bare arid plain, destitute of verdure or water.

28th April. Ten miles west-by-north from Loorabad, over a tolerably fertile plain, lies the city of Bumm, at which I arrived this morning a little before eight o'clock, and took up my quarters in a vacant dyer's shop in the outside bazar. After breakfast I went into the city and, by dint of enquiry, found my way to the citadel, the residence of Lootf Allee Khan, the Governor. I sent up Kureem Khan's letter, and waited full two hours under the gate-way among a pack of unmannered and boisterous matchlockmen, who were on guard, and annoyed me very much by their inquisitive impertinence. When I had abandoned every hope of either seeing the Governor or getting an answer to the letter, and was on the point of tracing back my steps, with very disconsolate feelings, to my people, a man came down to apprize me that the Khan would be in Durbar in a few minutes; and, conformably to this communication, he very soon walked across the court with a large retinue of servants. When pretty near the spot I was standing at, he turned to one of his train, and asked where the Firingee, or European, was. On my being shewn to him, he beckoned to me with his hand to follow, at the same time conveying, by a fixed gaze and a survey of me from head to foot, his astonishment at my garb, which was certainly uncouth enough to apologize for the rudeness of staring. It was composed of a coarse Belooche shirt, and trowsers that had been once white, but now, from being worn six weeks, bordered on brown, and were almost in tatters; a blue turband; a piece of cotton rope in lieu of a waist-band; and a bludgeon in my hand, which I found very useful in walking, as well as a protection from dogs.

We passed through two or three small flagged court-yards before we got to the Durbar, situated at the end of a larger area, with an alley on each side, between which there was a plat of ground with flowering shrubs, and three fountains playing. The room we entered was a very handsome square one, with a recess and bow window on each side, the floor covered with rich Persian carpets, and round the walls Numuds, or felts, for sitting upon. It was painted a pure white with gilt mouldings, and had altogether a very magnificent, but not gaudy, effect. The Khan sat down in the front recess, close to the window, and I placed myself on the opposite side of the hall, near the door. He made a number of enquiries pertaining to my journey, of which I gave him a very succinct narration, stating, in addition to what Kureem Khan had directed, that my ultimate wish was to join General Malcolm, the British ambassador at Teheraun, which I did in order that he might write to that effect to the Prince at Kirman. Kullyans were then introduced, and after he had detained me above an hour, he said, " I am about to dispatch a Chupper (a " mounted messenger) to the Shahzaduh at Kirman, and he shall be " ordered to keep company with you; he will set off this afternoon, "therefore you had better hasten such preparation as you will need "in the way of food, recollecting that there is nothing to be pur-"chased on the road." I professed my obligations to him, and took leave with a very favourable impression of the politeness of the Persians, from the specimen I had had in the complaisant conduct of Lootf Allee Khan, who is a young man for the situation he holds. His appearance did not bespeak him to be above twenty-two years old. I understood he was a native of Isfahan, and his manners are more polished and elegant than any of his fellow citizens that I afterwards saw.

My Hindoostanee man, during my absence, had in vain endeavoured to procure some flour, and I was therefore reduced to the necessity of buying a quantity of barley, the only grain to be had, and to trust to getting it ground elsewhere; however, I laid in a large stock of very fine dates and pomegranates, and the Chuppur coming at five *p. m.*, we set off and travelled three miles and a half, a good part of the way through heaps of rubbish and ruins, to a water mill on the road side, where we halted to pass the night, and were so fortunate as to get all our barley exchanged for flour, allowing the customary deduction for labour and waste.

An hour or two before I left Bumm, I was excessively irritated by the insolence of a bigotted Syyud * from the city of Mushed in Khorasan, who, learning that a Christian was baiting outside, strutted forth to expostulate with me on, and, as he said, to convince me of the manifest impropriety of my religion. At first he peeped into the room in which I was reclining, and dogmatically pronounced that I was not an European, but an Uffghan in disguise. I was aware of the danger of allowing that erroneous idea to be publicly entertained, from the implacable enmity existing between the two nations, and in consequence, arose and went into the verandah to disprove his affirmation; which having done, he began to harangue the crowd and talk very insultingly of all Christians or infidels, as he styled

* Syyuds are the descendants of Mohummud.

them. He then asked me how I dared to be in a Moosulman's habit, and not believe in his Prophet; whether I had any knowledge, who Allee was, and even seemed disposed to insist on my repeating the Sheea creed after him. This I firmly refused, after which he changed his subject, and desired I would truly inform him how many husbands were usually allotted to one female among my countrymen; whether brothers did not marry their own sisters and nearest relations, with several other infamous questions, the truth of which, he most solemnly swore to the multitude, he had heard admitted by two Europeans who had visited Mushed the preceding year *. All this was accompanied by a torrent of the most scurrilous abuse about hogs-flesh, wine, and other prohibited food, at which I had great difficulty in restraining my temper; but I knew, if I struck him, from the sanctity of his character, that I should most likely, and my people also, have been murdered in the scuffle that would have ensued. I therefore endeavoured, at one moment, by civil replies, to bribe him into silence; and the next, to intimidate him by denouncing on him the displeasure of Lootf Allee Khan, to whom I said I should prefer a complaint. Matters went on thus for a long while, and the whole people of the Bazar, to the number of two or three thousand, had collected round the house and were alternately ridiculing and execrating me for every thing that was despicable or wicked. At last, by good fortune, among his other interrogations, he sneeringly asked, if I knew where the Almighty was? I rejoined, that I had one query to put to him; and that, if he answered it clearly, I was ready to satisfy his curiosity. He assented to the proposition, on which I desired that he would inform me where the Almighty was not present? He instantly rose, and turning to the populace, said, in a very loud voice, "By God, if he was but a "Moosulman, he is a good man;" and, to my unspeakable satisfaction, walked off, followed by the whole of the crowd.

* The Europeans he spoke of were, I subsequently ascertained, two officers belonging to the French mission to Persia.

The province of Nurmansheer extends, in length, from the waste dividing it from Beloochistan to the city of Bumm, about eighty-five miles; and, in breadth, from thirty to seventy-five. Its boundary to the westward is the province of Kirman, of which, I believe, it is now deemed a component district; to the eastward it has the desert, as already mentioned; and, north and south, two ranges of mountains, the last of which are by much the highest, and I imagine, at all seasons, crowned with snow, as they were so when I saw them, at which period it was exceedingly hot in the plain beneath. I have dwelt so long on the description of the fort of Regan, in my diary of the *24th of April*, that it would be needless to say further here, than that it is applicable to all the others I saw or passed near, in this province. I may add, that I was informed, the town of Krook, which is the capital and seat of the Governor, is surrounded by a dry ditch, and is four-fold the size of Nuheemabad.

It is not more than nine years since the Ghiljyee Uffghans *, who had long possessed Nurmansheer, were expelled from it by the Persian government, which has invited the tribes inhabiting the frontiers of Beloochistan to re-people the deserted villages; and, since their colonization, they have all embraced the Sheea Islamism, and exult extremely at the empty honor of being subjects of the King of Persia. Of the Ghiljyees, who were thus driven from their homes, the greatest number fled to the province of Seistan, and the cities of Khubees, Neh, and Ghayn in Khorasan; a few of them are also settled at Kelat in Beloochistan. They were not themselves the original inhabitants of this province, but sprung from a colony that settled there, after the Uffghan invasion of Persia in 1719. Whether this settlement was effected by treaty, or from what tribe they wrested it, is a point that I am unable to decide; I however conjecture, that they obtained it amicably from Nadir Shah, for although, as the commander-in-chief of the armies of Shah Thamasp, the last and one of the weakest sovereigns of the Suffeveea dynasty, of whom,

* The Ghiljyees are a great class of the Uffghan nation.

in fact he was more the director than the submissive general; that famous warrior entirely subverted the usurped and unstable authority of the Uffghans in Persia; he did so as a step towards his own aggrandizement, and as all accounts agree, that he was exceedingly partial to his Uffghan subjects, after he had obtained the royal dignity, it may be justly concluded, that having removed the Ghiljyees of Nurmansheer from the scope of his ambition, by reducing them to the most abject obedience, he was happy to procure them an asylum in that empire, of which he, even at that time, calculated on being the future monarch. In support of this surmise, it appears that they continued to enjoy this fertile tract unmolested, throughout the zenith of his glory; they also conciliated his successors, and were on such friendly terms with the Zunds, that they assisted the later princes of that race in their quarrels with the ruling family, a circumstance to which their extirpation is to be ascribed. A longer historical notice of these people is here totally useless, and would diverge into a digression totally unconnected with my subject, as they were in truth but a very small colony of a great nation.*

The soil of Nurmansheer is chiefly a dark-coloured rich mould, but to the southward, as you approximate to the desert, it partakes of the same sandy and arid nature. It is on the whole, however, very fertile, and well watered by mountain streams, arising from natural springs, and likewise the progressive melting of the snow. These springs, beside answering all the purposes of cultivation, turn a great number of water-mills, of which I suppose I counted twenty between Regan and Bumm. During the summer and autumn months, the climate is reputed warm but healthy, which the looks of the people can testify. Were this province under an enlightened government, I should expect, at a future day, to hear of it as the

* The Ghiljyees are subjects of the King of Kabool. They are said to amount to nearly one million of souls. They are not on very good terms with their neighbours the Abdallis, or Douranees, of whose dominion they are jealous. Many of them are Sheeas, and they have always been esteemed a brave people.

most productive in the kingdom of Persia; but in a few years, when the people become rich enough to be objects of plunder, to satisfy the rapacity and avarice of the King and his ministers, its gradual improvement will be checked by extortion and injustice, and it will quickly go to decay.

The revenues realized from it in 1810, were above forty thousand rupees, after paying the military establishment that is kept for the protection of the different towns and villages; this probably may involve an expence of half a lac of rupees annually, so that the total may be computed at one lac, or twelve thousand five hundred pounds sterling.

Its productions are grain of all kinds, madder, cotton, roses for conserves and distilling, fruit, of which they export walnuts, almonds, and dried grapes; honey and gum; the latter is collected from the different species of the Babool tree, and is very valuable, being thought equal to, or better than that brought from the Red Sea; it is packed in leathern bags, holding seven pounds and a half each, and thus disposed of in the market of Kirman.

The city of Bumm was, until the expulsion of the Uffghans, as just related, the frontier town of the Province of Kirman; the reduction of it had repeatedly been attempted by them within the last twenty years, assisted by the neighbouring Belooches, as a retaliation for the inroads made by the royal forces into Nurmansheer; and the fortifications have in consequence been so vastly strengthened, that they are now accounted beyond any comparison the most defensible in Persia. They have an elevated site, and at present consist of a very high and thick mud wall, a deep, broad, and dry ditch, with six large bastions on each face, exclusive of those at the corners, which are higher by many yards than the others; the whole is built of mud mixed with straw and fibrous substances, and there is one gate between the two centre bastions of the southern face. The citadel is on the highest part of the eminence on which the town is built, and is well fortified with a lofty wall, and towers at each corner; the area thus enclosed, is entirely occupied by the Governor's palace, and buildings belonging to it. The Bazar is pretty large, and supplies are reasonable; a scarcity of wheat prevailed when I was there, but barley, dates, milk, and various sorts of fruit were procurable. The gardens here are famous for pomegranates, and they are undoubtedly superior in flavour and juiciness to any I tasted afterwards, either at Sheeraz or Bagdad, where the best in the world are supposed to be produced.

Of late years, the celebrity of Bumm has been increased in a high degree among the Persians, from being the place at which Lootf Allee Khan, the last of the Zund family who disputed the succession to the throne, was made prisoner about nineteen years ago. The spot where he was seized, when in the act of mounting his horse to escape, is marked, to this hour, by a pyramid of the skulls of his adherents, erected by order of his competitor, the merciless Agha Mohomed Khan Kajjar, the first of that tribe who reigned in Persia. I shall find occasion to advert to the particulars of that horrid transaction when I come to speak of Kirman, and need not detail further in this place.

The widely scattered ruins, and remains of demolished buildings, round the present fort, demonstrate the immense extent of the former city of Bumm, which is reputed to have been, in point of magnificence, in the days of its splendour, equal to any other in Persia. The Uffghans, when they invaded that Kingdom in 1719, are usually allowed to have been the original beautifiers, but not the founders of it, as the town itself was of much more ancient date. It is also quite certain, that, whatever might have been the state of it, when the Ghiljyees became masters of it, they were eventually the sole cause, if not the actual perpetrators, of its dilapidation. Some of the fountains here are said to have thrown water to an amazing height and distance, far beyond any thing that the science of hydraulics in Persia can at present accomplish, although much studied; for no house is considered complete without its marble cistern and *jet d'eau*. About three miles from the fort, my guide called my attention to a garden equal to several acres of ground, still retaining traces of having been walled in, with elegant summer houses at each angle, which he affirmed was, in the prosperous days of the Uffghans, regularly watered twice a-day by an artificial shower from one large central bason, that is now filled with rubbish. The situation of Bumm is doubtless very favourable to luxuries of this kind: built in a plain in the vicinity of high mountains, which are usually, if not always, covered with snow, it must have a vast and continual supply of water. I now return to a continuation of my Narrative.

CHAPTER XV.

ROUTE CONTINUED. — COUNTRY. — SURAE'. — VILLAGE OF SUBZISTAN. — TOWN OF TEHEROOT. — RIVER USHKOO. — DESCRIPTION OF IT. — BED CULTIVATED. — DESOLATE TRACT. — BAD ROAD. — OBLIGED TO TRAVEL ON FOOT. — TOWN OF MAHON. — DESCRIBED. — FLOURISHING. — KAREZES. — HOW FORMED — ADVANTAGES OF THEM. — THE AUTHOR ARRIVES AT THE CITY OF KIRMAN. — HIS FEELINGS. — GOES TO A KARWANSERAI'. — ANNOYED BY VISITORS. — BREAD. — FREQUENT DISAPPOINTMENT REGARDING IT. — MESSAGE TO THE PRINCE. — ANSWER. — LETTER TO BRIGADIER GENERAL MALCOLM. — VISIT THE PRINCE. — RECEPTION. — PRINCE'S QUESTIONS. — STATE. — PRINCE'S DRESS AND APPEARANCE. — HIS GENERAL CHARACTER — DOUBTFUL. — SOJOURN AT KIRMAN. — THE AUTHOR WAITS ON THE MINISTER. — VERY POLITE. — CAUSE EXPLAINED. — PERSIAN DINNER. — KULLYANS. — BOTH KINDS DESCRIBED. — COFFEE. — FRUITS. — MEATS AND STEWS. — SHERBET. — THIS THE PRINCIPAL MEAL. — INCONVENIENCES. — DISGUSTING MANNER OF EATING. — SKETCH OF THE PERSIAN CHARACTER — GUILTY OF EVERY SPECIES OF VICE. — SUM OF THE AUTHOR'S OPINION OF THE SOCIETY IN PERSIA. — IMPUDENCE OF A SERVANT BELONGING TO THE PRINCE. — THE AUTHOR'S BEHAVIOUR ON THE OCCASION. — ITS GOOD EFFECTS — BEAR DANCERS. — THEIR INFAMOUS LIVES. — THE PRINCE SITS IN JUDGMENT ON SOME MURDERERS. — DREADFUL PUNISHMENTS AWARDED. — CONSTERNATION OF THE INHABITANTS OF THE CITY — THE DRESS OF VENGEANCE. — ITS COLOUR. — TERROR IT INSPIRES. — CRUEL CALMNESS OF THE PRINCE. — CURIOUS PROPOSITION OF A PERSIAN TO THE AUTHOR. — HIS REPLY. — AFFECTING PENANCE PERFORMED BY THE SHEEAH MOOSULMANS. — FEELINGS CAUSED BY IT. — EXCESSIVE MEANNESS OF THE PRINCE. — THE AUTHOR'S CONDUCT ON THE OCCASION. — HE LEAVES KIRMAN FOR SHEERAZ. SUCCEEDING CHAPTER DEDICATED TO AN ACCOUNT OF THE PROVINCE AND CITY OF *KIRMAN*.

APRIL 29th. We mounted this morning before six, and travelled, in the course of the day, forty-four miles, about west by north. The latter twenty-eight afford no water, and are along a bare desert plain. The road was very good the whole way, and about eight miles from Bumm there is a Suraé with a very deep well of the most delicious water I ever tasted. I halted at midnight in the midst of a low range of hills near a small village called Subzistan, the town of Teheroot lying from us north-north-west, distant eight miles.

30th April. The first twelve miles of my route to-day were west, over a bare plain. I then entered a very broad river-bed, nearly dry, called the Ushkoo, in which, and parallel with the stream, the road led for upwards of six miles. We then crossed it, and continued along the plain ten miles further, and halted on it, near a pond of brackish water. The bed of the Ushkoo, which runs past Teheroot and loses its stream in the desert behind the mountains north-west from Bumm, is in some places above a mile in breadth, and in others not more than one hundred and fifty or two hundred yards; the banks are steep and high, and the whole had been at one time overgrown with brush-wood and jungul trees; but some industrious peasants had cleared away many large spaces, and were cultivating luxuriant crops of wheat, sugar-cane, tobacco, cotton, &c. The small town of Rayun, lying close under a range of lofty mountains, bore, from the spot we halted upon this night, west-by-south, twenty-two miles.

1st May. I journeyed twenty-nine miles these twenty-four hours, through a desolate and barren country; the direction varying between north-west and north-east: water was only to be had at a small spring in the side of a hill at the sixteenth mile. The mountains were very near us on each side of the road, which was stony and bad.

2d May. I was incessantly marching from five *a.m.* till nine *p.m.*, but the road, during the forenoon, was much worse than any that I had yet experienced in Persia, and in consequence of that, and my camels being reduced to the last stage of emaciation and weakness, we had to trudge on foot almost the whole way, and I do not therefore compute that we actually made more than thirty miles; though, had I judged by the complaints of my followers, and the soreness of my own feet, I should have felt inclined to say, double that distance. At the twenty-sixth mile, we passed through the town of Mahon, which is situated twenty-four miles east by south from Kirman. It is a very pretty little town, surrounded by numerous walled gardens, which are well stocked with all sorts of fruit trees. Shahzaduh Ibraheem Khan, who is governor of the province and city of Kirman, has a hunting lodge here, that appeared from a distance to be a very elegant mansion. This is likewise the place where all the horses and mules belonging to the Kirman government are kept, when not required for the public service, and there are five or six very large Suraés for the accommodation of the people attached to the establishment, exclusive of the stabling. This causes a considerable influx of strangers and trade; and the districts in the vicinity of Mahon are richly cultivated, and apparently very flourishing. I here first observed that curious mode of conducting water under ground, so much practised in different countries of Asia, called, by the Persians, Karezes. Pits from thirty to ninety feet in depth, and six feet in diameter, are dug one hundred, or one hundred and fifty, paces apart; and an under-ground excavation, or trench, afterwards made to connect them. By this method, as there is no evaporation, and springs are frequently found in the pits or trenches, the quantity of water is often rather increased than diminished by the extent it traverses from its original source, which is commonly at the base of some eminence abounding with springs or rivulets; and I have seen water, for irrigation, carried to a distance of thirty or forty miles. When any of these excavations chance to fall in, an angle is formed in the cut by digging another well a little way on either side, and leading the stream through it to the next one. It is apparent that Karezes are altogether attended by an amazing labour and trouble, but without them, cultivation would be nearly at an end in some of the most extensive provinces in Persia, and whole districts deserted.

3d *May.* I quitted my halting place at two *a. m.* and with mingled feelings of thankfulness for my safety, and exultation and pleasure at the completion of all that part of my journey which I considered hazardous, I reached the city of Kirman this morning at ten o'clock, having marched twenty miles over a plain that is tolerably well tilled, and interspersed with villages and gardens. My guide proceeded through the Bazars to a Karwansuraé, where I was immediately accommodated with a small room, round the door of which some hundreds of people soon collected to stare at me, and annoyed me very much by their officious and impertinent questions, to which however, I took good care to give them suitable answers. I next sent out to purchase some wheaten bread, after having been several times assured, it was that, (to me, rare) article that I had observed exposed for sale in shops in the Bazar; for the fact was, I had been so long habituated to starvation, and so frequently balked in my expectations, when I had been told I should get bread to buy at different towns, particularly in Nurmansheer, that I even was in doubt whether I should be able to procure it in the city of Kirman.

When I had breakfasted, I directed Lootf Allee Khan's man to go to the palace, and inform the Prince of my arrival, and also to request his permission for my remaining a short time in Kirman. To this message I received a reply, couched in all the overstrained style of Persian politeness, entreating me to look upon the city and every thing in it as my own; and adding, that as I was probably fatigued after my journey, the Prince would postpone seeing me until the following day. This was even much sooner than I wished to have an audience, as I had at that time no clothes whatever; but a friendly Hindoo, who lived opposite to me in the Karwansuraé, volunteered to dress me out for the occasion, and consequently I made no excuse. The necessity I was under of being thus obliged to the Hindoo, soon got abroad, and made a very sensible difference in the estimation in which I should possibly have been held during my sojourn at Kirman.

I was happy when it became dark, as I then got a little respite from my numberless visitors; and having dined off a very excellent Pilaow, that I got ready cooked from one of the shops, I lay down, and slept with more composure than I had done any night for the preceding three months.

4th May. I this morning dispatched a Kasid or courier to Sheeraz, with a letter acquainting Brigadier General Malcolm with my having arrived in safety at Kirman. I also had one in Persian written to Mohummud Nubee Khan, who was then minister of the province of Fars, and had been shortly before ambassador to the Government of India, requesting, in the event of General Malcolm not being at Sheeraz, that he would transmit my letter to him, and intimate to his Royal Highness the Prince, that it was my intention to advance to that city in the course of three weeks.

About ten o'clock a person came to acquaint me that the Prince was in Durbar, and would then receive me. I was soon trimmed out in borrowed clothes, and accompanied the messenger through several streets to the palace, and when we had crossed three or four inner courts, the Urz Begee, or master of the ceremonies, met us, and inquired my name, with which he returned to the Prince, who desired I might be called in. The Urz Begee instructed me to attend to his motions, and do exactly the same. When we came in sight of the Prince, who was sitting at a window about ten feet high, looking into a small court, with a fountain playing in the centre of it, we made a low bow, then advanced a few yards and made a second, and in like manner a third; all of which the Prince acknowledged by a slight inclination of the head. I expected I should then have been desired to enter the Durbar and seat myself, but my dress not being of the first order, I suppose I was not thought respectable enough for that honour, and therefore I was placed opposite the Prince in the court-yard, round the walls of which all the officers of government were standing, with their arms folded across their bodies. The Urz Begee whispered to me to do the same, but knowing it to be the etiquette for a servant before his master in Persia, and consequently not applicable to the Prince and myself, I refused compliance. When I had taken my station in front of him, the Prince called out in a very loud voice to know where I had been, and what could have induced me to undertake the journey I had performed, or how I had escaped from the dangers that must have attended it.

Before I went to the palace I had fabricated a story, of another officer and myself having been dispatched to Kelat, to approve of the horses for the Indian army, whence, by sea to join General Malcolm in Persia; but that as the season was too far advanced to go down to the coast and embark, I had preferred coming overland through Beloochistan. This was plausible enough to pass with the Prince, and after I had been there about half an hour, he dismissed me with the same forms as when I entered.

There is a considerable deal of state and magnificence about the palace, and there were a great number of well-dressed people in attendance. The room the Prince sat in was small, and inferior in decorations to many I afterwards saw, even in private houses, but some of the state-halls are very superb. The Prince himself is a handsome man, with an olive coloured complexion, and short black beard; he was dressed in a plain European Chintz Kubah or tunic *, and a black cap, made from the skin of the Bokhara kid, on his head. He is allied to the King in the three different degrees of consanguinity, of a son-in-law, nephew and step-son. In private life he is considered a humane mild man, and as a governor, very equitable and just. For a governor in Persia, perhaps he may be so, as in that country tyranny and extortion are so habitually the attendants of authority, that certain degrees of them are scarcely looked upon as evils; but there are anecdotes that speak to the contrary of him in both points. The severities he exercises are to be overlooked, being imperiously called for to check the enormities for which the city and province of Kirman are proverbial throughout Persia.

I remained at this city until the afternoon of the *25th of May*, in the expectation of being joined by Captain Christie from Heerat, but as the incidents which occurred during this long halt, were

* A Kubah is exactly similar to, and worn over, an Ulkhaliq, for which see Note on the 23d January.

neither so numerous or novel as to require a continuance of my diary, I shall briefly notice such as may be likely to amuse or interest, and pass from them to a short account of the province.

The day after I had been to the Prince's palace, I went to call upon the minister, who received me with every civility, and placed me on the same Numud or felt, on which he was himself sitting. His politeness I easily accounted for, when I was told that he had heard of the letter that I had sent to Mohummud Nubee Khan the foregoing day; for the man whom I had employed to do so, at first wrote an Ureezuh or petition, judging I suppose of my station in life from my shabby appearance; and on his reading it to me, when I told him it would not do, he desired I would explain the footing on which I stood with General Malcolm. I knew no better way of doing so, than by saying I was a relation of his, and therefore I replied that I was his nephew, which soon reached the minister's ears, and was the cause of his extreme civility to me. I chatted with him for nearly an hour, and when I came away, he asked me to dine with him the following evening, an invitation which I accepted. As all Persian entertainments are alike, by detailing the forms of this one, it will afford my readers a complete idea of their domestic habits on that head.

When I first went to his house about seven o'clock in the evening, Kullyans were brought. These are of two sorts; the Kurnyeé and Dustu, or snake and hand Kullyan; the one having a long pliant snake, similar to the Hookas of India, made of leather; and the other being, as its name denotes, held in the hand, and smoked through a short tube, often made of gold or silver, and beautifully enamelled. They are alternately changed and replenished with fresh tobacco, so that a person seldom takes more than ten or twelve pulls of either at a time. When water to wash had gone round, the eating and drinking commenced, by sweetmeats and two kinds of coffee, one of them is called sweet coffee, and made from syrup and the juice of different sorts of fruit; this and the real coffee are served up in small china cups, holding about a table spoonful each, placed in gold or silver ones, a size larger; these were succeeded by a variety of fruits, preserves, and pickles, in a green and dried state, and sherbets in bowls were handed round on trays, with a large wooden ladle to each, out of which every person drank what he pleased. A cloth was then spread in front of the party on the floor, and a quantity of bread in broad thin cakes thrown upon it, shortly after which the regular dinner, composed of all descriptions of pilows, stews, and other made dishes, was brought in upon trays, one of which was set before each guest. When every thing was thus arranged, the minister gave the signal to commence, by calling out Bismillah *, and in an instant the whole party was hard at work. The servants stood in the centre of the room, to help us to sherbet or water; and our host wanted very much to send for wine on my account, but I would not, of course, allow it; assuring him that I had not tasted it for many months, and infinitely preferred his iced sherbets. We had no less than three courses of meat, and as it was a very tedious business to remove and replace such a number of dishes, I was most happy when the time arrived for going home.

This meal, which is the principal one among Persians, corresponds exactly with our dinner. They eat nothing from that time until the following day at noon, which is their breakfasting hour, unless it may be a little green fruit very early in the morning. Two or three things are very inconvenient at their meals. You must dine off what happens to be next to you, or else have a person to put his feet in the midst of the dishes to reach at what you wish for; and, to Europeans, the method of sitting cross legged on a level with the victuals is, of course, always uncomfortable; nor do the Persians themselves seem to be much at their ease. From eating with the fingers, napkins also would appear to be indispensable, yet I never saw them introduced: many of the Persians use bread instead, and as it is very

* In God's name. Vide Note on Diary of the 8th April.

thin, and baked in pieces two or three feet square, it forms a tolerable substitute. Another vast objection is the want of spoons to help the different sauces: a fowl or a kid may be torn into scraps without much offence to our ideas of cleanliness; but, to see a person daub his greasy hand, that he has just licked, in a vessel of sauce, out of which his neighbour helps himself in the same manner the next minute, is truly barbarous and disgusting.

There are no people in the world who understand better the forms of politeness and etiquette to strangers, in their own houses, than the Persians; and were it not for their fancied pre-eminence, they would be exceedingly pleasant companions; but that spirit of egotism and false pride which they all inherit, from the highest to the lowest, makes them, even in their infancy, dogmatical to a degree sometimes bordering on rudeness.

Among themselves, with their equals, the Persians are affable and polite; to their superiors, servile and obsequious; and towards their inferiors haughty and domineering. All ranks are equally avaricious, sordid, and dishonest, when they have an opportunity of being so; nor do they care for detection when they have once reaped the benefit of their superior genius, as they term it. Falsehood they look upon, in all cases where it facilitates their ends, not only justifiable but highly commendable, and good faith, generosity, and gratitude, are alike unknown to them. In debauchery none can exceed them; and some of their propensities are too execrable and infamous to admit of mention. In short, to close this outline of the Persian character, I shall add, without the fear of confutation, that, from my own observation, I feel inclined to look upon Persia, at the present day, to be the very fountain-head of every species of tyranny, cruelty, meanness, injustice, extortion, and infamy, that can disgrace or pollute human nature; and have ever been found in any age or nation. *

* Perhaps a few of my readers may conceive what is here said to be too severe; but I think, of those who have had an opportunity of judging, there will be very few indeed of

A few mornings after my visit to the minister, I was conversing with a Hindoo in my room in the Karwansuraé, when a conceited fellow, dressed in fine silk cloaths, strutted in, attended by a servant carrying a Kullyan; he either was, or feigned to be, much surprized at my not rising to receive him, and inquired from the Hindoo why I did not do so, who referred him to myself, saying I understood and spoke Persian; on which he repeated his question in a most supercilious and contemptuous tone. "What!" said I to him, "do you "fancy I am come to Kirman to do nothing else than get up at the "entrance of every person who chooses to intrude himself upon me." He rejoined, that when people of rank came, I ought to pay them that compliment; and seeing that I made no movement to gratify him by doing so, he added, "but it is the behaviour I might have "expected from a Kafir Firingee *." I could hardly restrain my anger at the insolence of this upstart, who proved on enquiry to be a Peish Khidmut, or personal servant, of the Prince; however, I did so, and calling one of my Brahooes, desired him to shew the man of rank the door, and the fellow sneaked off. This fracas was soon blazed all over the Karwansuraé; and, thenceforward, my visitors were more scrupulous in their manners and observations; nor was I longer under the necessity of shutting the door of my chamber, and sitting in the dark; an alternative to which I had been obliged to resort to exclude strangers; for although I was always glad to see those from whose society I could derive either amusement or information, I found that they formed a very small portion of my visitors, and that the idle and ignorant, and not unfrequently the very dregs

that opinion. I speak from facts that I have either witnessed or heard of from unquestionable authority. I have known a Persian of education swindle a gentleman, to whom he was under the greatest obligations, out of a sum of money, and, on being taken to task, reply, that it ought not to have been left in his power to do so. Of every vice with which I brand them, I could adduce numerous instances within the sphere of my observation, and I am led to believe they are more prevalent in the precincts of the court than almost any other part of the kingdom.

* An infidel European.

of society, were my most common tormentors. I recollect, in particular, one morning, on my return from seeing a shawl manufactory, I found my room taken possession of by eight or nine Lootees, or bear leaders, and their bears, to whom I had to give a considerable sum to get rid of them, on their making a promise, which, to my surprize, they faithfully kept, of not returning. These Lootees are the buffoons of Persia, and perhaps the happiest race of beings in the empire, as they are privileged to say and act as they please, and not even the branches of the royal family, nor the great officers of government, venture to exasperate them. They are occasionally employed as the infamous medium of wreaking vengeance on such noblemen as fall under the royal displeasure, by giving up their wives and children, of both sexes, to them for the worst of purposes. *

On the 15*th of May*, the Prince sat in judgement on some people who were accused of murdering one of his servants; and the state of alarm and suspence in which the whole of the inhabitants were kept during the day is scarcely conceivable. The city gates were shut, at least to the egress of the public, and no business was transacted by the public officers of the government. People were sent for as witnesses, without any warning, and I saw two or three led away to the palace in as great agony as if they had been going to a place of execution. About three in the afternoon, the Prince pronounced sentences on those convicted; some were blinded of both eyes, had their ears, noses, and lips cut off, their tongues slit, and one or both hands lopped off. Others were deprived of their manhood, their fingers and toes chopped off, and all were turned out into the streets with a warning to the inhabitants not to assist or hold any intercourse with them.

On such occasions as these, the Prince always dresses in a yellow suit, and has a cloth of the same colour to cover the carpet

* I believe no instance of this Persian custom has occurred during the present reign. In Agha Mohummud Khan's time, it was very frequent.

he sits on; it is thence called the Ghuzub Poshak, or dress of vengeance; and when thus robed, not even his ministers are allowed to address him, unless spoken to. I learned afterwards that he sat at the same window at which I saw him, the day I went to the palace, throughout the whole of the mutilation of the miserable culprits, and gave his orders without evincing the smallest degree of compassion or horror at the scene before him.

One morning I had a visit from a middle aged person who came to my room followed by a servant, whom he presently dismissed, and requested leave to shut the door, as he wished to speak to me in private. To this I assented, and he commenced a long oration on the advantages of Christianity, and finally informed me that it was his earnest wish to become a convert to my religion, of which he begged I would state to him the leading tenets. I was a good deal surprized at so unexpected a declaration and request; but as I suspected the sincerity of both, I told him I was sorry it was out of my power to afford him any insight into those doctrines; that I was neither capable of instructing him, or had authority to do so; but that, if he really wished to be fully informed regarding them, he might proceed to India, where he would find many both equal and willing to afford him the necessary instruction. Finding he was not likely to make much progress on this head, he next assured me that there were six thousand men in Kirman expecting the English, and enquired when they were coming. The idiom of the Persian language admitting of my applying the sentence either to the British nation or myself*, I took his question in the latter point of view, and replied accordingly. "Come," said he very peevishly, "you don't confide in me. Why "will you not comprehend what I say to you? I wish to befriend "you all, and have six thousand men to back me." I persisted in pretending to misunderstand him; but at the same time remarked, that it was not customary with Europeans to make a confidant of a

Shooma, you, was the word he used for the English collectively.

stranger; to which he was about to reply, when a third person interrupted us by coming in, and the spy made off. *

The same evening, I witnessed a very extraordinary ceremony, which was repeated two or three times during my stay at Kirman. About five o'clock in the evening, a vast concourse, at least amounting to four or five hundred men, collected in the square of the Karwansuraé, and a Moollah, or priest, mounted up on the top of a pyramid of steps in the centre; he then commenced reading in a very loud and sonorous voice, the adventures and sufferings of Allee, the son-in-law of Mohummud; and the whole party gradually melted into tears and cried like children. I thought at first that their grief was only pretended, but soon became convinced to the contrary. The Moollah was repeatedly obliged to desist from reading, and sat sobbing with the tears running over his beard for ten minutes; nor were many of the auditory less affected. I confess I could not look on this scene with perfect calmness, and my people were nearly as much distressed as the Persians. The congregation was composed of persons of all ages, from boys of ten or twelve years old to men of seventy or eighty; and it was impossible to see such a number of them all weeping most piteously without feeling something like respect and awe for a religion, however erroneous, which had so sincere an effect on the believers of it.

A Karwan being expected to set out for Sheeraz on the *25th*, I prepared myself to accompany it, conceiving that it was needless to wait any longer at Kirman, in the hope of Captain Christie's arrival from Heerat. The minister hearing of this resolution, sent a man

* The employing of spies was very contrary to the general conduct of the Persian government towards General Malcolm's mission. It never betrayed the slightest jealousy of surveying, or any other steps that were taken to acquire a more complete knowledge of the kingdom and its resources. On this occasion, however, a doubt cannot exist. No person would have taken the trouble to come to me unless sent by the Prince's orders, and this was further corroborated by my ascertaining that the would-be Christian held one of the inferior offices of government.

to me on the *24th*, to inquire whether I wished to have an audience of leave previous to my departure or not; this honour I begged leave to decline, as the Prince had not shewn me the slightest mark of attention, and consequently I returned an answer to that purport. The messenger had left me about an hour, when the Darogha or overseer of the Karwansuraé made his appearance, and demanded the usual toll of one rupee on each of my camels, and likewise on a horse that I had purchased a few days before, accordingly, I paid him three rupees, and concluded, from the Karwansuraé being the private property of the Prince, that I should be exempt from any further charges. But the next morning he again called upon me, and said that he had forgotten the hire of the room which I had occupied. The amount of it being only half a rupee and a few copper coin *, curiosity tempted me to ask by whose directions he had returned for this *weighty* balance, and it was precisely what I had anticipated, when he most solemnly declared, by those of the Prince; adding, that had I agreed to visit His Royal Highness, I was to have been excused from paying this sum, and likewise the tolls levied on my cattle the preceding day. This confession I regarded as the very acmé of meanness; and I seriously interrogated the Darogha, how he could possibly imagine that the money, though multiplied by thousands, was an object in my estimation, or that of any other officer belonging to the British Government? I further reminded him that I had done my duty towards the Prince, by reporting myself on my arrival in his city; and that I was also capable of judging whether I had been properly treated and received. The Darogha, though a Persian, appeared ashamed of his royal master's conduct, and was about to make me a reply, I presume in extenuation of it, when I interrupted him by putting a rupee into his hand, and desiring that he would acquaint the Prince that he was welcome to the change.

About one shilling and ten-pence English money.

The Overseer pocketed the cash, made some remark to his servants on the justness of my sentiments, and marched off; after which adventure I heard no more of the Prince or his deputies, and about three in the afternoon of the same day, I quitted the city of Kirman, of which, as well as the province, the next chapter contains a succinct account.

CHAPTER XVI.

PROVINCE OF KIRMAN. — BOUNDARIES. — DIVISION. — LENGTH. — BREADTH. — SOIL. — FACE OF THE COUNTRY. — NO RIVERS. — SPRINGS. — KAREZES. — DESERT ENCROACHING. — MOUNTAINS. — SNOW LIES IN SUMMER. — BAD EFFECTS ON THE CLIMATE. — *GURMSEER.* — CITY OF KIRMAN. — SITE. — ONCE VERY OPULENT. — THE CAUSE EXPLAINED. — ANCIENT ACCOUNT OF IT. — TRADITIONS REGARDING ITS NAME. — CURIOUS. — WHAT THEY PROVE. — DIFFERENT CONQUERORS OF THIS CITY. — THE LAST SIEGE. — BY WHOM. — THE OVERTHROW OF THE LAST OF THE ZUND DYNASTY. — BARBARITY OF THE PRESENT KING'S UNCLE. — ENORMITIES COMMITTED BY HIS TROOPS ON THE CITIZENS. — THE CITY DEPOPULATED AND RAZED TO THE GROUND. — WHEN REBUILT. — GOVERNOR'S PALACE. — BAZARS. — KARWANSURAE'S. — POPULATION. — TRADE. — MANUFACTURES. — KARMANIAN WOOL. — SHAWLS MADE FROM IT. — CURIOUS FACT ABOUT THEM. — AMAZING FINENESS OF THE WOOL. — THE PROCESS OF PREPARING IT FOR THE LOOM. — EXPORTS AND IMPORTS OF KIRMAN. — REVENUES. — HOW REALIZED. — REVENUES OF THE PROVINCE. — TOWNS. — GOMBAROON OR BUNDER ABASS. — DISTANCE FROM KIRMAN. — STATE OF THE ROAD. — BRIEF HISTORY OF THIS TOWN. — IN WHOSE HANDS AT PRESENT. — TRIBUTE. — ACTUAL CONDITION. — POPULATION. — KIRMAN DESERT. — EXTENT. — SUFFERINGS OF THE UFFGHAN ARMY IN IT. — TOWN OF KHUBEES. — REMARKABLE SITE. — INHABITANTS. — THEIR PROFESSION. — ROUTE AND NARRATIVE RESUMED.

THE Province of Kirman is bounded on the east by a part of Seistan and Beloochistan; west by the Province of Fars; south by parts of Laristan, Mukran, and the Persian Gulph; and north by Eerak and Khorasan. It has from the earliest ages been partitioned into the habitable and desert regions, a division which I purpose adopting, proceeding, in the first place, to a consideration of the former. Its extreme length, from Regan in Nurmansheer, to Robat on the boundary of Fars, is about three hundred and sixty-five miles; and its breadth, from the southern limit of Eerak to the town of Gombaroon or Bunder Abass, on the shores of the Persian Gulph, about two hundred and eighty*. Even the soil of this tract is in many places very unprolific, and the face of the country barren and waste.

There is not a river in the province †, and were it not for a few springs in the mountainous districts, and the Karezes or aqueducts described in my diary of the *2d of May*, the natives could not possibly exist. As it is, water is procured with extraordinary pains and attention, and withal not more than is sufficient to cultivate a very trifling portion of the soil. Nurmansheer forms an exception to the aridity of the earth, but even there the vast supplies of water that formerly inundated that district, have decreased very much within these last twenty years; and the extensive desolate plains that I passed previous to reaching Bumm and Kirman, seem to argue, that the desert is fast encroaching in that quarter, which the inhabitants avow is undoubtedly the case.

Generally speaking, Kirman is a very mountainous province; the principal range of mountains is that which divides Nurmansheer from Laristan, and thence running in a south-westerly direction, approaches within four days journey of Gombaroon. It here seems to take the turn of the coast, and trending away to the west and north-west, joins the mountains of Fars in the latitude of 29° 40′ north, and longitude 54° east. In this course it throws out numerous ramifications, both to the northward and southward. Many of the former, particularly the more easterly ones, which stretch into the desert, terminate between the thirtieth and thirty-first degrees of latitude; while some

* I here speak of a direct line. The curvature of the roads rendered it nearly double the distance from Regan to Robat.

† As I travelled from east to west through this province, I assert this from indubitable evidence. The Ushkoo, which I passed the day after I left Bumm, (April 30th,) can only be looked upon as a mountain torrent, when filled by rain. There are three or four beds of the same description in the route from Kirman to Bunder Abass, but in my opinion it would be a misapplication of the word to call them rivers.

of the western arms reach the province of Eerak. They are in some places, from their height, scarcely worthy of being called any thing but hills, and in others are no way inferior to the great mass from which they have their rise. So entirely do they intersect the country, that the plains which they separate, are seldom seen to exceed ten or twelve miles in breadth, though often of an indefinite length.

The climate of this province is as varied as the face of the country, and it is accounted the least salubrious of any part of Persia; they have seldom any heavy falls of rain, but snow lies to a great depth on the mountains in winter, and from their loftiness it does not melt for the greater part of the year, so that it is not unusual to see the people in the plains panting from the extreme heat, while it is freezing on the summits of the mountains close to them. The air that blows down from them is very cool and luxurious, but brings agues, fevers, and other diseases as its attendants; and the natives dread it so much, and so often experience its baneful effects, that they prefer the most sultry weather.

To the southward of the great chain of mountains that I have described above, and between their bases and the sea, lies the Gurmseer or Hot Country, being a narrow stripe from thirty to ten leagues in breadth, which extends all along the sea-coast of Persia from Meenab, the capital of Laristan, to the mouth of the Shat Ool-Arab or Bussorah River. Within the limits of Kirman this tract is almost solely composed of saline sand, and the climate is peculiarly unhealthy. It produces nothing but dates, which are of a very inferior quality, and is in consequence nearly depopulated.

The city of Kirman is situated in north latitude 29° 56', and east longitude 56° 6', on the western side of a capacious plain, so close to the mountains, that two of them, on which there are ancient decayed forts, completely command it. It was once the most flourishing in Persia, and in size was second to none except the capital, Isfahan. Its situation in the direct road from Khorasan, Bulkh, Bokhara, Mawur Ool Nuhr, or Trans Oxiana, and all the northern part of the Persian empire to the sea-port town of Bunder Abass, gave it incalculable advantages as an emporium, and rendered it the centre of wealth, luxury, and magnificence. Of the original founder of this famous city there exists no positive record, and all that I have been able to trace with certainty is, that on the Arab invasion the last of the ancient Persian Kings fled to it, and made it his capital until the complete subjugation of the empire and dispersion of the followers of Zoroaster. I learn from a manuscript history of the conquest of Mukran, in the 90th year of the Hijree, that Kirman was then a very extensive city, full (according to the Oriental phrase) of riches, and celebrated for the excellence of the shawls and arms made in it. On the whole, it is probable that we may fix its foundation, or at least the first step towards that grandeur and opulence which it attained, both previous and subsequent to the introduction of Mohummudanism, as coeval with the city of Hoormuz (Ormuz) on the coast of Kirman, which was built by one of the earliest monarchs of the line of Sassan, and, according to the manuscript I have just quoted, takes its name from him. The traditions respecting the name of Kirman are various, some derive it from Khirman, a word signifying a granary, as allusive to the abundance which flowed into it; and others relate that its origin and appellation both arose from the trivial circumstance of a Guebre Princess eating an apple near the site of the present city, in the core of which she found a Kirm or worm, and thereupon vowed that she would build a city which, like the worm in the apple, should extract the benefit from all the surrounding parts (countries). These fabulous accounts, though deserving of no credit, are nevertheless curious, as they evince the opinion which has always been entertained of its happily selected situation; a fact that alone can have enabled it to withstand the dreadful shocks it has experienced, for no city in the east has been more subject to reverses of fortune, or oftener the scene of the most destructive wars, both foreign and domestic, than Kirman.

To enter into any relation of these, comes not within my purpose. The Khaliphas, Jungeez Khan, Tymoorlung, the Uffghans, and Nadir Shah, repeatedly and successively took, plundered, and destroyed it; in addition to the civil broils, in which it has still more frequently fallen to the victor by storm. The last event of this kind happened so recently as the year 1794, when it was betrayed into the hands of Agha Mohummud Khan, (uncle of the present King, and founder of the Kajjar dynasty,) who had besieged it for several months, during which period the magnanimous Lootf Allee Khan * held out with astonishing perseverance and courage, although reduced to such distress, that two-thirds of his troops and the inhabitants perished for want of food and water. At length, on the night of the *2d of July*, 1794, a Sirdar called Nujuf Koolee Khan, was induced, by promises of pardon and a large bribe, to allow a detachment of Agha Mohummud Khan's troops to enter the city by a sally-port in that angle of the works which he had charge of, and they, running to one of the gates which had unfortunately not been built up, broke it open, and made way for the entrance of the whole of the army. Lootf Allee Khan, finding that all was lost, mounted his horse, and, supported by a few brave adherents, cut his way under cover of the dark night, through the besiegers. He fled to Bumm, where he was most treacherously seized by the Governor †, and sent to Agha Mohummud Khan, who, with his own hands, put out his eyes, and had him ultimately strangled at Teheran ‡. The city was given up for

* Lootf Allee Khan was the last of the Zund dynasty. The bulk of the Persians, to the present day, regret his death, as he was brave, and, what is rare amongst his countrymen, very generous even in prosperity.

† Mohamed Alli Khan Seistanee was Governor of Bumm at the period above alluded to. He had a brother in Lootf Allee Khan's service. When that chief arrived at Bumm, the Governor inquired for his brother, and on being assured he was safe, did not attempt to seize Lootf Allee, but treated him with great distinction. The day after, however, it was ascertained that he was a prisoner with Agha Mohummud Khan, and Lootf Allee was instantly laid hands on, to serve as his ransom. This treachery was not attended with the proposed effect, as the brother was one of those put to death at Kirman.

‡ To commemorate this entire downfall of the Zund dynasty, Agha Mohummud Khan decided on forming a pyramid of skulls on the spot where Lootf Allee Khan was taken; and for that purpose having decapitated six hundred prisoners, he dispatched their heads

three months to the incessant ravages and plunder of an exasperated army that, under the sanction of its chiefs, committed the most unheard of enormities. The wives and daughters of the citizens, and of the latter class even children of a few years of age, were publickly exposed to the brutality of the soldiery, in presence of their husbands and fathers, who were afterwards forced to receive them, thus dishonoured, or destroy them themselves on the spot. All the fortifications and elegant structures, with which the city had been beautified by the Uffghans *, were razed to the ground, and Agha Mohummud Khan, after sacrificing to his revenge every person of whose zeal for his cause (for with him it was not sufficient to be neutral) he had the slightest suspicion, carried thirty thousand of the inhabitants into slavery, or at least exiled them on pain of death to the distant provinces of Mazenderan and Aderbejan.

The city lay desolate for some years until after the accession of the present King, who directed the fortifications to be rebuilt on a reduced plan. They are, however, still very large, and consist of a high mud wall, with nineteen bastions in each face, and a dry ditch twenty yards wide and ten deep. The works are entirely encompassed by ruins that extend, on the southern and eastern sides, for some miles, and there is a considerable angle, of the space within the walls, which is yet quite deserted. The gates are four in number, and the ark or citadel, in which the Governor's palace is built, lies on the southern face of the fort; it is defended by similar works. The Bazar is well supplied with articles of every description, and from every nation; one part of it is covered in with very elegant domes, built of a beautiful kind of blue stone, dug from quarries in the adjacent mountains. There are either eight or nine Karwansuraés

to Bumm by half that number, forcing each man to carry two of his comrade's skulls. These unfortunate wretches met the same fate by his orders on their arrival there, and the pyramid still existed when I was at that city in 1810, a horrid evidence of the conqueror's implacable and blood thirsty disposition.

* The Uffghans were masters of this part of Persia for many years after their invasion.

within the walls, beside many inferior ones outside: that which I resided in is the private property of the Prince, but is neither so spacious or handsome as some of the others.

The population of Kirman is not now more than thirty thousand souls, of which a small proportion are Guebres or Parsees; but there are neither Armenians, Hindoos, or Jews, resident in the place. Some of the two former classes occasionally repair thither on business. The trade of Kirman, though still considerable, has never revived in a manner to be compared to what it was previous to its last depopulation, and in all likelihood never will again, as the resort of merchants to the sea-port town of Abooshuhr or Bushire, farther up the Gulph of Persia, daily gains ground, to the prejudice of Bunder Abass, and, of consequence, Kirman. Its manufactures of shawls, matchlocks, and Numuds, or felts, are celebrated all over Asia, and are said to afford employment to upwards of one third of the inhabitants, whether male or female. The former are made from the wool known by the ancient name of the province (Karamania), and I have seen them, in delicacy of fabrick and texture, outrival those of Kashmeer; but they are not equal in downy softness and warmth. The sheep from which the wool is sheared, for it is a mistaken idea that it falls off, are very small and short-legged: they have been removed to different parts of the kingdom, by orders of Futtuh Allee Shah the King, where, although the animals appear to thrive, the wool loses its qualities; and, what is still more unaccountable, it cannot be wrought to any perfection elsewhere than at Kirman. From this undoubted fact it is to be inferred that the climate, or water, of that city has something very peculiar in its nature; and it is very curious that a similar circumstance occurs with regard to the Province of Kashmeer. I visited all the principal weaving manufactories at Kirman; but saw nothing in that process to merit description: at one of them I procured specimens of wool which were finer and softer than any cotton I had ever seen, and some of the shawls I purchased there were so even and beautiful, that they were valued by shawl merchants in India, to whom I afterwards shewed them, at five hundred per cent. more than they cost. The wool, when first cut off, is repeatedly and carefully scoured and picked; after which it is immersed for some weeks in a wash, the ingredients of which are unknown to any save the makers, but seem to be chiefly formed from a decoction of different leaves and barks; this renders it pliant and soft, and fit for spinning, which last operation is executed by women, and the thread is then ready for the loom.

The Kirmanees chiefly send their shawls, numuds, and matchlocks to Khorasan, Kabool, Bulkh, Bokhara, and the northern provinces; and, in return, receive asafœtida, gums, rhubarb, madder, and other drugs; Bokhara skins, furs, silk, steel, copper, and tea: the latter three articles are for home consumption: they export the remainder to India, Sinde, Arabia, and the Red Sea, also Pistachio nuts, rose leaves, and buds, for making conserve, gums, cotton, carpets, and bullion; and import, from the former country, tin, lead, iron, copper, steel, pepper, and all other spices; chintz (both European and Indian), indigo, muslin, tea, satin, Keemkhab or gold-flowered silks, Zureebaf or gold-cloth, cocoa nuts, china, and glass-ware, broad-cloth, &c. &c. From Sinde they have white cloth and coloured Loongees for turbands; and, from Arabia and the Red Sea, coffee, gold-dust, ivory, musk, frankincense, slaves, &c. &c. *

The revenues of the city of Kirman were, in 1810, only twenty-five thousand Toomans per annum †; but were said to be rapidly increasing; and are appropriated by the Prince, with the permission of His Majesty, for the maintenance of his court and a body of troops, that are exclusively kept in pay for the protection of the city and its neighbourhood. They arise from the Bazar duties, which are

* The tea which the Persians bring from the northward comes through Siberia.

† A Tooman is eight rupees or one pound Sterling. Just two centuries before (1610), a greater *monthly* sum was paid from the same source into the treasury of Shah Abass the Great!!

very high, and a heavy tax on shawls * and matchlocks: beside which, every camel or horse that enters any Karwansuraé in the city pays one rupee as a toll; a poney, half a rupee; an ass, one quarter, &c. Those of the province are regularly accounted for at the royal treasury; and one of the ministers had been called up to Teheran for that purpose when I was at Kirman. I have not been able to ascertain with any precision their exact amount, but should guess about fifty thousand Toomans yearly, exclusive of the tribute of Bunder Abass. These are collected by a tax on lands, and the imposts levied at different towns. It may seem a small sum for so great an extent of country, but we are to recollect that the province is naturally barren and thinly inhabited. Its aggregate population I am quite unable to speak to.

The towns in the eastern part of this province I have already touched upon, and those westward of the capital will be hereafter noticed in my Narrative. To the northward there are none, and Gombaroon or Bunder Abass is the only one to the southward that needs to be mentioned. It lies eighteen Munzils, or days' marches, from Kirman, which we may average at eight Fursukhs each stage; and, consequently, the whole distance, from five hundred and fifty to six

* The tax on shawls has not long been laid on, and was attended with a circumstance which deserves to be mentioned as, in my opinion, peculiarly illustrative of the present government, not only of Kirman, but all Persia. The Prince, finding that the manufacture was very much increased, and likely to be still more so, issued a proclamation apprizing the inhabitants of the city and province, that, after a certain day, any person who was found purchasing a shawl without the government stamp upon it, should be heavily fined. An office, at the same time, was opened for stamping the shawls, which it was the business of the purchaser to get done, before he received them from the maker. The people concluding that an order so couched was not to have a retrospective effect, continued to wear those shawls bought and in use before its publication. The Prince, however, meant very differently, and as soon as the necessary time had elapsed, he had the whole city searched, and fined every person in whose house a single shawl was discovered without the stamp. By this deep stroke of Persian policy, it is said, he netted above one lac of rupees, including the price of the shawls which were seized and sold on account of the government.

hundred miles. Gombaroon was anciently the seat of vast traffic, as it served for the continental Bunder, or emporium, of the island of Ormuz; and when Shah Abass, the Great, wrested that mart from the Portuguese, about the year 1623, he transferred the whole commerce of it, then the most extensive in Asia, if not in the world, to Gombaroon, and honoured that town by calling it Bunder Abass, or the port of Abass. It flourished for a short time, but on the death of Abass in 1629-30, his successors had either not the means or the wish to protect this colony, which was soon harassed by the people on the sea coast of Laristan, and other predatory and piratical tribes. The English and Portuguese companies gradually withdrew their agents and factories, and as other speculators were deterred from venturing there with their goods, owing to the imbecility of the government and its inability to afford them a safeguard, the place went rapidly to decay. It still carries on trade with Muskat, and several ports of India, the Red Sea, and east coast of Africa; and is garrisoned by the troops of the Imam * of the former town, who pays an annual tribute to the King of Persia of four thousand Toomans †, which amount is reported, in some years, to exceed the whole customs. The town is dirty and ill-built: the streets narrow, dark, and choked up with ruins; and, till within these six years, the works were equally neglected; but the alarm caused by the Juwassmee Arab pirates induced the Imam to repair them, and they are now capable of making a tolerable defence against an Asiatic enemy.

I have already said that the greater part of the intervening country between Kirman and Bunder Abass is barren and inhospitable, and there are only a few miserable villages. There was formerly a large and elegant Karwansuraé at each stage, built by Abass the Great, but they have been allowed to go to decay, and the systematic avarice of

* Imam, a religious leader. The title assumed by the Chief of Muskat.

† 4000l. Sterling, or 32,000 rupees.

the Persian government leaves no chance of their being repaired. The total population of Bunder Abass is about twenty thousand souls, and composed of Arabs, Hindoos, Persians, Indians, and other foreigners.

The desert region of the province of Kirman extends in length two hundred and seventy miles, from the northern boundary of Nurmansheer, in latitude 29° 30′ north, to the mountains of Khorasan, in latitude 34° north; and, in breadth, two hundred miles from the city of Yezd, in longitude 55° 40′ east, to a range of mountains separating it from Seistan, in 60° east. The soil of this tract is impregnated to such a degree with salt, and so decidedly barren, that it does not even produce grass, or any other vegetation, for eighty or ninety miles at a stretch; and water is entirely out of the question. The Uffghan army, on its march to invade Persia in 1719, suffered the most dreadful hardships in this waste, and after one third of the whole had perished, the remainder reached Nurmansheer with the loss of all their equipage and baggage. There is a path through it from Kirman to Heerat in Khorasan, by which couriers can go in eighteen days; but the risk of perishing is so great, that a person of that description demanded two hundred rupees to take a letter from me to Captain Christie, who had directed me to write to him.

The town of Khubees lies nearly in the centre of it, in latitude 32° 20′ north, on a spot which is verdant the whole year round, and has many pleasant gardens. It seems to have been founded as a place of refuge, or intended, in former times, to promote the trade between Persia and Seistan, as it is equi-distant from those countries. It formerly flourished, and was the residence of a Beglerbeg on the part of the chief of Seistan, but now is a miserable decayed place, and the inhabitants are notorious robbers and outcasts who subsist by infesting the highways of Khorasan and Persia, and plundering Karawans. When they are pursued, they retire by paths only known to themselves, through the desert to their homes.

It is very remarkable, that the water in the gardens at Khubees, and to a distance of three or four miles round that town, should be very fresh and plentiful; but, beyond that circle, the desert stretches on every side for many days' journey, without a blade of grass or a bush. I now resume the Narrative of my route.

CHAPTER XVII.

LUCKY DAY. — MESSENGER FROM SHEERAZ. — VILLAGE OF ROBAT. — INTERMEDIATE TRACT. — FORT OF BAGEEN. — VERY LONG MARCH. — ARRIVAL AT KILLAHE' AGHA. — COUNTRY. — BAZAR. — CHIEF. — HIS DOUBTS REGARDING THE AUTHOR. — POLITENESS. — FORT OF PA KILLAH. — ROAD. — CITY OF YEZD. — ROUTE INFESTED BY THIEVES. — PRECAUTIONS TAKEN. — KOTHULS OR PASSES. — TOWN OF MEENAM. — FORMED OF CAVERNS. — DESCRIPTION OF IT. — ITS INHABITANTS. — NOT ORTHODOX MOOSULMANS. — THEIR TENETS. — TOLERATION. — GREATER IN PERSIA THAN ELSEWHERE. — THE CAUSE EXPLAINED. — THE HABITS OF THE MEENAM PEOPLE. — ROUTE CONTINUED. — COUNTRY. — SHUHRI' BABIC. — BEAUTIFUL GARDENS. — INCREDIBLE PRODUCE IN FRUIT. — BAZARS. — PLAN OF THE TOWN. — THE SEAT OF A LIEUTENANT GOVERNOR. — ARRIVAL AT ROBAT. — CAPITAL ROAD. — RICH PLAIN. — TOBACCO AND ROSES. — SOORSANT. — SYUDS OF ROBAT. — RESPECTABLE MEN. — LUDICROUS AFFRAY. — WRESTLING. — VILLAGE OF KHURRAH. — UNCULTIVATED PLAIN. — HAMLET OF KHOONSAR. — RIVER OF LIQUID SALT. — APPEARANCE OF IT AND THE PLAIN. — COUNTRY VERY PICTURESQUE. — ELYAUTS. — ROMANTIC VALLEY OF KHOONSAR. — VILLAGE OF MUZAR. — NO BAZAR. — ADVANCE. — HALT. — BAD ROAD. — DEFILE OF URSINJAN. — WHENCE SO CALLED. — TOWN OF URSINJAN. — GARDENS. — STREAMS. — VILLAGE OF KUNJAN. — BUND UMEER RIVER. — FERTILITY AND RICHNESS OF THE CIRCUMJACENT DISTRICTS. — ROAD. — CANALS. — GREAT DEPTH. — BRIDGE OVER THE BUND UMEER. — RUINOUS STATE. — REFLECTION ON THIS RIVER. — FACT PROVED BY IT. — THE AUTHOR ARRIVES AT SHEERAZ. — MINISTER'S ATTENTION. — VISITS TO HIM AND THE PRINCE. — AUTHOR'S REASONS FOR CLOSING HIS NARRATIVE. — GARDEN OF THE JUHAN NOOMA. — TOMB OF HAFIZ. — DEPARTURE FROM SHEERAZ. — TOWN OF ZERGAN. — PERSEPOLIS. — SURHUD ROAD. — BOUNDARY OF THE PROVINCE OF FARS. — TOWN OF YEZDIKHAST. — GREAT COLD AT NIGHT. — STAY AT ISFAHAN. — THE AUTHOR IS JOINED BY HIS FELLOW TRAVELLER, CAPTAIN CHRISTIE. — HIS FEELINGS ON THAT EVENT. — PALACES AND OTHER CURIOSITIES OF ISFAHAN. — PAINTINGS. — STAINED GLASS. — ENAMELLING. — BAZARS OF ISFAHAN. — EXTENSIVE. — EQUALLED BOTH AT SHEERAZ AND KIRMAN. — LEAVE ISFAHAN. — ARRIVAL AT KASHAN. — ACCOUNT OF THAT CITY, ITS PRODUCTIONS AND SCITE. — RAPID MARCHES MADE BY THE

AUTHOR AND HIS COMPANIONS. — VILLAGE OF MEEANA. — KAFILAN KOH. — KUZL-OOZEEN RIVER. — BRIDGE. — STRIKING SCENERY. — JOIN GENERAL MALCOLM AT MURAGHA. — CAPTAIN CHRISTIE SELECTED TO STAY IN PERSIA. — FOR WHAT PURPOSE. — ABSTRACT OF HIS ROUTE AFTER HE LEFT THE AUTHOR AT NOOSHKY. — THE MISSION QUITS MURAGHA. — ARRIVAL AT BAGDAD BY THE ROUTE OF SENNA AND KIRMANSHAH. — PASSAGE DOWN THE RIVERS TIGRIS AND SHATOOL ARAB. — THE AUTHOR'S DETENTION AT BUSSARAH. — RETURN TO BOMBAY.

MAY *25th.* We moved only six miles as a commencement to our journey, the day being exceedingly lucky, according to the belief of my fellow travellers, and stopped near some ruins and a garden. I met the Kasid, or messenger, whom I had dispatched to General Malcolm on my first arrival, a little way from the city; and by the letters that he brought me, I had the first intimation of his having left Sheeraz on his advance to the Persian court.

26th May. We mounted at one *a. m.* and after a tedious march of forty miles, halted at noon at a small village called Robat, where there is a very large Karwansuraé, with stabling for five or six hundred horses, falling to decay. The direction of this march varied from west south-west to west by north; it is reckoned ten Fursukhs (Parasangs), and the road is level and excellent the whole way. Thirty miles from Kirman we passed close to Bageen, a small fortlet, and the first stage for laden cattle; but our mules were light, and therefore we proceeded ten miles further.

27th May. We left Robat at eight *p. m.* on the *26th*, and arrived at the fort of Killahé Agha *, at noon on the *27th*; the intermediate distance being sixty-three miles, of which upwards of fifty were over a hard level tract, interspersed with jungul; the remainder a well cultivated and level plain between the mountains (which here approach), with abundance of water. Killahé Agha was once considered a strong place, and made a stout resistance against the army

* The fort of the master or lord.

of Agha Mohummud Khan, when he passed here on his way to besiege Kirman. The fort has been since repaired, and there is a tolerable Bazar, in which all kinds of supplies requisite for a traveller are to be had. The Kud Khoda or chief man of the town, hearing that I was an European, came to visit me, and seemed much amazed to find me in the Persian costume, which I now completely assumed. He was in the room some time staring about, before he asked where I was, and to the last expressed his doubts of my being a real Firingee or European; nevertheless he was extremely polite, and sent me a large dish of remarkably fine cherries, in return for which I gave his man a small present of money.

28th May. From Killahé Agha to Pa Killah *, a small fort built on the summit of a rocky precipice. This stage is above thirty miles, whereof the first fifteen were across a fertile plain, and the latter among, or over mountains with an excessively intricate and bad road. These mountains stretch to the northward to the city of Yezd, the road to which branches off about three miles from Killahé Agha. The average direction was a little to the southward of west; and there is plenty of forage for horses and camels in this route; but it is hazardous to travel it without a well armed party, being a famous rendezvous for highwaymen. My fellow-travellers fully expected to have encountered some of them; and we all rode while it was dark (having set out about three *a. m.*) with our pieces loaded, and the matches ready lighted.

29th May. We left Pa Killah at two in the afternoon, and having clambered and toiled over a continued series of difficult and rocky Kothuls or defiles, at the end of eight miles we came to the town of Meenan, consisting of three or four hundred caverns excavated out of the face of the mountain, along which they extend for a quarter of a mile. Some of these subterraneous dwellings were dug one above another, with a shelving path or steps, to ascend to the upper

* The firm fort.

ones; but in general they were all on one floor, with a large apartment in the centre, and recesses on each side. I went into several of them, under pretence of purchasing barley and forage for my cattle, and found they were kept in the filthiest state imaginable. The population seemed to have been formerly larger, as there were many caves unoccupied. The inhabitants of Meenan are not orthodox Moosulmans, but of a sect known by the name of Alioollyahs *, who hold, as the leading tenet of their faith, that the Almighty deigned for the benefit of mankind, to appear upon earth in the person of Allee, the son-in-law of Mohumud; they believe the latter to have been an inspired person, but regard almost all the doctrines of the Koran, as interpolations of the Imams †, who had it transcribed in its present shape. This sect meets with greater toleration in Persia, than in any other part of Asia, owing to the reverence with which the Sheeas are used to consider the character of Allee; but even that does not entirely protect them, and they are often persecuted, and always spoken of with detestation and abhorrence. Their habits are pastoral, and they keep vast flocks of goats and sheep.

30th May. A westerly march of twenty-six miles, of which ten were over a continuation of the range of mountains, and the remainder a fertile, though chiefly uncultivated plain, brought us at eleven *a. m.* to Shuhré Babic ‡ or Bababeg, which has formerly been a very handsome city, though now gone entirely to ruin. The avenues into the town from all parts, are planted on either side with orange, lemon, mulberry, almond, walnut, cherry, and pomegranate trees; and the profusion of those fruits, beside grapes, apples, apricots, peaches, nectarines, quinces, currants, plums, figs, and pears, produced here, is so incredible, that the natives make a proverb of

* This cannot be translated literally. It means people who believe that Allee is God.

† The immediate successors of the Prophet were called Imams, or leaders in a religious sense.

‡ The city of Babic or Bababeg.

it, and say, If all Persia, save this district, were a desert, Shuhré Babic would supply it with fruit. The gardens are said, notwithstanding, to be much fallen off; but, in my opinion, they still far surpass those of Isfahan or Sheeraz, in beauty and taste.

The city has four gates, from each of which long streets lead to a market-place in the centre, and divide it at right angles. The principal streets, as well as the market-place, have been covered the whole length with domes; but the greater part of those over the streets have tumbled in, and what remain are in a tottering state. The dome over the market-place is still very perfect, and is the largest in Persia.

Shuhre Babic lies equi-distant from Kirman, Sheeraz, and Yezd, and the bulk of the merchandize from the two latter cities was, some years back, conveyed by this route to Bunder Abass; the customs of it were then very considerable; and a Lieutenant-Governor still resides here, who officiates under the superintendance of the Prince at Kirman.

31st May. From Shuhré Babic to a small walled village called Robat, on the western confine of the Province of Kirman, the distance twenty-eight miles, a capital road leading over a spacious plain with many villages, and much culture, particularly in tobacco and roses; the latter were at this time in bloom, and as we rode among the plantations, diffused a delightful fragrance. The cultivators pluck those intended to make rose-water before they are full blown, and the buds for conserve still sooner. The tobacco of this and the neighbouring districts is the mildest and best in the world: it is usually sold under the name of Sheeraz tobacco, from an erroneous idea that it grows at that city; but what is produced there, is not comparable in flavour or delicacy.

My companions regretted quitting the Province of Kirman, being provided with a warrant of the Prince for demanding Soorsaut * for

* Soorsaut is an allowance authorized by Government to be levied on the inhabitants of towns and villages, by travellers and others. It is supposed that a deduction is made

themselves and cattle, of which they took especial care to avail themselves with uniform regularity. The village of Robat is peopled by Syyuds, who appear an industrious well-behaved set of men, and wanting that arrogance and contempt for their fellow-creatures, which so often distinguishes those who claim the same descent *. There is not a Karwansuraé, or any accommodation for travellers here, and we were therefore allowed to put up in the mosque.

A most ludicrous affray occurred during our halt here, between the muleteers and a man who happened to be travelling with us under a feigned name. One of the former had a dispute with him on some trifling point, which terminated in a challenge to decide it by a wrestling match, and they set to in the mosque, the floor of which was made of burnt tiles; the muleteer strove in vain to throw our disguised companion, who at length seized a good opportunity, and tossed his unskilful opponent several yards up into the air, whence he fell with such violence on the flags, that he lay quite stunned. His fellow-drivers, who had previously enjoyed the fun, now thought of punishing the victor, and having prefaced their actions with a torrent of abuse, three of them assailed him; but they all shared the same fate with their discomfited brother-whip, and were pitched into different corners of the mosque, with joints almost dislocated. Subsequent to this rencontre, the winner offered to wrestle with six of them at one time, but they had not the temerity to enter the lists against him. †

in the collection of the revenue on this account, whenever it occurs, but the cultivators never reckon upon any remuneration, for, even though it should be admitted, the chief of the place usually appropriates the advantage to himself. This ruinous system is peculiarly distressing, when a mission passes through the country, as all the followers fancy they have a right to the same indulgence, and, if not checked, would not hesitate to help themselves. I saw the mules of one party driven into fields of standing grain, when the villagers refused to obey the warrant.

* Syyuds are lineal descendants of Mohummud.

† This man, whose real name was Allee Uskur, confessed to me that he was the champion wrestler of Persia: his disguise he accounted for by the following story, which Cap-

1st June. We made two marches within these twenty-four hours; the first from Robat to Kurrah, thirty miles over an uncultivated plain, overgrown in some spots with jungul; and the second from Kurrah to the deserted hamlet of Khoonsar, a distance of fourteen miles. Half-way between the two former places, we crossed a river of liquid salt, so deep as to take my horse to the knees; the surface of the plain, for several hundred yards on each side, was entirely hid by a thick incrustation of white salt, resembling a fall of frozen snow, that crackled under the horses' hoofs; the stream was likewise covered with large flakes of a similar nature, but not compact enough to prevent the horses and mules from walking through it. Khurrah is a neat village, and travellers can be supplied with every thing in its bazar.

The country from Khurrah to Khoonsar is picturesque and romantic beyond imagination. It consists of low and luxuriant vallies or plains, intersected and separated by ranges of low mountains that were green to their very summits, with beautiful turf. Through one of these the path is cut out of the rock for fifty yards and upwards, so very narrow that only one mule can pass at a time. The road was otherwise very tolerable, and forage may be had in every vale from

tain Christie afterwards told me he had heard at the city of Yezd, his native place. The King's principal wrestler about two years before, had challenged any man in Persia to a trial of strength in the King's presence, and Allee Uskur travelled up to court for the purpose of coping with him. The yard in which they wrestled, had a fountain in the centre of it; and after some exertions on both sides, the acceptor of the challenge took his antagonist up in his arms, and dashed him into the fountain with such tremendous force, that he broke his thigh, and otherwise so dreadfully bruised him that he died in a few weeks. The King banished Allee Uskur from the empire, but he lay concealed, and in the autumn of 1809, when the King was on his return from the plain of Sooltaneeah to Teheran, he met him four Fursukhs, or nearly sixteen miles from that city, and walked backwards in front of his horse, playing a pair of immense clubs round his head, without the slightest intermission, or ever looking at the ground. The King was so pleased at this display of strength, that he pardoned him, and he once more appeared in public, but the relations of the deceased wrestler still vowed vengeance against him, and at the time I saw him, he was flying from Kirman, to which city they had traced him.

the Eellyauts, or wandering tribes, who reside under black felt tents. We found an encampment of them at Khoonsar, which is, without exception, the most beautiful spot I met with in any quarter of Persia. A brook glided down the bottom of the dale through fields of wheat and rice; the tents were erected on the brow of a hill, close to a grove of large walnut trees, that extended along the whole side of the valley; flocks of sheep and goats were browsing on lofty precipices within a few yards of the shepherd's door; and the complacent looks and active industry of the inhabitants, taught me, for the first time, to know, that it was possible to live contented in Persia.

2d June. From Khoonsar to Muzar, fourteen miles west, through a country, as yesterday, abounding with fine scenery. Muzar is a miserable village, without bazar or supplies, although the Eellyauts have cultivated a considerable portion of ground in its neighbourhood.

3d June. We left Muzar at three *a.m.*; and, after a march of forty-two miles, halted at sunset in the plain, there being no village within two Fursukhs. The whole of this day, mountains were near us on both hands, and the road was stony and rugged; it lay principally through a valley varying from four miles to four hundred yards in breadth, with a great deal of impenetrable jungul, but no water. At the western end of it is the defile of Ursinjan, so called from a town of that name which bore north of us at the thirty-eighth mile. This defile, in some places, does not exceed fifty yards in width, and is nearly one league in length. The mountains on each side ascend perpendicularly to a great altitude; and, were its natural strength aided by artificial improvements, I think it might be rendered tenable by a very small division against the largest army.

The town of Ursinjan is the seat of a Hakim or governor, and seemed to be a large place encompassed by extensive gardens. It is situated in a valley, encircled by hills that are in the highest degree cultivated, and abundantly stored with running streams, one of which turns ten or twelve water-mills in the course of half a mile.

4th June. We left our halting-place this morning at four *a. m.*, and proceeded over a fertile and highly improved level tract, twenty miles; at the twelfth of which is a neat village named Kunjan; and three miles in advance from it we passed a bridge over the Bund Umeer river * (here called, by the natives, the Koolbar). The cultivation of rice in this plain is inconceivably great, and my fellow travellers informed me that these districts were admitted to be by far the richest and cheapest in the Persian empire; a distinction to which they bear sufficient evidence of their claim, as I could at one time distinctly count upwards of thirty towns and villages entirely encompassed, and connected with each other by tilled ground. The road was excellent throughout; but there are numerous small bridges built over the canals, that intersect the plain in every direction for the purposes of irrigation, that, if broken down, would (for a time at least) obstruct all intercourse. Some of these canals are thirty and forty feet deep, and usually not more than five or six in breadth. The bridge over the Bund Umeer is (like every other work of that kind that I saw in Persia) in a state of ruin, and must very shortly fall in. When I crossed it, there were many large apertures through the pavement of it, across which some one had laid branches of trees to warn travellers at night. It consists of twelve arches, and the river has a most beautiful appearance from the top of it, gliding down between vast districts of rice cultivation, and diffusing plenty over the soil.

Since landing at Sonmeany, I had now performed a journey of upwards of one thousand five hundred miles, of which thirteen hun-

* The Bund Umeer river, or the river of the dyke of the Noble, is so called from a Bund, or dyke, built across it about eight centuries ago by the Umeer Azad ood Doulee, in the reign of Ul Kadir, the twenty-fifth Khalipha of the house of the Abbassides. This Bund was formed for the purpose of confining the waters to one channel, until they entered the plain of Meerdusht, in which the ruins of Persipolis stand, whence they are diverted by canals all over the face of the country.

dred were in as direct a line, as the paths would admit, from east to west; and yet this was the first place in which I had seen a running stream sufficiently deep to have taken a horse above the knee, a conclusive proof of the extraordinary aridity of the intermediate countries; and furnishing an example perhaps unparalleled on the face of the globe, when the diversity of soil, temperature, and appearance of the surface, that I found in them, is taken into consideration.

After passing the Koolbar, we advanced five miles, and having halted for a few hours, moved on again six miles across the plain. Here we entered a narrow valley, between two high ranges of mountains, which continued in a direct westerly line thirty-four miles to the plain of Sheeraz, which city I had the satisfaction of reaching about nine *a. m.* on the morning of the *5th June.* I immediately went to the palace of Mohummud Nubee Khan, the minister of Fars, who directed one of his servants to accompany me to the house occupied by Lieutenant Little of the Madras Native Infantry, which officer had remained at Sheeraz, on the advance of the mission to court, as one of the political assistants of Brigadier General Malcolm, to transact any business that might arise between the Ambassador and the Government of Fars. About two hours after my arrival, the Minister sent several trays of sweetmeats and fruit, as a present of welcome to me, together with his formal inquiries after my health, and I once more began to fancy myself a British officer.

On the *6th of June* I visited the Minister, who received and treated me with great cordiality and attention. On the 11*th* I was introduced to Prince Mohummud Allee Meerza, who is Beglerbeg of the Province of Fars, and Governor of the city of Sheeraz. He is a remarkably handsome young man, and was most superbly dressed in a vest entirely covered with pearls and precious stones; and the style and etiquette of his court was quite correspondent in magnificence and splendour with his own person. There was, however, nothing in the reception different from the common forms. I chatted for some time with His Royal Highness, through the Urz Begee or master of the ceremonies, and after Kullyans were brought, he signified his wish for me to take leave.

I have now brought to a conclusion all that portion of my tour through Beloochistan and Persia, which has the advantage of novelty to recommend it for perusal, and shall therefore close this Narrative with a few very brief memoranda of my subsequent proceedings, until my return to India.

The works which have lately appeared from the pens of Mr. Morier and Lieutenant Macdonald Kinneir, of the Madras Native Infantry *, combined with those which the world have reason to expect from some of the literary gentlemen of the various missions that have of late years been deputed to the Persian court, will complete our knowledge of the present state of that empire, in every point of view, to a degree that could scarcely have been hoped for; and although I did not cease, while in Persia, to prosecute my inquiries on such subjects as I have included in the preceding sheets, yet, for the above reason, I feel that it would be most unnecessarily increasing the size of this volume, to enter into any discussion regarding them, and more especially so, as others have had much longer and better opportunities of qualifying themselves for the task.

During my stay at Sheeraz, I availed myself of so good an opportunity to see and visit every place worthy of attention. Those which principally struck me, were the garden of the Juhan Nooma, or displayer of the world, and the tomb of Hafiz. The former was made by the Wukeel Kureem Khan, Zund, and the summer houses erected in it, command a most enchanting prospect of the city and circumjacent country. One of them is called the Koollahé Firingee, or European's hat, from its fancied resemblance in shape to a cocked hat. The tomb of Hafiz is a gloomy and, in my opinion, ugly

* Morier's Travels in Persia, and Kinneir's Geographical Memoir of the Persian Empire.

building, but the transcript of one of the poems of that poet, which is cut on it in the most exquisite Persian character, renders it an object of great curiosity. It is said, how truly I know not, that the best and oldest copy of his works extant, is kept within the tomb, but on my asking to see it, I was informed that the person who had charge of this relique was absent. The white marble with which the tomb is formed, is become from exposure to the weather, very much discoloured, and adds to the sombre effect produced by the cypress trees that surround it.

I quitted Sheeraz on the 11*th of June*, in company with John Cormick, Esq. surgeon on the Madras establishment, and attached to Brigadier-General Malcolm's mission. Our first march was to Zergan, a very nice town, built immediately at the base of a lofty mountain, and the second to a garden within one mile of the far-famed ruins of Persepolis, where we halted two days to admire them. In this second stage we passed the Bund Umeer river, by a ruinous bridge of nine arches. It is neither so broad or deep here, as in the place I crossed it at on my route from Kirman. From Persepolis we took the Surhud or cold road to Isfahan, where we arrived on the 27*th of June*, having made in all ten marches from Sheeraz, seven in the Province of Fars, and three in that of Eerak. The dividing boundary is a very deep water-course at the town of Yezdé-Khast, a part of which literally overhangs the bed beneath. There is an excellent new Karwansurae here, but all the others on this road are in the most dilapidated condition. Although this was the warmest season in Persia, we frequently found it so exceedingly chilly, while marching at night, that we were glad to dismount, and walk for some miles to warm ourselves.

We remained at Isfahan eight or nine days, and, in the interim, had the sincere pleasure of being joined by Captain Christie from Heerat and Yezd. It seldom falls to the lot of man to experience sensations of such perfect gratification as this meeting afforded us both, and, if possible, those sensations were augmented by its being quite unexpected. Captain Christie arrived in the city about dusk, unknowing and unknown, and went to the governor's palace to request a lodging, which was ordered, when, by accident, one of the attendants observed that there were two Firingees in the Chihul Setoon *; and that he would possibly like to join their party; he accordingly came to the palace, and sent up a man to say that he wished to speak to one of us. I went down, and as it was then quite dark, I could not recognise his features; and he fancying me a Persian, from my dress, we conversed for several minutes ere we discovered each other. The moment we did so, was one of the happiest of my life.

The greater part of each day we spent in viewing the palaces and other curiosities of this immense city. In one or two of the palaces there are some very good paintings by European and Persian artists. Those of the latter are chiefly of historical subjects, and many of the figures are said to be excellent likenesses. The groupes in one or two battles are admirably managed, and though the whole is deficient in the very essential point of perspective, yet they convey a correct idea of the costume and manner of fighting in Persia during the last two centuries. There is likewise one palace built by the present Intizam ood doulu, Mohummud Hoossein Khan, and presented to the King five or six years ago, which gives a perfect notion of the present style of architecture in Persia. The windows of it display some very beautiful specimens of stained glass and enamelling, arranged in couplets in honour of the Shah, and quotations from the Koran. Beneath this palace there is a complete range of Surdabs, or subterraneous apartments, intended to reside in during the hot weather.

The Bazars of Isfahan are more extensive than any other in Persia, but I look upon the Bazari Wukeel, or Wukeel's Bazar, at Sheeraz, and the Bazari judeed, or new Bazar, at Kirman, to be no way inferior with regard to style or beauty of materials. There are several

* One of the palaces in which Doctor Cormick and myself were permitted to put up.

glass manufactories at Isfahan, and some of the bottoms for Kullyans blown and cut there, would do credit to an English artisan.

Mr. Cormick, Captain Christie, and I, resumed our journey from Isfahan on the *9th of July*, and, on the *14th*, reached the city of Kashan. This city, from being nothing more than a heap of ruins, is become, within these few years, by the exertions of Mohummud Hoossein Khan, Intizam Ood doulu, the most flourishing place in Persia. Its staples are copper ware, carpets, and coloured and flowered silks, which latter are exquisitely beautiful. I purchased some of them made in scarfs, in imitation of the richest Kashmeer shawls, of which they had all the brilliancy of colour combined with the glossy appearance of the silk. Kashan is situated on the southern extreme of the great salt desert that extends northerly to the mountains of Mazenderan. The soil around it is sandy, and abounds so plentifully with scorpions and tarantulas, that the sting of a Kashan scorpion is proverbial.

A rumour reached us the day we halted at Kashan, that Brigadier General Malcolm was shortly to have his audience of leave from the King, preparatory to the return of the Mission to India; and being very desirous of getting up to Oojan, at which place the Oordoo or royal camp was then established, previous to that event, we travelled with all possible expedition, ten very long marches to Meeana, a village built at the foot of a pass over the Kafilan Koh, or mountain of Tigers. At the bottom of this mountain runs the Kuzl Oozeen or golden stream, across which there is a very ancient bridge of eight arches of different dimensions. The height of the bridge is immense, and the scenery from the top of it strikingly picturesque. As you ascend the pass there are some ruinous bastions and walls on the right side of the road, which is partly formed by a very substantial causeway, begun by Shah Abass the First, and finished by Shah Abass the Great. The Kuzloozeen forms the boundary of the provinces of Eeraké Ujumee or Persian Eerak and Aderbejan.

The day we arrived at Meeana, we were met by a Chuppur, or mounted messenger, with letters directing us to join General Malcolm by the nearest cross route, at Muragha, twenty Fursukhs to the south-westward of Tabreez. We accordingly struck off the high road leading to the latter city, and at the end of the third march found ourselves once more in the society of our numerous friends, from whom we had parted just seven months antecedent at Bombay. Within this period Captain Christie had traversed a distance computed by him at two thousand two hundred and fifty miles, while the aggregate of my routes amounted to two thousand four hundred and twelve.

Captain Christie having been selected by His Majesty's Envoy at the Court of Persia, as one of the officers to remain in that country, to fulfil that part of the treaty relative to organizing the Persian troops, he wrote out a hasty Memoir of his journey in the course of a halt of five or six days made by General Malcolm at Muragha for the express purpose of affording him an opportunity to do so. I have annexed an abstract of that report after our separating at Nooshky, as an Appendix to this Narrative, conceiving it a respect due to the memory of my friend who, had he lived to revisit India, would probably have enlarged and amended it * into a form for publication.

The mission moved from Muragha on the *8th of August*, and arrived at Bagdad, by the route of Senna and Kirmanshaw, on the *20th of September* following: thence it proceeded by boats down the Tigris and Shat-ool Arab to Bussorah, where the public service de-

* Captain Christie was unfortunately killed in an attack made by a body of Russian troops on the Persian camp on the night of the *31st of October*, 1812. No officer ever died more universally regretted, as none had ever lived more beloved and respected. His acquirements and talents were of the very highest order, and his untimely death was not only felt by his numerous friends to be an irreparable loss, but was justly considered such, in a public light, to his country and his employers.

tained me for a period of nearly three months. I then embarked on board the Honourable Company's Cruiser Psyche, and landed at Bombay on the *6th of February*, 1811, after an absence of thirteen months and some days.

PART THE SECOND.

A SHORT

HISTORICAL AND GEOGRAPHICAL

MEMOIR OF THE COUNTRIES EXPLORED

DURING

A TOUR

THROUGH

BELOOCHISTAN, AND A PART OF PERSIA,

COMPRISING

CURSORY OBSERVATIONS ON THEIR BOUNDARIES, EXTENT, GOVERNMENT, CLIMATE, SOIL, AND NATURAL HISTORY;

TO WHICH IS ADDED,

A SUMMARY ACCOUNT

OF

THE PROVINCE OF SINDE,

AND THE PROCEEDINGS OF THE MISSION TO ITS RULERS IN 1809.

WITH A MAP.

CHAPTER I.

BELOOCHISTAN. — NAME EXPLAINED. — EXTENT. — NUSSEER KHAN'S TERRITORIES. — *GRANT BY NADIR SHAH.* — *GEOGRAPHICAL DIVISIONS.* — BOUNDARIES. — VARIETY OF FEATURES IN THE KINGDOM. — PLAN PROPOSED TO EXPLAIN THEM. — PROOF OF ITS MOUNTAINOUS NATURE. — THE BRAHOOICK *MOUNTAINS.* — WHY SO CALLED. — *DESCRIPTION OF THEM.* — *CONJECTURE* REGARDING THEIR SOURCE. — HINDOO KOOSH, OR INDIAN CAUCASUS. — TUKHTE' SOOLEMAN. — MOUNTAINS OF MUKRAN. — DESCRIPTION OF THEM. — *CONNECTED WITH THE HAZARUH MOUNTAINS.* — *WILD SHEPHERDS THAT* INHABIT A PART OF THEM. — PROVINCE OF LARISTAN. — ITS MOUNTAINS. — CAPES MOOBARUK AND ARABAH. — KOHISTAN. — HOW FORMED. — BUSH-*KURD.* — *NAME EXPLAINED.* — *INHABITANTS.* — *KOHE' NOUSHADIR, OR SAL-*AMMONIAC HILL. — COMPARATIVE MAGNITUDE OF THE MOUNTAINS OF BELOOCHISTAN. — DETAIL OF IT. — DUSHTI BE DOULUT. — KOHUN WAT. — DIAGONAL MEASUREMENT. — ALLOWANCE TO BE MADE FOR INFLEXIONS OF THE ROAD. — INSTANCE OF ITS NECESSITY. — ALTITUDE OF THE BRAHOOICK RANGE. — NATIVE OPINION. — HOW PROVED. — THE CITY OF KELAT, ITS HIGHEST POINT. — THE AUTHOR'S CONJECTURE RESPECTING ITS PERPENDICULAR HEIGHT ABOVE THE SEA. — THE GROUNDS OF HIS REASONING. — DEFILES. — TEMPERATURE OF KELAT. — COMPARISON BETWEEN THE BRAHOOICK MOUNTAINS AND THE PYRENEES. — RECENT DISCOVERIES TEND TO ESTABLISH THE MOUNTAINS OF ASIA AS THE HIGHEST IN THE WORLD. — FURTHER DISCUSSION DEFERRED. — MOTIVE. — THE SAME APPLICABLE TO THE BROOKS.

BELOOCHISTAN, *or the country of* the Belooches, comprehends all that space within latitudes 24° 50′, and 30° 40′ north, and longitudes 58° 55′, and 67° 30′ east; in addition to which there are one or two of its provinces stretching far east and west, whose exact longitudinal limits cannot be defined, until I come to treat of them respectively.

The whole of this vast tract constituted at one time the dominions of Nusseer Khan, father of the Khan of Kelat, on whom it was bestowed in the year one thousand seven hundred and thirty-nine by the Persian conqueror Nadir Shah, together with the title of Beglerbeg of all Beloochistan. On the authority of that grant, I have availed myself of that general term; but as the political state of the country has undergone an entire change since the period of its date, it becomes requisite to establish geographical divisions in attempting a description of it.

The boundaries of Beloochistan, in its largest acceptation, are to the southward, the Indian ocean or Erythrean sea; northward, Seistan and the country of the Uffghans; westward, the provinces of Laristan and Kirman; and to the eastward, a part of Sinde and Shikarpoor, a district in the hands of the king of Kabool. Within these bounds are comprised the under-mentioned divisions, which shall be discussed in the order in which they stand; and I afterwards purpose annexing a summary account of the present state of the province of Sinde, of which the ruling chiefs and a large portion of the population are Belooches.

Division I. The provinces of Jhalawan and Sarawan and the district of Kelat.

Division II. The provinces of Mukran and Lus.

Division III. The province of Kutch Gundava and district of Hurrund Dajel.

Division IV. Kohistan, (the country of hills), or the Belooche country, west of the desert.

Division V. The desert.

Division VI. The province of Sinde.

It may be readily conjectured, that in regions of such great extent, the features would vary so much, as to render inadequate any essay that might be made, to give a correct delineation of the whole under one head; and I shall therefore confine myself in this place, to an introductory view of the principal mountains, their connexion with those of circumjacent kingdoms, their various ramifications and tendencies within the limits of Beloochistan, their comparative altitude, length and breadth, with such other facts of a general nature as may enable my readers to comprehend with greater facility, the more detailed remarks that the divisions will severally demand.

In traversing Beloochistan from the province of Lus to the frontiers of Uffghanistan, between the sixty-fifth and sixty-seventh degrees of east longitude, I found it uninterruptedly mountainous. This stupendous range, to which I venture to assign the appellation of the Brahooick mountains, from the people (the Brahooés) who inhabit them, is the primitive root of almost all the others, and consequently, merits peculiar attention in this disquisition, in which, influenced by its formation, though contrary to usual practice, I shall commence from the southward, and trace its progress from the coast to the inland extremes.

It springs abruptly to a conspicuous height and grandeur out of the sea at Cape Mowaree, (Monze) in north latitude 25°, east longitude 66° 58', whence it assumes a north-easterly direction for ninety miles; it there projects a ridge east by north, the base of which is washed by the river Indus at the fort of Sehwan; however, this is so secondary in size that it only deserves notice as being the most easterly point of the whole. From the separation of this arm, in latitude 25° 45' to that of 30°, the primitive body runs due north; now marking the western limits of Sinde, Kutch Gundava, and a part of Seeweestan, as it formerly did that of Hindoostan; it thence once more regains its original inclination to the north-east, and decreases in magnitude and elevation so rapidly, that in the course of forty miles it sinks to a level with the hills inhabited by the Kaukers and other Uffghan tribes, with which it becomes incorporated.

Were I to extend my inquiry farther in this quarter, or had I begun this examination of the Brahooick mountains from the upland regions to which I have followed them, I hope with sufficient explicitness, instead of the coast; it is evident, that in either cases, it would be necessary to investigate the origin of the hills with which they unite; but, as doing so would induce a lengthened dissertation totally irrelative to the geography of Beloochistan, for that, and other reasons, I purposely avoid interfering with the subject.*

To the westward, the Brahooick mountains are far more complicated. At their emergence from the ocean, their breadth does not amount to thirty miles from the base at one side to the other; an extent strikingly diminutive with their comparative loftiness, but, from the latitude of twenty-five degrees and a half, they progressively sweep round to north, north-north-west, north-west, and west-north-west, expanding over several degrees of longitude, and sending forth many collateral piles, all inferior to the original, some of which pass west the whole length of Beloochistan, and conjoin with the mountains of Persia, others elongate southerly till they touch the sea, or come within a few miles of it, and then either take the inclination of the coast, or subside in the low and barren plains in its vicinity, while the main body, or rather its western face, stretches away north-west by north, to the twenty-eighth degree of north latitude, where it meets the south-eastern corner of the sandy desert, about the sixty-fourth degree of east longitude: thence it inclines with a northern aspect between the north-east and north points of the compass to Nooshky, in latitude 30° north, from which place it runs more easterly, till at length it gradually sinks, like the eastern front, to a size of equality with the Uffghan hills, and can no longer be treated as a distinct series.

Among these hills, however, there are, in this quarter, interspersed numerous towering ridges, generally coming from the north-eastward, and terminating, on the edge of the desert, between the sixty-sixth and seventh degrees of longitude. And it is not at all improbable, but the Brahooick range, the extreme limits of which I have now defined, might have been traced to a coalition with them, and cor-

* The geographical and historical account of Uffghanistan lately published by the Honourable M. Elphinstone contains the fullest particulars of these mountains, &c.

rectly denominated an enlargement of a southern branch of that enormous pile, known by the name of the Hindoo Koosh, or Indian Caucasus, whence the Hazaruh or Paropamisan range has its origin, and extends westerly to the borders of the Caspian sea. A branch of it is also often called Kohé Sooleemanee, or the mountains of Solomon, from a celebrated peak called the Tukhte Sooleman *, that constitutes its most elevated point; these lying, however, far beyond the bounds, I have assigned to this sketch, demand no further notice from me.

Within a few leagues of the same spot at which the western face of the great body is repelled by the sandy desert, an immense mass disengages itself, and diverges in a variety of ramifications to the southward and westward; one of the latter, of a superior bulk and elevation, establishes a barrier against the further encróachments of that desolate waste, which I have allotted as the fifth division of Beloochistan, by running along its southern base, in a direct westwardly line, for upwards of two degrees; thence it suddenly alters its course, from a cause that shall be hereafter exhibited, to north-west, which direction it retains for fifty miles, and then gradually recedes still more westerly, converging with divers lesser ranges, that here advance from the westward, to one focus. These all become consolidated, about the thirty-first degree of north latitude, into a narrow, though, at intervals, very lofty ridge, which extends between the fifty-ninth and sixtieth degrees of longitude, so far to the northward, that it seems to be in some measure united, by detached hills, with the Hazaruh or Paropamisan mountains, to the westward of the city of Herat, the capital of the province of Khorasan.

This chain divides the provinces of Seistan and that part of Kirman called the desert † from each other; and likewise marks the extent

* The throne of Solomon.

† See the account of that province, Chapter XVI. Part I.

of the existing titular authority (for it can here only be called such) of the Kings of Persia and Kabool. It partakes of the unproductive and desolate nature of the regions which encompass it, is ill supplied with wood or water, and thinly inhabited by a race of shepherds so wild and uncultivated, that even the Belooches designate them savages.

. The next range, in point of size and distinction, originates at the south-western angle of the Brahooick mountains, about one degree and a half to the southward of that last mentioned, with which it runs parallel for upwards of two hundred and thirty miles, both reciprocally protruding arms, that connect them so intimately, that had it not been for the intervention of some capacious and barren flats, added to their eventual total disjunction, they might have been accurately examined as one mass. After holding the same course for the distance I have stated, they meet a weighty and powerful pile of mountains opposing their further westerly progress; which obliges one of them, as I have already shewn, to wind to the northward: that, which is now under consideration, splits into two portions, each of which having made a short circuit, they again unite in a body; which, hence, tends to the southward of west, and progressively forces its way, spreading or contracting according to the height and variety of the eminences it surmounts, to a conjunction with the mountainous regions of the Persian province of Laristan, amongst which it is completely overwhelmed and lost. From the commencement to the final disappearance of this range, many branches likewise shoot from it to the southward, and form headlands on the coast of Mukran. Of these, Cape Urboo (Arabah), within fifteen leagues of Sonmeany, and Cape Moobaruk (the Bumbarrack of our nautical charts), on the confines of Persia, are the highest. *

* The Rasool Moobaruk, or Cape Moobaruk of the Arab navigators, has been strangely perverted by etymologists. It is so called from the Kohé Moobaruk, viz. the mountain of welcome, situated about nine miles inland, and first seen by ships at sea, when coming from the southward. Niebuhr writes Cohum-barrick and calls it loose sand,

Those mountains that have their source to the westward of Mukran, finding no exit in the quarter towards which they first incline, recoil, as it were, on their primary body, and coalesce in a very confused heap, which the native Belooches call Kohistan, or the land of mountains *. The most western district of this tract, according to the late Captain Grant †, is named Bushkurd, a compound word, importing it to be the residence of the Kurd or Koord Belooches ‡. Some of its towering peaks are visible from Bunpoor, a distance exceeding one hundred miles.

Previous to the junction of the several piles composing the Kohistan, they disperse numberless inferior ledges of rocky hills, that stretch in uneven and often interrupted lines across that part of Mukran which I journeyed through. These are by slow and imperceptible degrees compressed, on one side, by the wilds of Kirman; and, on the other, by that range which the Kohistanee mountains turn northerly, until they unite in the manner and place detailed in a preceding paragraph. A few of them likewise bend to the southwest, and constitute that continuation of mountains that I passed the day I quitted Basman §, and in which the Kohé Noushadir, or salammoniac mountain, is situated. These all end in abrupt cliffs on the edge of the sandy waste that separates Bushkurd from Nurmansheer, and are excessively rugged to their very foundations.

The comparative magnitude and height of these stupendous chains now claim our regard, and here we find that the Brahooick again outvies all the others. At its utmost expansion, in the twenty-eighth

from which we find that, although he had some idea of the orthography, he had none of the derivation of the word. His errors have misled others at a distance; and those English officers who have visited this coast have been too inattentive to rectify the mistake. There are not ten places, from the Indus to the Shatool Arab, that would be intelligible to a native, pronounced according to our maps !!!

* From Koh, a mountain; and Stan, a seat or place.

† Vide Narrative. Diary of the 18th *April* (note).

‡ From the Persian verb Bashudun, to dwell; and Koord, the name of the tribe.

§ Vide Narrative of the 21st *April*.

degree of north latitude, it is nearly two hundred miles broad, and from Nooshky, to the low and fertile champaign of Seweestan, along its northern front, it may perhaps be one hundred and thirty. In this line, however, there is a gap, nearly mid-way, of thirty miles, caused by a bare plain, whose sterility is sufficiently indicated by its appellation of the Dushtibedowlut * or desert of poverty. The Brahooick range contracts itself quickly as we approach the sea; and at "Kohun-wat," the southern extreme of the province of Jhalawan, it is not above forty miles from east to west; a breadth which it holds nearly to Cape Mowaree (Monze).

Lengthwise, or perhaps, more strictly speaking, diagonally, its greatest measurement is from south-south-east to north-north-west, in which parallel it exceeds two hundred and eighty miles; and, if we draw a line due north throughout the whole, it will not be under one hundred and ninety. In this and the foregoing paragraph, it is to be recollected, that I speak exclusively of direct bearings, and make no allowances for the inequality and curvature of the roads, of which a partial idea may be framed from the following circumstance. Measuring, on the map from Bela, the chief town of Lus, to Kelat, it does not appear to be quite one hundred and sixty miles; whereas, the absolute distance between these two places proved, by the most accurate computation that Captain Christie and I could make, to be two hundred and ninety three, or nearly as much more.

This range is admitted to have attained its greatest altitude at Kelat, from which city, agreeable to the natives, whatever route he may pursue, a traveller must descend; but the country seemed to me to verge in so very trifling a degree, for a long way on either side of that capital, that it is not perceptible by the eye. It consequently requires some other expedient to ascertain the level; and, as none can be more decisive or simple than to trace the brooks, I made the fullest search on that principle, and afterwards established my

* Sometimes the Dushti bedar, or uninhabitable waste.

opinion, which is almost wholly coincident with that above alluded to.

The streams in the valley of Kelat run to the north-east; and, at Kapotho, nine miles to the southward, they take an opposite direction. To the westward, the equality of height appears to be so well ascertained, that I have every reason for believing it to be an exact table-land from the village of Koor, seven miles north-west of Kelat, to the mountains of Sarawan, on the edge of the desert. This is not, however, by any means, to be deemed a flat tract, on the contrary, it abounds with lofty precipices, and ridges whose summits are often obscured with clouds; but, taken in a large sense, the bases of all these form a surface so even, that the torrents caused by heavy rains force their passage in every direction, except immediately towards Kelat, nearer to which they do not approach than the village above-mentioned. Eastward of that city, the same feature characterizes the country for twenty-five or thirty miles; whence the slope becomes gradual into the plain of Kutch Gundava. I cannot, however, say, that it is uninterrupted; rather the reverse; for many of the least accessible Lukhs, or defiles, in Beloochistan lie in these parts, and obstruct the mountain rivulets on every hand. But I collect what I have here affirmed, from finding that the waters of a Munzilgah *, called Sirri Kujjoor, situated about seventy miles north-east of Kelat, make their way, sometimes above, sometimes under ground, through a succession of narrow glens, to the same level territory.

As I was unprovided, during my tour, with a barometer, or other instruments, that might have assisted me in finding out the perpendicular height of Kelat, as the most elevated spot of the Brahooick mountains, it is only by a comparison of facts that I am prepared to offer my sentiments on that head. Although the obliquity be not, as I have before stated, visible in the immediate vicinity of that capital, yet to the southward we found a very marked one, in places

* A halting place; from Munzil, a stage; and Gah, a place.

amounting to steep defiles and hills, for a day's journey at a time, until we reached Rodenjo within twenty-five miles of it. Hence, to Gurruk, seven miles north of the city, I conceive the slope to be undistinguishable; but, in travelling from the latter village to Nooshky, we crossed over six lofty Lukhs, or passes, whose descent to the northward was invariably double, and on one or two occasions fourfold the ascent on the southern face. The accumulated difference of these would, alone, be equal to a very great declension; and yet, after we had got to the bottom of them, and came in sight of the desert, we found ourselves prodigiously elevated above its surface, and a seventh Lukh remained to be passed down, the declivity of which was, apparently, double that of all the others *. Even then we were on a raised plain, the waters of which, when augmented from any cause, such as rain or the melting of snow amongst the neighbouring mountains, escape towards the sea, by various outlets, in the province of Mukran, with excessive velocity.

The temperature of Kelat likewise serves to corroborate its amazing elevation; however, as I mean to offer, in the sequel of this memoir, some observations on the seasons of all the divisions, I shall be very brief in my deductions from that source at present. That city and the neighbouring districts, though scarcely more than five degrees and a half removed from the summer solstice, are subjected to a most rigorous winter; and snow lies, even in the vales, from the close of November till the beginning of February. Rice, and certain other vegetable productions that require warmth of climate, will not thrive here; and wheat and barley do not ripen so soon as in the British Isles †. From a philosophical estimation of all these concurrent particulars, it is inferible, that the extreme altitude of the Brahooick mountains is not inferior to that of some ridges, which are celebrated as the loftiest in Europe ‡; nor shall we long admit this with sur-

* Vide Diary of the *9th March*, Part I.

† Kelat is in latitude 29° 6' north.

‡ To offer a conjecture on a point of this kind may appear futile; but I do so with cautious diffidence; and yet allow it will probably be very erroneous. Judging from the

prize and doubt, when we find that recent discoveries teach us to look to Asia as the seat of the most sublime and stupendous piles on the face of the earth. *

I am not aware that any of the other ranges of mountains within the boundaries of Beloochistan are entitled, either from their magnitude or elevation, to a critical recapitulation in this introduction; and more especially, as a review of each province will afford me an opportunity of particularizing any observable localities that may have been heretofore neglected with respect to them. For a similar reason, I shall likewise defer the unimportant observations that the streams will require; here merely premising, that there is not a single body of running water in the northern parts of this country, worthy of a more eminent appellation than a rivulet, unless when swoln by partial floods to a tumultuous and unfordable torrent, nor one, even of that description, that can be said to flow through a regular and unbroken channel to the main, as will be seen when they come forward in the fixed rotation of the divisions, to a consideration of which I now turn my thoughts.

eye, of the Lukh or pass nearest the desert, and comparing its apparent length and steepness with some of the Ghauts of India, of whose ascertained height I am apprized, I should pronounce its summit to be five thousand feet from the sandy flat beneath. If we moderately, add one moiety of this for the other six passes, between that spot and the city of Kelat, and grant the desert as the base of the whole, to be elevated of itself five hundred above the level of the ocean, it produces an aggregate of eight thousand feet, an elevation exceeding by one eighth the altitude of the loftiest point of the Pyrenees.

* The late Lieutenant Macartney of the Bengal army who went as surveyor with the mission to Kabool in 1809-10, estimated the mountains of Hindoo Koosh at more than twenty-two thousand feet; and Lieutenant Webb of the same service, who was deputed in 1807 to discover the source of the Ganges, by a mean of observations makes the Himalayeh range twenty-one thousand feet above the plains of Rohilkund.

Vide Asiatic Researches, vol. xi. p. 644. Calcutta edition.

CHAPTER II.

FIRST DIVISION OF BELOOCHISTAN. — THE PROVINCES OF JHALAWAN AND SARAWAN AND DISTRICT OF KELAT. — THEIR EXTENT. — BOUNDARIES OF THE FIRST. — THUKS OR DISTRICTS. — CHIEF TOWN. — RIVERS. — SARAWAN. — ITS BOUNDARIES. — DISTRICTS. — TOOMUNS OR VILLAGES OF TENTS. — DISTRICT OF KELAT — WHY DISTINGUISHED FROM SARAWAN. — KHANUZADS OR HOUSEHOLD SLAVES. — COMPARISON BETWEEN JHALAWAN AND SARAWAN. — EXTRAORDINARY RUGGEDNESS OF THE LATTER — POPULATION GREATER. — PROBABLE CAUSE. — KELAT THE CAPITAL OF ALL THREE. — HISTORY OF IT INCLUDES THAT OF ALL BELOOCHISTAN. — PLAN OF DETAIL PROPOSED. EARLY ACCOUNTS. — UNKNOWN AND UNEXPLORED STATE OF THE BRAHOOICK MOUNTAINS — GREEKS. — THEIR IDEAS. — INDO SCYTHIA. — ITS EXTENT. — AUTHOR'S SURMISE. — ALEXANDER THE GREAT — SHORT SKETCH OF HIS MARCH. — NATURE OF THE COUNTRY DEMONSTRATES IT. — CRATERUS. — HIS MARCH — REASON FOR THE ROUTE HE PURSUED. — ALEXANDER'S DEATH. — BELOOCHISTAN FORGOTTEN. — HINDOO EMPERORS. — PERSIAN DYNASTIES. — RECEIVE TRIBUTE. — INTERCOURSE HOW CARRIED ON. — THE KHALIPHAS OF BAGDAD — THEIR ARMY INVADES SINDE. — MOTIVES. — ROUTE ADOPTED. — WHY BRAHOOICK RANGE STILL UNEXPLORED — MUHMOOD OF GUZNEE. — HIS CONQUESTS. — HIS SONS. — THEIR EXAMPLE FOLLOWED. — REASONS FOR THIS BEING THE CASE — HINDOOS DRIVEN OUT OF SINDE. — AUTHOR'S SURMISE. — IMPERVIOUSNESS OF THE BRAHOOICK MOUNTAINS. — RECENT PROOF. — A BLANK IN ALL THE MAPS HITHERTO PUBLISHED. — HISTORICAL EVENTS BEGIN TO BE ORALLY PRESERVED. — DISCUSSION PROPOSED REGARDING THE ORIGIN OF THE NATIVES OF BELOOCHISTAN. — FOUNDED ON CONJECTURE. — PRECAUTIONS OBSERVED. — LANGUAGES. — BELOOCHES DENY BEING OF UFFGHAN EXTRACTION. — THEIR REASONING AND CLAIMS TO ARAB DESCENT. — NOT ADMITTED. — THE COUNTRY WHY CALLED BELOOCHISTAN. — SELJUKE TARTARS. — TOORKUMANS. — THE BELOOCHES SPRUNG FROM THEM. — REASONS FOR THIS OPINION. — SHORT ACCOUNT OF THE MOGHULS AND THEIR COLONIZATION IN SINDE. — ALL DISAPPEAR. — THE AUTHOR'S OPINION. — GROUNDS OF IT. — BRAHOOES. — WHENCE MIGRATED TO BELOOCHISTAN. — NATIVE IDEA. — THEIR TRADITIONAL DESCENT. — VISIT FROM MOHUMMUD. — THEIR IGNORANCE. — SLIGHT KNOWLEDGE OF RELIGION. — WHENCE ACQUIRED. — DEHWARS. — BRIEF ACCOUNT OF THEM. — AUTHOR AT ONE TIME CONCEIVED THEM TO HAVE BEEN GUEBRES OR

ANCIENT PERSIANS. — HIS REASONS DETAILED. — OBJECT IN STATING THEM. — HINDOOS EXPELLED FROM SINDE. — WHERE SETTLED. — ULTIMATELY SUBDUED BY THE BRAHOOES.

THE provinces of Jhalawan and Sarawan, together with the interjacent district of Kelat, which I have appropriated as the first division of Beloochistan, are exactly comprised within the compass of the Brahooick range of mountains, after we have rejected that portion lying to the southward of the twenty-sixth degree of latitude. To define their boundaries, in addition to what has been said, may therefore appear superfluous; but I am induced to do so, as it will enable me to circumscribe their several extents with greater precision.

Jhalawan, which is the most southerly, and likewise the largest, has to the southward the province of Lus and a part of Mukran; northward, the district of Kelat and Sarawan; eastward, parts of Sinde and Kutch Gundava; and westward, Mukran. It contains the Thuks, or districts of Wudd, Khozdar, Nal, Punduran, Zuhree and Zedee, beside two or three others of less importance; and, even to enter into a long description of these would be to no purpose, they have each a chief, whose authority is limited by, though not derived from, the Khan of Kelat, as I shall hereafter explain.

Zuhree is the largest town in this province, it gives a name to a Thuk or district, also to a tribe of Brahooes, of whom Qadir Buksh is the Sirdar or leader, and contains from two to three thousand houses, protected by a mud wall. In the province of Jhalawan, there is not a brook larger than the Oornach, which I saw in February, when it was not more than three yards wide and ten inches deep in dry seasons; it frequently ceases to flow, but abundance of water, even for cultivation, can at all times be procured by digging a few feet in the bed of it, and of many similar mountain streams.

Sarawan is bounded to the northward by the Uffghan hills, and the eastern side of the desert separating it from Kandahar; southward it has Jhalawan and Kelat; eastward, Seeweestan and Kutch Gundava; and westward, the desert; its divisions are Nooshky, Koor,

Koohuk, Paeenkothul, Sirroh, Kishtan, Kharan, &c. these need no remark, save the general one I have made on Jhalawan; they have neither towns or villages of a fixed nature, and the Brahooe Toomuns are constantly moving in search of pasturage.

The district of Kelat, strictly speaking, belongs to the province of Sarawan, from which it has become customary to distinguish it, because the Khans of Kelat have usurped the privilege of bestowing the revenues accruing from it on their Khanuzads * and dependants, without reference to the chiefs of the Kheils that dwelt within its precincts, the result has been, that they have insensibly withdrawn from it, and persons of the former description exclusively cultivate and enjoy the soil.

In drawing a comparison between these two provinces, I find one of them possessing some natural advantages over the other; Jhalawan, though amazingly mountainous, boasts of two or three small plains or vallies, such as those of Wudd, Soherab and Khozdar, while, in Sarawan, it is said, that there is actually not a level space, the circumference of which would exceed a few miles, except the desert tract of the Dushti be Doulut, alluded to in the preceding chapter; the climate of the former province is also more temperate, and rain falls so frequently, that it makes the soil, otherwise poor and stony, in a greater degree arable and productive; notwithstanding these favourable circumstances, it is calculated, that the population of Sarawan, exclusive of the Kelat district, is twofold that of Jhalawan, a fact to be attributed to some unaccountable predilection in favour of the northern countries.

The city of Kelat is at present, and has been for generations, the capital of these provinces; it also held, at one period, that pre-emi-

---

* Khanuzads are household slaves. The term is derived from Khanuh, a house, and Zaeedun, to be born. Some account of the customs of the Belooches with regard to their slaves, will be found in Chapter IV. Part I. The Khanuzads being of a superior class, are always kept near the persons of their chiefs, and employed on all affairs of great trust. Their character and station is considered highly respectable, and, even after they are enfranchised, and rewarded with a portion of soil, they retain the appellation.

nence over all Beloochistan, and from being the seat of the only regular form of government, that I have been able to come at a knowledge of, among the Belooches, its modern annals are connected with, and will include most essential points in those of the other divisions. I therefore purpose attempting to compress the whole into this and the following chapter, in the most regular and perspicuous manner that my unconnected and scanty materials will permit; but prior to commencing that endeavour, a few summary remarks on the earlier accounts we have of these regions, may seem requisite in a treatise of this kind.

In the course of my investigations on the Belooches, it has frequently recurred to me, that there was no spot in the ancient hemisphere, the interior of Africa excepted, that had remained so long unexplored, and of which such erroneous and contradictory opinions had been formed, as the first division of Beloochistan. The Greeks, from whom we possess the earliest knowledge of the western frontiers of India, were either so totally ignorant of this tract, or found it by report to be so inhospitable a waste, that they have been almost silent with respect to it; they saw that it was mountainous, and learned that in it there was a race of natives, whose manners and occupations resembled the Scythians, whence they denominated it Indo-Scythia, though that would seem to have been only strictly applicable to a very small portion of the south-eastern skirts of the Brahooick range, in common with a tract extending to the confines of the Province of Mooltan, the ancient Malli; and, in fact, I am very dubious whether the upper parts of it were at all inhabited until long subsequent to the period of the Macedonian conquest, my reasons for which I shall hereafter assign.

Alexander himself, on quitting Pattala (said to be Tattah) on the Indus, proceeded, with his army, through the dominions of the Arabitæ, a part of the present Province of Lus, and in it forded the Arabis (Poorally) river. To the westward of that diminutive stream, he traversed the territory of the Oreitæ, and thence, crossing over one range of mountains, he entered the Province of Gedrosia (Mukran), in which his troops were thinned by the accumulated hardships of thirst, famine, and fatigue. This march was incontestably to the southward of the Brahooick chain, and had the Greek historians been even less explicit, the nature of the country alone must have decided any question that might have arisen on this point *.

Craterus, who was charged with the guidance of the heavy baggage and invalid soldiers, by Arachosia and Drangiana, as certainly marched far to the northward; for those provinces are included within the modern ones of Kandahar and Seistan, no part of either of which lie even in a parallel of latitude with Beloochistan. We may beside unequivocally conclude, that as that General was purposely detached to shun the deserts of Gedrosia (Mukran), he would not shape his progress through a region in which all the obstacles experienced by the divisions headed by the King in person, would have been augmented, by the labour of forcing a passage among inaccessible cliffs and deep defiles.

Posterior to the Greek invasion, and the partition of that vast empire, on the demise of Alexander, we meet with no further mention of these countries, unless in the unconnected and fabulous legends related of the Guebres or ancient Persians, for a lapse of above nine centuries and a half. The Hindoo emperors of India were obliged to pay tribute to, and acknowledge the supremacy of, the monarchs of the successive dynasties of the Seleucidæ, Arsacidæ, and Sassanides, who sat on the throne of Persia, within that round of time; so that the communication between the two nations, must have been defined and frequent, but being carried on either by sea or the northern route of Khorasan, it threw no light on the intermediate

* Had Alexander come to the Poorally river in the rainy season, he would in all likelihood have found it unfordable. My Diary of the 30th January, will demonstrate this fact, and had he once entered the Province of Jhalawan, the most southern exit his army would have found, had been the road from Khozdar, in latitude 27° 54′ north, to Punjegoor. Vide Map.

countries that form the basis of this inquiry, and they sunk into their original and possibly merited obscurity. *

Ninety-two years after the epoch of the Hijree †, the Khaliphas of Bagdad, incited by the combined motives of zeal for the Mohummudan faith, and desire to revenge an insult that had been offered to their dignity by the idolators ‡ of Sinde §, dispatched an army against that kingdom, by the same route that the Macedonian hero had selected on his return to Babylon, nearly one thousand years antecedent. This force is expressly stated to have kept close along the sea-coast, that it might be certain of a supply of water, which is always procurable, by digging a foot or two deep in the sandy beach; it consequently knew nothing of the inland regions, nor was any attempt made, as far as I can learn, during the administration of the Kaliphas of the houses of Oommyuh and Abbass, to explore them.

When Muhmood, the successor of Subuktaghi, the first Sultan of the Ghaznuwee dynasty, in the plenitude of his power, turned his arms towards India, he subjugated the whole of the level districts, west of the river Indus, to the very base of the Brahooick mountains. His son Musaood, extended these conquests still more westerly into Mukran; he adhered, however, to his father's plan of not ascending those lofty ranges; and all subsequent invaders of Sinde seem to have been guided by their example; or if they did penetrate a short way, it was merely a casual inroad, generally made in pursuit of a

* In an ancient Manuscript History of Guzeratte, I find that Shah Behcram Gore, King of Persia, came to the former kingdom in disguise, and returned through Neemroz, the present province of Seistan, with a large army, having been discovered in India on a hunting party. This was in the reign of the Hindoo Emperor Rajdeo, and in the fourth century of the Christian era. Seistan was then a fertile and populous country, now it is a desolate sandy waste.

† A. D. 677.

‡ Hindoos, such is the appellation bestowed on them by Mohummudan writers.

§ Vide Division V. Chapter XII.

discomfited enemy, and without any aim at a permanent conquest.*

This is ascribable to two distinct causes, the poverty and the imperviousness of this tract; the former was so well ascertained at an early date, that the compiler of the Chuch Namuh, the best history of Sinde extant, states that those infidels (Hindoos) who would not conform to the doctrines of the Koran, were driven to the mountains, there to perish by famine and cold. Wilds thus spoken of, I presume were void of people, and from this epoch I shall hereafter fix the first regular settlements in the provinces of Jhalawan and Sarawan, or at least their most elevated districts. Ample proof of the second operative cause may be collected from all that I have noticed regarding these regions, and were it necessary to strengthen what I have advanced, on the certain grounds of ocular demonstration, numberless instances might be adduced, of their having been retired to as a place of temporary refuge, during the wars between the Tartar, Puttan, and Moghul competitors for the sovereignty of Hindoostan and Persia. So lately even as the year 1806, Prince Kysur, one of the royal family of Kabool, fled to Beloochistan, and his security in these fastnessess was so confessedly understood, that no means were taken to pursue him, although unattended by any force. In conclusion, I may observe that the utterly unknown state in which this country has heretofore remained, is evident from a glimpse of all maps either ancient or modern, that include it. In none of them has it any designation † except in the term Belloo-

* Musaood, the son of Muhmood, had collected an army in Mukran, to invade these countries, but the appearance of the Seljuke Tartars, who then first began to make a figure, called him off.

† Major Rennel has carried the province of Mukran to so high a degree of north latitude, that it includes both Jhalawan and Sarawan, but the information obtained by that able, and generally correct geographer, relative to the southern parts of Sinde, and the countries westward of that province, seems to have been defective, and has led him into mistakes. I may perhaps occasionally differ very materially both

gees, or Bloatchees, which are mere orthographical corruptions of the denomination of one class of its natives, in my opinion, less proper than the Brahooés, (who are all mountaineers,) to bestow a name on the land they inhabit.

We are now arrived at that period when some indistinct memory of the historical events of Beloochistan begin to be orally preserved; but to render them intelligible, it becomes not merely proper, but indispensable, that I should subjoin a few words on the origin of the various classes of the natives, the reasons and date of their primary emigrations to this uninviting land, and the manner in which they seem to have apportioned the soil. My readers will perceive, as they advance, that my sentiments on these points are mostly conjectural. More cannot be expected of people destitute of letters, and that spirit of curiosity which leads less barbarous tribes to investigate, whence they sprung. I have not however neglected to draw my information from the best sources, and to exclude all that was fabulous and uninteresting.

As neither the Beloochekee or Brahooekee are written languages, all accounts are traditional, and entitled to little credit. The Belooches, or people who speak the former, ascribe their own origin to the earliest Mohummudan invaders of Persia, and are very desirous of being supposed to be of Arabian extraction. They spurn the idea, usually entertained, that they are descended from one stock with the Uffghans; and a circumstance, which they always urge, almost demonstrates the truth of this denial, namely, their proximity to that nation, and their nevertheless speaking a distinct dialect.

from him and Monsieur d'Anville, who is just here in fewer errors, but I have neither the abilities nor the wish to criticise the valuable geographical labours of those learned authors in any degree, my aim is to detail facts as I found them. The inhabitants may have changed since the days of Alexander, the face of the earth cannot reasonably be supposed to have done so, and as I have seen the latter, I may claim, without arrogating to myself, a right to speak positively.

I am not, however, by any means willing to admit, implicitly, their claims as the first propagators of Islamism, an honour to which every petty tribe aspires; at the same time, there can exist little doubt, but they came from the westward. The affinity of the Beloochekee to the Persian language, affords, of itself, strong evidence in favour of this position; to back which, we still see that the majority of the Belooche nation dwells on the western frontier; a fact to which, they say, Beloochistan owes its present name; for Nadir Shah, who conferred the title of Beglerbeg on Nusseer Khan, knowing more of that people than the Brahoóes, named the country after them. Admitting this minor question, of their having migrated from the westward, to be established, the principal one stands yet undecided. Under what description of the natives or conquerors of Persia are we to range the Belooches? My unacquaintance with any of the Turkish or Tartarian dialects, deprives me of one great clue to a solution of this query; but as neither their features, their manners, nor their language, bear the smallest similitude to those of Arabs, I reject them totally.

In the beginning of the fifth century of the Hijree, the Seljuke Tartars appeared, for the first time, in Khorasan; and, in the short space of ten years, their leader, Toghrul Beg, wrested that kingdom from the house of Ghaznuwee. It was ceded to his successor Alp Aarslan, and constituted a part of the Seljukide dominions, until the extinction of that race, about one hundred and fifty years posterior to Toghrul Beg's having assumed the title of emperor. Within this lapse of time, the Belooches are alluded to, both by that general term and particular tribes; and, what is even more decisive, as *dwelling in the very districts* which they people at this hour.

To think of following the frequent bloody revolutions, which extinguished one body of freebooters to make room for another, is quite foreign to my purpose. We learn, from the most authentic relations of the Greek and Asiatic historians, that as these armies became dismembered, either by the death of their generals or a defeat, the barbarians who composed them wandered over the country until they found an advantageous place to fix themselves, or entered the service of some more fortunate chieftain than their own, as mercenaries. Such, in my opinion, was the case with the Belooches; and, that they are of Toorkuman * lineage, various circumstances go to prove. Their institutions, habits, religion, and, in short, every thing but their languages, are the same: this last anomaly is easily explained. The Seljukes had long settled in Persia, which was then justly considered the richest and most delightful clime in Asia, where they naturally adopted the colloquial dialect, and brought it with them, on their expulsion by the Kharizmian Princes; who, in their turn, gave way to the Moghuls of Jungeez Khan. This dialect has not yet undergone more alteration than an intercourse with bordering nations might be expected to bring about.

As it may seem feasible, to some of my readers, to trace the Belooches from a Moghul origin, I shall summarily offer my additional reasons, to those stated above, for giving the preference to the Toorkuman; and leave the point, if deserving of further inquiry, to be settled by some one better qualified for the task. The former nation, whose history is more fully recorded than any of the others I have adverted to, first began to make a figure under the great Jungeez Khan; and he, or his immediate descendants, overturned all preceding dynasties. The unremitting enmity of the Kharazmian kings forced vast hordes of them to fly from Persia, after they had been colonized there for many years. The fugitives are said to have gone to Seistan and the neighbouring countries, which are those of Sinde, Seweestan, and the Brahooick mountains; and in the Mujmuool waridat, or *compendium of occurrences*, which includes an abstract of the history of the two former, it is mentioned, that there were upwards

* The Seljukes I call Toorkumans, in conformity with the native authorities I have consulted. They, as well as the Moghuls, are of Tartarian origin; but to speak of them as the same nation would be as likely to confound, as a person writing on Europe, to include Spaniards and Frenchmen under the common term of Europeans.

of ten thousand Moghuls residing in the city of Tattah, so long ago as the year of the Hijree 743 *, where they had a Muhul, or quarter, assigned to them, called the Moghulwarra, a distinction it retains at this time. From the same source, I also learn, that in A. H. 734, Jillodah Khan, a Moghul chief, marched from Seistan with six thousand men, and coming unawares through the mountains, ravaged all the plain on the west of the Indus, between the twenty-sixth and twenty-ninth degrees of north latitude; but, at last, being surrounded by the army of Noosrut Khan, then the viceroy of Mooltan, Outch, and Sinde, he capitulated; and, on swearing allegiance to the emperor's Ullawuddeen †, was granted a Jageer ‡ for himself and followers, and pardoned.

These examples suffice to shew, that the Moghuls were, in one era, resident in these countries; but the successive invasions of Hindoostan, which ultimately subverted the Puttan dynasty, and established the ancestors of the reigning monarch, afforded those restless and insatiable plunderers too fair an opportunity of enrolling themselves, once more, under the banners of their countrymen, to be missed; and they quitted their newly acquired possessions to partake of the spoils of India. So universal was this impulse, that no trace of their progeny now remains; at least, that can be positively ascertained to be such, or is acknowledged: and it seems improbable that any cause for the total disappearance of the colonies I speak of, save a voluntary migration, would have been passed over in silence by the Asiatic historians of the day, who are the only authorities I have to rest upon.

The particular manner in which I have dwelt on the descent of the Belooches, prompts me to hasten over that of the other tribes of Beloochistan. Had I been directed by the relative bulk of the population, or the existing rank of the chiefs, the Brahooes ought to have

* A. D. 1328.

† Alla I. Vide Dow's Hindoostan.

‡ A grant of land.

taken precedence; but their history is peculiarly obscure and uninteresting, and therefore calls for little notice. They seem to have been a nation of Tartar mountaineers, who settled at a very early period in the southern parts of Asia, where they lived an ambulatory life in Kheils, or societies, headed and governed by their own chiefs and laws, for many centuries, till at length they became incorporated, and attained their present footing at Kelat, and throughout Beloochistan, by an event which I shall presently describe.

It is impossible to form more than a supposition, nor is it in any way material to this enquiry to know, what the nature of the region was from which they migrated to Beloochistan; but their pursuits and way of domestic life afford the strongest reason for believing that they were originally mountaineers; and some among themselves affirm, that their very name demonstrates this by its signification, being a compound of the affix Bu, on; and Roh, a word said to mean a hill, in the dialect still spoken in some parts of Thibet. Such reasoning is, however, not entitled to any great dependence, though supported by the collateral evidence of the Belooches being called, in one quarter of the country, Nharooes or Nurohees, which, if we admit the former derivation, means lowlanders, i. e. "literally not hill-men;" a name they received from the Brahooes when they came amongst them, and evinced a preference for the champaign districts, low vallies, and plains.

In the observations made on the Brahooe nation, in the first part of this work, I have stated that its remote annals are highly embellished with fabulous traditions *. I had it, at one time, in contemplation to have inserted a succession of those fictions; but I soon discovered that it would have been an unprofitable task to scrutinize a series of absurdities, that, taken in any shape, are irreconcileable to common reason. The sum of them appears to be, that they imagine themselves the aborigines of the country, and peculiarly favoured by

* Vide Part I. Chapter IV.

the Arabian Prophet; who, they aver, paid them a visit one night, mounted on a dove, and left several Peers, or saints, amongst them for their spiritual guidance *. The remains of forty of these deified preceptors are believed to be buried under a mountain about seventy-six miles north of Kelat, whence it is called the Kohéchihultun, or mountain of forty bodies †, and flocked to, as a place of Zearut, or pilgrimage, by both Moosulmans and Hindoos.

Removed as it were from the world, among their native mountains, the greater number of Brahooes have not the slightest conception of any thing anterior to Islamism; except, that an universe did exist. Thus much they learn from the Koran, and that, even, most superficially; for, as few or none of the wildest of them can read that book, they necessarily trust to the interpretations of illiterate mendicants, who find it a lucrative profession, independent of the commendation they fancy due to their zeal, to travel from one Kheil to another, propounding the divine law, as it best suits their purposes. A religion so uncertain and ill understood, quickly paves the way for idle romances, and a superstitious proneness to the marvellous and incredible legends of their forefathers keeps this people in utter barbarism.

Of the Dehwars I shall say but a few words. I had, at one period of my inquiries on Beloochistan, conceived them to be a colony of Guebres or ancient Persians, that had been forced to embrace the Mohummudan faith, and fled from their persecutors; but by more recent investigations, I discover that the same people are to be recognised in many different parts of Asia by various names, that they all speak the same pure Persian, coincide in manners and occupations, and, what is even more remarkable, they all, as far as I know, live under the same restrictions and immunities as those of Beloochistan ‡,

* I have heard the same tradition applied to the Uffghans, but most likely when the Prophet was abroad he would take a circuit.

† From Koh, a mountain; Chihul, forty; and Tun, a body.

‡ Vide Part I. Chapter IV. Account of the Dehwars.

which is of itself presumptive proof that they have been at one time refugees from another country, and allowed to settle, on entering into a compact with the ruling authority.

The first hostile appearance of the Arabs in Persia, as the propagators of the Koran, is usually allowed to have taken place about the eighteenth year of the Hijree, (A. D. 603.) but it was not before the thirtieth or thirty-first, that they penetrated into the south-eastern parts of the provinces of Kirman, Eeraké Ujumee, and Mukran, where they met with little or no opposition, for Yezdigerd, the last of the Persian Kings, who had, according to some accounts, resided for many years at Yezd, and to others, at Kirman, being deserted by all his troops, who, to use the words of the Moosulman historian, eagerly grasped at the Light of Heaven, which the Prophet had sent amongst them: fled through Seistan, and was eventually assassinated by some of his apostate subjects.

After his death, the dispersion of the Guebres became universal, and the Mooslim forces drove that unhappy sect before them, in their advance to the eastward, until it entirely disappeared *. Subsequent to this period, the histories which I have looked into, contain no further notice of the Guebres till the reign of Musaood, about the year of the Hijree 427, who found a few of them scattered here and there in the provinces of Mukran and Seistan, whence it would appear they have since returned into Persia, and are chiefly settled at Yezd. †

---

* I have here given the literal translation of the original in the Mujmuool Waridat, or Compendium of Occurrences, because it is somewhat enigmatical. The compiler quotes the Mirat ool Juanan (Mirror of Paradise), and Gozeedah Namah (Select History), but writes with all the virulence of an enthusiast, in lieu of the impartiality of an historian. I fancy that he here means to assert that the proselytes, refugees, and martyrs, included the whole race. His style is elsewhere exceedingly obscure; he speaks undistinguishably of the Parsees and Hindoos, as Kafirs and Guebres, both words signifying infidels, and I have, in following him, supposed a meridian to divide those people. I have done so at the sixty-fifth degree of longitude, as I shall hereafter prove that the Hindoos extended far west of the Indus.

† Vide Part I. Diary of the 27th *March*. Note on Atush Kudus.

The two foregoing paragraphs contain an epitome of the arguments on which I had grounded my belief of the Dehwars being descendants of the Guebres, and as I can perceive nothing but their numbers to militate against the possibility of that still being the case, I have thought it worth stating my opinion, as a clue to others who may be inclined to prosecute the inquiry.

The Hindoos are the remaining class of the natives of Beloochistan, and I shall simply add, that I deem them to have been the first colonizers in the upper part of the Brahooick mountains, on their being expelled from Sinde, Lus, and Mukran, by the armies of the Khaliphas of Bagdad. This event more properly appertains to the account of the former province, which is comprized in the sixth division of this Memoir, and to it I refer my readers.

From the period of that expulsion which took place, as I have stated in a preceding place, in the ninety-third and fourth years of the Hijree, I have no records whatever of Beloochistan for many centuries. The natives say that the Hindoos followed their mercantile avocations, and that their Rajahs exercised a lenient authority over those Brahooes who ventured to settle near their towns. The latter people, and the Belooches, gradually spread over the country; and at length the Hindoo power was subverted by a revolution, which placed the ancestors of the present Khan of Kelat on the Gaddee *. This revolution and subsequent events up to this day, may be styled the Modern History of Beloochistan, and I shall proceed to an examination of it in the next chapter.

* Gaddee literally means a pillow, but it is applied, as well as Musnud, to the throne on which Hindoo and other princes usually sit.

CHAPTER III.

GENEALOGICAL DESCENT OF THE KHANS OF KELAT. — HISTORY OF THAT PLACE PREVIOUS TO THE RISE OF THE REIGNING FAMILY. — HINDOO GOVERNMENT SUBVERTED. — DEATH OF THE HINDOO RAJAH. — THE BRAHOOE CHIEFS SEIZE THE GOVERNMENT. — UNCERTAIN ACCOUNTS OF SUBSEQUENT EVENTS. — SYSTEM OF GOVERNMENT. — ABDOOLLAH KHAN. — INVADES THE PROVINCE OF KUTCH GUNDAVA. — HIS SUCCESS. — NADIR SHAH'S INVASION OF HINDOOSTAN. — TAKES KELAT. — DEATH OF ABDOOLLA KHAN. — HIS SUCCESSOR. — TYRANNICAL AND LICENTIOUS LIFE. — OPPRESSIVE LAW REVIVED BY HIM. — NUSSEER KHAN. — DEPOSES HIS BROTHER AND PUTS HIM TO DEATH. — NOMINATED BEGLERBEG OF BELOOCHISTAN. — REFORMS THE GOVERNMENT. — MAKES A CIRCUIT THROUGH HIS DOMINIONS. — FORTIFIES KELAT. — THE MONARCHY OF KABOOL FOUNDED. — NUSSEER KHAN'S POLICY. — REASONS FOR IT. — CONSEQUENCES. — WAR WITH AHMED SHAH ABDALLI. — KELAT BESIEGED. — SIEGE RAISED. — TREATY. — ANECDOTE OF NUSSEER KHAN. — HIS DISTINGUISHED AND GALLANT SERVICES WITH AHMED SHAH. — REWARDED BY LARGE PRESENTS. — CIVIL WAR IN BELOOCHISTAN. — QUELLED. — NUSSEER KHAN DIES. — HIS FAMILY. — HIS CHARACTER CONSIDERED AS A SOLDIER, A STATESMAN, AND A PRINCE. — THE AUTHOR'S IDEAS REGARDING HIM. — HIS SUCCESSOR. — ANOTHER CIVIL WAR. — COMPROMISE BETWEEN THE COMPETITORS. — BREACH. — DEFEAT AND DEATH OF ONE OF THEM. — FAMILY DISSENSIONS. — RESULT OF THEM. — DEFECTION OF CHIEFS TRIBUTARY TO KELAT. — CAUSE. — CLOSE OF THE HISTORY TILL THE YEAR 1810. — INTESTINE BROILS SINCE. — THEIR SANGUINARY CONSEQUENCES. — THE AMBITIOUS PROJECTS OF THE PRESENT KHAN OF KELAT. — THE AUTHOR'S SENTIMENTS ON THEM.

IT is impossible to fix, with any degree of precision, the period at which the revolution just alluded to occurred, but I am led to conjecture it was not two centuries ago. I offer this surmise, on the grounds of the reigning family having held the chief authority ever since. Its genealogical descent is said to be

1. Kumbur, father of

2. Sumbur, father of
3. Mohummud Khan, father of
4. Abdoolla Khan, father of
5. Hajee Mohummud Khan, brother of
6. Nusseer Khan, father of
7. Muhmood Khan, the present ruler;

And as the six former chiefs, with the exception of Hajee Mohummud Khan, died or were killed at an advanced age, I think we may estimate their lives at one hundred and fifty years, or rather more.

Previous to the aggrandisement of this family, Kelat had been governed by a Hindoo dynasty for many centuries, and the last Rajah was either named Sehwa, or that had always been the hereditary title assumed by the princes of his race, on mounting the Gaddee. This last surmise seems to be the best founded, because the city of Kelat is, at this hour, very frequently spoken of as Kelaté Sehwa, an appellation it is more likely to have derived from a line of governors than one individual, unless, as was the case with Nusseer Khan, he was distinguished for great talents and virtues.

Sehwa himself resided principally at Kelat, while his only son, Sungeen, officiated in the capacity of a Naeb or lieutenant-governor at Zuhree. The administration of both those princes is avowed to have been very equitable, and affording every possible encouragement to merchants or other sojourners in their territories. Sehwa was at length obliged to invite to his aid the mountain shepherds with their leader, against the encroachments of a horde of depredators from the western parts of Mooltan, Shikarpoor, and Upper Sinde, who headed by an Uffghan chief, with a few of his followers, and a Rind Belooche tribe, still famous for its robberies, called the Muzarees, infested the whole country, and had even threatened to attack the seat of government, which was then nothing better than a straggling village.

The chief who obeyed the summons was the Kumbur, whose name stands at the head of the genealogical list, at the commencement of this chapter; his ancestors were believed to have been originally Abyssinians *, and he was considered the lineal descendant of a famous Peer or saint, who worked many miracles in his time. This gave Kumbur and his adherents a weight and respectability among their countrymen, to which neither the numbers of the latter, nor the hereditary possession of the former, gave them any claim, for his paternal property was very trifling indeed, and lay in the district of Punjgoor in Mukran.

On their first ascending the lofty mountains of Jhalawan and Sarawan, these auxiliaries were allowed by Sehwa a very small pittance, on which they could scarcely support life; but in a few years, having either extirpated or quelled the robbers against whom they had been called in, and finding themselves and their adherents the only military tribe in the country, and consequently masters of it, Kumbur formally deposed the Rajah, and assuming the government himself, forced numbers of the Hindoos to become Moosulmans, and put others, under the cloak of religious zeal, to death.

Sehwa, the Rajah, with a trifling portion of the population, fled towards Zuhree, where his son Sungeen was still in power; but their new enemies daily acquired fresh strength by the enrollment of other tribes under their banners, and at length succeeded in driving them from that retreat, whence they repaired to the cities of Shikarpoor, Bhukor, and Mooltan, and obtained an asylum among the inhabitants, who were principally of their own persuasion.

Sehwa is said to have died during the latter part of this rebellion, and his son Sungeen, being made a prisoner, abjured his faith, and embraced Islamism, which example was adopted by a good number of his followers, who still retain evidence of their former religion in the name of their tribe, being Gooruwanee †. These are now settled in Kutch Gundava, and are reputed to be a quiet laborious

* The word Kumbur in the Belooche language signifies an Abyssinian, thence Kumburanee, the name of the tribe to which Muhmood Khan belongs.

† Gooruwanee, disciples of a Gooroo or Hindoo priest.

set of men, more like the Noomrees of Lus, than mountain Belooches.

Subsequent to the accession of Kumbur to the Musnud, the history of this country is involved in the same obscurity it was in during the Hindoo dynasty; and indeed it would have been useless to have made further inquiry among a people who have no written documents. His successors appear to have gradually laid aside their enmity to the followers of Brahma, and by holding out every inducement, succeeded in recalling many of them to reside and trade under their authority. At the same time they did all in their power to incorporate the wandering shepherds into tribes, rewarding those who acceded to this plan with large tracts of land, free of taxes or any kind of stipulation, save that of acknowledging the paramount authority of the head of the Kumburanees, and furnishing him with quotas of troops, regulated by the exigency of the service they might be needed for, and the extent of the tribes on whom he might be pleased to make a call.

This peaceable system was, according to all oral accounts, for we have no other to depend upon for these points, persevered in till the time of Abdoolla Khan, the fourth in descent from Kumbur, who being an intrepid and ambitious soldier, turned his thoughts towards conquering Kutch Gundava, then held by different petty chiefs, obedient to the authority of the Nuwwabs of Sinde, to whom the most of them likewise paid tribute. A very large levy was accordingly called forth, and after various successes on both sides, the Kumburanees possessed themselves of the sovereignty of the portion of that fruitful plain which they still hold, including many fine districts, and the chief town Gundava.

It was during this contest, that the famous Persian conqueror Nadir Shah, commonly called in Europe Thamas Koolee Khan, advanced from Persia to the invasion of Hindoostan, and while at Kandahar *, dispatched several detachments under experienced gene-

* Kandahar, the capital of the Douranee country, lies about three hundred miles north by west of Kelat.

rals into Beloochistan, who established the monarch's authority in that province, and sent the two sons of Abdoolla Khan, the chief of Kelat, to the royal camp, as hostages for the good behaviour of their father, who was continued in the government of the country by Nadir's orders, but was very shortly after killed in a battle fought at Khanpoor in Kutch Gundava, between the forces of the Nuwwabs of Sinde and his own army. The victory was, however, decidedly in favour of the Brahooes, and the Sindians finding they could no longer make a stand against them, retired, after ravaging the country, and destroying all the towns and villages.

On the death of Abdoolla Khan, his eldest son, Hajee Mohummud Khan, who, as already related, was in the camp of Nadir Shah as a hostage, having been invested by that king with the usual Khilăăt *, repaired to Kelat, and took into his own hands the reins of government; he soon, however, evinced his total incapability to support the dignity of his late father, and, in a few months, the Sindians seeing this change, returned with an army into Kutch Gundava, but the Belooches and the other inhabitants of that province were so exasperated by the cruelties and devastation they had unnecessarily practised on flying from it the preceding year, that they rose in a body and chased them across the Indus, along the eastern bank of which river they marched home.

In the interim, Hajee Mohummud Khan had abandoned himself to the most tyrannical and licentious way of life: amongst other duties, he levied nearly treble the Bazar tolls that had been collected by his father, who had made them as light as possible, in order to give encouragement to trade; he ordered that no Hindoo should be allowed to live within a distance of his palace, which was so great, that it expelled them all from their shops, and when they expostulated, or fled, he confiscated their property to his own use. In fact there was no proceeding, however nefarious, to distress that class of his subjects, that he did not aim at; he revived a very oppressive and

* An honorary dress.

disused custom, by which he, as the lord paramount of Kelat, had a right to enjoy the bride's company on the night of a Hindoo's nuptials, and even wished to extend this law, evincing the abject state to which the Hindoos had been reduced *, to all his Moosulman Ryots.†

The people had groaned under this system for the space of two years and some months, the town of Kelat was nearly deserted, and the heads of tribes had ceased to attend at the Durbar, or to pay even the semblance of obedience to the commands of Hajee Mohummud Khan, when Nadir Shah, on his march from Sinde, passed within seventy or eighty miles of the seat of government, and dismissed Nusseer Khan, the second son of Abdoolla Khan, and brother of the tyrant, with a Khilăăt and other honourable marks of the royal favour: this prince had accompanied the victorious monarch to Delhi; and, on every occasion, shewed such proofs of courage and sagacity, that Nadir, it is said, advised him at a public levee to depose his brother, and restore the country to its former prosperity and quiet; on his arrival at Kelat, he was, therefore, hailed by the few inhabitants it contained, and, indeed, the whole population of the province as their deliverer; and finding that expostulation had no effect on his brother, he one day entered his apartment when alone, and stabbed him to the heart ‡; the guards made not the slightest opposition to this scene, and the moment the tyrant was dead, they declared Nusseer Khan their chief: he accordingly mounted the Musnud amid the universal joy and rejoicing of his subjects, and immediately transmitted a report of the events that had taken place to Nadir

---

* This law was said to have been established by Kumbur on his first seizure of Kelat, more to deter Hindoos from settling there, than from any other motive or passion.

† Ryots, subjects.

‡ This transaction is told in two ways. One as above, the other that Nusseer Khan took the palace guards into the room with him, and made them dispatch his brother. This seems at first to be the most probable, but Nusseer Khan ever after spoke of the act he had committed with sincere grief, and said, that nothing but the welfare of his country and countrymen could ever have induced him to do so.

Shah, who was then encamped near Kandahar. The Shah was gratified by the intelligence, and dispatched a Furman*; by return of the messenger, nominating Nusseer Khan Beglerbeg of all the territories comprising the first five divisions of this memoir.

Nusseer Khan commenced his reign by such acts as were likely to secure the fidelity and esteem of his subjects. He revoked the greatest part of the taxes imposed on merchandise by his brother, fixing them at the present moderate standard; and the tolls on horses and cattle of all descriptions he entirely abolished; he publicly expressed his disapprobation of religious controversies, whether between the two sects of Moosulmans, or either of them, and the Hindoos, whom he invited by every encouragement from Shikarpoor and other trading towns, being well aware that they would prove an incalculable benefit to his dominions. As an inducement for them to settle at Kelat, he not only allowed them the free exercise of their religion, but re-established a grant, supposed to have been made by the immediate successor of Kumbur, empowering the Hindoos to levy for the maintenance of Brahmins, and a pagoda, one quarter of a rupee on every camel load of goods that entered the Bazar.

His next step was to call upon all the chiefs, who held by military tenure to furnish their quotas of troops, and having, by that measure collected a very large force, he marched from Kelat, passing through Khoadar and Punjgoor, and proceeded to Kedge, the capital of the province of Mukran, where he remained some time; thence he moved westerly as far as the town of Kussurkund, on the frontier of his territories; and taking a circuit to the northward, came back to his capital by the route of Dizuck and Kharan. In the course of this progress, he inquired into and arranged the internal government of all the provinces and districts in his dominions, and on reaching Kelat, applied himself to the improvement of that city, building the present fortifications, and forming, at his own expence, many gardens in the valley, which, having stocked with fruit trees brought

* A royal letter or order.

from Kabool and Persia, he made presents of them to deserving people, offering rewards for the finest specimens of fruit, grain, &c. He likewise received the submission of all the Belooche and other chieftains in Kutch Gundava, and came to the determination of passing a part of every winter in that province, a practice still adhered to by his son.

On the death of Nadir Shah, an event that took place in 1747, Nusseer Khan acknowledged the title of the King of Kabool, Ahmed Shah Abdalli, who then founded the dynasty which still reigns in that country. In doing so he seems to have been actuated by a consideration of the proximity of that kingdom to his own dominions, and a wish to avoid a war; for he did not consider himself tributary to that monarch, but rather an inferior participator in the division of Nadir Shah's empire. In 1758 he declared himself entirely independent, and Ahmed Shah dispatched a force under one of his ministers to chastise this alleged presumption. The Khan again levied his feudal troops, and totally routed the Uffghan army at the village of Pringowadh, seventy miles north of Kelat. On the news of this discomfiture reaching court, the King himself marched with strong reinforcements, and Nusseer Khan was worsted in a pitched battle, fought at Mustoong, three miles from the former field of action. He retired in good order to Kelat, where he had previously made every preparation for a vigorous resistance; and the victor, as he had anticipated, followed him, and invested that place with his whole army. The siege was protracted by the intrigues of some chiefs in the Douranee service; and after the royal troops had been foiled in three attempts to take the city by storm or surprize, a negotiation was proposed by the King, which ended in a treaty to the following purport: "That the King was to receive the cousin of "Nusseer Khan in marriage, as a pledge of their future friendship; "and that the Khan was to pay no tribute whatever; but, when "called upon, was to furnish troops, and to transport them at his "own expence to the royal camp; after which, he was to receive an "allowance, in cash, equal to half their pay." The Khan also expressly stipulated, "that he and his successors were never to assist "in a civil war; a clause to which they have strictly adhered "throughout all the dissensions respecting the Kabool dominions *." This treaty having been ratified, the King returned to Kandahar with his new wife and some of her relations, among whom were the Khan's mother, and Beheram Khan, a brother of the lady that the King had espoused.

It is related as an anecdote of Nusseer Khan's military talents, and also one that tended to shorten the siege of Kelat, that he one day observed Ahmed Shah saying his prayers on a carpet spread in front of his tent: he instantly loaded and pointed one of the cannon of the fort, and struck, with the ball, the spot on which the King had just before prostrated himself. The monarch, as it is said, made immediate overtures for the negotiation, and afterwards complimented the Khan on this proof of his skill in gunnery.

In 1761-2, Nusseer Khan was called upon, by Ahmed Shah, to accompany him, on his second expedition into Hindoostan. He joined that monarch, with his troops, at the city of Lahore, in the Punjab, and was present at a battle fought between the Seikhs and the Uffghans, in which the former were defeated with great slaughter. The Khan afterwards returned to Kelat; while the King advanced to the relief of Delhi, which was then threatened by the remnant of the troops of the Mahratta confederacy that had escaped at the battle of Panniput †. In 1769, the whole of the Persian chiefs formed a coalition to attack the Uffghan dominions to the westward, and Nusseer

* When Captain Christie and myself were at Kelat in 1810, Shah Muhmood, one of the competitors for the throne, wrote to Muhmood Khan, desiring his aid against Shoojaool Moolk. The Khan's reply was, that he was ready to assist in expelling invaders from the dominions of the Kings of Kabool, or to provide his troops for foreign service; but, that his father's treaty with Ahmed Shah was a sufficient answer to the present demand.

† The battle of Panniput was fought in January 1761. An excellent and detailed account of it is to be found in the Third Volume of the Asiatic Researches, London, Fifth Edition, Page 91.

Khan again attended Ahmed Shah to meet this invasion. The Prince Tymoor, and some experienced generals were detached to give the Persians battle, near the city of Mushed in Khorasan; and when the day had taken a decided turn against the former, Nusseer Khan, with three thousand choice Belooche cavalry, made a most desperate charge, and beat the Persians back. A second instance, of similar gallantry and judgement, occurred at Tubbus * during this campaign; and on the close of it, the King bestowed upon Nusseer Khan, as a reward for his eminent services and a proof of his own gratitude, the districts of Shal and Mustoong, north of Kelat, and that of Hurrund Dajel, on the eastern bank of the Indus; to hold in perpetual and entire sovereignty. In return for these princely donations, the Khan voluntarily agreed to send a thousand men, as a yearly subsidiary for the protection of the province of Kashmeer.

Some years after these events Beheram Khan came from Kabool, whither he had attended his sister on her marriage with Ahmed Shah, and began to foment disturbances by claiming a greater portion of the revenue than his rank gave him a title to; at last, nothing less than an equal share of the government with Nusseer Khan would satisfy him, and both parties necessarily took the field, to decide the question by the sword; Beheram Khan was defeated in several skirmishes, and eventually sustained a complete overthrow in a desperate engagement fought at Koohuk near Kelat; he retired to Kabool, and did not again appear in Beloochistan during the life of Nusseer Khan, who died, after a very happy and prosperous reign, at an extreme great age, in the month of June, 1795, leaving three sons and five daughters. Muhmood Khan, the present chief of Kelat, his eldest son, was then a boy about fourteen years old.

* Nusseer Khan, by a feint, led the Tubbusee troops into an ambuscade; and, when in confusion, charged at the head of his cavalry. The consternation became universal, and the whole Persian army was literally destroyed. Tubbus lies about three hundred and twenty miles from Herat. Vide Appendix, Captain Christie's Journal, date *7th June*.

If we contemplate the character of Nusseer Khan, whether as a soldier, a statesman, or a prince, and call to mind the people among whom he was placed, we shall find in him a most extraordinary combination of all the virtues attached to those stations and duties. He began his career under the odium of having put his own brother to death; and yet such were the pangs he suffered, when he had leisure to reflect on that act, that even his enemies pitied him; and his conduct throughout life proved that he had believed it to be a duty incumbent on him to sacrifice his brother in order to save his country; he could not have been dazzled by the hopes of wealth, as he never lived in better style than his attendants when in the field, and shewed a total disregard to riches, except as the means of rewarding merit and improving the condition of his subjects; he seldom made presents in money, and frequently said he had remarked, that doing so encouraged idleness; but when any artizan brought him a specimen of his handiwork, he would order him ten or twelve times the value of it in cloth and other necessaries. As a statesman, he reconciled to his authority in a few months an immense kingdom, bestowed upon him by a cruel conqueror; and what proves his address was, that the most distant districts were always equally alert in obeying his orders with those at hand; his justice and equitable discharge of his duties as a prince were so conspicuous, that his name became and is a proverbial phrase amongst his immediate countrymen, and all classes of the population of Beloochistan, to the most western extreme. In short, had Nusseer Khan governed an enlightened nation, or one with which Europeans were better acquainted, he would, during his life, have been regarded as a phenomenon among Asiatic princes; he was liberal, brave, just, and forgiving, patient under adversity and distress, and so strict was his veracity, that he had never been known to break, or attempt to evade, the most trivial promise.

On the demise of the illustrious chief, whose character I have imperfectly sketched, his cousin Beheram Khan made another struggle to obtain the government, and the ministers of Muhmood Khan, who, as I have already said, was a child, were obliged to cede to him the province and town of Kutch Gundava, by a treaty, in which he agreed not to molest the remaining dominions of the latter chief; but he only adhered to this fcr a short time, and then raised a very large force, principally consisting of Sindians and other mercenaries. Muhmood Khan applied to Zeman Shah, then King of Kabool, for assistance, and that monarch dispatched a nobleman of his court to mediate the business. Beheram Khan would, however, hear of no terms, except those of Muhmood Khan resigning the government to him during his life-time, and accordingly war was declared. After various skirmishes, in most of which the rebel chief was successful, the two armies, led by the Khans in person, met at Duhunédurruh* in Kutch Gundava, and Beheram Khan's troops were totally defeated by the treachery of several tribes that deserted him during the engagement: he was himself wounded, and fled to Hyderabad, the capital of Sinde, where the Umeers refused him a refuge, dreading the anger of Zeman Shah; he accordingly proceeded on towards Buhawulpoor, but died from fatigue, at the Tanda or village of Kulundur Shah, within one hundred and twenty miles of that city. †

In addition to this competitor, Muhmood Khan had also to contend against his half sister, who, as soon as she heard of Beheram Khan's death, took that chief's only daughter to Larkhanu in Sinde; whence she sent a messenger to Meer Gholam Allee Talpooree, the principal ruler of that country, and stipulated with him that his army should assist in deposing Muhmood Khan, and placing his youngest half brother on the Musnud, in return for which he was to receive Beheram Khan's daughter in marriage. Her motives for this have never been clearly explained, but they most probably originated in some private quarrel. Meer Gholam Allee made every promise

* Literally, the mouth of the valley.

† The city of Buhawulpoor lies on the eastern side of the Gurruh river, in latitude 29° 25′ north longitude, 71° 59′ east. It is the capital of the territories of Buhawul Khan, usually called Daood Pootra, or the sons of David.

that was demanded, and came to Larkhanu, where his nuptials were celebrated; but, the moment he had got possession of his bride, he declared his resolution of not meddling with the internal government of Kelat. When Muhmood Khan heard of the Sindian Umeer's intention of uniting himself to a female of the Kumburanee tribe, he was highly exasperated at his presumption; but, as the Sang or agreement * had been made, and could not be broken off without going to war, to do which he was not then prepared, he was obliged to be silent; he, however, wrote to the King of Kabool, vowing eternal vengeance against the Talpoories † for the insult their head had offered to his family. To add to this feeling, the Umeers of Sinde availing themselves of these family dissensions at Kelat, seized the sea port town of Kurachee, which, before Nusseer Khan's death, belonged to the Belooche government; the governors and Hakims of several other provinces and districts, seeing the inability of their lord paramount to chastise their defection, also ceased to pay tribute to him, or even acknowledge his nominal authority, and, since that period, the dominions of the Khans of Kelat have so gradually diminished, that they are now comprised in the first and third divisions of this memoir.

Such is a summary sketch of the history of Beloochistan from the earliest ages to the year 1810. Since the latter date, intestine broils have been attended with much more sanguinary consequences; and, of the three sons of Nusseer Khan, only the eldest is now alive. The second, Meer Mustapha Khan, was killed in the year 1811, at a hunting party, by his younger brother, who afterwards raised troops and took possession of the rich district of Hurrund Dajel. Muhmood, who is a very humane and indolent man, wished to persuade this fratricide to return to his allegiance, and even offered him an unconditional pardon, but he would hearken to no terms; and, in

* For an account of the Sang, see Part I. Chapter IV. Marriage ceremonies.

† The Talpoories are a very low tribe, which added to Muhmood Khan's ire. Vide Account of the province of Sinde, Division VI. Chapter XII.

the month of November, 1812, a force, under Qadir Buksh, the chief of Zuhree, was sent to quell him. A battle was fought at Moonee, a village in Hurrund Dajel, in which the Kumburanee Khan was killed, with forty of his Khanuzads, or household slaves. The other part of his troops, the moment they saw him fall, which he did very early in the action, laid down their arms and called for quarter. Subsequent accounts state that Muhmood Khan contemplates an attempt to re-establish his authority throughout Beloochistan, on the same footing that his father bequeathed it to him; but, from my own observation while in that country, combined with the known indolence and irresolution of that chief, I am convinced he has not the slightest prospect of success; and, were the Belooches to the westward to direct their exertions against him, I should fully expect to see him expelled from his present limited territories.

CHAPTER IV.

GOVERNMENT. — LIKELY TO FLUCTUATE. — DESPOTIC AUTHORITY OF NUSSEER KHAN. — HIS POLITIC METHOD OF SOFTENING ITS RIGOUR. — TRIBES SELECT THEIR CHIEFS. — WAR. — TREATIES. — MADE BY THE KHAN OF KELAT. — CHIEFS BOUND TO OBEY. — BOUNDARY DISPUTES. — REFERRED TO THE KHAN. — HOW TO BE ADJUSTED. — LAW FOR RESTRAINING THE CHIEFS OF KHEILS OR SOCIETIES. — FEUDATORY CHIEFS MUST ATTEND WITH THEIR QUOTA OF TROOPS IN PERSON. — DISPOSITION AND DISTINGUISHING BANNERS OF THE ARMY. — RESPECT SHEWN TO THE KHAN OF KELAT OR HIS REPRESENSATIVE. — ANCIENT CODE OF LAWS. — CAUSE OF THEIR INADEQUACY. — NUSSEER KHAN FORMS ANOTHER. — LAWS RESPECTING MURDER. — BURGLARY. — THEFT BY DAY. — SHOP-LIFTING. — ADULTERY. — SEDUCTION. — PETTY OFFENCES AND THEFTS. — APPEALS TO THE KHAN. — ADVANTAGES AND SALUTARY EFFECTS OF THE LAW OF APPEAL. — EXCEPTION TO THE RESTRICTIONS ON THE LAW OF MURDER. — STRENGTH OF THE BELOOCHE ARMY. — EXAGGERATED. — PROBABLE STRENGTH. — REVENUES OF THE KHAN OF KELAT. — DUTIES. — LAND TAXES. — DIFFERENT RATES OF IT. — DEDUCTIONS MADE BY THE COLLECTORS. — HINDOO BROKERS. — FOR WHAT PURPOSE EMPLOYED. — CURRENCY OF KELAT. — TRADE.

THE general complexion of the government at Kelat, and all over Beloochistan, cannot very easily be defined; and must necessarily be always fluctuating with the different views that the chiefs may have, or revolutions that occur. When Nusseer Khan was in his full power, the whole kingdom might have been said to have been governed by a complete despotism, because no one could dispute or abrogate any of his orders and laws; yet, at the same time, that ruler so tempered the supreme authority, by granting the feudal chiefs privileges within their own tribes, that, to a casual observer, it bore the appearance of a military confederation.

The tribes all exercise the right of selecting their own Sirdar or head; but that office, when once fixed, appears to be hereditary. The Khan of Kelat, nevertheless, reserves to himself the nominal power of disapproving, or otherwise, of this selection; but I could not hear of a single instance of Nusseer Khan having attempted such a measure as refusing to confirm the nomination of the people; and, since his son has been at the head of the government, it is hardly looked upon as necessary to report to him their proceedings on this subject.

The city of Kedge and town of Gundava, the capitals of the provinces of Mukran and Kutch Gundava, were obliged to receive a Hakim, or governor, appointed by and subject to the pleasure of Nusseer Khan, although those places were inhabited by different tribes; which was deemed by the people to be so great an infringement on their natural rights, that the governor's authority had to be upheld by a considerable body of troops; and the moment Nusseer Khan died the inhabitants expelled them from both places. Muhmood Khan succeeded in enforcing his father's regulation in Gundava; but since that event Kedge has simply paid him a titular homage.

The power of declaring war and making treaties, connected with the whole of Beloochistan, rested with the Khan of Kelat; and the Sirdars of tribes had no option with regard to assisting him with their troops; indeed, they were not only bound to do so, but also to carry into execution such parts of the treaties entered into as had any relation to the tribe to which they belonged, even though detrimental to what they conceived to be their own interest or advantage; but if the common weal demanded a sacrifice of that nature from any particular community, the Khan of Kelat was expected to make it an equivalent compensation. He was, by the same reasoning, empowered to fix the limits of all landed property; and where disputes on the subject of boundaries arose, whether between tribes or individuals, reference alone was had to the Khan as lord of the soil. It then became his duty to make the strictest investigation, to examine the whole of the witnesses brought forward on each side; for they seldom, perhaps never, had any other means of supporting their claims; and afterwards to pronounce his opinion, which was conclusive.

When a complaint happened to be made to him, by a man of any Kheil against the Sirdar of it, he had the option of either enquiring into the merits of and deciding the matter, or referring it to the head of the tribe to which the Kheil of the complainant and defendant belonged. He was, however, not likely to resort to the latter plan; because, if either party, as was almost inevitably the case, fancied himself aggrieved by the judgement of the Sirdar of his tribe, he could still appeal to the Khan of Kelat. The only benefit, consequently, to be derived from a reference to the head of the clan, was, that it brought the true state of the case at one view to the highest court.

Another very strong evidence of the absolute supremacy of the Khans of Kelat, is their being enabled to order the Sirdar of each tribe to attend in person with his quota of troops. When the collective army takes the field they are divided into three divisions, each distinguished by a particular banner. The troops of the province of Kutch Gundava and the districts of Kelat and Nooshky, move under the immediate command of Muhmood Khan or his Naeb (deputy), and bear a red flag; those of the province of Sarawan are led by Rysar Khan, and are known by a green forked pennant. Qadir Buksh Khan, Zuhree, and Wulee Mohummud Khan, Mingull *, jointly share the honour of heading the auxiliaries of the provinces of Jhalawan and Lus, and their distinguishing flag is yellow. If any of these divisions are detached, the leaders beat the Nukharah or kettle-drum, and should the armies of Sarawan and Jhalawan be serving together, their different generals do the same in their own quarter of the camp; but the moment the Kelat troops join them,

* Zuhree and Mingull are the names of their tribes.

whether headed by the Khan in person or his deputy, that distinction appertains alone to them.

A code of regulations for the administration of justice was formed by one of the earliest Princes of the Kumburanee tribe, which entailed the entire task of that important duty on the person at the head of the government; and, consequently, when the dominions of that family became so widely spread, as they were during Nusseer Khan's reign, the laws were found inadequate to the proposed end. That wise legislator, therefore, set himself about remedying this evil; and the part of his territories which now remain to his son is governed by his regulations. In cases of murder the Khan always sits in judgement; nor is any other chief in the country considered competent to do so, unless by special permission. The usual laws on that head are as follow.

If a man kill another, and the relations of the deceased are willing, it is usually expiated by imprisonment and heavy fines. In the extreme case of not being able to come to terms, blood for blood may be demanded; and, as the Khan endeavours to evade actually passing sentence of death himself, he usually delivers the offender over to the friends of the person whom he has killed, to do as they like with him. This plan is usually successful in saving the man's life, and he is kept as a slave at hard labour, To this latter law there is, however, one unerring exception, which speaks highly in praise of the feelings and policy that dictated it; that is, when the murdered person is a foreigner, for then, every one concerned in his death is immediately executed. Next to murder, burglary and robberies at night are the crimes most severely punished; and when either are clearly proved, death is always awarded. Theft by day, and ordinary crimes, such as shop-lifting, picking pockets, &c., are subject to flogging and imprisonment, according to the extent or value of the articles stolen.

A man who discovers his wife committing adultery, may put her and her lover both to death; but he must bring two respectable witnesses to attest the fact, else it is treated as a case of murder. In the same manner, if he can produce four creditable eye witnesses to his wife's infidelity, though he himself should not have suspected it, he is at liberty to destroy her, and her paramour if he can get hold of him. The circumstance is then reported to the Khan, who, assisted by the Moollahs or priests, examines into it, and if the proofs are valid, the matter is settled; but should any doubt arise respecting the evidence, the man, who has revenged his own supposed wrong, is doomed to the most severe penalty for murder, and the witnesses are given up to the family of the accused person until they can prove their assertions. This salutary law equally restrains revenge and false accusation. — If a man seduces a girl, and her father should discover it before she is pregnant, he may insist on both parties being put to death, and the Khan is bound to condemn them, in support of parental authority; but this is a case that had never been known to occur, and the measure is usually obviated by marriage.

Petty quarrels, thefts, and, in short, disputed points of every description, among the inhabitants of a Kheil or society, are adjusted by the Sirdar; and, from him, the parties may appeal to the chief of the tribe to which the Kheil appertains. Should it be of considerable importance, a third appeal lies to the Khan at Kelat; but, as he seldom finds it necessary to reverse the first sentence, and both time and trouble are required to obtain a hearing, very few think it adviseable to make the attempt. It is this voluntary feeling that throws a great part of the jurisprudence of the country into the hands of the Sirdars and chiefs, thereby relieving the Khan of a vast pressure of business, which is, naturally, more easily and equitably decided on the spot where the disputes arise, while it does not deduct in the least from the actual liberty of the subject, and makes the heads of the first tribes amenable for their acts.

The only case in which a criminal can be executed, without the previous licence or decree of the Khan of Kelat, is when a traveller is way-laid and murdered: on such an occasion, the nearest chief is authorized to carry the law into execution and make a report of the circumstances immediately. Serious disputes between tribes, or

Kheils, are always brought before the Khans of the Kumburanee tribe, at an assembly composed of Muhmood Khan and his relations.

A register of the Belooche army that I saw at Kelat, exhibited an aggregate of two hundred and fifty thousand men, but it had been drawn out at the period when Ahmed Shah first threatened to invade Beloochistan, unless Nusseer Khan would agree to pay him a tribute, and it was sent to that monarch in answer to his furman; it was, therefore, most probably much exaggerated, though even now, the same documents comprise a list of one hundred and twenty thousand troops, after rejecting all the revolted provinces and districts. I should, however imagine that, on the greatest emergency, Muhmood Khan could not muster more than half that number of fighting men. His total revenues, in their present reduced state, I should suppose fairly estimated at 350,000 rupees annually *, a large portion of which is paid in produce. In Nusseer Khan's time, the revenues exceeded thirty lacks of rupees per year, but Mukran, Lus, Punjgoor, Dizuk, Kharan, &c. &c., then paid tribute, exclusive of the customs of the sea port town of Kurachee in Sinde.

The duties levied at Kelat are exceedingly moderate. A camel-load, (whatever it may be), pays five rupees on entering the city to the government, and one quarter of a rupee to the Hindoos; there is also a Bazar toll on all goods sold, which does not amount to one and a half *per cent.* on their cost; horses or cattle pay nothing whatever throughout the Belooche territories: land watered by wells or trenches, which require labour and trouble to keep them in repair, pays about one twentieth of the produce; and that which is otherwise cultivated by rain, fluctuates between a sixteenth and a tenth, according to the season. Where there are chushmuhs or springs, the tax is still higher; and in some of the gardens of Kelat it nearly amounts to one-fifth. The whole of this is not paid into the Khan's treasury, as a very small portion of it is appropriated by the Sirdars of the tribes and

* Forty-three thousand seven hundred and fifty pounds sterling.

Kheils, who are usually employed to receive the government customs, and forward them to Kelat. When the receipts in kind exceed (as they must always do), the consumption of the Khan, the overplus is made over to a Hindoo broker, who supplies him with articles of foreign manufacture or growth, in return for the produce of his own country.*

The currency of Kelat is in Kureem Khanee rupees, to one of which there are forty-eight copper pice. Gold sequins pass here for six Kureem Khanee rupees, of which five are equal to four Zeman shahees. The exports from Kelat itself are very trifling; but it was once the great channel for merchandize from Kandahar, Kabool, and Khorasan to India, the traders being induced to prefer this route on account of the low customs; its imports are iron, tin, lead, steel, copper, indigo, beetel-nut, cochineal, sugar, spices, silks, keemkhab, gold-cloth, chintz, and coarse woollens from India. Fruit, &c. they receive from Kabool and Khorasan, and sometimes steel and copper from Seistan. Dates from Punjgoor and the southern parts of Mukran, and white cloth, chintz, loongees, turbands, and salt they have from Sinde, Mooltan and Shikarpoor.

I shall include my remarks on the climate, soil, and natural history of Beloochistan, under one general chapter, at the close of this memoir, and in the mean time, proceed to a geographical notice of the different divisions.

* This is the constant practice with chiefs of every rank and description, from Muhmood Khan downwards; and even Eidel Khan, the Surdar of the small Kheil of Nooshky has his Hindoo agent to transact all business.

CHAPTER V.

SECOND DIVISION OF BELOCHISTAN. — PROVINCES OF MUKRAN AND LUS. — BOUNDARIES. — LENGTH. — BREADTH. — FACE OF THE COUNTRY. — HIGHEST MOUNTAINS. — HINGLATZ TEMPLE. — MUKRAN HOW DIVIDED. — MUCH. — WHY SO CALLED. — THE PROVINCE OF LUS. — ITS EXTENT. — BOUNDARIES. — LUKHS OR DEFILES. — RIVERS. — POOR ALLY (ANCIENT ARABIS). — THE HUBB. — WUTTA. — SANGANEE. — DESCRIPTION OF THEM. — FACE OF THE COUNTRY. — THE CHIEF. — HIS REVENUES. — WHENCE DERIVED. — A FEUDATORY VASSAL OF KELAT. — ARMED FORCE. — DREAD OF THE BELOOCHES. — TOWNS AND VILLAGES OF LUS. — EXPORTS AND IMPORTS. — PROVINCE OF MUKRAN. — DISTRICTS. — UNKNOWN STATE OF THIS PROVINCE. — EXPLORED BY CAPTAIN GRANT. — THE AUTHOR'S ROUTE THROUGH IT. — RECENT INVESTIGATIONS. — RIVERS. — ERRONEOUS BELIEF HITHERTO ENTERTAINED REGARDING THEIR SIZE. — GENERAL DESCRIPTION OF THEM. — MINUTE DETAIL FROM EAST TO WEST. — THE RIVERS. — AGHOR. — MUKLOO. — BHUSOOL. — ROOMRA. — SUDUK. — DUST OR DUSTEE. — THE GREAT LENGTH OF THE LATTER. — ITS VARIOUS NAMES. — SURMISE REGARDING IT. — FARTHER DETAIL OF THE RIVERS. — NIGAR. — NEEM KHOOR. — GAYANEE. — SIRRAH. — BUNTH AND SUDJEE. — KEDGE THE CAPITAL. — SITE. — SIZE. — SITUATION FAVOURABLE FOR TRADE. — GONE TO DECAY. — THE CAUSE. — NOW IN REBELLION. — LAST HAKIM PUT TO DEATH. — REVENUES ARISING FROM IT. — TRACT TO THE SOUTHWARD OF KEDGE. — ITS NATURE. — PUNJGOOR OR PUNJER. — FINE DISTRICT. — CELEBRATED FOR ITS DATES. — THE CHIEF. — HIS REVENUES. — MUCH. — ITS POSITION. — RUGGED TRACT. — POPULATION. — DELICATE RACE. — THEIR CHIEFS AND HABITS. — KUSSURKUND. — A LEVEL DISTRICT. — FORT. — PRECAUTIONS PRACTISED BY ITS NATIVES. — WHY NECESSARY. — NOT ALWAYS EFFECTUAL. — BUSHKURD. — VERY MOUNTAINOUS DISTRICT. — ITS INHABITANTS. — WHENCE EMIGRATED TO IT. — DISTRICTS OF DIZUK. — SIBB. — KALPOORUKAN AND JALK. — AGGREGATE POPULATION OF MUKRAN. — — NOT TO BE ASCERTAINED. — AUTHOR'S OPINION OF THE NATIVES OF THE COAST. — COMPARED TO THE BELOOCHES AND BRAHOOES. — SENSUAL LIVES. — WOMEN. — UGLY. — ABANDONED. — THE CONSEQUENCES. — LITTLE REGARD PAID TO THEIR ADULTEROUS PRACTICES. — LAWS. — UNKNOWN. — ANARCHY AND DREAD OF ATTACK. — TRADE. — BY WHOM CONDUCTED.

DIVISION II.

THE second division of Beloochistan, which includes the provinces of Mukran and Lus, is bounded on the north by parts of Jhalawan, the sandy desert, and the Kohistan; south by the Indian ocean; west by the province of Laristan; and east by that of Sinde. Its extreme length, from the range of mountains separating it from the latter province to its western boundary, exceeds five hundred and fifty miles, and in the broadest place from the sea-coast to the village of Jalk in the latitude 28° 34′ north, it is about two hundred and twenty. The nature of this tract, when compared with the first division, is much less mountainous; but there are, nevertheless, many great ranges running through and across it. These, fortunately, assist in fertilizing the soil, which is otherwise remarkably sterile, for it is to be observed, that wherever the plains of Mukran exceed ten or twelve miles in width, they are found to be, except at the immediate bases of the hills which encompass them, little better than complete deserts. The loftiest chain of mountains in Mukran are those to the westward, within the district of Bushkurd; whence, as I have shewn in a preceding chapter, they advance easterly until they encounter a southern arm of the Brahooick mountains, and the coalition of both forms the Kohistan *. The next range, as to elevation, is that very short one, which projects from the south-western angle of the Brahooick mountains, directly southward to the coast, forming the cape, called by Europeans Arabah, and by the natives Urboo. On the summit of this range, within view of the sea, stands the celebrated Hindoo temple of Hinglatz, dedicated to Kalee, the goddess of fate, to which many thousand pilgrims yearly resort.

* The district of Bushkurd is looked upon by the natives as a part of the Kohistan, and the Koords, who inhabit it, are never spoken of by the term Mukranees or people of Mukran: but as it lies to the southward of the parallel I have drawn as the southern line of the Kohistan, and is also unquestionably in Mukran, I include it in this Division.

Of the two branches of the Brahooick mountains, that run nearly east and west throughout the greater part of Mukran, one divides it into the northern and southern portion, and the other separates them both from the desert; the northern one is called by the natives Wushutee or Much, the last of which words signifies a palm tree, and we accordingly find that the date begins to flourish there * in great perfection. To the westward, a large range inclines nearer the sea-coast than the mountains lie in general, and forms the head lands of Cape Moobaruk and Cape Jask, which is the western limit of what is considered by the inhabitants to be in Mukran.

The province of Lus or Lussa might, perhaps, with great propriety, be looked upon as the eastern division of Mukran; but as it is entirely independent, and always spoken of as a distinct tract, I have assumed the same grounds for doing so. It is called Lus, or Lussa, from the former word meaning in the Judgalee language, a valley or plain; it extends about ninety miles by fifty, and its boundaries are Jhalawan on the north, the bay of Sonmeany on the south, and ranges of mountains on the east and west, separating it from Sinde and Mukran. Three sides of it are consequently encircled by mountains, and these are only accessible by five Lukhs, or Passes, two of which lead into Mukran, two into Sinde, and one to the northward into Jhalawan; the two former are called the Lukhs of Hinglatz and Bela, because the road over one of them passes close to the temple of that name, and the other commences within five miles of the latter town; those into Sinde are distinguished by the names Kurachee and Hyderabad, affixed to Lukh, from lying on the roads to those places, and the one towards Kelat is styled "Kohun Wat," or the mountain road, owing to its direction through the lofty piles of Jhalawan.

The rivers of Lus are two, the Poorally and Hubb; the former, which is known in ancient geography as the Arabis, rises in the mountains north-east of Bela, whence after leading along the base of the Jhalawan mountains, until near that town, it there takes a

* Wushutee is a term synonymous with the Persian "Khoosh Amudee;" You are welcome, or, how do you do?

southerly bend, passes close to it, and falls into the bay of Sonmeany, about two miles south-west of that village. The water of this river is very fine as far as Lyaree, twenty miles north-north-east of Sonmeany, where it is impregnated by the sea, and becomes navigable for small boats, and the deeper places of it abound with fine fish: at Bela, in the very dry season, it is only from fifteen to twenty yards wide, and a foot or two deep, while, in the rains it is above a quarter of a mile across, and completely unfordable. The Hubb is a very small stream, having its source in the mountains separating Lus and Sinde, and thence it runs directly west into the sea: beside these, there are two or three rivulets, such as the Wutta, the Sanganee, &c. that rise in different places in the mountains, and empty themselves into the Poorally; they are frequently dry, or nearly so, unless in the rains.

The whole face of the country of Lus is perfectly flat, as its name indicates, and it is in general barren, except on or close to the banks of the different streams, but there it produces very abundant crops of grain, sugar-canes, &c. The chief of this little state is Jam Meer Mahomed Khan, who enjoys a revenue of fifty thousand rupees per annum, arising chiefly from the Bazar duties of Bela, and the customs of Sonmeany, and the port of Urboo, which lies at the back of the mountains of Mukran. He, at one period, sent a large part of this as tribute to Nusseer Khan of Kelat, but on his marriage with one of the daughters of that ruler, he was exempted from the payment, and now holds his government under the feudatory tenure of furnishing four thousand five hundred irregular troops, for the service of his lord paramount: these are more men than, I believe, he could muster, and in fact, the whole conditions have become little more than nominal. His territories, however, are subjected to all the restrictions, already detailed, of the other heads of tribes in Beloochistan, and an appeal may be made by any of his subjects, even against himself, to the Khan of Kelat; nor should I think it likely he would attempt to call in question the validity of, or resist, any orders he might receive from that court: his country lies so open to the inroads of the Bezunjas, Mingulls, and other Brahooe tribes, who would rejoice to receive Muhmood Khan's sanction to overrun it, that he is held in the utmost awe and subjection.

The chief town of Lus is Bela, of which I have given a description in the first part of this work. Next to it ranks Lyaree, a small place lying about twenty miles north-north-east of Sonmeany; it is situated on the bank of the Poorally river, and contains from sixteen to eighteen hundred houses. A Darogah or overseer resides here, to receive the Bazar tolls and other customs. Ootul, of which an account will be found in my Diary of the *20th of January*, is the third place in the country; and there are, altogether, not more than twelve fixed villages within the whole province. The people reside in huts, or tents, that are constructed to be removed at pleasure.

The exports of this country are grain, in considerable quantities, and a few felts, and coarse carpets; these articles are chiefly sent to Mukran, and the coast of Arabia, whence are received in return, dates, almonds, and Caffre slaves; the latter are very valuable here, and do most of the outdoor labour. Its imports from Bombay consist of iron, steel, tin, sugar, beetel-nuts and cocoa-nuts; and from Sinde, they are supplied with coarse white cloths, chintzes, loonges, and a little raw cotton, intended to be worked into a stuff called Khargee, which the very poorest classes wear; broad cloth and other European manufactures, are highly prized, but the poverty of the natives, and consequent trifling sale, will not authorize the importation.

In reverting to the province of Mukran, I shall commence by an enumeration of a number of its districts, but as many of these are either uninhabited, or exceedingly unfertile, I mean to confine myself to observations on those most deserving from their nature, of that attention. The principal inland districts of Mukran are Kedge, Punjgoor, Much, Dizuk, Kussurkund, Bushkurd, Sibb, Jalk, Kalpoorukan and Kohuk, and on the sea-coast, there are those of Urboo Koolaj, Choubar, Teez and Gwak.

The whole of this country was unknown to Europeans, except the sea-coast, until the latter end of 1809, when Captain Grant of the

Bengal Native Infantry, was dispatched into it by Brigadier-general Malcolm, and made a considerable circuit into the south-western parts of it: a part of my route from Kelat to Bunpoor lay through the most northern districts; and, with these to direct my inquiries, I have, since my return to India, gained so considerable a stock of native information, corroborative of what I had myself seen, that I may venture to write with great certainty on subjects connected with this province.

As I have already treated of the mountains of Mukran in different preceding places, I need add nothing further with respect to them. There are a vast number of river mouths along the sea-coast, which have led to a belief, that the inland part of the country was well stocked with streams; but so far from that being the case, there is scarcely a brook in it that runs throughout the year, and not one that extends in an uninterrupted channel from its source to the sea; they all, usually, have a broad and deep channel from the coast, until they reach the mountains or stony hills, where they become contracted into narrow and intricate water-courses, that are quite dry the greater part of the fair season, and in the wet one, swelled to terrific torrents, which run off in the course of a few hours after the rain that has filled them ceases. The beds of all these water-courses are usually overgrown with a thick and impervious jungul of tamarisk, Farnesian mimosa, and other bushes, that afford browsing for camels and goats, besides harbouring many different descriptions of wild beasts.

In order to render the most perspicuous view in my power of these river beds, I shall begin with the most easterly, and point them out with their various meanderings, as I move westerly.

Immediately on ascending the range of mountains, separating Lus from Mukran, we come to the Aghor Nudee*, which runs under the pagoda of Hinglatz, and thence through a succession of narrow beds

* Nudee, a river.

to the sea; close to the temple, in the bed of the Nudee, is a famous well, which is called from its depth, the "Uneel Ka Koond," or unfathomable abyss; a man who had been there, assured me he had seen some hundred fathom of rope let down without coming at the water, and the natives believe it to have been dug by the tutelary goddess of the temple. The water of the pagoda is very fine, and esteemed good for many diseases. Two stages farther on we find the Muckloo Nudee, which has its source forty-five miles from the sea, and receives two or three rivulets in its course. In the succeeding forty miles west from this place are the Bhusool, Roomra and Suduk nullahs or streams, the two former of which traverse a distance of twenty or thirty miles from the nearest hills, and the latter about eighty. Within one mile of the Suduk is the village of Pusunee, which once carried on some trade, and the river was sufficiently deep to admit of canoes going ten or twelve miles up it, to cut timber for knees for boats and fire-wood; but the village was burnt in 1809 by the Arab pirates, and the Hindoos have left the place. Thence to the Dust Nudee is upwards of seventy miles, in which extent of coast there is only one very small rivulet. The Dust is the largest stream we have yet come to, and the reader will form an idea of the others, when he is told, that the depth of the stream in it at low water, within one hundred yards of the beach, is about twenty inches, and the breadth from ten to thirty yards. When the tide flows, the sea rushes up for a mile or two, and a person who should then see, and pass his opinion on it, would pronounce it a fine river.

Notwithstanding its diminutive depth and breadth, where it disembogues, the Dust * may be traced under different names, to a distance of between six and seven degrees in a direct line from the coast, and from the various enquiries I have made on this point, I should conjecture, that water running from its northern extreme into the sea, would traverse little less than one thousand miles. In my

Sometimes the Dustee.

journey across the sandy * desert, I passed a river bed called the Boodoor, which was at least a quarter of a mile in breadth, and I was informed, that it extended in various windings to Gurmysyl, a country on the banks of the Helmind river in Seistan. To the southward of my path, it forces egress between the mountains, and turning more easterly, fertilizes the district of Punjgoor, three miles to the northward of which, an abundant and never failing stream springs from its bed; thence it winds through a series of glens and ravines past Kedge, the capital of the province; at which place it is called the Mooleedanee river, and a little farther southerly, we discover it with the title of the Bhugwar: this it retains, until it becomes the Dust or Dustee, under which name it falls into the ocean.

On consideration of what I have stated above, I am inclined to imagine, that the Dustee, or by whatever other name we may distinguish it, has been formerly the bed of a river much larger than any now in Mukran, that has either been drained by its waters flowing into some other channel, or the original source of them being exhausted. †

Westward of the Dustee are the Nigar, the Neem Khoor, the Gayanee, the Sirrah, the Bunth, the Sudgee, and various other nullahs or brooks, all of which empty themselves into the sea. They are sometimes so much increased by rains in the mountains, as to be unfordable; but in general they contain very little water.

Kedge, which I have already stated to be the chief town of this province, gives its name to a district that is well watered by the

* Vide Part I. Diary of the *1st of April.*

† The waters of Lhoreh river, which runs through the district of Shorawuk, to the north-east of Nooshky, are lost in the sand, and do not, it is said, again appear, unless in the Boodoor; but from the position at which I met with that river bed, and the information I received regarding it, I rather conceive it to be a branch of the Helmind, which has lost its stream by the sinking of the bed of that river. Captain Christie describes the high cliffs on each side of it, so as to give an idea of its having been once much more on a level with the desert than it is at present. Vide Appendix, Diary of the *20th of March.*

Dust Nudee. The fort of Kedge is built on a high precipice, under which the river runs; and, from its natural strength, the natives deem it impregnable. The town entirely surrounds three sides of the base of the hill on which the citadel stands, and once contained three thousand houses; but, since the death of Nusseer Khan of Kelat, the trade which was carried on through it between Kandahar, Kelat, Shikarpoor, Khozdar, Bayla, &c., and the sea-port towns of Gwuttur and Choubar has entirely ceased, and the Hindoos and other opulent dealers, have quitted the place, so that it is gone to decay. The Hakim or governor of Kedge, in 1810, was Abdoollah Khan, Bezunja Brahooe, who then pretended to acknowledge the authority of Muhmood Khan, but paid no tribute; and, since that period, I am informed he has ceased even to show outward respect. His predecessor was put to death about seven years ago, in the most faithless manner, by Meer Mustapha Khan, who finding that even nominal obedience was not paid to the orders of his brother the Khan of Kelat, sent a messenger to direct the governor's attendance at that city, which demand was replied to by a peremptory refusal. After some discussion, and a solemn promise being made, by the Kelat chiefs, of personal safety, a meeting was agreed to be held at Punjgoor. The Hakim was punctual in his attendance, but came never to return, as he was murdered by the troops that had accompanied Mustapha Khan.

The revenues of Kedge are very trifling, and the governor, who supported, as an officer of the Kelat government, four or five thousand men, has not, now-a-days, so many hundred Arabs in his pay.

The country immediately to the southward of Kedge is described as an arid *Dusht*, or tract of waste land; though in some spots, great quantities of dates are produced; but it seems to be the peculiar nature of the palm tree, to flourish in the most sterile and forbidding soil.

Punjgoor, or Punjer, is a small and fertile district lying about nine days' journey north-north-east from Kedge. It is a valley amid mountains, and contains twelve or thirteen villages of tents, that are abundantly supplied with water from the Boodoor river: they are all well peopled; and the district produces dates that are esteemed better than any others in Mukran *. The chief of Punjgoor is now Ruhmootoollah Khan, a nephew of Muhmood Khan of Kelat. Notwithstanding his relationship, he has followed the example of his countrymen at Kedge, and has declared himself independent. His revenues are said to amount to twenty thousand rupees per annum; but that sum I should conceive to be exaggerated.

Much is the term applied to that country, lying to the westward, and on the parallel of Punjgoor; and forming the southern barrier of the sandy desert which I travelled over. It is a very rugged, mountainous tract; producing, however, in some of its vallies, grain sufficient for the use of the few wandering shepherds that inhabit them. Water is said to be plentiful in Much, except in the months of April, May, and June, when it becomes scarce until the springs and rivulets are replenished by the rains; and, when they fail, the natives are obliged to retire to the southward. They also cùltivate some dates here; and have a few camels, goats, and sheep. They are described as a smaller and more delicate race than the Mukranees in general. Their arms are a matchlock, sword, and shield; and each village has its own chief, who decides all controversies that arise among the people.

Kussurkund is a plain twenty-five miles long, and nearly as broad; having a small river running through it. The fort defends the village, which is built all round it; and the cultivated grounds in the plain are likewise protected by low bastions, built at distances of four or five hundred yards, in which matchlockmen keep watch throughout the ripening season. This precaution is rendered indispensable, from the proximity of this district to the Nharooes of Bunpoor and the Kohistan; nor does it even always preserve their lands from being laid waste by those plunderers. All that can be said of Bush-

* For an account of the culture of the date tree, see Chapter VII.

kurd is, that it is one uninterrupted and rugged mass of mountains, that afford pasturage for the cattle of the Koord Belooches, who depend on the lower countries for grain and other supplies. These people are a tribe of Koords that have advanced out of Laristan, and are doubtless the descendants of a colony who conquered that province some centuries back *. They retain their inherent predilection for upland regions; and many of them have now settled in the Kohistan. Some mention of the districts of Dizuk, Sibb, Kalpoorukan, and Jalk, has already been made in the first part of this Work, and I deem it useless to enter into further detail †, either with regard to them, or any of those on the sea-coast, which are mere flat, bare, plains, extending to the bottom of the nearest mountains, without a symptom of vegetation.

The population of Mukran is so likely to fluctuate, from being composed of wandering tribes, that it would be ridiculous to guess at its extent; those of its natives who dwell on the sea-coast appeared to me to be of larger proportions and blacker complexion, than the northern ones, a circumstance that may probably be attributed to their frequent intermarriages with the Caffres of Muscat and Arabia; but still, all the Mukranees whom I saw, were a puny and delicate race of men, when compared to the Belooches, or Brahooes, and diseases were prevalent among them; these, however, may be owing to the climate, and their sensual lives, for which both sexes are notorious; they likewise drink great quantities of an intoxicating beverage, made from fermented dates, which must be exceedingly pernicious in its effects. The women of Mukran are, usually, very ugly, and proverbially unfaithful, they set no bounds to the gratification of their passions, and in consequence, at an early period of their lives, they are tottering under decrepitude and premature old age. The men do not seem to be remarkable for longevity. They pay so little regard to the

* Kinneir's Persian Empire. Page 83.

† Vide Narrative of the *4th, 7th, 8th,* and *9th April.* The village of Kullugan is in the Jalk district.

infidelity of their wives, that a sheep or two is always looked upon, in cases of discovery, to be an ample offering to appease the husband's wrath. The code of laws prepared for Beloochistan, by Nusseer Khan, was introduced into this province, with some necessary modifications by that Prince, but at his death they ceased to be respected, and all is now anarchy and bloodshed: each district has its own system of revenge, and travellers or merchants can only move from one part of the country to another when accompanied by an armed party, sufficiently strong to repel attack. The only trade carried on from the ports of Mukran, is the exportation of a part of the annual crops of dates to Bombay, and other parts in the peninsula, whence the returns are made in articles similar to those specified in my account of Lus; this commerce is conducted by Hindoos, who retail the imports by barter to the native Mukranees.

CHAPTER VI.

THIRD DIVISION OF BELOOCHISTAN. — THE PROVINCE OF KUTCH GUNDAVA AND DISTRICT OF HURRUND DAJEL. — LAWS, CUSTOMS, AND TAXES, SIMILAR TO THOSE IN KELAT. — BOUNDARIES OF KUTCH GUNDAVA. — EXTENT. — RIVERS. — THE NAREE AND KANHEE. — CHIEF TOWN. — SIZE AND FORTIFICATIONS. — TOWN OF DADUR, BHAG, AND LHEREE. — IMMENSE NUMBER OF VILLAGES. — POPULATION. — JETHS, OR JUTS. — THEIR HABITS. — SYSTEM UNDER WHICH THEY LIVE. — HINDOOS. — THE ONLY TRADERS. — THE DISTRICT OF HURRUND DAJEL — BOUNDARIES. — CHIEF TOWN. — THE HAKIM. — HIS UNLIMITED POWERS. — EXTENT OF THE DISTRICT. — FERTILITY. — GREAT REVENUE. — CLIMATE. — TRAFFICK — FOURTH DIVISION OF BELOOCHISTAN. — THE KOHISTAN. — WHENCE NAMED. — BOUNDARIES. — MOUNTAINS, THEIR PRODUCTIONS. — THE KOHI NOUSHADIR, OR SAL AMMONIAC HILL. — VOLCANIC APPEARANCE. — RIVERS OF THE KOHISTAN. — BUNPOOR RIVER. — KASKEEN RIVER. — DISTRICTS OF THE KOHISTAN. — MYDANEE, OR THE PLAIN. — KOHUKEE, OR THE HILLS. — TOWNS AND VILLAGES. — TOOMUNS. — NATIVES OF THE KOHISTAN. — GOVERNMENT. — ALMOST UNKNOWN. — STATE OF SOCIETY. — PUNISHMENTS HOW EVADED. — NECESSITY FOR ITS BEING SO. — TRADE OF THE KOHISTAN. — FIFTH DIVISION OF BELOOCHISTAN. — EXTENT. — BOUNDARIES. — REFERENCE TO THE NARRATIVE. — CONCLUSION OF THE GEOGRAPHICAL REMARKS ON BELOOCHISTAN. — PROVINCE OF SEISTAN. — ITS NATURE. — CAPITAL. — CHIEF. — REVENUES. — POWER. — THE RIVER HELMIND. — FORMS A LAKE. — EXTENT OF IT. — WATER. — FLIES. — PRECAUTIONS REQUISITE. — NATIVES OF SEISTAN. — THEIR LANGUAGE. — DRESS AND RELIGION. — DISTRICT OF GURMSYL. — FERTILITY. — INHABITANTS. — THEIR EVIL PRACTICES. — REVENUES OF THIS DISTRICT. — THE DISTRICTS OF KHOONCHEE, SHAL, AND MUSTOONG. — THE TWO LATTER CELEBRATED FOR THEIR FRUITS. — POPULATION. — CURIOUS FACT ATTENDANT UPON IT. — DISTRICT OF SHORAWUK. — ITS SITUATION. — REVENUE. — GOVERNMENT.

DIVISION III.

THE province of Kutch Gundava and the district of Hurrund Dajel, which I have apportioned as the third division of Beloochistan, being as unconditionally amenable and obedient to the authority of Muhmood Khan, as the district of Kelat, it naturally results that all points with respect to laws, customs, and taxes, which I have touched upon, in the third chapter of this Memoir, are equally to be applied to them; and it only remains for me to make my readers acquainted with their geographical extent and boundaries.

Of Kutch Gundava, the latter are Seeweestan on the north, Sinde on the south, the Brahooick mountains west, and a desert tract, lying between it and the river Indus, on the east. Its utmost length, from north to south, is about one hundred and twenty miles; and in breadth, the habitable and fertile part of it is little more than sixty.

There are two rivulets in Kutch Gundava; the Naree and the Kauhee. The former issues from the mountains north-west of Sebee, and runs past the following villages in succession, Mittree, Eree, Hajee, Buddha, Bhag, Nusseerabad, Pullall, Munjhoo, Kunduh, and Tumboo, close to which last place, it loses itself in the sand and impenetrable jungul. This brook has an immense quantity of water in it when heavy rains prevail, or the snow is melting on the mountains, but, commonly, it is for months at a time almost dry. The Kauhee runs down the valley of Boulan; which is the high road from the Dushtébe Doulut to Kutch Gundava, and at the Duhuné durruh * divides into two branches; one of which winds by the villages of Kauhee, Khanpoor, Myhésur, and Bhugaee; where it is banked up for purposes of cultivation; the other branch passes Dadur, and falls into the Naree, about four miles from the village of Eree. There are many aqueducts dug from both these rivers, that lead the water over the face of the plain, to irrigate the soil, and various natural branches of them are enclosed by bunds or embankments for the same end.

The chief town of this province is Gundava, which is not so large

* Duhuné durruh, literally the mouth of the valley. It is a halting place, and known by no other name, which induces me to use this in preference to the English meaning of it.

as Kelat, but built with greater regularity, and kept in better repair. The Khan of Kelat has a palace here, and he, with his family, and all the principal Sirdars, and people of the provinces of Jhalawan and Sarawan, come down every winter, to avoid the extreme cold of those lofty regions; the town is surrounded by a very high mud wall, that is always kept in repair, by the Jeths, or cultivators; and there are some small swivels mounted over the three gates, which are called those of Kelat, Kurachee, and Shikarpoor, from leading to the roads to those places: the second town is Dadur; and after it rank Bhag and Lheree, but none of these are of any considerable size; they severally contain from one thousand to fifteen hundred houses, protected by a mud wall and bastions pierced with loop holes. The villages in this fine plain are almost innumerable, and are increasing in number every year.

The great bulk of the population of Kutch Gundava are Jeths or Juts, a people whose manners, appearance, and customs, prove them to be descended from the aboriginal Hindoos, that have either been converted to, or forced to accept the Mohummudan faith. They reside, like the Dehwars of Kelat, exclusively in villages; and cultivate the adjacent soil under certain restrictions and immunities imposed upon and allowed them by the Belooche and Brahooé chieftains, to whom Muhmood Khan has granted the lands in fief. Most of the Belooches, and all the Brahooes, who possess ground in this province, only reside here during a few of the cold months in the year; and, as soon as the spring appears, they repair to the hills, leaving the Juths to till the country and transmit them their share of the crops, or keep it in readiness for their return. There are also a few Hindoo settlers in Gundava and the smaller towns and villages, who carry on a trade by barter with the cultivators, and dispatch the grain and other products to the sea-coast for exportation to Mukran, or elsewhere, according to the demand.

The district of Hurrund Dajel is bounded on the north by that of Derué Ghazee Khan; south, by the hills inhabited by the Goorchanees and other Rind Belooches; west, by the districts of Tul

Chuteealy and various independent Uffghan tribes; and, east, by the river Indus.

The chief town in this district is Hurrund, and the second Dajel; at the former of which a Hakim resides, on the part of Muhmood Khan, who is entrusted, owing to the distance of his government from the capital, with the fullest powers on all subjects connected with the laws and execution of them, even to the matter of life and death. The Hakim, in 1810, was Oolfut Khan Kumburanee, a cousin of Muhmood Khan, but I understand he has since been disgraced for not holding out against the rebels headed by Mahomed Ruheem Khan, the youngest brother of the latter prince, when he seized the towns of Hurrund and Dajel in 1811.*

This district does not exceed fifty miles, either in length or breadth, but the soil is so very fruitful that the Khan of Kelat is said to derive a greater revenué from it than from the whole of the province of Sarawan. The population is entirely composed of Juths, unless it may be a few Uffghans and other incidental colonizers. The climate is cooler in summer than that of Kutch Gundava †; and, in winter, is quite as mild and agreeable. There is a considerable traffick carried on from this district by means of boats on the Indus, that go up to Mooltan and Attock, or down to Hyderabad and Tattah.

DIVISION IV.

THE Kohistan, or land of mountains, which is the name given by the native Belooches to that part of Beloochistan lying to the westward, has, for its boundaries on the north, east, and west, nothing else than sandy deserts, with the exception of one very narrow range

* Vide Chapter III. † Vide Chapter VII.

of mountains projecting from its northern extremity, as already described in the first chapter of this Memoir. To the southward it is bounded by various districts of Mukran, of which province, strictly speaking, it ought to form a component part; but as the population of the two differ both in manners and language, I have found it adviseable to distinguish them entirely.

The principal mountains in this division are those called the Surhud, or cold mountains, which are situated between the twenty-ninth and thirtieth degrees of north latitude, and may be perceived, towering over all the others, at the distance of eighty or ninety miles. The whole of these mountains abound with mineral productions: in several places there are brooks of liquid salt, and pools of water, covered with a scum, similar to the naptha, or bitumen, found near the Caspian Sea. They also produce iron, copper, and other metals, of which the natives dig a sufficient quantity to serve their own uses. The Kohé Noushadir, or sal ammoniac mountain, that I saw when at Basman, and of which I have made particular mention in my Diary of the *20th April*, bears many symptoms of containing subterraneous fire. On one face of the hill, the soil and stones are perfectly black, and the mould at particular times is so heated and dry as to crumble to atoms on being touched; and on the opposite side, as I have already stated, there are springs of hot water and exudations of sal-ammoniac, brimstone, &c.

This division is equally devoid of rivers, with the others I have described. There is a brook near Bunpoor, which the natives call a river; but when I visited that place in *April* 1810, it had almost ceased to run; and if the dry season continued two months longer, must certainly have done so altogether: the water of this brook is lost in the sandy desert to the westward. The river Kaskeen is formed by the junction of several mountain streams that come from the eastward. It was perfectly dry when I passed it on the 18*th April*, 1810. The brooks to the northward of it, and those that rise in the Surhud mountains, run westerly also, and terminate in the desert of Kirman, as does the Kaskeen in that of Bunpoor.

The two principal districts in the Kohistan are those of Mydanee, or the plain; and Kohukee, or the hills. The former includes the towns and villages of Huftur, Puhra, Bunpoor, and Basman, beside a great number of Toomuns of felt tents, which are the only abodes used by the mountaineers of the other district. The natives of both, likewise, adopt local terms amongst themselves, to discriminate particular quarters of these districts; but as these are likely to be changed with every new Kheil, it would be answering no purpose to enumerate them *. The Kohistan is exclusively peopled by Belooches, who are not intermixed with any other classes; neither do Hindoos, or foreigners, venture to colonize under their authority. There are not above eight or ten tribes of note in the whole of this Division, which is but thinly populated, owing partly to the general infertility of the soil, and partly to the migrations that have taken place, of late years, from it into Persia, as well as to the eastward, towards Kutch Gundava.

It might with safety be affirmed, that the forms of government and the common laws of society are equally unknown and disregarded by these people, as they both depend solely on the caprice and temper of the heads of the various tribes composing the population; but that distinction being hereditary, and the sons being bred up with the prejudices and views of their fathers, they naturally imbibe all their principles and habits, so that, in the course of time, the system which was at first the effect of chance, assumes something like an air of regularity, that passes down from one generation to another. Viewed in this light, we find that the Kohistan comprises a number of petty republics, in which every member of the community feels that he has a right to revenge his own wrongs, and give his vote on all points relating to the common good; in fact, there is a most perfect equality as to sentiments and actions, from the highest

* These local distinctions are such as Surhud, or the cold district, also applied to it as the boundary. "Sirrirood," or the district on the river. "Pooshté kohee," or behind the mountain, &c. &c.

to the lowest; and although the measures proposed by the chiefs are more frequently adopted than those of any other adviser, this circumstance seems to be the result of a belief, that they have had better means of judging of the subjects under discussion (which are commonly connected with incursions into neighbouring districts) than any other member of the commonwealth. A similar feeling, combined with that awe and respect which the wealth and station of the head of each tribe must superinduce, to a certain degree, impels those who reside under his guidance, to look to him as the arbitrator of all trifling differences amongst themselves, and the general conveniences and tranquillity of the society lead them to consider his award as conclusive. This is, however, confined to the most trivial disputes, above which scale every man judges for himself. When any person commits a crime that is likely to draw upon himself and his family the opprobrium or displeasure of the whole Keil to which he belongs, he usually avoids the consequences, by flying to another part of the country, knowing that any attempt to expostulate against his being protected or harboured there, would be treated with ridicule and contempt; but, indeed, no such step would be contemplated for an instant, for, in a society, where every man is by birth, and education, a professed robber, and where there are no laws to protect either property or person, it is obvious, that partial condign punishment would prove unavailing for the suppression of outrage, and that, if every instance of the latter were visited by its concomitant award, the province would soon be depopulated.

Dates and other produce of this division are sent by the Belooches down to the sea-coast of Mukran, where they are purchased by the Hindoos, and exported. A small share of the returns for these are made in a few articles of foreign growth or manufacture, but the great bulk is in silver rupees, which are the only coin in circulation.

DIVISION V.

The tract that may strictly be denominated the Sandy Desert of Beloochistan, I estimate to be about three hundred miles in length, and rather more than two hundred in breadth. To the northward, it is merely divided by the Helmind river, from a continuation of the same sandy waste, which prevails in some places to the very base of the Paropamisan mountains, and on the west it is all but connected with the desert of Kirman, and would be entirely so, were it not for one narrow range of hills. In the event, therefore, of our rejecting these two nominal boundaries, we shall find, that the absolute extent of desert is, from north to south, nearly of five hundred miles; and from east to west in a diagonal direction, upwards of six hundred. Its boundaries on the east are, the mountains of Uffghanistan and the province of Sarawan; and to the southward, those of Mukran. I have been so particular on the nature of these deserts in my diary, that it would be superfluous to dwell further on the subject in this place, and as I am therefore about to close my geographical remarks, I shall do so, by subjoining a few words on those countries adjoining Beloochistan to the northward of my route, and on which I have not yet touched. The principal one of these is Seistan, throughout which province Captain Christie journeyed, and found it to answer exactly the description I had heard of it: that is, a flat sandy country, in some places overgrown with Jungul. The capital is Dooshak or Jullallabad, which latter name it has received in honour of the son of Beheram Khan, who assumes the royal title of Badsha, or King of Seistan, and lives in as magnificent a style as his trifling revenues will admit of; his territories are divided into petty districts, to each of which he formerly appointed a governor, whose authority was nearly equal to his own; and I am informed, that many of them have of late years declined paying tribute.

The river Helmind runs through Seistan, and about two days journey for a horseman to the westward of Dooshak, forms a lake, which, at some seasons overflows its banks, so as to extend eighty or ninety miles in length, and thirty or forty in breadth, usually it is not above thirty the former and twelve the latter way; there is an island in the center of it, the water is bitter, and the banks overgrown with weeds and brushwood, which engender myriads of flies, that infest the whole province from April till the beginning of October, during which period, the horses, and even camels, belonging to the natives, are obliged to be covered with quilted cotton cloths down to their very hoofs. The people of Seistan dress like Persians, and have the same colloquial dialect; they are all Sheea Moosulmans, and on the very worst terms with the Uffghans.

Gurmsyl is a very narrow tract, lying on the southern bank of the Helmind river, and five days journey north-westerly from Nooshky, on the edge of the desert. It has all the appearance of being the dry bed of a river, and is exceedingly productive in wheat, rice, and other grains. The inhabitants of this district are notorious for their robberies, and are composed of the outcasts from society, of all the neighbouring countries, who are said to be induced to settle here, from the trifling labour with which they raise their crops, partly owing to the yearly supply of water they derive from the overflowing of the Helmind river, and partly to the amazing fertility of the earth rendering vegetation remarkably quick. This district formerly paid four thousand rupees annually to the king of Kabool, but of late years it has been in a state of rebellion.

Khoonchee is a small district adjoining Gurmsyl, and, at present, similarly situated. There is a village in it of the same name, at which a body of troops were, until very lately, maintained and commanded by a partizan of the Kabool government. To the northward of Kelat lie the districts of Shal and Mustoong, which were given to Nusser Khan, by Ahmed Shah for his services when in Hindoostan; they are both celebrated for the profusion and excellence of the fruit that they produce, beside madder and scented rice: the population of these districts is a medley of Brahooes, Uffghans, and Dehwars; and it is a curious fact, that some of the villages have been peopled for many generations by these three classes, which are still unmixed and speak distinct dialects. Eastward of Mustoong is situated the district of Shorawuk, which is now the most southern of the Kabool dominions. An agent resides here on the part of that government to receive the revenues, which are very trifling, and likewise assist at the arbitration of any disputes between the subjects of that monarch and those of Muhmood Khan.

CHAPTER VII.

CLIMATE AND SOIL OF BELOOCHISTAN IN GENERAL. — SEASONS OF THE FIRST DIVISION. — TEMPERATURE. — PERIODICAL RAINS AND WINDS. — SALUBRITY. — SEASONS OF THE SECOND DIVISION OF BELOOCHISTAN. — HOW DISTINGUISHED. — THEIR CONTINUANCE. — TEMPERATURE. — WINDS. — INSALUBRITY OF THE PROVINCE OF MUKRAN. — LUS AN EXCEPTION TO THIS. — THE KOHISTAN, OR FOURTH DIVISION OF BELOOCHISTAN. — ITS CLIMATE LIKE THAT OF THE FIRST DIVISION. — MILDER AND HEALTHIER. — SEASONS. — RAINS. — KUTCH GUNDAVA, OR THE THIRD DIVISION OF BELOOCHISTAN. — CLIMATE. — SOIL OF BELOOCHISTAN. — GENERALLY ACKNOWLEDGED TO BE STONY. — WITH THE EXCEPTION OF KUTCH GUNDAVA. — MINERAL PRODUCTIONS OF THIS KINGDOM. — METHOD OF SMELTING THE ORE. — FRUITS. — GRAINS. — MADDER. — COTTON. — INDIGO. — AGRICULTURAL REMARKS. — DETAIL OF THE CULTURE OF MADDER. — PRICE IT SELLS AT. — OOSHPOOST, OR CAMEL GRASS. — HOW CULTIVATED. — QUICK VEGETATION OF KUTCH GUNDAVA, LUS, AND MUKRAN. — DATE FRUIT — PROCESS OF ITS CULTIVATION. — THE DIFFERENT METHODS OF PRESERVING THE FRUIT. — VARIETIES OF IT. — GREAT VALUE JUSTLY PLACED ON IT BY THE NATIVES. — TIMBER OF BELOOCHISTAN. — ENUMERATION OF DOMESTIC AND WILD ANIMALS. — VERMIN AND REPTILES. — FISH. — THE HORSE. — ASS. — MULE. — BLACK CATTLE. — SHEEP. — GOATS. — CAMEL. — DROMEDARY. — SHEPHERDS' DOGS. — GREYHOUNDS. — WILD DOGS. — LION. — TIGER. — HYENA. — WOLF. — JACKALL. — EAGLES AND HAWKS.

IT was once my intention to have inserted a few remarks on the climate and soil of each division, under its particular head, but doing so, I found, would have subjected me to the necessity of repeating the same observations very frequently, and I therefore judged it better to include them all in a separate chapter. The diversity of situation of the various provinces of Beloochistan, and the consequent irregularities of climate and soil, will, however, frequently induce me to revert to them, in order to discriminate with greater precision.

The seasons of the two mountainous provinces of Jhalawan and Sarawan are, like those of European countries, divided into spring, summer, autumn, and winter. The former is usually supposed to commence between the middle and end of February, and continues two months, or perhaps longer, a circumstance which rests entirely on the forwardness, or otherwise, of the season. The summer lasts till the beginning of August, and the autumn then follows, until the cold, or a fall of snow, announces the arrival of winter, an event that commonly happens in October; that portion of the year is, consequently, accounted much longer than any of the others.* The heat is at no time unpleasantly great, unless it may be a few days at the close of summer; but, on the other hand, the cold is intense during the winter, and attended by a north-easterly wind, that blowing without intermission, and sometimes with extreme violence, not only throughout that season, but the spring months, brings with it heavy falls of snow, sleet, and rain, and it may also be remarked as a thing rather unusual in Europe, that here the very hardest frosts are experienced during the height of these winds, which appear to be the only periodically prevailing ones in these provinces.

Captain Christie and I were at Kelat, from the *9th of February* till the *6th of March*, 1810, and towards the latter end of our sojourn there the natives were in daily hopes of a fall of rain, which was to them the harbinger of spring, and expected to last for three weeks or a month; this is the only annual fall they have, but, in addition

* None of the natives of Beloochistan seem to be aware, that any unerring principle can be laid down, to mark the commencement of the seasons, which they contend must depend on the state of the weather, a mode of calculation that renders it a mere accident whether any two years correspond. In February, 1811, it snowed incessantly for fifteen days in the vicinity of Kelat, and the frost set in early in October following: so that rejecting the winter, the other three seasons of that year agreeable to the Belooche theory, did not include more than seven months and a few days.

to it, the months of September and October are showery, and indeed, the whole of the cold season is more or less so, four or five days seldom passing without either sleet or rain, save, during frosty weather, when the air is keen and bracing. The salubrity of these provinces appears to be regulated by the seasons; the summer and autumn are said to be delightful, but in winter and spring, fogs, rain, snow, and cold, are the origin of many diseases among the poorer classes, who have not means of protecting themselves against the effects of a climate that is equally fluctuating, and more severe, than that of England.

In Mukran and Lus the seasons are likewise four in number, but they are not to be distinguished like those of the province just named, as they consist of two wet, one hot, and one cold one, the latter of which is very moderate, especially on the sea-coast. The wet seasons are in February or March, and June, July, and a part of August; the former comes from the north-west, and only continues for a fortnight or three weeks, but the latter comprises all the fury of the south-west monsoon. The hot season begins in March, and lasts till October, (the south-west monsoon intervening,) and in it, occasionally, the heats are so excessive as to prevent, even, the inhabitants from venturing abroad during the days called the "Khoormu Puz" or date ripening, which take place in August. The months of November, December, January, and February, are looked upon as the cold season, but even then it is much warmer than at any period of the year in the upper parts of Jhalawan and Sarawan: * north-west winds prevail at this time, and are particularly strong towards the close of the cold weather; during the remaining eight months the hot winds blow continually, inland, and though

* Wherever two provinces lie contiguous to each other, as Jhalawan and Lus, it necessarily results, that they must in some degree partake of the advantages and disadvantages of climate which prevail in each. Thus, the southern districts of Jhalawan are not so cold as Kelat, and the part of Lus, adjoining them, is much colder in winter than the sea-coast.

they are seldom known to be fatal to life, they destroy every symptom of vegetation, and will, even after dusk, scorch the skin in a most painful manner. Mukran is considered by the people of the adjoining countries to be peculiary unhealthy, except on the immediate coast, where the atmosphere is tempered by the sea breezes. To the European constitution, it has, even there, been esteemed extremely prejudicial, as was proved (in the only instance I have heard of) by the late and much regretted Captain Grant, of the Bengal military service, who was about three months in this province, while acting under the orders of Brigadier-General Malcolm, and quitted it in a state of extreme bad health. The small province of Lus is reputed to be an exception to the general insalubrity of this division of Beloochistan; and it is a very extraordinary fact, that the range of mountains that separate it from Mukran, has also drawn a grand line of distinction between their natives, in manners, customs, and appearance. The Kohistan, or that division of Beloochistan, lying to the westward of the sandy desert, being of a mountainous nature, resembles in climate the provinces of Sarawan and Jhalawan, unless that it is much milder, and consequently healthier. The seasons here, are like those of Mukran; but the rains, in June and July, which are always regular in that province, are here often partial, and at other times so heavy as to destroy the crop; such was the case in 1809, and a famine succeeded, while in Sarawan, the same calamity occurred from drought.

In Kutch Gundava, the climate is oppressively hot throughout the summer, and during the winter it continues so warm that this province is resorted to by all the chiefs and inhabitants (who can afford the expence) of the provinces of Sarawan and Jhalawan.

I am not prepared to offer any detailed observations on the soil of Beloochistan, which, in fact, is a subject peculiarly devoid of variety or interest. It generally appears to be exceedingly stony; and in the provinces of Sarawan, Jhalawan, Lus, and Mukran, this is evident to the most common observer, unless on the sea-coast of the two latter, where it is sandy and arid. The mountains of all these are chiefly composed of black or grey rock of a very hard nature, and the earth of the plains and vales, amongst them, is mixed with such a profusion of pebbles and small stones, that there is often not the slightest appearance of mould; yet, in spite of this disadvantage, some of them produce plentiful crops of wheat and barley; and in others, where they are not tilled, grass grows luxuriantly and to a great height. The soil of the Kohistan is very diversified. In the vallies, it is usually of a black loamy description, and even some of its loftiest mountains have fine earth to their very summits; whilst others are nothing else than a mass of black rock, destitute of verdure. Of Kutch Gundava, the soil is rich and loamy; and so exceedingly productive, that it is said, were it all properly cultivated, the crops would be more than sufficient for the consumption of the whole of Beloochistan: even as it is, they export great quantities of grain, beside cotton, indigo, and oil. The Badé Sumoom, of which I have made very particular mention in another place *, blows in Kutch Gundava during the summer months; and many people lose their lives by it.

Gold, silver, lead, iron, copper, tin, antimony, brimstone, alum, sal-ammoniac, and many kinds of mineral salts, and saltpetre, are found in various parts of Beloochistan. The precious metals have only been discovered, in working for iron and lead, at mines near the town of Nal, about one hundred and fifty miles south-south-west of Kelat. The different other minerals, I have enumerated, are very plentiful. Rock salt is very common to the westward, and saltpetre is likewise dug up in a native state: at Kelat they make the latter ingredient from the soil, and esteem it much the strongest.

*. Vide Narrative of the 2d *of April.* Part I.

On the high road from Kelat to Kutch Gundava there is a range of hills, from which a species of salt, perfectly red in its colour, is extracted, that possesses very great aperient qualities. Sulphur and alum are to be had at the same place. I saw quantities of white and grey marble in the mountains to the westward of Nooshky; but it does not seem to be at all prized by the Belooches. The method they have of smelting ore is very simple; and although it may sometimes leave a trifling portion of the soil mixed with the metal, it is, from its ingenuity, worthy of description. When a sufficient quantity of the ore for one process has been collected, it is placed on a pile of dried wood, which is kindled and kept replenished with fresh fuel till the ore melts and forms a mass at the bottom; it is then separated from the rubbish, and is much cleaner than when taken out of the mine. They next place it in a pit made of tiles or highly tempered mortar, that is so constructed as to admit a fire under it. When the ore melts the second time, all the dross and dirt that can be removed by skimming and picking, is taken away; the metal is afterwards lifted out, in a liquid state, and poured into hollow moulds of clay, in which state it is sold, in the Kelat market, about one half cheaper than European metal of similar description. The Belooches do not attempt to purify the gold and silver ore, and therefore dispose of it, in its native state, to the Hindoos, who transmit it secretly to the cities in the Punjab to avoid the duties.

The gardens of Kelat are planted with many sorts of fruit trees, of which, all the finest were brought from Kabool during the government of Nusseer Khan, who paid vast attention to their rearing, and excited an emulation among his subjects by offering rewards for the best productions. The following sold at a very moderate rate, in due season, in the Bazar of Kelat, will shew how far successful his endeavours have proved: apricots, peaches, grapes of various kinds, almonds, pistachio nuts, apples many different kinds, as also of pears, plums, currants, and cherries; quinces, figs, pomegranates, mulberries, plantains, melons *, guaivas, &c. &c.

At Shal and Mustoong, to the northward of Kelat, they have almonds of so delicate a quality, that they are blanched by simply rubbing them in a dry cloth. All kinds of grain † known in India, are cultivated in the different provinces of Beloochistan, and they have abundance of vegetables. ‡ Madder, cotton and indigo are also produced in Beloochistan, particularly to the northward and eastward of Kelat, and the latter is considered superior to that of Bengal, and sells for a higher price.

In the upper parts of Sarawan and Jhalawan, and the districts of Shal and Mustoong, the wheat is sown in August or September, and reaped the June following; barley is put into the ground one month later, and the crop is gathered earlier, so that it comes to perfection in about eight months; maize in three or four, provided it be planted in the heat of summer, and in a sheltered place. Indigo will not thrive here at all, and rice only in low dales where there is a supply of water to keep it flooded. The madder does not become fit to use under three years, and as the culture of it requires some pains, by describing the process, it will afford an idea of the Belooche system of agriculture. The ground being prepared and lined off into small trenches, the seed is put into them and flooded, and, while in

* Melons of all kinds are cultivated to astonishing perfection, and some of the water-melons come to so large a size, that a man can hardly lift one. The Belooches pluck all the flowers, except one or two, off the stems, and nourish them with manure, alternately keeping the fruit above the earth, or covered with it, which makes it sweet and juicy. The same plan is adopted for the musk melons.

† The grains cultivated in Beloochistan are rice, wheat, barley, bajree, *(Holcus Spicatus.)* Jowaree, *(Holcus Sorghum.)* Moong, *(Phaseolus mungo.)* Maize, *(Indian corn.)* Dal, *(Vetch.)* Oorud, Muttur, *(A kind of pea.)* Til, *(Sesamum.)* Chunna, *(Cicer Arietinum.)*

‡ Vegetables to be had at Kelat are turnips, carrots, cabbages, lettuces, cauliflowers, peas, beans, radishes, onions, celery, parsley, garlic, egg fruit, cucumbers.

that state, the trenches are filled with earth and rich manure. The plants appear in nine or ten days, and in the course of the first summer the stalks increase to three or four feet in height; they are cut down in September and given as fodder to the cattle. After this the ground is repeatedly flooded and manured until spring, when the plants again shoot forth, and such as are intended for seed, are set apart, as this second year is deemed the best for that purpose; the remainder are cut every month or six weeks, which throws all the vegetation into the roots, and adds to their size. Each stalk of those selected for seed, produces one flower on the very top of it. In the pod, which succeeds, are two seeds; this, when ripe, is plucked off and laid apart, the stems are then taken away, as in the first year, and similar precautions adopted to enrich the soil. In the third summer the stalks are pruned as in the two preceding, and in September the roots are dug up; they are quite straight, without any ramifications whatever, and usually from three to five feet long, but very thin; these roots are immediately cut into small pieces and dried, in which state they are sold, about ten pounds for a rupee in the Kelat bazar. Ooshpoosht or camel grass is a particular kind of clover, that grows with a stalk a foot or two high, and leaves like shamrock; it will produce twice in a month, from the commencement of spring till the end of autumn, and remains in a withered state during the winter, at the close of which it is flooded and manured. This plant lasts in great perfection for six or seven years, but after that period the roots are pulled up, and the soil allowed to lie fallow for two or three seasons. The straw of the different grains constitutes a very principal food of the cattle, and is commonly chopped with Ooshpoosht. The southern provinces of Mukran and Lus have the advantage of two annual crops of grass, owing to their two wet seasons.

In the low champaigns of Kutch Gundava, Lus, and part of Mukran, the crops are much sooner ripe. Wheat is reaped in six months, and barley in less than five; the oriental grains vary from five to two months; and cotton and indigo are proportionably quick. It is a remarkable fact, that rice will not grow in Kutch Gundava, although the soil there affords the most luxuriant crops of every other description; nor is there any deficiency of water. In Mukran the culture of the date fruit is conducted with great attention; and as the process is somewhat remarkable, and proves in the most incontrovertible manner the existence of the male and female trees (a point I have heard disputed), I shall here detail it, premising that I had several opportunities of being an eye-witness to the fact. The trees, both male and female, generally begin to blossom the end of February or early in March. The flower grows out of the stem, between the topmost leaves or branches, and has much the appearance of a bunch of wheat ears, except that it is larger and quite white. The male flower is sweet and palatable, but that of the female bitter and nauseous to the taste. As soon as the trees are completely in flower, they are pruned of all exuberant branches; beside which, it is often found adviseable to remove a certain quantity of the blossoms from the female, otherwise the fruit will not come to the same perfection. When this has been done, a stalk of the male flower is inserted into a small incision made in the core of the top of the female tree, and the dates gradually increase in size till the "Khoormu Puz" or date ripening, which is a term applied to a period of extreme hot weather, seldom exceeding three weeks, that occurs in August or September. Without this agency, the female blossoms will form into the shape of dates, but never ripen; and those of the male tree are of no other use, unless I may add that the Belooches eat them as bread, either in their green state or roasted. One tree of the latter sex is sufficient to fecundate many hundred females, as the minutest particle of farina will answer for that purpose; and I was even assured that the same portion might be removed, in case of necessity, from one to another with equal effect. When the "Khoormu Puz" is past, the dates are pulled, and appropriated according to the views of the owner. Some are dried on mats in the sun, in the state they come off the tree; the same method is pursued with others after extracting the stones, and they are then strung on small lines made of goats' hair. Those that are intended to be kept in a moist state are immediately packed into baskets made from the palm leaf, and the abundance of saccharine matter that they contain preserves them from spoiling. There are numerous different kinds of the tree and fruit, as the conjunction of any two varieties forms a third, distinguished by another name; yet a person, to be deemed well versed in the cultivation of dates, must be capable of pointing out and mentioning, on seeing each tree, the name and description of the fruit it bears. The most esteemed in Beloochistan are called Lur, Puppoo, Moojwatee, and Shinguskund. The date tree is looked upon by the natives of these countries, and with great reason too, the most important blessing they enjoy; the value of which is enhanced by its thriving best in soil of a gravelly and barren nature, and consequently of no other use.

The best timber the Belooches have is of the Upoors * and tamarind trees, both of which are remarkably hard and durable; and the former resembles teak so greatly in grain, weight, and appearance, that Captain Christie and myself mistook it for that wood. Both these trees grow to a very large size, and to them may be added the Babool, Lye, and Mulberry, as they are all used for building. To the westward, the natives principally appropriate the palm tree to the same purpose. The Neem, Peepul, Sissoo †, Chinar, Mango, walnut, and sycamore, are also all found in various divisions of the country; but the oak, ash, fir, &c. are unknown.

The domestic animals of Beloochistan are horses, mules, asses, camels, dromedaries, buffaloes, black cattle, sheep, goats, dogs. and cats; beside fowls and pigeons: they have neither geese, turkeys, or

* A species of the Zizyphus Jujuba.

† The Babool, Farnesian mimosa; Lye, tamarisk; Neem, melia azadirachta: Peepul, ficus religiosa; Sissoo, dalbergia sissoo (Roxburgh); Chinar, platanus orientalis.

ducks. The wild animals are lions, tigers, leopards, hyenas, wolves, jackalls, tiger cats, wild dogs, foxes, hares, moongooses, mountain goats, antelopes, elks, red and moose deer, wild asses, &c. &c. Of the feathered kind there are eagles, kites, vultures, magpies *, crows, hawks, wild geese, and ducks, flamingos, herons, bustards, florikens, rock pigeons, lapwings, plovers, snipes, quails, partridges, and almost every class of small bird to be met with either in Europe or India. Vermin and venomous animals are not so common as in Hindoostan, and fresh fish is, it may be said, unknown, except on the sea-coast, where the inhabitants subsist on it the greatest part of the year.

The horses of Beloochistan are strong, well boned, and large, but usually extremely vicious. Those which are brought to India from that country, are mostly bred to the southward of Kelat, and in Kutch Gundava. The breed of this animal, in Lus and Mukran, is small and deficient in spirit. Westward of the desert, the Belooches chiefly get their horses from Khorasan; and those chiefs, who have brood mares, cross them with Arab or Persian horses, from which circumstance they are very superior in mettle, docility, and beauty. There is nothing observable in the ass or mule of this region; nor do the black cattle, sheep, or goats, require any particular notice. The sheep are mostly of the species called, in Persia, Doomba, or the fat-tailed; and the goats are rough and covered with black hair, which serves to protect them from snow and cold. Of all the domestic creatures I have enumerated, the camel and dromedary are the most highly prized by the Belooches. The camel is of the species with two humps, and is only serviceable for burthen, being heavy in his make, with enormous bones, shaggy coat, and amazing strength. The

* I have never seen magpies in any part of Asia except at Kelat. I believe they are unknown in Persia or the Kabool dominions, and it seems unaccountable that they should be confined to the district of Kelat alone.

dromedary, or one-humped camel, is trained by these people to travel at an incredible rate for many successive days, and their abstinence from food or water peculiarly suits them for the Chupaos or marauding expeditions of their owners, in which they have a decided advantage over horses. The camel is never seen in any of the lowland countries, and even in the upper provinces they are rarely employed or reared. The dromedaries vary exceedingly in form and appearance, according to the clime of which they are indigenous. In Mukran and Lus they are slender, light in colour, and usually beautifully proportioned; while at Kelat and to the northward of that city they are, comparatively speaking, heavy, very black, rough, and cross made. These latter are by much the best, and are more patient of heat and cold than any others I have ever heard of. Shepherds' dogs and greyhounds are the most valued of the canine species, and the Belooches are as attentive to their pedigree and rearing as a sportsman in England could possibly be to his pointers. The former are very large and powerful, and, when irritated, exceedingly ferocious; but, in common, the most docile creatures imaginable. The wild or jungul dog is of this description, and unless a man be very well armed, it would be dangerous to molest one of them. They frequently hunt in packs of twenty or thirty, and will seize a bullock and kill him in a few minutes. Fortunately their timidity is so great, that they keep in the most impenetrable junguls, and they are therefore little to be apprehended.

The lion and tiger are seldom found in the mountains of Beloochistan, and I imagine, their real haunts may be traced to the forests on the banks of the Indus, and other parts of the desert waste lying between Sinde and Guzerratte. Hyenas, wolves, and jackalls abound all over this country, and make sad havoc amongst the flocks; none of them, the hyena excepted, will attack a man, and that only, if urged by severe hunger, or irritated by opposition. Eagles are alone seen in Jhalawan and Sarawan. Hawking is a favourite pastime with some of the Belooche chiefs to the westward, and they instruct their birds with great care, principally to take bustards, jungul * fowls and black partridges.

* The jungul fowl are a wild species of the common barn-door fowl, but considerably smaller, and very like bantam fowls. They are game birds, and a small sized hawk, it is said, will not venture to attack a full grown cock.

CHAPTER VIII.

DIVISION SIXTH. — THE PROVINCE OF SINDE. — CAUSE OF THE MISSION TO ITS UMEERS OR RULERS. — THE ENVOY AND HIS SUITE. — PREPARATIONS — DEPARTURE FROM BOMBAY. — ARRIVAL AT THE PORT OF KURACHEE IN SINDE. — VISIT FROM THE GOVERNOR. — HIS APPEARANCE AND DRESS. — OBJECT HE HAD IN VIEW. — HIS SECOND VISIT. — APOLOGY TO THE ENVOY. — HIS ALARM DURING THE VISIT. — UNCEREMONIOUSNESS OF HIS FOLLOWERS. — DISEMBARKATION OF THE ENVOY. — REFUSAL TO ADMIT THE PUBLIC SERVANTS INTO THE FORT OF KURACHEE. — DISCUSSIONS ON THAT TOPIC. — INSOLENT ASSUMPTION OF THE UMEERS. — MEASURES ADOPTED TO REPEL IT. — REPORTS IN CIRCULATION. — DISPATCH OF AN AGENT TO TREAT WITH THE ENVOY. — HIS COMMUNICATIONS. — REPLY GIVEN TO THEM. — ORDERS TO FORCE THE BRITISH SHIPS TO LEAVE THE HARBOUR OF KURACHEE. — MEASURE RESORTED TO. — ABSURD ASSERTIONS REGARDING THE IDIOM OF THE PERSIAN LANGUAGE AS USED IN SINDE. — IMPROPER CONDUCT OF THE GOVERNOR'S PEOPLE. — HIS EXPLANATION. — ATTEMPTS TO IMPOSE ON THE ENVOY. — HIS DECIDED REMARKS. — JEALOUSY OF THE SINDIAN GOVERNMENT. — ARROGANCE OF THE GOVERNOR. — STATE OF AFFAIRS DESCRIBED. — A SECOND LETTER FROM THE UMEERS. — THEIR INSOLENCE AND BRAVADO. — THEY WITHDRAW THEIR STIPULATION RELATIVE TO THE ADVANCE OF THE MISSION TO COURT. — PREPARATIONS FOR LEAVING KURACHEE. — MEANNESS AND DISHONESTY OF A SINDIAN CHIEF. — HIS IMPUDENCE. — THE SHIPS TRY TO GET ACROSS THE BAR, BUT FAIL.

DIVISION VI.

THE causes that led to the mission to the King of Persia in 1808,* rendered a similar precaution requisite on the part of the supreme government of India with regard to the rulers of Sinde; and Nicholas Hankey Smith, Esquire, of the Bombay Civil Service, then resident at Bushire, was selected by the Right Honourable the

* Vide Introduction, Part I.

Governor-general to fulfil the duties of envoy. Henry Ellis, Esquire, Bengal Civil Service, was nominated his first assistant; Lieutenant Robert Taylor of the Bombay Native Infantry, and myself, the second and third assistants. Captain Charles Christie to command the escort. William Hall, Esquire, surgeon, and Captain William Maxfield of the Bombay Marine, marine-surveyor. Preparations were made at Bombay in the early part of 1809, in a suitable style of magnificence, and the Maria, country ship, was hired for the conveyance of the envoy and his suite to the port of Kurachee, whither the Honourable Company's cruizer, the Prince of Wales, Captain Allen, and three armed gallivats, were ordered to attend her. The envoy embarked on board the Maria, under the customary salutes, on the afternoon of the *27th of April*, and the whole of the vessels immediately weighed and stood out of the harbour.

On the *9th of May*, at day-light in the morning, the Prince of Wales being a-head, made the signal for land in sight, which proved to be the lofty mountains extending inland from Cape Monze (Mowaree). At 10 *a. m.* the western point of Kurachee harbour was distant three leagues. It is a remarkably bluff headland, and there is a small fort on it, which has the appearance of a square house. Several very high rocks within the harbour appeared over the low land that connects this promontory with the continent, like ships under sail. At noon we came to anchor in twelve fathom water, and Captain Maxwell went on shore, to announce to the Governor of Kurachee the arrival of the mission, and to demand pilots to carry the ships over the bar without delay, as it was blowing fresh from the south-west, with a heavy swell, and other indications of the commencement of the south-west monsoon. The Governor made some demur regarding the admission of the ships into the harbour; but his objections were over-ruled, and on the 10th both weighed and stood for the bar, gradually shoaling their soundings from twelve to two and three quarter fathoms, which was the lowest cast, as they immediately deepened to four and five. On passing the fort on the point, the Maria was saluted with two guns, to which an equal number were returned. About an hour after she had anchored, the Governor came on board to visit Mr. Smith, attended by several matchlockmen, and brought some sheep and vegetables as a present. He neither spoke Persian or Hindoostanee, but made numerous inquiries through his interpreter, regarding the vessels and the number of men they carried; and after sitting half an hour, seemed very happy to get away. He was a mean looking little man, with a dress corresponding, and the only point in which his costume differed from that of his followers was, that he wore an immense turband. The two succeeding days were lost in discussions respecting the disembarkation of the mission, which the Governor was anxious to protract, until he should receive instructions from the Umeers. On the 12th, he visited Mr. Smith a second time, when the latter took occasion to reprehend some improper assumptions, in the correspondence that had taken place relative to the titles and rank of the Governor-general and the Umeers, at which he professed his regret, and said it arose from his ignorance of the Persian language, but, that he was willing either to put the person who had written them to death, or blind him, as the envoy chose. He was of course requested not to proceed to such violent measures, but to give orders for greater circumspection in future.

The Governor seemed under great alarm throughout this visit, and after his boat was along-side, hesitated whether he would come on board or not. His attendants shewed him little respect, and when Mr. Smith and he went into the cabin, one of them instantly rose off the deck, and placed himself in the chair in which the Nuwwab* had been sitting, another wished to occupy Mr. Smith's, but was prevented.

On the 13*th* and 14*th of May* the tents and public stores of the mission were landed, and the former pitched on a spot pointed out by the Governor. Several of the gentlemen had gone on shore, and

* The governor's official title.

learned that great consternation had been excited by our arrival, that orders had been issued not to let any of our people enter the fort of Kurachee; and, that a large body of troops, under one of their most distinguished Sirdars, had encamped within eight miles of the place, with the evident intention of watching our motions; indeed, the whole of the Governor's conduct had evinced a medley of terror and dissimulation, and a jealousy of our acquiring the slightest information, which could not have been exceeded had we come with declared hostile intentions. On the *16th of May*, the envoy disembarked under salutes of fifteen guns from the two ships, and was received on the beach by the escort and gentlemen of the mission, amidst the acclamations of a vast concourse of natives, to whom money was distributed according to the oriental custom. In the afternoon the Nuwwab sent a man to intimate his intention of paying his respects to the envoy, but as the order for debarring our servants from ingress to the fort was still in force, he was informed he would not be received. Mr. Ellis went to the Governor to explain the cause of this refusal; and had an interview with him at a house outside the walls. The Nuwwab wished us to believe that a similar prohibition extended to all strangers: he said that he was very sorry it should give such offence; that whether Mr. Smith saw him or not, he would daily attend at his encampment; that he had his orders from the Umeers, his masters, and must obey them, and that when a Mihmandar * was sent from Hyderabad, to conduct the mission to court, we should be convinced of the necessity of his non-compliance. A few days after, a letter was received from the Umeers, acquainting the envoy with their determination to depute two officers of government to treat with him at Kurachee, and that he was to accept all they said as strictly official; but, as the style of their language was in that strain of arrogance and superiority, which it

* Mihmandar from Mihman, a guest, and Dar, a keeper. He is a person appointed to conduct envoys, and see that they are supplied with the productions of the country. Usually his powers are very much abused, by making them a cloak for extortion.

was so much the object of the mission * to check in its infancy, the letter was returned, accompanied by a polite communication, acquainting the Umeers, that as it contained, not merely an unwarrantable assumption of rank on their behalf, but a want of due acknowledgment of that of the exalted government, of which the envoy was the representative, it was impossible its contents could be attended to in any form. Reports of various natures now daily reached us. At one hour it was confidently affirmed, that the mission was to advance to the capital, escorted by a large body of Sindian horse, and to be received with every mark of attention. At another, that the envoy would be called upon to negociate with officers that were to be dispatched to him for that purpose, and, at a third, that we were to be forced by a body of troops, then reported to be on its march to Kurachee, to re-embark on board the ships, and sail for India. All of them corresponded in one great feature, which was, that the Umeers entertained the utmost apprehensions of our designs on their territories, and in fact, the hourly arrival of reinforcements for the garrison and defence of Kurachee, would have afforded sufficient evidence of this dread.

Some days subsequent to the transmission of the letter to the Umeers, a friendly note reached the envoy from Akhoond Mohummud Bukka Khan, who had been at Bombay a few months before as an agent on behalf of the Sindian government, announcing his being deputed to confer with Mr. Smith, and his intention of making all possible haste to join him. The same messenger who brought this letter, confirmed intelligence that we had obtained some time before, of an army of three thousand men having been collected in

* An envoy on the part of the government of Bombay had been deputed to Sinde the preceding year, and treated in a manner that was not deemed at all warranted by the relative rank of the two powers. The envoy from the Governor-general had therefore the most pointed instructions to repress every attempt at similar impropriety, and to be scrupulously exact in resenting any omission of that respect due to the British power in India, as well as any superiority claimed by the rulers of Sinde.

the neighbourhood of the city of Tattah, and the probability of its moving towards us, in order, as we presumed, to enforce the Akhoond's terms, which officer arrived at Kurachee on the *23d of May*, and the following morning came to the British encampment, where he had a very long conference with the envoy. He dwelt much on the fears that had been engendered in the minds of the Umeers by the presence of two armed ships in the harbour of Kurachee; and concluded by avowing that their being dispatched to Bombay, or at least out of the Sindian dominions, was a *sine qua non* previous to the mission being allowed to move towards Hyderabad.

Other subjects were also discussed of a political nature, and the consultation ended by a positive declaration of the envoy, that in preference to proceeding to the capital, under the most trifling stipulation, he would go on board of ship; and, however great the risk might be of venturing to sea at that advanced season of the year *, sail for Calcutta to lay the business before the Governor-general. That with regard to that part of the communication, made by the Akhoond, which related to his powers to treat with the envoy, it was entirely out of the question, as the latter could only do so with the rulers of Sinde, to whom he was accredited. On the *26th of May*, the Governor sent a verbal message to the envoy, desiring he would issue orders for the ships to quit the harbour immediately; but he, as well as the Akhoond, evaded, in the most artful manner, giving any written document to this effect. At length the former proposed to shew any of the gentlemen of the mission the official instructions he had received from the Umeers, to enforce this demand; however, when Mr. Ellis and Captain Christie proceeded to the usual place of meeting, he declined to fulfil his proposal, on the grounds of not being authorized to do so by his masters. Under these perplexing circumstances, Mr. Smith came to the determination not to have any

* The south-west Monsoon had set in with great violence, and it was then blowing a tremendous gale.

further official intercourse either with the Nuwwab or the Akhoond; but to write a letter to the Umeers and regulate his future measures in conformity with their answer. At the same time he announced this resolution to those officers, and requested that the latter would attend at the British encampment, in order that he might hear the proposed letter read, ere it was sent off to Hyderabad. He accordingly came, and, while it was preparing, a very long conversation took place, in which he laboured to convince the envoy that the mission had been received in the most friendly way, that the simple fact of its being permitted to land, and hoist the British flag, was decisive evidence of this assertion, "for," added he, "if you had "attempted to enter the port without leave, the guns of the fort "would have sunk your vessels." To this bravado it was replied, that had affairs come to that crisis, it would have been seen whether English or Sindian guns were best, and that the result was very obvious.

The Akhoond next adverted to the expressions which were complained of in the Umeers correspondence, and endeavoured to prove that they were according to the idiom of the Persian language as used in Sinde: he swore repeatedly that "Moolazimat," (services) meant a friendly meeting; that "Mowuddut," (friendship) was highly disrespectful as used in the envoy's letters; and that "Hoozoor," (the royal presence) had been the title of the Umeers for twenty years, and could not be altered without putting every man in Sinde to death. Mr. Smith reminded him that it was absurd to expect that he should be acquainted with the peculiar idiom of Sinde, or adopt it, even admitting he were so; that he used the two first words pointed out, and all others, agreeable to their general acceptation; that "Hoozoor" was only applicable to an independent sovereign, and not to a tributary government like that of Sinde. The Akhoond here interrupted the envoy by saying that the tribute was of late years only nominal, and that he might attribute his not receiving answers to his former letters to the diction used in them. The letter about to be dispatched to the Umeers was then read aloud by one of the Moonshees, or Persian writers, and the Akhoond made the same ridiculous objections to the use of various words inserted in it, after which he took leave.

All the Sindians, who had entered the public service, were this forenoon expelled with their families, from their houses in the fort of Kurachee, and one of them, who was bringing some provisions for the use of the envoy's table, was seized and tied to a post, in the centre of the Sindian camp, which now nearly encompassed our tents; but as we had Kunauts * all round our encampment, it did not inconvenience us. A remonstrance was instantly sent to the Nuwwab, who ordered the man to be released, and expressed his dissatisfaction at the act; but a few hours after his own people committed one of much greater insolence, by beating the Lascars who were filling water for the consumption of the two ships' crews, and spilling all that was ready to be sent on board. Another expostulatory message was resorted to, but the reply that was returned rather augmented the outrage, by corroborating what the people had said, that it was done by the Nuwwab's instructions; he, however, condescended to explain, that he had only intended the Lascars should not waste the water, and promised nothing similar should again occur. In the evening the Akhoond came to our encampment, accompanied by a person whom he introduced by the name of Moosa Khan, informing the envoy that he was empowered to communicate the Umeers desire, that the ships should quit the harbour, and that the mission might afterwards advance to Hyderabad, with every honor and attention. The envoy called to the Akhoond's recollection, that he had apprized him of his sentiments on this subject, and therefore further discussion was unavailing. Moosa Khan seemed, throughout this interview, to be a stupid ignorant man, and continually referred his obervations to the Akhoond, for his approbation. He was dressed in a plain white shirt, a pair of blue silk trowsers, and a quilted cap;

* Kunauts are tent walls, made for the purpose of keeping tents private.

in one hand he held his sword, and he found employment for the other, all the time he sat with us, in rubbing his beard and mustachios. The people who came with him crowded into the tent without ceremony, and would have taken possesion of the couches, but were ordered to seat themselves on the carpet.

We had been so narrowly watched, since our arrival here, that it was quite unpleasant to venture beyond our camp limits; and matters began to assume so hostile an appearance, from the increasing arrogance of the Nuwwab, and the real, or affected, imbecility of Akhoond Bukka Khan, that it was judged adviseable to re-ship all the valuable part of the public property. Boats were consequently requested of the Governor, who avowed his positive determination not to permit a single article to be sent on board, and effectually prevented any such precaution, by denouncing the displeasure of the Umeers, against whatever boatmen might dare to serve us. We were in reality now nothing better than prisoners at large, for the only communication we could have with the ships was by means of their boats, and every time that one of them came to the landing place three or four armed men were placed near her, to prevent things being put on board; we now also discovered that a guard was stationed at each corner of our encampment every night, which was so unequivocally meant to observe our proceedings, and consequently so undisguised an insult, that one of the Chobdars* was sent with a message, to direct that they might not again come there, under any circumstances, which was attended with the proposed effect. The Hindoos and other inhabitants of the town, who had been, at first, in the habit of occasionally visiting our encampment, had of late ceased to do so; and the Sindians, who had been entertained in different capacities, were threatened with harsh treatment, unless they quitted our service, but as the envoy apprized them of his intention of making this unwarrantable threat a subject of discussion

* Chobdar, a native mace-bearer: from Chob, a mace, and Dar, a bearer.

with the Umeers, they were all content, under this assurance, to remain.

About a week after the transmission of the envoy's letter to the Umeers, their reply was received, in which they entered into a very prolix review of the behaviour they had adopted towards the mission from the government of Bombay, the antecedent year, contrasting it with the increased attention and respect they wished to impress on Mr. Smith, had been observed with regard to the present one; the style of their letter was, however, highly domineering and imperious, and, among others, it contained an observation, that they knew not how to write to a person who had returned the Purwanué Hoozoor (royal mandate): they, however, revoked their orders respecting the dispatch of the ships, a matter, which they endeavoured to treat in the lightest manner, by inquiring of what importance it could be to them, though there were twenty British ships of war in Kurachee Harbour?

Political considerations induced the envoy to overlook, or at least to view in a secondary light, the exceptionable style of this communication, which was instantly returned, and as the question of any compromise of the dignity of the British government, was laid at rest, by the rulers of Sinde having waved their stipulation on the subject of the vessels, he announced his determination to set out for Hyderabad in a few days. We were now anxious to procure horses, and in proportion as our demand for them became known, they rose in price, so that a tolerable poney, which might have been had a week earlier for eighty or ninety rupees,* was seldom offered for less than double that sum. Circumstances occurred in the purchase of some of them, that will serve to illustrate the general character of the Sirdars of the Sindian army; one of them, called Buhadoor Khan, sent three horses for sale, together with a written memorandum, implying that he had no wish to dispose of them, farther than to

* Ten or eleven pounds sterling.

oblige the envoy. They were on examination deemed scarcely worth one thousand rupees,* which was the price put upon them, but, as the avowed civility of the owner bespoke him something above the common class, that sum was dispatched by one of the Chobdars, and a message expressive of thanks. In the course of two hours the Chobdar brought back five rupees, that the Khan requested might be changed, as they were four or five pice † short of their value, and we learned the whole had been counted over a dozen times, and each rupee examined with the most scrupulous attention. A gold mohur ‡ was instantly sent, and the Sirdar desired to pay himself out of it, whatever sum there might be deficient in the thousand rupees, when to our astonishment he kept the whole, and returned an answer, to say, that he wished he had been paid the total amount in similar coin, and that he had retained it to cover his risk of some more of the rupees proving defective. This man, we afterwards found, was really a person of some rank, and a great favourite of the Umeers. He came to visit the envoy at our encampment, a short time subsequent to this fraud, without evincing the slightest symptoms of shame at the meanness of his behaviour.

The weather had been unusually mild for some days, and the commander of the Prince of Wales, conceiving that that cruizer and the Maria might put to sea, they were ordered to proceed to Bombay, as their longer detention at Kurachee was uncalled for by any circumstance. They accordingly made an attempt to cross the bar on the *7th of June*, in which the Maria was in imminent danger of being lost, and Captain Allen then stated, as his official opinion, that the ships would not be enabled to prosecute their voyage to India, until the close of the monsoon, unless a northerly wind should take place, which was very improbable.

---

* One hundred and twenty-five pounds sterling.

† A Pice is about twopence.

‡ A gold Mohur is equal to fifteen Rupees.

CHAPTER IX.

KURACHEE TOWN.—ITS SITUATION.—HARBOUR.—BAR.—HOW PROTECTED.—SUGGESTION.—THE FORTIFICATIONS OF KURACHEE.—VERY IRREGULAR.—NUMBER OF HOUSES AND INHABITANTS.—CUSTOMS.—HOW REALIZED.—THE PROGRESSIVE INCREASE OF THEM ACCOUNTED FOR.—EXPORTS AND IMPORTS OF SINDE.—FACE OF THE COUNTRY ABOUT KURACHEE.—ABOUNDS WITH GAME.—THE MISSION MOVES FROM KURACHEE.—ARRIVES AT TATTAH.—INTERMEDIATE COUNTRY.—WELLS.—BY WHOM DUG.—VILLAGES OF GAHRAH AND GOOJAH.—RIVER BEDS.—NAMES OF THEM.—SAID TO BE NAVIGABLE IN THE RAINS.—RUINS OF THE ANCIENT CITY OF BUMBHORA.—ERRONEOUS CONJECTURE REGARDING IT.—TOMBS AT TATTAH—DESCRIPTION OF THEM.—DATE.—REMARKABLE WELL.—FIRST APPEARANCE OF TATTAH.—IMPOSING.—DELUSIVE.—RAISED CAUSEWAY.—ENTRANCE OF THE MISSION INTO THAT CITY.—LETTER FROM THE UMEERS.—JUMPTEE OR STATE BOAT.—SOJOURN AT TATTAH.—ACTS OF ONE OF THE OFFICERS OF THE SINDIAN GOVERNMENT CALLED WULEE MOHUMMUD KHAN.—DISCUSSIONS IN CONSEQUENCE.—RESULT OF THEM.—THE ENVOY VISITED BY WULLEE MOHUMMUD KHAN.—RETURNS THAT COMPLIMENT.—MAGNIFICENCE OF THAT NOBLEMAN.—APPEARANCE.—DRESS—MANNERS.—TRIBE.—LIBERALITY.—TATTAH ONCE THE CAPITAL OF SINDE.—ITS PRESENT DEPOPULATION.—CAUSE.—EXTENT AT PRESENT.—EARLIEST ACCOUNTS OF IT.—SUPPOSED TO BE THE PATTALA OF THE GREEKS.—UNCERTAINTY.—POLICY OF ITS PRINCES.—DECAY OF ITS OPULENCE.—TO BE TAKEN IN A MODIFED SENSE.—MANUFACTURES.—SHOPS.—BAZAR.—MANNER OF BUILDING.—BADGEERS.—GOVERNMENT.—CUSTOMS HOW COLLECTED.—LATITUDE AND LONGITUDE.—FACE OF THE COUNTRY IN THE VICINITY.—STATE OF THE WEATHER IN JULY, 1809.—THE MISSION QUITS TATTAH FOR HYDERABAD.

THE fortified town of Kurachee, is situated in latitude 24° 52' north, longitude 67° 17' east, nearly at the south-eastern extremity of the province of Sinde, of which it has become, of late years, the principal Bunder, or sea-port. Its harbour, which is sometimes distinguished by the name of Khoor Allee *, is very confined, and owing to the bar at the mouth of it, it would not be prudent for vessels drawing more than sixteen feet water, to attempt entering it, though, when once over the bar, they would find deep, smooth water inside.

A fort, built in 1797, on the promontory that forms the western side of the bay, is judiciously placed to defend the entrance, and if good cannon were mounted on it, and well served, I should suppose that no ship could approach it with impunity, and certainly not with effect, for her guns would require to be so greatly elevated, to avoid striking the brow of the hill, that nine shot out of ten would pass over, and fall into the sea on the opposite side. The same circumstance would undoubtedly screen her from the fire of the fort; but, as she would be close under the hill, her decks might be cleared by matchlockmen, who would be completely protected by the masses of rock, and therefore, in the event of its ever becoming necessary to take this place, the only plan would be, to land troops at some distance from it, and carry it by escalade. The fortifications of the town are very mean and irregular, being in some places not above five or six feet high, and even there so broken down, that a horseman might ride up to the top of them; while in others they are lofty, and kept in excellent repair. The whole are built of mud mixed with straw, and a long creeping weed, that grows in the marshes in the neighbourhood; and on that side towards the creek, which flows up from the head of the harbour, they have observed the necessary precaution of facing the works to a certain height with stone and mortar. The houses inside the walls were ascertained by an actual numeration made in 1813 by order of the Umeers, to amount to three thousand two hundred and fifty; beside which, there are some straggling huts around the fort that were not included in the calculation. The resident population, excluding sojourners, at the same period, had in-

* Khoor Allee, the harbour of Allee. Vide Chapter XII. Part II.

creased to thirteen thousand souls, which is more than one-half greater than when the mission was there in 1809. The majority of the inhabitants are Hindoos, who prosecute a most extensive commerce, in despite of the heavy customs and duties that are levied by one of their own tribe, who farms the revenues of Kurachee, a species of destructive policy that obtains throughout this country. The sum received into the public treasury in 1809, on account of Kurachee, was ninety-nine thousand rupees * annually, and the Ijarudar, or renter, was said to clear about twelve for his trouble. The former has since been advanced to one lac twenty-three thousand †, and the present farmer is estimated to pocket nearly twenty; from which it would appear, that this place is in a progressive state of improvement, a fact solely attributable to the advantages of situation it possesses, lying, as it does, nearly central between India and the whole of the dominions of the King of Kabool, together with Persian Khorasan, Bulkh, Bokhara, &c. The unsettled and decreasing authority of Muhmood Khan of Kelat, also tends to augment the revenues of his enemies, the Sindians; for the northern merchants seeing his power unable to protect their property within his territories, have no other alternative, than to take the route through Sinde, notwithstanding the exactions imposed upon them.

The exports of Sinde are chiefly made from Kurachee, and therefore this seems the most eligible opportunity to enumerate them. Those of home produce consist of saltpetre, salt, rice, cotton, ghee, oil, oil-seed, sharks' fins, bark for tanning, alkali, calico, and felts; and from the kingdoms and provinces to the northward, they bring chiefly for exportation, assafœtida, saffron, horses, leather, hides, madder, musk, alum, drugs of various kinds, Kashmeer shawls, dried fruit, diamonds, lapis lazuli, turquoises, and other precious stones, bdellium, and gums. The imports from India are, iron, tin, steel,

* 12,375l. sterling. † 15,375l. sterling.

lead, copper, ivory, tea, sugar, spices of all descriptions, chintz, broad cloth, glass, and china-ware, cocoa-nuts, indigo, areca-nuts, muslin, gold cloths, shields, &c. &c. &c., a large portion of which are forwarded as returns for the articles above enumerated. From Khorasan, Mukran, Persia, and Arabia, the Sindians have, for home consumption, swords, silk, carpets, dates, rose-water, conserve, tobacco, coffee and Kullyans.

The face of the country in the vicinity of Kurachee is a perfect level (on the sides of the fort facing north, east, and south) which extends, in each of the two former directions, at least eight or ten miles, and in the latter down to the sea. As there had been a want of rain for three seasons, previous to the mission into Sinde, the earth seemed to be quite burned, without the slightest trace of vegetation, some small stunted bushes, scattered over the plain excepted; but I observed one or two wells that were encompassed by large trees covered with luxuriant foliage, and the inhabitants assured us, that within eight and forty hours after a plentiful fall of rain, the ground would be a perfect grass plat. This plain is a delightful place to ride upon, as there are no stones or fissures in the ground; this circumstance frequently tempted us to go out with the grey-hounds, but we were only once fortunate enough to meet a jackall, that gave us a good run, and escaped by leaping into a well, although we understood, that jackalls, foxes, wild hogs, deer, and various other kinds of game were plentiful some miles further inland than we usually proceeded.

The mission quitted Kurachee on the morning of the 10*th of June*, and in five marches arrived at the city of Tattah, which was formerly the capital of Sinde, though at present in a state of desolation and ruin. The intermediate country between Kurachee and this place might, with great truth, be styled a desert, being bare and sandy, without trees or any vegetation to relieve the sterile appearance it presents to the eye. except some bushes of the Babool, Lye, and Doodhul.* At the two first stages there are Tandas or Suraés, dis-

* Doodhul, Euphorbia antiquorum.

tinguished by the names of their founders, who deserve the gratitude of their countrymen, and more particularly for having dug very deep wells, whence the thirsty traveller may procure a draught of deliciously cold water in the warmest weather. Our latter halting places were at the villages of Gahrah and Goojah, the former of which is built on a small stream connected with the Indus. We crossed, in the course of this route, several river beds, such as the Bakran, Gungara, Gorlukee, Peepul, and Koaknee, that were of various breadths from fifty to five hundred yards, and then perfectly dry, although they were all described to us, as navigable during the rainy season. The ruins of Bumbhora, which was formerly a very large city, lie within four miles of the village of Gahrah, in latitude 24° 46', longitude 67° 50' east, on the southern side of a very large hollow, in the shape of a bowl, the sides of which are beautifully verdant and over-hung with large spreading trees. On the northern base of this mound are the tombs of several chiefs, who fell in a battle fought here between the competitors for the government of Sinde. Bumbhora has been hitherto usually considered to have been the very ancient city of Brahminabad; but, from the situation in which the latter is spoken of, in the histories of this province that I have read, I have no doubt but that conjecture is erroneous. About three miles from Tattah, on the side towards Kurachee, there is a hill called Mukulee, covered with tombs, which are now the only remaining evidence of the ancient opulence of that city. I shall describe one of them, which had better withstood the ravages of time than the others. It was erected in an area enclosed by a high wall, the stones of which were neatly engraved and inlaid. The building itself was about eighty five feet square, with a cupola seventy feet high, that was partly hid by two balconies, or verandahs, the fronts of which were supported by pillars. The whole, as well as the outside wall, were of yellow free stone, and inside, immediately beneath the centre of the dome, was a mound of black stone, on which were the names of the people interred there: the most modern we could decypher was engraved above a century and a half ago. One of the Umeers had sent people who carried away the stone door of the entrance into the dome, on which we were told the period of the building being founded was noted *. Several tombs were built of a similar kind of stone, and others highly ornamented with enamelled tiles of beautiful green, purple, and blue colours; but the exquisite engraving of chapters of the Koran on the stone door-frames surpassed every thing else that we found worthy of observation in these sepulchres. There is likewise dug out of the solid rock, on the southern side of this hill, a very remarkable well with a chamber all round it, about fourteen feet below the surface, to which you descend by spiral steps. The water of this well has a strong medicinal taste that renders it unfit for ordinary purposes.

From the summit of the eminence, in which this excavation has been made, Tattah has the appearance of an immense city. The houses are of a mud colour, and the heaps of dilapidated walls and mosques, seem at that distance to form a part of the dwellings; but, as you approach, the delusion soon ceases, and nothing is to be observed, on either side, save long streets of uninhabited and ruinous houses. The latter two miles of the road led along a causeway about seven or eight feet high, which was formerly found necessary to ensure a communication between the city and the hill, at the period of the swelling of the Indus, which annually overflowed its banks so as to encompass Tattah by water; but for some years past this has not happened, from causes which I shall endeavour to account for, when I describe that river; and the embankment, like the city, is going to decay.

At seven o'clock in the morning of the *16th of June* we entered the suburbs surrounded by a large concourse of the inhabitants, who followed us through the streets praying aloud for the success of the mission, and testifying their joy by acclamations. We rode a long way, after we got among ruins, before we came to the habitable part

* It was built by Meerza Eesa Toorkhan. Vide Chapter XII.

of the city; and nearly as far thence, until we reached the Honourable Company's factory *, where we dismounted and took up our quarters.

A second letter was received by the envoy from the Umeers while we were on the road, acquainting him that one of their Jumptees, or state boats, was about to be dispatched for the conveyance of himself and suite, by water, to Hyderabad; and that he might expect her in a few days. It had been previously decided, that some plausible excuse should be fabricated to enable the gentlemen of the mission to separate here, in order to proceed to court by two routes, and thereby acquire the utmost geographical knowledge of the country possible under so jealous a government; and, therefore, this act of politeness was deemed rather unfortunate; but it proved so exactly the reverse, that our plan was perfected by it, as the boat was found too small even to contain one half the mission; and Mr. Ellis, Captain Maxfield, and myself, were eventually accommodated on board of her, with some difficulty, while the envoy and the remainder of the officers proceeded by the land route.

Our stay at Tattah afforded us ample leisure to see every corner of it, and the surrounding district offered to the sportsmen of the party abundance of shooting at hares and partridges. We were not, however, exclusively indebted to these recreations for means to pass our time, as some acts of the officers of the Sindian government, again called for all the firmness and address of the envoy to combat them, and had nearly led to the mission abruptly leaving the country. Shortly after we had taken up our residence at Tattah, a nobleman of high rank and station, of the name of Wullee Mohummud Khan, came to that city on official business; and, the very next morning, sent a body of his troops, who made prisoners of all the Sindians that were employed by the mission.

* The Honourable East India Company had a commercial residency in Sinde for many years.

Mr. Ellis immediately waited on him by the envoy's directions, and reprobated in strong terms this unfriendly and unjustifiable measure. A very long conference ensued, in warm language, in the course of which the Khan asked Mr. Ellis who we (the English) were? and whether we fancied ourselves the lords of the land? He added that he would do as he chose with the subjects of Sinde. That he would flog them, cut their ears off, and put them to death; nay, that he would burn Tattah if he thought proper!

Mr. Ellis pointed out to the Khan the absurdity of his vehemence, and told him, that had any objection been known to the envoy, to exist against Sindians being entertained in the British service, it would of course have been attended to; but that as nothing of the kind had been intimated, the Khan's conduct in seizing those people was, in the most favourable view of it, very unfriendly and indecorous.

The nobleman then asked Mr. Ellis whether he had been instructed to say so, or was acting from the natural giddiness of a young man; to which Mr. Ellis replied, that he had come there by desire of the envoy, for the purpose of expostulating on what had occurred; that he had no defined instructions how to express himself, as that must depend on the tenor of the arguments opposed to him; but that he conceived it required little discrimination to distinguish right from wrong in a case like the present.

The Khan then began a prolix enumeration of his titles and powers, avowed that he had been employed on negotiations of vast moment with the King of Kabool, and had succeeded in the objects for which he was deputed; that he therefore conceived himself, and his opinions, entitled to the highest consideration and respect; and could only account for the latter not being duly appreciated by Mr. Ellis by his youth and inexperience.

Mr. Ellis, in reply, said that wisdom was by no means a necessary consequence of age, and that the recital of dignities was not likely to bias his judgment or alter his ideas of the merits of so self-evident a case as that under discussion.

The Khan next spoke of the envoy visiting him; suggested the expediency of his being made acquainted with the final objects of the mission; and hinted at the influence and patronage he might be disposed to exert in favour of it, if properly solicited.

In answer to these observations, Mr. Ellis informed him, that the idea of the British envoy condescending to solicit the patronage of any person was quite ridiculous; that it was equally so to imagine he would communicate to any person, save the Umeers, the objects of the mission; and with regard to visiting, that it was the Khan's duty to wait upon him first; after which the conference ended, and Mr. Ellis returned to the factory.

The Sindians, who were imprisoned for entering our service, being unconditionally released, the envoy was induced to receive a complimentary visit from Wullee Mohummud Khan, which he returned the following day. At both these visits there was a considerable deal of high language regarding the style of writing that had been persevered in towards the Umeers, but it forms such a repetition of what I have already detailed, that it is unnecessary to say more than that the controversy terminated without the slightest compromise on the part of the mission, and that Wullee Mohummud Khan left Tattah a few days after, professing the greatest personal friendship for the envoy, and good wishes for the general interests of the British government. The retinue and appearance of this nobleman was much more magnificent than any thing we had before met with in Sinde. When he came to the factory he was attended by several Sirdars, who treated him with the utmost deference. He was very elegantly dressed in a white tunic, with a superbly rich Loongee * tied round his waist as a sash, and another of finer texture he wore as a turband. His sword was carried by one of his attendants, and delivered into his hand as he entered the room. His manners were

* Loongees are cloths made in Sinde for sashes, turbands, &c. Some are of silk, others silk and cotton, and many of them are exceedingly rich and costly, with a vast deal of gold embroidery.

dignified and affable; and his person tall and well formed, and calculated to impress the idea of the rank he held. We afterwards learned that his clan is that of the Lugharee Beloches, a branch of the tribe of Goorchanee, who inhabit the hills to the northward of Kutch Gundava, and belong to the great class of Rinds. At the visit which the envoy paid him, all our attendants, amounting to upwards of two hundred people, were entertained with sweet-meats, sherbets, and rose-water, and indeed every trifle was conducted in a princely style.

I have remarked, in a preceding place, that Tattah was once the capital of Sinde, a distinction it held till the present rulers built the fortress of Hyderabad and removed their court thither, since which event the population has decreased so rapidly, that upwards of two-thirds of the city is now uninhabited. It is, however, still a considerable place, being by computation nearly six miles in circumference, exclusive of the ruins, which extend a long way on either side.

I have in vain attempted to trace by whom this city was founded, as the earliest mention I find made of it is in the year of the Hijree 92 *, when it had fortifications, and made some slight resistance against the troops of the Khaliphas of Bagdad. The site it is built upon is commonly supposed † to identify it with the Pattala of the Greeks; but the whole of the lower districts of Sinde have undergone such astonishing changes, even within the memory of man, that all such conclusions must rest on mere conjecture. When the native princes of Sinde regained their independence from the Arab yoke, they fixed their capital at Tattah, which soon became one of the richest cities in Asia, and the emporium of all commerce carried on between the peninsula of India and all that part of Asia lying to the northward and westward of it. They spared no expence or labour to beautify it by the erection of handsome buildings, and the establish-

* A. D. 677.

† Vide Chapter XII. Part II.

ment of fine gardens, and were equally provident of the more important objects of affording facility to trade by cutting canals from the Indus, which runs four miles east of the town, through which the goods were brought and landed from boats at the very doors of the merchants' houses. All traces of the ornamental improvements of those sovereigns are now almost entirely obliterated, and the only aqueduct that yet remains is choked with rubbish, and has no longer pretensions to any other designation than a common drain.

The wealth and dignity of this city seem to me to have gradually declined from the period at which the province of Sinde became a tributary of the empire of Hindoostan; but this is to be understood only in a comparative view with its pristine wealth and power, for even so recently as the period of Nadir Shah visiting Tattah on his return from Delhi *, it is said there were forty thousand weavers of calico and loongees in that city, and artisans of every other class and description, to the number of twenty thousand more, exclusive of bankers, money-changers, shop-keepers, and sellers of grain, who were estimated at sixty thousand †; whereas the aggregate population of it, at the present day, is believed to be overrated at twenty thousand souls, and the revenues derived from it are not equal to one lac of rupees (12,500l.) per annum, a sum which falls short of the monthly collections made at the period I have just alluded to. ‡

* That event took place in 1742.

† This being a native calculation, allowances should *perhaps* be made for exaggeration. I say *perhaps*, because we have the testimony of Captain Hamilton, who visited Tattah in 1699, with regard to the immense population of that city. I have not been able to procure a copy of his voyages, and cannot therefore quote volume or page; but from some extracts sent me by a friend, I find he writes that the citadel was capable of lodging fifty thousand men and horses; and in another place he adds, that in consequence of a failure of rain a dreadful plague had raged there, of which malady above eighty thousand people died of those who manufactured cotton and silk; or, in other words, calico and loongees, which latter, as I have frequently had occasion to mention, are formed from a mixture of those productions, or silk alone.

‡ A curious anecdote is told of Nadir Shah which will exemplify the natural resources of Sinde, and almost demonstrate what I have asserted on the opulence of Tattah in

The only manufactures now carried on in Tattah are those of a few white cloths and coloured loongees; and in lieu of the bustle of a great trading city, the streets are deserted, the few shops that remain open are scarcely worthy of being called such, from the disreputable figure they cut, and the whole Bazar exhibits a deplorable picture of poverty and depressed commerce. The houses here are built on a plan that I have never met with in any other country, as the walls are made hollow, by small pieces of sticks being nailed across each other, from the outer edges of a small frame of wood; these bits of stick are usually from eight to sixteen inches long, and are placed diagonally, so that they form a very strong frame on both sides, which is plaistered over with mud, or mortar, and afterwards has all the appearance of a solid wall. Some of the dwellings erected on this principle are three or four stories high, with heavy flat roofs, which is a proof that they are very strong; but I should doubt whether they would last long, as the instant two or three of the bits of wood get decayed, in the walls, the whole must necessarily give way. Many of the better sort of houses are also built with brick and

those days. When the monarch arrived at that city, he ordered Meer Noor Mohummud, the governor of the province, into his presence; who came with his turband round his neck, a wisp of hay in his mouth, and his feet covered, all customary tokens of submission, which the conqueror required; when he had prostrated himself before the throne, Nadir called out in a loud voice, and asked him, if he had a well full of gold. The governor replied laconically. Not one, but two! Nadir then demanded if he had the Lal, a celebrated large ruby belonging to the Umeers of Sinde. Meer Noor Mohummed again made his former answer. The King threw up his handkerchief, and desired to be informed what the Meer saw on looking at it. He replied nothing but troops and arms, which were naturally the ideas uppermost in his thoughts. Then said Nadir, "Produce your gold and rubies." The governor called for a Koolee, or very large basket, made in divisions, and used for holding grain and flour, which he had filled, and placed on his right hand; he next ordered a skin of ghee, or clarified butter, to be put on his left, and said to the Shah, "I am a cultivator of the soil, and these are my gold and rubies, in which I shall not fail you." The King was gratified by the frankness of the answers he had received, and bestowed on him an honorary dress. Meer Noor Mohummud afterwards entertained the whole army and followers, (exceeding 500,000 people,) for sixteen days in the most princely manner, and without a symptom of scarcity.

mortar, on a frame of timber; and all of them, from the governor's palace to the lowest hovel, have Badgeers; which are a sort of ventilators, like chimnies, down which the wind blows cool and refreshing in the most sultry weather; at that time it is the common practice to shut up every other aperture, so as to exclude the hot wind and dust. The government of Tattah confers the official title of Nuwwab on the person holding it, who was in 1809, a cousin of the Umeers, but his appointment is a complete sinecure, as there are no troops permanently stationed there, and the customs are farmed by a Hindoo, who takes his own measures for collecting them. The latitude of this city is 24° 44′ north, longitude 68° 17′ east, both of which are fixed by the mean of numerous observations taken by Captain Maxfield. The country immediately around it is perfectly level, except the hills of Mukulee, on which the tombs are built that I have already described, and they extend to the southward till within fifteen or twenty miles of the sea. These hills, as well as the plain, are covered with thick jungul, principally of the tamarisk, and a species of bastard myrtle.

The rains had now set in with great violence, and it poured so heavily, that the streets frequently ran like rivulets, which quite put a stop to our riding out morning and evening. The heat had been, previous to this fall, excessive, for in the coolest apartment in the factory, the thermometer usually ranged from 94° to 102° throughout the twenty-four hours, but towards the middle of July it became much cooler, and we were greatly surprized by the frequent recurrence of strong northerly gales, one of which enabled the ships to cross the bar of Kurachee harbour, and make a very quick passage to Bombay. The latter end of the same month, the mission left Tattah for Hyderabad, where Mr. Ellis, Captain Maxfield, and myself, arrived, by water, several days sooner than the envoy and his party, they having been detained on the road by the severe indisposition of the envoy.

CHAPTER X.

RIVER INDUS. — SUPPOSITION REGARDING IT. — RECENTLY PROVED INCORRECT. — PARTICULAR DETAIL OF. — ITS SOURCE. — COURSE. — TRIBUTARY STREAMS. — PUNJNUD. — WHENCE SO CALLED. — THE DIFFERENT NAMES BY WHICH THE INDUS IS KNOWN. — WHERE IT ENTERS SINDE. — KUMBURGUNDEE, OR LARKHANU RIVER. — LAKE THAT IT FORMS. — FERTILE DISTRICT THAT IT ENCOMPASSES. — KHYRPOOR, OR DOORLEE RIVER. — RAPIDLY FILLING WITH SAND. — FUI FLEE RIVER. — ITS ORIGIN AND COURSE TILL IT REUNITES WITH THE INDUS. — THE GOONEE RIVER. — FORMERLY DISEMBOGUED INTO THE SEA. — BUND OR EMBANKMENT BUILT ACROSS IT. — WHEN. — FOR WHAT PURPOSE. — LONEL, OR SALT RIVER. — BREADTH AND DEPTH OF THE GONEE. — NATIVE ASSERTION RESPECTING IT. — FURTHER DETAIL OF THE COURSE OF THE INDUS. — IT HAS ONLY ONE MOUTH. — CREEKS CANNOT BE CONSIDERED IN THAT LIGHT. — CURRENTS IN THE INDUS. — SOUNDINGS. — TABLE SHEWING ITS ACTUAL DEPTH AND BREADTH. — SAID TO HAVE NO BAR. — FLAT-BOTTOMED BOATS USED. — ADVANTAGES OF THIS CONSTRUCTION. — GENERAL DESCRIPTION OF THE FACE OF THE PROVINCE OF SINDE. — UMEERS GREAT PASSION FOR HUNTING. — ITS CONSEQUENCES. — PROCEEDINGS OF THE MISSION CONTINUED. — THE ENVOY REACHES HYDERABAD. — COMPLIMENTARY MESSAGES FROM THE UMEERS. — LITIGIOUSNESS OF THOSE PRINCES. — HOW SILENCED. — OUTRAGE COMMITTED BY A SINDIAN. — MEASURES TAKEN TO PREVENT A SIMILAR OCCURRENCE. — THE BRITISH ENCAMPMENT. — DESCRIPTION OF IT. — BUFFOONS. — JUGGLERS. — FAKEERS. — THE PERSEVERANCE AND RIDICULOUS THREATS OF THE LATTER. — DISCUSSION REGARDING THE CEREMONIALS OF THE ENVOY'S FIRST AUDIENCE. — ASSUMPTION AND UNWARRANTABLE PROPOSITION OF THE UMEERS. — THE ENVOY'S BEHAVIOUR ON THE OCCASION. — FINAL ARRANGEMENT. — FORMS A CORRECT PICTURE OF THE SINDIAN GOVERNMENT. — NECESSITY FOR GREAT ATTENTION TO PUNCTILIOUS CEREMONIES. — THE ENVOY AND HIS SUITE INTRODUCED TO THE UMEERS. — DETAIL OF THAT CEREMONY. — CONFUSION IN THE DURBAR. — PROBABLE CAUSE OF IT. — AUTHOR'S OPINION. — DISPLAY OF JEWELS. — ORDER OF

RANK OF THE THREE PRINCES. — THEIR APPEARANCE. — DRESS. — IMMENSE TURBANS. — STATE OF THE WEATHER AT HYDERABAD IN AUGUST, 1809. — OPPRESSIVE HEAT.

BEFORE I proceed further in the abstract from my journal, of the proceedings of the mission till its final return to Bombay, I shall, in this place, detail the sum of Captain Maxfield's and my own observations on the river Indus, and the adjacent districts, together with the information I have derived from other sources.* That celebrated river was once supposed to have flowed in nearly a direct south line, from its source into the ocean, but the successful investigations that have of late years been pursued, regarding the geography of Asia, have rectified this error, and thrown a light on the north-western frontier of Hindoostan, which could scarcely have been anticipated by the most sanguine promoters of science. From these researches we are led to think that the Indus rises between the thirty-fifth and thirty-sixth degrees of north latitude, whence it runs a little to the southward of west, for a distance of seven or eight degrees, forcing its way among the snowy mountains that separate Kashmeer and Little Thibet. About the seventy-second degree of east longitude it suddenly turns more southerly, being denied a further westerly progress by the mountains of Kashkar, and thence it varies its course, between south and south-west, to the fortress of Attock, in north latitude 33° 55'. To the northward of that place it is distinguished by the title of Aboo Seen, or Father River, and there it is usually called the Roodé Attock, or river of Attock, by which name it is known until joined by the Punjnud, or five streams, that water the provinces within the Punjab; † here it may be said to

* The sources whence I have received information on the Indus, exclusive of the surveys to Kabool and Sinde, I shall touch upon in a short notice, regarding the construction of the Map that I purpose affixing to this volume.

† The five rivers of the Punjab, passing from west to east, are the Behat, or Chelum, anciently Hydaspes. The Chunaub, or Jenaub, anciently Acesines. The Rauvee, or ancient Hydraotes. These three unite about 70 miles north-east of Mooltan, and take

enter Sinde, and, accordingly, it seems to be thenceforward exclusively spoken of as the Duryaé Sinde, which we must interpret the river of Sinde, though, in reality, it signifies the sea of Sinde. That is, however, used metaphorically to convey an idea of its magnitude.

From the spot at which the Indus receives such a vast addition to its waters, by the Punjnud disemboguing into it, I am informed that it flows south-south-west, almost without a curve, for a distance of one hundred and sixty miles, passing the cities of Sukor, Rohree, and Bhukor; the latter being situated on an island in the midst of the stream. Seventeen miles to the southward of these places it sends off a branch to the westward, that forms a circuit, and rejoins the main body at the town of Sehwan, fifty miles lower down than where it is disengaged. This branch is known by the two different names of the Kumburgundee and Larkhanu river; which last it derives from running past the town of that name, and in one place it expands into a lake, ten or twelve miles across, that lies immediately at the foot of the Brahooick mountains, and has its edges overgrown with impenetrable jungul and reeds, the haunt of lions and other ferocious animals. The district of Chandookee, that is encompassed and fertilized by this branch, is the finest in the territories of the Umeers, who receive from it a revenue of eight lacs of rupees per annum,* an amount, not equal to one half what it was thirty-five years ago. To the eastward, about half way between Bhukor and Sehwan, the Indus receives a tributary stream that is generally called the Khyrpoor river, from running near that town, as far as which, boats of light burthen navigate in the rains. Its proper name, I am told, is

the name of the centre one, or Chunaub. The fourth river is the Beah, and the fifth the Sutledge. These two, when united, form the Hyphasis of ancient geography. They are sometimes known by the name of the Sutledge, but most frequently, now a-days, called the Gurru, or Gurrah. They run into the Chunaub, in latitude 29° 10′ north, longitude 71° 28′ east, and the whole receive the title of the "Punjnud," or "five streams," until they enter the Indus, as stated in the text.

* One hundred thousand pounds sterling.

the Doorlee, but that I have reason to think originates in the source of it lying in the district of Durelee, where it is joined by two other small rivulets, one of which is said to have run to the southward along the edge of the sandy desert, and eventually reached the sea; but the original bed of it has now disappeared in the sand, and the Khyrpoor river is rapidly sharing the same fate.

The next branch, if it can be called such, is immediately opposite the fort of Sehwan, where the river forms an island of some extent that affords capital pasturage in dry weather, but is overflowed when the waters rise. From this branch other minor ones disengage themselves, and irrigate the districts to the extent of thirty or forty miles; while the main body is swoln, though in common they are perfectly dry. We next come to the branch called the Fulelee, that encircles the island on which the capital, Hyderabad, is built. This is a larger stream than any I have yet described, and the cause is evident, for the Indus, immediately above its separation, skirts along the edge of the hills, and acquires such velocity from being confined on the western bank, that the moment it finds an exit to the eastward it throws off all the increased and superfluous water by it. The Fulelee re-unites with its mother stream ten miles south-west of Hyderabad, though it is more than double that distance to follow the winding of the water. At its most eastern point it detaches the Goonee, which once disembogued into the ocean, about a degree to the eastward of the great mouth of the Indus; but in 1799, Futtuh Allee, a late Umeer, threw a bund or embankment across it at Allee Bunder, where there was an island in the centre of it, and now, the fresh water presses against the dam, on one side, whilst the tide regularly flows up to it on the other; indeed, previous to the erection of this bund, which is the only work of public utility ever made by any of the reigning family, the salt water found its way twelve miles higher up during the springs, and tended to ruin the fine crops, which the circumjacent plain now produces. The river below the dam is called the Lonee or Salt river, in contradistinction to the Goonee, which signifies efficacious or useful. The usual breadth of the Fulelee is from two to four hundred yards, and the depth of water varies between two and six fathoms; the Goonee is much narrower and shoaler, and the natives declare, that it is drying up every succeeding season, an assertion that is demonstrated by our finding that there are not more than four months in the year, during which boats of any burthen can ply between Hyderabad and Allee Bunder, whereas, some years back, there was a never failing intercourse by water, and considerable trade flowed through that channel into the eastern parts of the province.*

After the Fulelee rejoins the Indus, the latter winds a little to the eastward of south, but soon regains its predominant inclination to the south south-west, which it increases still more westerly after passing Tattah, and enters the Indian ocean with nearly a western aspect, in one vast body; I say one body, for, although some trifling streams separate about eighteen miles from the sea, and, after various windings and intersections, empty themselves into it by three or four mouths, they cannot strictly be called any thing else than creeks, being full or empty according to the state of the tide and river, and overgrown with thick junguls of mangrove. The rapidity of the stream in the Indus fluctuates with the seasons, whether dry or otherwise, and the nature of the districts it runs through also seems to affect it. I should estimate it to be above Tattah, usually between two and a half and four miles per hour; lower down it is influenced by the tide, which causes it sometimes to run off at the rate of eleven or twelve, but this is said only to be the case, when great freshes, and spring tides happen at the same period. The soundings of this river are subject to the same remark, but in a greater degree, as the currents, and therefore, I have framed a medium table of

* When the mission that was deputed to Sinde by the Bombay government returned in *September*, 1808, the boats were dragged through the mud for several miles down the Goonee. A part of our heavy baggage was sent by the same route to join us in Kutch, but as it was a month earlier, the people who had charge of it experienced no such difficulties.

them, at various positions, that will better illustrate this matter, than a long paragraph. * The actual breadth of its channel I have likewise included in this table, and it only remains for me to add, that the natives affirm there is no bar at the mouth of the river, nor any obstacle so high as Lahoree Bunder, (to which place in fact, it is an arm of the sea,) that would prevent even a line of battle ship from going up, provided she was in charge of a skilful pilot. Notwithstanding the great depth of water, which the table exhibits in the Indus, the commerce is entirely carried on between Sinde and the Punjab and Uffghanistan in flat bottomed boats that carry from one to three hundred tons, and yet are so constructed, as to draw but a

---

* TABLE of the Depth and Breadth of the Channel of the River Indus. (*a*)

		DEPTH.		BREADTH.	
Latitudes.	Places.	Dry Season.	Wet Season.	Dry Season.	Remarks.
▽33° 55′ N.	Attock			260 yards.	When the mission to Kabool crossed the Indus at Attock, on the 21st of June, 1809, the depth was unascertained, from the rapidity of the current, which is here confined by banks 40 feet high, to the top of which the waters often rise during the freshes. At Kalabagh the stream is slow, still, and extremely deep. I have adopted the breadth exclusively of the dry weather, as the really narrowest places often seem the broadest in the floods.
▽33° 7′ N.	Kalabagh			380 do.	
▽31° 52′ N.	Derue Ismael Khan	2 fath.		1000 do.	
▽31° 28′ N.	Kuheree	2 do.		1200 do.	
29° 54′ N.	Derue Ghazee Khan	3 do.	7 fath.	1000 do.	
29° 20′ N.	Rajunpoor	3 do.	7 do.	1400 do.	
28° 27′ N.	Conflux of the Punjnud	8 do.	16 do.	2200 do.	
27° 13′ N.	Bhukor	5 do.	10 do.	1600 do.	
26° 6′ N.	Sehwan	3 do.	6 do.	900 do.	
Δ25° 22′ N.	Hyderabad	5 do.	8 do.	2000 do.	
Δ25° 9′ N.	Fulelee river	5 do.	10 do.	2200 do.	
Δ24° 44′ N.	Tattah	4 do.	6 do.	1800 do.	
Δ24° 40′ N.	Peer Putta	7 do.	18 do.	700 do.	
24° 32′ N.	Lahoree Bunder	11 do.	16 do.	4 miles.	
24° 29′ N.	Dharajay Bunder	13 do.	16 do.	9 do.	
24° 8′ N.	Extreme of the land	13 do.	16 do.	12 do.	

(*a*) The depth and breadth in the dry season of those marked thus ▽, were ascertained by the Kabool mission. Those thus Δ, by that to Sinde, and the remainder are from the best native information I could procure.

few feet water *. This construction enables them, when proceeding upwards, to keep close to the edge, where the current is hardly perceptible; and on their return to the southward, although their passage might be accelerated by being of greater draught of water, and consequently having more hold of the stream, yet this defect is more than counterbalanced by the advantage I allude to. These boats set a large square sail that is hoisted abaft the mast when going before the wind; but they never attempt to haul upon it, and are, in the event of its being contrary, dragged up the stream by men.

To the eastward of the Indus the province of Sinde is a perfect level from its most northern boundary to the sea-shore, with the exception of two or three low hills called the Gunjah hills, on the island in which Hyderabad is situated. On the western bank of the river, from the latitude of Sehwan in 26° 6', there is a variety of feature in the face of the country, some districts being mountainous, some flat, and some intersected by ranges of low hills until we reach the sea. Northward of Sehwan the plain extends to the hills of Seweestan. The present rulers of Sinde being passionately fond of hunting, and feeling no scruple at impoverishing their dominions and oppressing their subjects, when placed in the scale with the gratification of that passion, have enclosed all the finest districts along the banks of the river for the preservation of game; and places that were within these last twenty years in the most luxuriant state of cultivation, are now impervious junguls of the most useless description of trees and bushes.

The morning after the envoy reached Hyderabad, the Umeers each sent a formal deputation out to our encampment, which was pitched on the bank of the Fulelee river, about one mile south-east of the

* The trade on the Indus is now almost nominal. The ignorant and short-sighted policy of the Umeers of Sinde has crushed it in that province, and the unsettled state of the countries to the northward renders is precarious there. At present it amounts to little more than a few boats passing up and down with grain, saltpetre, salt and firewood.

fortress, to congratulate him on that event and enquire after his health; but as it was ascertained that none of the persons who brought these complimentary messages, and who were also charged with the delivery of many large trays of sweetmeats, were of higher rank than Khidmutgars*, it was not deemed consonant with the situation of affairs that Mr. Smith should receive them in person, and Mr. Ellis accordingly did so; at which arrangement they appeared considerably disappointed, though, when they found that they had a present notwithstanding, this feeling ceased, and they returned in perfect good humour. The Umeers did not, however, allow this alledged disrespect towards themselves to pass without a long expostulation, which was delivered by one of their Deewans, or managers, called Mooshtak Ram, who particularly enlarged on the policy of the envoy courting the favourable opinion of the Umeers by acts of pointed external respect, on which subject, he added, they were very tenacious. He likewise adverted, most opportunely, to its having been omitted by the envoy to make a return of complimentary enquiries for the Umeers, and was informed that that had not been neglected, but that the Moonshee who was dispatched for that purpose had in vain endeavoured to gain entrance into the fort, and was actually obliged to wait outside until he sent a person back to Mr. Smith, to ask what steps he should take towards delivering his messages; and that that gentleman had even waved ceremony so far as to direct he would do so to any of the officers of government he should happen to meet with, in order that they might be conveyed to the Umeers through that channel.

The Deewan was further reminded, that previous to the arrival of the envoy at the capital, Mr. Ellis found occasion, more than once,

* Khidmutgars are personal servants, and we usually apply the term to every description of attendants at table. In Sinde the word appears to be more confined in its acceptation, and to signify inferior Deewans or stewards. They, however, wait on their masters and perform servile offices in the household. The Peish Khidmuts of Persia are of the same class, and seemed to me to be employed on similar errands and duties.

to have intercourse with the Umeers on official topics, and that the Moonshee who was employed on those errands was invariably refused admission into the fort, and obliged to remain in the bazar, outside, until an answer was brought to him. It was therefore evident, if any unfriendly omission had occurred, that it originated on the side of the Sindian government; and, it was equally obvious, that the Umeers had no cause to feel any sort of chagrin at their Khidmutgars not being seen by the envoy, when they had declined to admit a Moonshee, who was a person of much higher station and respectability, into their presence, even when charged with important verbal communications.

A serious quarrel had nearly occurred among our people and the Sindians, one of whom attempted to rush past a sentinel, and, on being prevented, struck him and knocked off his cap. Exertions were made to seize the offender, but he effected his escape in the crowd; and the envoy's anxiety to obviate any similar occurrence, which might have led to the most fatal consequences, only for the forbearance displayed by the Sipahee, suggested the expedient of the sentries being posted inside the Kunauts, which was accordingly resorted to.

Our encampment might have been thought at this time to be pitched in the centre of a fair, from the vast numbers of people of every profession and description that were continually hanging about it, and we were serenaded night and day by the unceasing vociferations of buffoons, jugglers, bear-dancers, and Fakeers, the latter of whom diversified the concert by sounding horns and trumpets. Many of them evinced astonishing perseverance in their profession, and took post as near the envoy's private tent as the outer skreens would permit them to approach it, where they continued for days at a time, bellowing forth their demands and occasionally denouncing the vengeance of the Prophet and the Umeers against the mission, unless they were satisfied. Others reserved their attack until we rode out, which was generally the case every evening when the weather was fair; and then they would run before the envoy's horse, assuring him, if they were well remunerated, they were ready to intercede with the Umeers in behalf of the mission; but, that on the other hand, if their offers were neglected, he might as well go back to India without delay, as nothing could be effected without their concurrence. At first these vagabonds, who were almost of every nation in Asia, gave us considerable annoyance by the noise they made, but we soon became reconciled to their shouting and hooting, and latterly their exclamations and denunciations were rather a source of laughter and amusement.

The second day after the envoy had got to Hyderabad, the ceremonials of his first audience at court were brought forward; when, as we had foreseen, the proposals made by the Umeers, through various people, induced a negotiation that delayed the final arrangements for nearly a week; and had once or twice led us to anticipate quitting Sinde without a personal interview of its rulers.

It had been understood that the Musnud or throne was considerably elevated from the ground *, and the envoy therefore deemed it proper that he should have a chair to sit upon, and also that the three Umeers should rise on the entrance of the mission; while they, on the other hand, not only declined shewing any outward mark of respect by standing up, but actually proposed that we should all be disarmed, previous to coming into the hall of audience, grounding this unwarrantable proposition on a plea that proved it a still greater insult, of an attempt having once been made by two Vakeels † of the Jypoor Rajah, to assassinate one of the Umeers at a public levee.

Mr. Smith reprehended, in the most unequivocal terms, this degrading demand, and acquainted the deliverer of it, that had he even felt inclined to submit to it himself, than which nothing could be farther from his thoughts, he was not at liberty to insist upon the

* This mistake was immediately rectified, and the stipulation regarding the chair withdrawn, as it was ascertained that the Umeers sat upon a Fursh or quilted matrass, that did not raise them above two inches from the ground.

† Vakeels, agents.

gentlemen of his suite following his example; and that in preference to compromising, in the most trifling degree, the dignity of the government he represented, he would immediately depart out of the Sindian territories.

Wullee Mohummud Khan, the same chief who had met us at Tattah, at length came to try his powers of persuasion, vested, as it was said, by the Umeers with full authority to conclude any terms he might judge fit; but, on the first mention of the above subject, he found the envoy so decided, that he gave up the point, and reverted to the minor one already touched upon.

After every reasoniug that the subtilty of the Khan could adduce to convince us of the absolute impossibility of the Princes getting up to receive the mission, he artfully descended from that high tone by a gradation of offers, commencing with their making a motion as if in the act of rising, until it was finally fixed that they should stand up on the first appearance of the envoy, and remain in that position till he had advanced to the spot at which he was to be seated, on the right hand of the Umeers; and that they were to observe an equal token of respect when we took leave.

The result of this debate forms a most correct commentary on the government of Sinde, and indeed it may be said, on that of all other Asiatics who estimate their successful policy by the impositions they can put upon foreigners, regarding punctilious ceremonies, which it should be peculiarly the aim of every person acting in a public capacity to crush by the most explicit and immoveable measures; otherwise he may calculate, not merely on entailing on himself the derision of the court he is employed at, but that his future negotiations will be cramped and interrupted by every species of litigious etiquette that can be devised; and possibly, from that very circumstance, prove in the end equally unavailing and derogatory.

The evening after the forms of our reception had been agreed upon, we were introduced to the Umeers by Akhoond Mohummud Bukka Khan, who came to the British encampment for the purpose of conducting us to court, and severally announced the rank and station of the envoy and the gentlemen of his suite. The precipice on which the eastern face of the fortress of Hyderabad is built, the tops of the houses, and even the fortifications, were covered with a multitude of people of both sexes, who testified their good will towards us by exclamations and applause. From the first gate at which we entered the fortress, the path led up a steep ascent, that was lined on both sides with ranks of matchlockmen, until we came to a second tower with a winding passage under it; whence, to the palace, the streets were so filled with armed men, that it was with much labour, and at the risk of trampling many under our horses feet, that we made way through them. At last we got to the place where we were to dismount, and were there received by Wullee Mohummud Khan and several other officers of the highest rank, who preceded us to a large open platform, at the further end of which sat the three Umeers. The platform was spread with the richest Persian carpets, so that we here put off our shoes, and the moment the envoy made the first step to advance towards the princes, they all rose and stood upright until he reached his allotted place, which was distinguished from that of the remainder of the party by having an embroidered cloth laid over it.

As soon as we had sat down, a scene of confusion ensued which it is difficult to describe, and could only be attributed to a distrust of our real designs, for the mass of attendants, matchlockmen, and swordsmen crowded into the place, and nearly overwhelmed us by their pressure. The foremost of them even placed their feet on the scabbards of our swords and skirts of our coats; which, from the manner we were sitting, lay along the carpet; but whether this was a preconcerted plan, or the effect of chance it was impossible to guess. Subsequent interviews, however, incline me to lean to the former idea. The princes, individually, made polite enquiries for all our healths. Indeed nothing but compliments and expressions of politeness took place, as it was a mere audience of ceremony; and after we had been in the Durbar about half an hour, the eldest verbally signified their wish that we should retire, a hint that is given at all Indian levees by the introduction of Pan Sooparee* and Utr, or oil of roses; but in Sinde they have no such custom, nor even the Persian one of Kullyans and coffee.

The Umeers wore a vast number of jewels, exclusive of those which were set in the hilts and scabbards of their swords and daggers; beside which, their waist-belts displayed some extraordinary large emeralds and rubies. They were seated, agreeable to age, the eldest in the centre, the second one on his right hand, and the youngest on his left, on a thin felt that extended all round the circle, and over which was laid, only under them, a silk mattrass, about an inch thick, spread with a muslin cloth embroidered in a most exquisite manner with gold and silver flowers. At their backs there were three large pillows covered with similar embroidery to that they sat upon, which, with their display of jewels, gave the whole Durbar an inconceivably rich effect. Many of the officers of government also appeared in very good style; and the general splendour and richness of the scene, far surpassed any thing we had expected to see at the court of Hyderabad.

In person, the Umeers are corpulent middle-sized men. The eldest, Meer Gholam Allee, did not appear to be more than forty-five years of age; and his two brothers, who are called Meer Moorad Allee and Meer Kureem Allee, are several years younger. The youngest, Meer Kureem Allee, has a pleasing open countenance, with a constant smile that conveys the idea of great affability and good humour, both of which he was † said to possess in contradistinction to the two senior princes, who were described as sullen and unforgiving men; but, at the same time, by no means cruel.

Except in the decorative parts of their dresses, the three brothers were habited alike, in fine muslin tunics with very costly loongees tied round their waists. Their turbands were of thin transparent

* The Pan is the leaf of the piper betle. The Sooparee, the fruit of the areca tree.

† Meer Gholam Allee is since dead. Vide Chapter XII. Note.

gauze, and exceeded in dimensions any thing I had ever beheld in the form of head dresses: speaking within bounds, I should imagine they were from two to two and a half feet in diameter, and yet so neatly folded up as to have by no means either a heavy or an unbecoming appearance. *

We had experienced excessively heavy falls of rain during the period we had been at Hyderabad, and the Fulelee river suddenly overflowed its banks, and nearly inundated our encampment, but by opening a few trenches for the water to escape into the canals that intersect the country, we were enabled to remain on our ground, which was for some hours very doubtful. The sultriness of the weather was greatly augmented by the violent exhalations from the earth, after it had been saturated by water, and numbers of the followers of the mission were attacked by fevers and other complaints incidental to such a change. The gentlemen, however, by taking regular exercise and using requisite precautions, contrived to keep in good health, though all suffered, in a greater or lesser degree, from the heat, which had attained such a pitch that the thermometer seldom fell below 102°, and the atmosphere, particularly at night, was oppressive beyond any thing I had ever felt in India.

* An idea may be formed of the extraordinary size of the turbands worn by the great men of Sinde, from the fact of some of them containing upwards of eighty yards in length of the gauze they are formed from. It is usually from eight to twelve inches in width.

CHAPTER XI.

FORTRESS OF HYDERABAD. — LATITUDE AND LONGITUDE. — SITUATION. — DISTANCE FROM THE INDUS AND FULELEE RIVERS. — WHEN BUILT. — BY WHOM. — ESTIMATED VERY STRONG. — FORTIFICATIONS. — SHAPE IRREGULAR. DESCRIPTION OF THEM. — EASILY STORMED. — GATE. — DITCH. — CANNON MOUNTED. — PETTAH, OR SUBURBS. — POPULATION. — MANUFACTURES. — PRESENTS SENT TO THE UMEERS. — REFUSAL TO RECEIVE SOME OF THEM. — THE ENVOY'S MEASURES ON THE OCCASION. — ITS GOOD EFFECT. — PRESENTS MADE IN RETURN. — A SECOND AUDIENCE OF THE UMEERS. — DECORUM WITH WHICH IT WAS CONDUCTED. — THE CURIOSITY OF THOSE PRINCES ABOUT SWORDS. — ITS PUBLIC UTILITY. — SUPERB PEARLS AND JEWELS THEY WORE. — THE ENVOY HAS A PRIVATE AUDIENCE. — NEGOCIATIONS COMMENCED. — THEIR ULTIMATE CONCLUSION. — AN ENVOY DEPUTED TO THE GOVERNOR-GENERAL OF INDIA, ON THE PART OF THE UMEERS. — THE MISSION QUITS HYDERABAD FOR BOMBAY. — ARRIVAL AT THE VILLAGE OF KUDDEEN. — PROCEED ACROSS THE DESERT TO LUKPUT BUNDER, IN KUTCH. — MOHUMMUD KHAN'S TANDA. — DESCRIPTION OF IT. — ITS CHIEF. — HIS REVENUES. — IMPROVING STATE OF HIS COUNTRY. — INTERMEDIATE TRACT BETWEEN HYDERABAD AND KUDDEEN. — ARRIVAL AT BOMBAY. — GENERAL POPULATION OF SINDE. — VARIOUS CLASSES. — HINDOOS. — JUTHS. — BELOOCHES. — CHARACTER OF THE SINDIANS. — VICES. — APOLOGY FOR THEM. — GOOD QUALITIES OF THE SINDIANS. — WHENCE INHERITED. — THEIR RELIGION. — COLOUR. — STATURE. — FEATURES. — WOMEN. — VERY BEAUTIFUL. — FACE AND FIGURE USUALLY VERY STRIKING. — DRESS OF THE MEN. — THE WOMEN.

HYDERABAD lies in latitude 25° 22′ north, longitude 68° 41′ east, on the eastern side of an island that is formed, as I have already stated, by the streams of the Indus and Fulelee. The nearest point of the former river bears from the fort west by south four miles, and the latter runs within one thousand paces of the foot of the precipice on which it is built, but sends off a creek sufficiently large to admit boats within a few yards of the fortifications, when the river itself is swoln. This fortress was built by Meer Futtuh Allee, an elder brother of the present princes, and is looked upon by the Sindians as strong enough to defy any attempt that might be made to reduce it, but it would make a poor defence against the regular approaches of an European enemy. The shape of the fortifications is entirely irregular, as they have been so fashioned as to correspond with the curves and angles of the hill. The walls are of brick, from fifteen to thirty feet high, and the foundations of them are placed on the very edge of the summit of the hill; there they are pretty thick and solid, but taper off so much towards the summit, and are so weakened by embrasures and the loop-holes with which they are pierced, that a very few well directed shot would demolish any part of them, and expose the people on the ramparts to the fire of musketry. The round towers that flank the whole are erected in judicious positions, at intervals of three or four hundred paces, and combined with the steepness of the hill have an imposing appearance; but the latter is of too soft and friable a stone, to be scarped, and the slope is such that the rubbish, from a breach made in the wall, would rest upon it and materially assist troops, in storming the place, by affording them secure footing.

On the northern side there is a dry ditch, that has a bridge across it leading to the gate, which is protected by an immense bastion built over it. There are about seventy pieces of cannon mounted on the works of Hyderabad, but with the exception of eight *or ten pieces of heavy metal, in the bastion over the gate*, they are all said to be small and in bad order. The Pettah, or suburb, lies to the northward of the fortress, on a rising piece of ground, and consists of two thousand five hundred houses, with a population of ten thousand souls. Inside the fort there is nearly an equal number of houses, but not one half so many people, who are chiefly soldiers. The principal manufactures of Hyderabad are of various kinds of arms, such as matchlocks, spears, swords, &c. and embroidered cloths. The former alone are stated to afford occupation to one-fifth of the inhabitants of the suburbs, and some of their workmanship is hardly to be distinguished from that of European artists.

The morning after we had been received at court, the presents brought from India for the Umeers, were dispatched to their different palaces in charge of the Chobdars of the mission. They consisted of mirrors, gold watches, clocks, fowling pieces, telescopes, pistols, velvets, and chintzes, to a considerable value, and were all thankfully received, except the latter article, which they threatened to return, as beneath their dignity to accept. The fact was, they did not consider it sufficiently costly, and had recourse to this scheme, in expectation of getting something in lieu of it more valuable; but as their declining to take it would have been a mark of great disrespect towards the donor, the envoy combated their objection, by remarking to the person whom they deputed to express their feelings on this subject, that the chintzes, in common with all the other presents, were tokens of the friendship of the government he represented; that they were rather intended as specimens of the various manufactures of England, than as gifts, the prices of which it was conceived could not have been any object to the rulers of Sinde, but as that did not appear to be the case, he was quite prepared to receive back the whole of the presents, and transport them to India on the return of the mission, and that it would of course rest with the Umeers to account to the Right Honorable the Governor-General for this measure having proved requisite. These observations, which were so well calculated to work on the inherent avarice of the Umeers, as well as to awaken their apprehensions of disobliging the British government, had the effect of completely silencing their scruples, and the customary presents in return, were subsequently sent to our encampment; those for the supreme government were only horses; the envoy had one from each of the brothers, and a handsome sword; and the remainder of our party, various productions of Sinde to a trifling amount.

We had a second audience of the Umeers, a few days after our introductory one, at which every thing was conducted with the utmost regularity and comfort. They received us on the same terrace, and with similar attention; but instead of the guards and attendants crowding forward, as they did at our first visit, only a few of the latter were admitted, and they stood at a great distance from us, ranged round the walls, with their hands folded across their breasts in the most respectful manner. The three princes were exceedingly chatty on this occasion, having, I suppose, got over that alarm for their personal safety, which there could be no doubt they entertained on the previous one; and not only seemed perfectly reconciled to our appearing with our swords, but successively requested the whole of the party to draw them, in order that they might judge of the quality of the metal and workmanship. They afterwards produced their own, and also their daggers, all of the very finest steel, to purchase which article they informed us that they annually dispatched agents into Persia and Asia Minor, with instructions to spare no cost in procuring the very best kind; indeed, we soon found from their conversation, that this rage for swords and other arms, was the only species of extravagance that got the better of their excessive cupidity for accumulating money; and that they carried it to a most extraordinary pitch, vying with each other who should be possessed of the highest priced curiosities of that description. This rage is, however, like most other fashions, attended by its peculiar public benefits; for as the chiefs about the court see the rulers of the country engaged in this emulation, they naturally strive to imitate them. This feeling has spread to the lower classes of the population, and thence has arisen the vast employment for armourers at Hyderabad, as well as the elegance and superior style of their handiwork.

At this levee the Umeers were dressed still more superbly than when we first saw them; however, there was nothing so remarkable in the change of any part of their costume as to merit description. The eldest brother had some very long strings of beautiful pearls round his neck, and one in his hand, which he used as a rosary, the size of which I should have before regarded as perfectly incredible.

One of the younger princes had a dagger in his sash, from the hilt of which was suspended a perfect emerald considerably larger than a pigeon's egg.

Towards the close of this audience, the envoy retired with the Umeers, and had a private conference, when he explained to those princes the nature of the negotiations he was entrusted with by the Governor-general, and intimated his desire that they would nominate such officers of their government as they deemed qualified to conduct on their behalf the consideration of the various topics connected with his mission; to which proposal they gave their ready assent, and promised that their ministers should attend daily at the British encampment until all matters were finally arranged.

The ministers fixed upon by the Umeers were Wullee Mohummud Khan, Akhoond Bukka Khan, and a Hindoo called Mooshtak Ram, all persons of acknowledged abilities, and high in the confidence of their masters; but it would be equally uninteresting and unprofitable here to enter into a prolix narrative of the progress of the negotiations, which almost wholly engaged the attention of the envoy during our further stay at Hyderabad. The very nature of them, although extremely delicate and perplexing, rendered the whole peculiarly devoid of interest *; and as the rulers of Sinde had desisted from assuming the tone of imperious superiority that had guided their counsels on our first arrival in the country, the discussions thenceforward were purely of a political nature. It therefore is sufficient for me to add, that the result of them was in the highest degree

* The great object of the mission from the supreme government was to annul a treaty of offensive and defensive alliance, that had been entered into the preceding year by the envoy from Bombay, through misconception of his instructions. To debar the agents of the French from admission into Sinde, and to re-establish the proper relative rank of the British and Sindian governments, were, though highly important, of secondary consideration. The former was secured by the result of the negotiations, and the latter effected even before they commenced: in fact it had been, as I have shewn, exclusively attended to for a length of time, even after our reaching the capital, as no other business could proceed till it was adjusted.

satisfactory to the supreme British authority in India, and that the envoy received the merited approbation and thanks of his superiors for the firmness, dignity, and sound judgment he had evinced in fulfilling the orders with which he had been furnished. An envoy to the Governor-general was likewise appointed to return with the mission in order to receive the ratified copy of the treaty that was made.

Having had an audience of leave, we embarked on board three Jumptees, or state barges, provided by the Umeers, on the morning of the *25th of August*, the baggage being shipped into boats hired for the purpose, and dropped down the Fulelee from Hyderabad in a south-south-east direction till we entered the mouth of the Goonee, which stream I have already described; thence, the third evening, we reached the village of Ḳuddeen, lying almost at the extreme end of a branch of the Goonee *, and as the water here had become so shallow that the boats would scarcely float, we landed the trifling baggage that had been brought with us; and, after halting some days to shoot, proceeded across the salt marsh separating Sinde from Kutch to the fort of Lukput Bunder, on the western limit of the latter country, where we arrived on the *7th of September*. The boats conveying the bulk of the baggage and the greater number of natives attached to the mission went directly down the Goonee to Allee

* The mention of this furnishes me with a proper opportunity of remarking, what I have omitted in its proper place, that some of the minor branches of the Indus run off from the mother stream into the interior of the country, and suddenly terminate like the one I speak of in the text; while others, of less size, always flow into the great stream, even when it is full. This at first surprizes an observer, but is owing to the declivity of the soil through which they meander. Were the former to empty themselves into the sea or any large channel, there would be nothing observable even in this circumstance; but to see a stream forcing its course across several districts and gradually tapering away till it becomes a brook of a few inches in depth, and that too without any visible cause for such a diminution of its waters, is certainly very extraordinary. A part of them is doubtless expended in irrigation, but the most probable theory appears to me to attribute their consumption to absorption by the sand.

Bunder, where all were re-shipped into others on the Lonee River, and joined us eventually in Kutch.

The only place we passed during this passage worthy of being noticed was Mohummud Khan's Tanda, which is a large and flourishing fortified town, the residence of Meer Sooltan Allee, a relation of the reigning Umeers. He holds several fine districts, and his capital is the great rendezvous of all the northern merchants, who bring horses yearly to the market of India. His revenues are now (1813) from four to five lacs of rupees (50 to 62,500 pounds sterling) annually; and his territory is in so rapid a state of improvement, that if he continues unbiassed and unmolested by the intrigues of the other princes, he may soon expect to double them. The country between Hyderabad and Kuddeen on the immediate banks of the rivers, is generally speaking very fine, and capable of producing rich crops, but the husbandmen are dispirited where it belongs to the Umeers, and the soil lies waste.

From Kuddeen to Lukput Bunder the road lies over a bare salt marshy flat that extends within four miles of the Tanda or seat of Mohummud Khan. From Lukput Bunder we made eight very easy stages to Mandavie, a sea-port town on the western side of the gulf of Kutch, to which place the Honourable Company's ships of war, the Benares and Teignmouth had been ordered to transport the envoy and his suite to Bombay, where we arrived the latter end of *October*. The annexed Chapter, on the history and extent of Sinde, also includes some observations of a geographical and statistical nature, that I have not found it convenient to introduce before. The population of Sinde now consists of a medley of Hindoos, Juths, and Belooches, or more properly speaking, a third race sprung from the two latter. The Hindoos were the original possessors of the country, and the Juths are the descendants of those of that persuasion, who embraced Islamism *; their habits were strictly agricul-

* See the account of the Juths of Kutch Gundava in Chapter VI.

tural or mechanic, which induced them to entertain Belooches for the protection of their property, and the offspring of the frequent marriages that were contracted between them, soon became the bulk of the natives, the term Juth fell into great disrepute, and is now generally used to signify a low inoffensive creature, who is unable to support his own rights. The Sindians, notwithstanding their enmity towards the subjects of Muhmood Khan of Kelat, are fond of tracing their origin to them, and, in extolling the prowess or abilities of any of their chiefs, it is not unusual to hear them remark, that he is "Usl Belooche," viz. a genuine Belooche. To define the character of a people, unless it be marked by extreme good or bad qualities, is, I am aware, at all times that part of a traveller's duty, in which he is most likely to fall into error, and therefore, judging with due caution, I offer my opinion, that the Sindians at the present day, are a race among whom the latter predominate in a lamentable proportion. They are avaricious, full of deceit, cruel, ungrateful, and strangers to veracity; but, in extenuation of their vices, it is to be recollected, that the present generation has grown up under a government, whose extortion, ignorance, and tyranny, is possibly unequalled in the world, and that the debasement of the public mind, is consequent to the infamy of its rulers, seems to be an acknowledged fact in all countries. I do not, however, wish it to be inferred, that I ascribe the gross defects I have stated in the Sindian character, to that cause alone, because I am more disposed to attribute the majority of them to that moral turpitude which may almost be pronounced, to pervade in a greater or lesser degree, the population and society of every nation in Asia, of which we have the slightest knowledge.* The good qualities to which the

* Among the people of the countries bordering on Sinde, the term "a Sindian dog," is synonymous with "a treacherous liar." This feeling has gained greatly of late years, from the abhorrence with which the government of that province is regarded. I hope I shall not be stamped as a misanthrope on account of the sentiments I entertain of all Asiatics. I am convinced, the farther our researches spread, and the more inti-

Sindians lay claim, are entirely physical, and if admitted even to the fullest extent, will make a poor figure when compared with those of an opposite nature: they consist of personal bravery, abstinence, capability of making great exertion, and unqualified submission, and obedience to their superiors, which combine to give them, at least the credit of being the best mercenary soldiers, that are found in the service of the native powers of Hindoostan. The most of these, however, they inherit in common with their neighbours and ancestors the Belooches; but, whether from the effect of climate, the oppressive government they are born under, or their more frequent intercourse with other nations, the Sindians have certainly lost many traits of fine feelings that are to be observed in the former nation. In manners they are generally forward and unpolished, in intellect dull and unapt, and in hospitality and fidelity, equally regardless and deficient. The majority of them are Soonnee Moosulmans; but the Umeers and some of the great men about the court are of the Sheeah persuasion.

The men of Sinde are dark in colour, but, taken collectively, may be called exceedingly handsome; they are above the medium height of Asiatics, have good features and well formed limbs. The beauty of their women is proverbial, and deservedly so. When we rode out, during our sojourn at Tattah and Hyderabad, we had only casual opportunities of seeing any of the higher class of females, who were attracted by curiosity to look at us, but among the numerous sets of dancing girls, who came at different times to exhibit before us, I do not remember to have seen one who was not distinguished by loveliness of face, or the symmetry of her figure, and in most instances, both these requisites to beauty were strikingly combined.

mately we become acquainted with the East, we shall discover stronger, clearer proofs of the general application of the conclusion I have drawn, I should be happy to have any evidence to the contrary, but do not anticipate it.

The men's dress consists of a loose shirt, a pair of trowsers puckered at the ancles, and a quilted cotton or cloth cap, in shape like the crown of a hat, ornamented with flowers of silk or gold round the bottom. That of the women is very similar, with the exception of the cap; beside, underneath their shifts they wear a silk jacket, made to fit the form, that laces behind, and when abroad, a Saree or cloth that wraps round the body, having one end brought over the crown of the head, whereby it serves as a veil to cover up the face when they meet strangers.

CHAPTER XII.

THE PROVINCE OF SINDE. — BOUNDARIES. — RESEMBLANCE TO EGYPT. — AN OBJECT OF GREAT POLITICAL CONSIDERATION TO THE BRITISH GOVERNMENT. — REASONS FOR THIS. — WHY SO LITTLE KNOWN. — AUTHOR'S MOTIVE FOR INCLUDING ITS HISTORY. — GREEK ACCOUNT OF SINDE. — THE SOGDI. — BHUKOR. — MUNSOORAH. — MUHMOOD OF GHUZNEE. — REMARKABLE PROOF OF THE AUTHENTICITY OF THE GREEK HISTORIANS. — MINNAGARA. — MONSIEUR D'ANVILLE. — LARKHANU THE CHIEF TOWN OF THE DISTRICT OF CHANDOOKEE. — GRECIAN ACCOUNT CONTINUED. — TERRITORIES OF SAMBUS — PROOF OF THEIR POSITION. — FORT OF SEHWAN. — CONJECTURE REGARDING IT. — PATTALA. — DELTA. — AUTHOR'S DOUBTS RELATIVE TO PATTALA. — ARRIAN'S DESCRIPTION OF THE RIVER INDUS DEMONSTRATED. — NEARCHUS TAKES CHARGE OF THE FLEET. — VARIOUS UNDENIABLE INSTANCES OF THE VERACITY AND CORRECTNESS OF THE GREEK HISTORIANS. — KROKALA OR KUKRALU. — HISTORY VERY OBSCURE AFTER THE GREEK INVASION. — NOUSHERWAN OR KHOOSROO KING OF PERSIA. — SASEE RAJAHS. — SUHEERSINGH. — REVOLUTION IN SINDE. — DOWNFALL OF THE SASEE DYNASTY. — RISE OF THE CHUCH DYNASTY. — ITS HISTORY AND SUBVERSION. — KHALIPHAS OF BAGDAD. — CONQUER SINDE. — ACCOUNT OF THAT CONQUEST. — GOVERNMENT OF THE KHALIPHAS OF THE OOMYUH AND ABBASSIDE DYNASTIES. — THEIR ULTIMATE ABANDONMENT OF SINDE. — MUHMOOD OF GHUZNEE APPEARS. — SUBDUES THIS PROVINCE. — TRIBE OF SOOMRUH. — GHOORIAN EMPERORS. — TRIBE OF SUMUH. — SEIZE THE GOVERNMENT. — SINDE REDUCED TO A PROVINCE OF THE EMPIRE OF HINDOOSTAN. — VICEROYS APPOINTED. — THEIR AUTHORITY. — MOGHUL INVASION UNDER BABER. — ITS CONSEQUENCES IN SINDE. — URGHOONEEU TRIBE. — TOORKHANEE TRIBE. — THE LATTER REBEL. — SINDE CEDED TO ITS HEAD. — HE DECLARES HIMSELF INDEPENDENT, AND ASSUMES THE TITLE OF NUWWAB. — HUMAYOON UNABLE FROM CIRCUMSTANCES TO CHASTISE HIM. STATE OF AFFAIRS FOR SOME YEARS. — THE EMPEROR AKBAR ENTIRELY SUBJUGATES SINDE. — CHANGE IN ITS NUWWABS. — THE FAMILY OF KULORA. — NADIR SHAH INVADES HINDOOSTAN. — SINDE AND ALL THE PROVINCES WEST OF THE INDUS CEDED TO HIM. — NADIR MURDERED. — AHMED SHAH ABDALLI FOUNDS THE MONARCHY OF KABOOL. — CONDUCT OF THE NUW-

WABS OF SINDE. — THE PUNJAB AND SINDE GIVEN TO PRINCE TYMOOR. — MAHRATTAS IN GREAT POWER. — ADVANTAGE TAKEN OF THIS BY THE KULORAS. — ULTIMATE CONSEQUENCES OF THEIR POLICY. — TALPOORIES. — IN REBELLION. — SEIZE THE GOVERNMENT OF SINDE, AND EXPEL THE KULORAS. — WHO ARE RE-INSTATED. — AGAIN EXPELLED. — MEER FUTTUH ALLEE TALPOOREE CONFIRMED IN THE GOVERNMENT. — HE REBELS. — ZEMAN SHAH'S IMPOLITIC COMPROMISE WITH HIM. — ITS EFFECTS. — DIVISION OF SINDE ON THE RISE OF THE TALPOORIES. — MEER SOHRAB. — — MEER THARA. — THEIR TERRITORIES. — REVENUES. — ARMIES. — MEER FUTTUH ALLEE DIES. — PARTITION OF THE REVENUE. — EXTRAORDINARY COMPACT ENTERED INTO BY THE THREE REIGNING UMEERS. — REFLECTIONS ON IT. — ALLEDGED INCREASE IN THE REVENUE. — RAPACITY AND INSOLENCE OF THE UMEERS. — THEIR VIEWS ON KUTCH BOOJE. — INTERPOSITION OF THE BRITISH GOVERNMENT. — PRESENT STATE OF SINDE. — THE AUTHOR'S OPINION REGARDING ITS UMEERS. — IMPOLITIC FORBEARANCE ON THE PART OF THE BRITISH GOVERNMENT. — ITS EFFECTS.

THE province of Sinde is bounded on the north by the province of Kutch Gundava, the district of Skikarpoor and the territories of Buhawul Khan, commonly called Daood Pootra, to the southward it has the Indian ocean and a part of the country of Kutch Booje; eastward, an extensive desert separating it from the kingdoms and provinces of Agimere, Marwar, Oudipoor, Joudpoor, Bickaneer, &c., and westward, the provinces of Lus and Jhalawan.

The resemblance which this country bears to Egypt is so great, as to strike the observer with surprize; a level plain, with a noble river fertilizing each bank to a certain distance, when the face of the earth becomes on one side a sandy desert, and on the other, a pile of barren mountains, that are quite as inhospitable both as to soil and climate.

The natural situation of this province, as lying on the western frontier of the British possessions in India, and the grand barrier which its river would oppose to an invasion from that quarter, combined with the facilities that the very same obstacle would afford to our governments, as masters of the ocean, in carrying on such military operations as the advance of any hostile power towards Hindoostan should call for, ought always to render Sinde an object of vast political consideration; while its contiguity to Guzeratte and other countries, that have been for some years subject to the executive authority of the British East India Company, seems to have entitled it, even a sa point of curiosity, to a stricter investigation of its history and geography, than has yet been bestowed upon it. This has doubtless, with regard to the latter question, principally resulted from the unexampled jealousy of the chiefs, who have governed it for thirty years past, and who still persevere in the same suspicious policy. My recent examination of Beloochistan having, however, led me to make some trifling historical Inquiries regarding Sinde, because it adjoins the former kingdom, and more especially as a part of the natives of both are descended from one common stock, I am induced to insert a short abstract of the result of them, wishing it, however, to be understood, that I do not by any means offer it to to the public as a conclusive account, but rather one that may possibly assist future investigators. When I originally began to dedicate my leisure hours to these inquiries, with a view to publishing, it was my aim to have collected and written a copious history of Sinde; but as I soon discovered it would have formed a large volume of itself, and moreover that the trifling manuscripts I had procured on it, for the last two centuries, were very imperfect, and that the other topics included in this work would afford me ample employment, I was deterred from the attempt, and am now so conscious of the slight knowledge I possess on that subject, that I should entirely omit this chapter had I not in various preceding places made reference to its contents.

In the fourth century, before the Christian era, the province of Sinde first became known to the Greeks, by the refusal of the troops to follow Alexander into India Proper; who was consequently induced to drop down the Indus, until he came to the ocean. At that period we are informed, that the regions through which he passed, from the Punjab to the sea, were the seat of several governments, of which, the most northern was the Sogdi, supposed to be the present fortress, or city of Bhukor, built on an island in the centre of the Indus, and having the two towns of Sukor and Rohree as its suburbs on each bank of the divided stream. The Ayeen Akberry informs us, that this place was afterwards called Munsoorah; but that was most probably a mere temporary title bestowed on it, by the Arabian conquerors of this country *, in consequence of a victory obtained there over the native Hindoos. It is yet a place of some note, although the fortifications have fallen into decay, but at what period it obtained its present name of Bhukor no record is discoverable. I find it so mentioned in the year of the Hijree 416, (A. D. 1001,) when it was taken possession of by the army of the celebrated Emperor Muhmood of Ghuznee, having been some few years before given up to the native chiefs by Ul Kadir Billa, the twenty-fifth Khalipha of the Abbasside dynasty; who was the last that held any territories to the westward of the present empire of Persia.

Alexander rebuilt the capital of the Sogdi, and having left a garrison in it, proceeded on his voyage to the territories of a chief called Musicanus, which are so clearly and incontestibly identified with the present district of Chandookee, that it would alone demonstrate the authenticity and correctness of the historians of those days. I have before alluded to the extraordinary fertility of this district and the river that encircles it, and accordingly we find that the ancients here fixed a spacious island, formed by a stream that rejoined the Indus, on which they bestowed the appellation of Prasiane or the verdant †. The name of the ancient capital of this tract is not expressly stated; and Minnagara, which Dr. Anville gives us, is

* Munsoor in Arabic signifies either victorious or defended. Perhaps from the strength and situation of Bhukor, the last is the meaning we ought to assign to it; but this is mere surmise, as well as that in the text. Monsieur D'Anville thinks Munsoorah was lower down the river; and my conjecture is equally applicable to the site he fixes upon, or possibly it was called Munsoorah, after the Khalipha "Ul Munsoor," in whose reign he states it to have been added to the dominions of Bagdad.

† I have great pleasure in stating, that I was not aware of this circumstance until after I had made my previous remarks on the district of Chandookee, as it not only corroborated my own information, but established a remarkable coincidence with ancient geography. The word Chandookee, implies, in the present dialect of Sinde, literally silvery,

doubtless intended for Meeannuggur, or the centre city *, but for my own part I have been unable to discover any place that corresponds with the site he allots to it.

The chief town now-a-days is Larkhanu †, which lies on the river of the same denomination, and is a post of great importance to the Sindian Umeers, as they there first levy tolls on merchants entering their dominions; beside keeping a considerable garrison stationed there to guard against the encroachments of the Belooches of Kutch Gundava.

While Alexander remained with Musicanus, he undertook expeditions against two chiefs, called Oxycanus and Sambus, which latter dwelt among mountains stated to be immediately adjoining the principality of the former; and it is therefore evident that he was the head of the tribes who then inhabited that chain of mountainous districts that run easterly from those of Jhalawan, and touch the Indus at Sehwan ‡. In fact there are no other mountains or even

---

that is, by metaphor, opulent or beautiful to the eye. Had I extended my remarks to the rivers of the Punjab, I could have adduced proof that wherever our geographers have departed from the ancients they have fallen into mistakes.

* Minnagara, or Meeannuggur, from Meean the middle, and Nuggur a city. This D'Anville speaks of as the modern capital.

† I have fruitlessly endeavoured to trace the origin of Larkhanu, in hopes to identify it with some former place. Lar, in Shanskreet, means saliva; and Khanu is a dwelling, in modern Persian. Were we to apply the former, figuratively, to the Ooze or mud of the river, we have a local fact established, as the natives manure the adjacent districts with it.

‡ I cannot sufficiently express my regret at my own unacquaintance with the language in which the originals of the subjects I am now considering are written. To the extreme kindness of a learned and esteemed friend, I am indebted for the interpretation of various details I have touched upon, and I have also made every use of the labours of Monsieur D'Anville, and Dr. Vincent. I am led to make these remarks by a very striking similarity that I have just observed between Musicanus and Moo, Sehwan. The two latter are the names of contiguous districts, lying exactly where we are told the Greeks found that chief's territories; and it is usual to this day to connect them. I am so fully aware of the general futility of etymological researches, that had I even been qualified to make them, I should have dedicated little time to that object; but in this instance the resemblance is too obvious to escape notice. Dr. Vincent alludes to the same words without being aware

hills in the neighbourhood to the westward of the river; and on the eastern side lies a level plain until we cross the desert and reach the hills of the Rajpoote territories in Hindoostan. After the subjugation of one, and the death of the other of these chiefs, the Macedonian hero returned to the river, and, as we are informed, built a citadel at a commodious and commanding point; from which particular notice I have no scruple in saying that it must have been at the present Sehwan, that fortress being seated on a high hill that overlooks the ferries across the Indus and Larkhanu rivers, and otherwise admirably situated to awe the surrounding tracts.

The land and water expedition then moved down to Pattala, lying at the head of the Delta, formed by the branches that the river separated into; but to the ancient description of this position there does not exist, at the present day, the most remote affinity in any part of Sinde, and whether we are to place it at Tattah or Hyderabad appears to me equally dubious.*

During the halt of the forces at Pattala, the King himself made two excursions with a part of his fleet to the ocean, and visited, by Arrian's account, the only two mouths of the river. It is very remarkable that the same two mouths, the most easterly and westerly were navigable within these thirty years, and no others, and had

that they are the names of districts, instead of a title, as he will have them. The learned divine has confounded Sewee, the capital of Seeweestan, with Sehwan on the Indus; and naturally finds it impossible to reconcile the accounts of Arrian and the Ayeen Akberry.

* The great length of two hundred and ten miles, which Major Rennel assigns to the Delta, is only to be reconciled by supposing that the sea has encroached above two degrees on the coast; and that even after we have placed Pattala at Hyderabad. From Tattah to that city Captain Maxfield found the distance, by actual survey to be, by the course of the river, but fifty-three miles; and an intelligent Hindoostanee man who went from Kurachee to Tattah by water with the heavy baggage of the mission, estimated the passage at thirty or forty Sindian Kos, after he entered the large river, which he did at Dharajay Bunder. The utmost we can allow for this is fifty miles, and I have before me a medium of information acquired from above two hundred natives of the lower parts of Sinde, that fixes Tattah seventy-nine miles from the sea. This I deem conclusive, but should others be still sceptical, the latitudes of Kurachee and Tattah will demonstrate the fact.

not the dyke at Allee Bunder been erected, as I have mentioned in the preceding chapter, they would have both been so at this hour.

When every necessary preparation had been made for the march of the troops through the provinces of Lus and Mukran, the fleet was placed in charge of Nearchus, with orders to put to sea, and eventually join the land forces at Babylon. To follow the vessels in their progress down the river and along the coast of Sinde, till they arrived at the promontory Eirus, now Cape Monze, the western extremity of that province, would be quite irrelative to my purpose; and I shall dismiss this subject by adducing two more undeniable proofs of the veracity of the Greek historians. One, the alarming turbulence of the sea at the conflux of the fresh and salt water, of which I have taken notice in an early part of this volume *; and the other, the absolute identity of the port of Kurachee with that which Arrian denominates Krokala. The present name of the district, in which Kurachee is situated, I learn from a native manuscript, written in 1809, to be Kukrala; and I have reason to imagine that the very modern appellation bestowed on this harbour of Khoor Allee, is a bigoted corruption of that word. †

It would merely be corroborating the remark I have made on the history of Beloochistan, subsequent to the Macedonian, and prior to the Arab, invasion, were I to attempt to give any thing in the shape of a detailed account of the events that occurred in Sinde

* See Narrative of the 16th January, Part I.

† Khoor Allee, I have before stated, signifies the harbour of Allee, and is therefore a religious title. I take this opportunity of avowing, that in proportion to the extent and number of the comparisons I have been able to make, between the Greek and modern accounts of Sinde, I have found the former increase in minute correctness. The expanded breadth of the river near the sea, the creeks being choked by marshy bushes, so as to render them unnavigable, the Delta not being intersected by rivers, and the brackishness of the water that they were forced to dig for, and take up immediately, are a few of the many instances that have occurred to me. I may add, that in general the conclusions drawn by the reverend author of the *Voyage of Nearchus* are correct. *Had he been* implicitly guided by Arrian, I venture to say they would have been still more so.

during that period. The native Hindoo princes are not even mentioned by name, in all the manuscripts I have perused, until the time of the celebrated Khoosroo (usually called Nousherwan), King of Persia *, who sent a large army and ravaged the western frontier of Sasee Rajah's dominions; which are described, including his tributaries, to have extended on the north to the present provinces of Kashmeer and Kabool, southward to Surat and the island now called Dieu, westward along the sea coast of Mukran, and eastward to the provinces of Marwar, Bickaneer, &c. The Rajah, whose name is stated to have been Suheersingh, opposed this invasion in person at the head of his troops, and a pitched battle was fought in Mukran, in which he was killed and his forces totally routed. The Persians, however, seem to have had no further object than plunder, for having loaded themselves with spoils they marched back, carrying with them some thousands of the most beautiful of the women whom they had made prisoners. After this event, two princes of the same dynasty, neither of whose names are given, succeeded to the throne, and we are told that they governed their extensive dominions with great judgment and equity; the first of them made many wise regulations for the defence of this kingdom, and in lieu of paying revenues he obliged his subjects to build some forts, and repair others that had fallen to decay during the peaceable reigns of his progenitors. † The second Rajah was, in the early part of his government, equally attentive, but the prosperity of his empire soon became so great, and appeared so well established, that he gave himself up to sensual pleasures, and passed whole weeks in his seraglio, leaving the conduct of public affairs to his minister. About the period of this change in the policy of the prince, the minister fell sick, and a young Brahmin, who had been appointed to an inferior

* Noushorwan flourished about the middle of the sixth century of the Christian era. He was contemporary with the Roman Emperors Justinian and Justin.

† The names of some of these forts are mentioned: such as Sehwan, Moo, Oocha, Naraen Kott, or the Fort of Naraen, &c. &c. the three former of which are still known by the same designations.

situation in the government, had occasion to wait upon the king, to receive his orders on some important business. He was admitted into the seraglio for this purpose, when he and the queen became so enamoured of each other at first sight, that after various disappointments they succeeded in indulging their criminal passions; and on the death of the king, which happened soon after, the queen married the Brahmin, who had, in the interim, been promoted to prime minister, and in concert with him, brought about a revolution which placed him on the throne. "Such" says the historian, "was "the close of the race of Rajah Sasee, which had governed the "kingdom of Sinde for upwards of two thousand years; whose "princes at one period received tribute from eleven dependant king-"doms, and who had set the threats of the greatest monarchs of the "world at defiance." *

The Brahmin, whose rise I have briefly related, was called Chuch; and from him the dynasty took the name of the Chuch Rajahs. His aggrandizement disgusted the relations of the late king, and the Rajahs of Chitoor, Jesselmeer, Joudpoor, &c. entered into a confederation to invade his usurped dominions; but Chuch, by means of his vast riches and popular manners assembled an army, and encountered their combined forces, on the frontier of the Jesselmeer Rajah's territories. Just as the battle was commencing, the general of the allied princes challenged Chuch to single combat, which he accepted, and they fought in front of the two armies; the latter was triumphant, and the confederated troops, on beholding the death of their commander-in-chief, immediately dispersed, and were cut up in great numbers by those of Sinde. No further molestation was offered, from this quarter, to Chuch in his new kingdom; he lived to an advanced age, and at his death, in the 86th year of the Hijree,

* In speaking of the greatest monarchs of the world, allusion is doubtless made to those of Persia, who were a part of that time struggling with the Romans for the empire of Asia.

(A. D. 671,) his son, Daher, quietly mounted the throne; but his repose was soon disturbed by an invasion of the troops of the Khalipha of Bagdad. The causes that led to this are heretofore stated to have been a combination of religious zeal and insulted pride *; in explanation of which latter remark. I must now add, that the immediate successors of the Arabian prophet, had been in the yearly habit of dispatching people to Sinde for the purpose of purchasing Hindoo slave girls, who were highly esteemed for their beauty; and that one of these parties on its return from the city of Brahminabad, to the Bunder of Wueel †, was set upon by the Rajah's troops, and all either made prisoners or killed in the conflict. This happened in the Khaliphat of Abdool Mulik, the third of the sovereigns of the house of Oommyuh, and seems to have been intended to revenge several unsuccessful attempts that had been previously made to conquer Sinde, for even so early as the time of Omar and Allee, those potentates had directed their views towards this rich kingdom, and had sent detachments of troops to it by sea, which were invariably repulsed.

The command of this ultimately successful expedition, on the part of the Khalipha, was entrusted to Hoojaj Bin Yoosoof, then governor of the two Eeraks, but as the public service required his presence in Persia, he deputed his son-in-law, Mohummud Bin Kasim, to carry the orders of the Khalipha into execution. The Sindian Rajah was advised by his ministers to await in his capital, Ooloor, the approach of the Mohummudans; and the consequence of this was, that his subjects became dispirited, while the enemy carried fire and sword throughout his dominions, and crossed the Indus flushed with victory; at length the Rajah's patience was exhausted, and on the 10th of the month of Rumzan, in the year of the Hijree 93, he

* See Chapter II. Part II.

† Now Lahoree Bunder. It appears to me to be the same as Debil, but I have learned no meaning for it. In all the manuscripts I have read, it is clearly written Wueel.

left the city with all his war elephants and choicest troops, to make one grand effort towards recovering his country; but this step was taken too late, as he lost both his kingdom and life in the battle which ensued *. The entire subjugation of Sinde quickly followed this defeat; and an immense number of curiosities, together with two daughters of the Rajah, who had fallen into the hands of Mohummud Bin Kasim, were sent to Bagdad †, as presents to the

* The account of this battle is given in great detail in the Mujmuool Waridat, or compendium of events, and as it will serve to shew the pomp and state of the Rajahs of Sinde, I annex an abstract of it. "We are told (says the writer) that the Rajah appeared on an elephant, in a chair covered with a canopy, set with precious stones; and that he had two beautiful slave girls with him, one to serve him with wine, and the other with beetel leaf and areca nut. This elephant moved in the midst of one hundred more, and the palace guards, to the number of one thousand, clad in polished steel armour, surrounded the whole. The total of the Sindian army was thirty thousand foot and horse, and that of the Khaliphas between twelve and thirteen thousand. The battle began at break of day and lasted till dusk, when the Rajah's elephants took fright, from the rockets that were thrown amongst them, and threw themselves into the river (Indus). That which bore the royal canopy stuck in the mud, and at the same moment the Rajah was shot through the neck, by an arrow, and instantly expired. The rout then became universal, and the city gates being shut, by those who remained inside, all the Brahmins and nobles of the court were made prisoners. The Mohummudans slept on the field of battle, after returning thanks for this great victory; and the following morning after some negotiation, took possession of Ooloor, in the name of Khalipha Wulud Bin Abdool Mulik."

† These princesses were esteemed the most beautiful women in Asia, and on their arrival at Bagdad, they falsely accused Mohummud Bin Kasim of having slept one night with each of them, and afterwards having dispatched them to the Khalipha. That monarch was highly enraged at this supposed insult, and sent an order to the general, who was second in command, to sew Mohummud Bin Kasim into a raw hide, and thus forward him to the presence. By way of rendering this mandate more premptory, the Khalipha wrote with his own hand in the margin of the letter, "Mohummud Bin "Kasim, wherever this finds you, you are to sew yourself into a cow's hide, and appear "so before me! Fail not in this!" This letter reached him at Oodipoor, and though consciously innocent, he allowed the unjust and cruel punishment of his sovereign to be inflicted on himself. He died the third day after, and when the Khalipha discovered that the Sindian princesses had merely fabricated the tale, to be revenged on their father's conqueror, he was so exasperated that he had them tied by the hair of their heads to the tails of horses, and dragged, naked, through the streets of Bagdad, until they were dead. Their mangled bodies were afterwards thrown into the river; and a superb mausoleum

Khalipha. One fifth of the prize-money was appropriated to building mosques, and the remainder divided among the troops and their generals. Two sons of the Rajah, who had escaped from the field of action, fled to the fort of Alexander *, where they held out until it was taken by storm, and every soul in it put to the sword, which was the last struggle that Sinde made against the Arabs as an independent kingdom.

The bulk of the people seeing that the ancient system of things was at an end, in so much, that the Khootbu † was read in the name of the Khalipha; and likewise, that those that made early submission to the conquerors were treated with attention, although obliged to accept the Mohummudan faith, flocked to the camp of Mohummud Bin Kasim in whole tribes; while some, either through fear or detestation of the tenets of Islamism, refused to acknowledge his authority, and were eventually driven into the mountainous regions of Beloochistan, where they colonized, as I have detailed in my account of that kingdom. Mohummud Bin Kasim then set himself about extending his conquests over the countries to the northward and eastward of Sinde; and appointed to the government of the latter province a nobleman of the house of Ansaree, which family continued to fill that situation, hereditarily, until the transferring of the Khaliphat from the Oommyuh to the Abbasside dynasty, an event that occurred about forty years after the subversion of the Hindoo authority. The whole of the dependants of the first were then turned out of power, and subsequently to that revolution, the governors of Sinde, on behalf of the Abasside Khaliphas, were nominated and removed at the pleasure of the reigning sovereign; so that the history of this province, for a period of nearly three centuries, is without novelty, and comprises a

was erected to the memory of Mohummud Bin Kasim, which was to be seen at Damascus (his native place) for many centuries.

* In the original, the Killahé Sekundur: it is spoken of as a very strong place.

† The Khootbu are the prayers read in all Moosulman countries, for the safety and preservation of the sovereign and his authority.

mere statement of the causes that led to the removal and in general the execution of one Hakim to make place for another favorite, who usually shared the fate of his predecessor. It may, however, be added, that the internal quiet of the province was very frequently disturbed, by the incursions of hordes of adventurers, who on more than one occasion were so powerful as to take and keep possession of the greatest part of the country, until strong reinforcements were sent to the aid of the government from Bagdad.

In the early part of the fifth century of the Hijree, the Khalipha Ul Kadir Billa, found it necessary to withdraw his troops from Sinde and the contiguous countries, for the protection of the less remote parts of his dominions, which had been invaded by the forces of the Emperor Muhmood of Ghuznee; and for some years the province of which I am now treating, seems to have been the scene of extreme anarchy and confusion, owing to the innumerable tribes that laid claim to the right of nominating a leader for the whole; this competition was, at last, only effectually suppressed by the arrival of the legions of the last named potentate, which quickly subdued all the claimants, and added the territory that was the object of their dispute, as a tributary to the empire of Ghuznee. Hakims were regularly sent from court to this province, until the reign of Musaood, the son of Muhmood, when a great tribe, called Soomruh, appeared in arms and expelled all the partizans of the king; but their chief, whose name was Sunghar, immediately making an apology for this outrage, and offering to pay tribute to the amount of the revenues before collected, he was pardoned and appointed governor, in the stead of the person he had deposed.

The tribute was paid with great regularity for one hundred and fifty years after this arrangement, when *the empire of Ghuznee was* overturned by the Ghoorian dynasty; on which the Soomruhs, in whose tribe the government of Sinde had gradually been allowed to become hereditary, declared themselves in a state of independence, and although they were repeatedly worsted in the wars that followed this declaration, yet they managed to preserve their liberty till the final extinction of the race, or at least the princes of it, in the person of Duhooda, who died without children in the year of the Hijree 694, about three hundred and thirty-five years from the time his ancestors had first made themselves so conspicuous.*

On the demise of Duhooda, numerous candidates for the vacant government started up; and it was a continual struggle, for nearly a century, who should succeed to it. Among the last of them, two brothers, called Kheeramull and Urukmull, successively held it for a time, but at length the tyranny of the latter became insupportable, and the head of the tribe of Sumuh went to his palace, accompanied by the ministers of the country, and put him to death. The populace with one accord elected this chief, who had relieved them from so dreadful a scourge, their king; and he was accordingly placed on the throne with the title of Jam, or leader, which he was said to have adopted from his family being descended from the celebrated Jamsheed, King of Persia.

He began his reign by trying to reduce the forts of Sehwan and Beherampoor, which were then in the hands of two generals of the Ghoorian Emperor; in the former of which he was successful, but in storming the second he lost his life, three years and six months from his accession to the throne. His eldest son, Jam Joonuh, succeeded him, and not only carried his father's meditated conquests into effect, but possessed himself of Bhukor and Oocha. His health was, however, so very delicate, that he could not always be on the

* The Ayeen Akberry states that the Soomruhs reigned 500 years, and that there were no less than thirty-six princes of that race; but its learned author, Abool Fuzl, does not give either their names or his authority. I have, by dint of search, discovered the names of twelve or fourteen of them, but deem it unnecessary to mention them in an abstract of the kind I am writing. I should guess there may have been about ten more princes, making in all twenty-four; and with regard to the period of their government, I am as certain as native information, well corroborated by various authorities, can make me. To account for the apparent inconsistency in the chronology in the text, to which this note alludes, it is requisite to say that the Soomruhs were the great fomenters of the disturbances previous to the invasion of Muhmood of Ghuznee, and seem frequently to have had the government in their hands. To this, no doubt, the Ayeen Akberry alludes.

field of battle, therefore his troops were often depressed by his absence; and, after governing sixteen years, he saw, ere he died, all the fruits of his hard earned victories lost, and his territories limited to the original possessions of his father.

On his death an interregnum ensued owing to the rightful heir having been made prisoner in one of the last battles fought during his father's reign, and carried to Delhi, where he publickly acknowledged the paramount authority of the Emperors of Hindoostan, of whom he offered to hold his kingdom in fief; but when the other heads of the tribe were made acquainted with the terms on which he was to be released, they formally deposed him and placed his next brother on the Musnud. This chief, whose name was Jam Babeenuh, did not, however, long taste the pleasures of unlimited sovereignty, for after twice repelling the army of Feerooz Shah III., he was, in the year of the Hijree 779 (A. D. 1364), reduced to capitulate; and was taken to Delhi, where, in his conduct, he evinced so many amiable and princely qualities, that the Emperor, in A. H. 781, having invested him with a Khiläät and a royal umbrella *, sent him back to Sinde as his viceroy, on the very same conditions that his brother had agreed to enter into a few years before. His reign as an independent prince comprised a period of four years, and he officiated as viceroy, fifteen, reckoning from the date of his return from Delhi.

The history of Sinde, from the date at which we are now arrived, is so interwoven with that of Hindoostan, that it would be almost impossible to separate it in the form of an abstract; and, in fact, the barrenness of the subject would ill repay either my readers or myself, were I to do so. I consider it, therefore, sufficient to say, that the Jams of the family of Sumuh became the hereditary vicegerents of the province on behalf of the Emperors of Hindoostan, and filled that station by an uninterrupted succession of twelve princes, until the year of the Hijree 926 (A. D. 1511), when the same revolution

---

* Khiläät, an honorary dress. The permission to carry an umbrella, of a particular shape and value, is alone granted to the blood royal.

that placed Baber on the throne of Delhi, led to their entire downfall. The nature of the government which subsisted in Sinde, throughout the period I have stated, must be explained, to have been a vicegerency with the most unlimited powers. The Jams seem to have held and availed themselves of the right of enlarging their dominions by invading the territories of neighbouring chiefs, not subjects of their lord paramount. One or two of them who visited Delhi were allowed to appear in that capital with various ensigns of regal authority; and, in short, had it not been for the circumstance of the reigning Emperor conferring the Khiläät of confirmation on each of these princes on his accession to the viceroyalty, and occasional large Peshkushes *, that they all sent to court; it would have been a misapplication of the term to have called Sinde a tributary province †.

In A. H. 923, (A. D. 1508,) Baber came to Kandahar, and Shah Beg Urghoon, the prince of that country, seeing himself thus dispossessed of his paternal inheritance, ‡ raised a large force and con-

* Peshkushes are offerings from an inferior to a superior, and are sometimes, from their amount, merely a different term for tribute.

† The Jams of the Sumuh tribe, who reigned after Jam Babeenuh, were,

Jam Jumajee	13 years
Jam Sulahooddeen	7
Jam Nizamooddeen	2
Jam Sher Ulee	4
Jam Kurun	1
Jam Futuh Khan	10
Jam Tughulook	21
Jam Sekundur	2
Jam Raedhenu	5
Jam Sunjur	1
Jam Nizamooddeen	60
Jam Feerooz	4
	130

‡ Shah Beg was the son of Meer Zulnoon Beg, Prince of Gurmseer, a tract lying on the banks of the river Helmind. This was a tributary province of the kingdom of Samarkand, but in the struggle between Baber and the Oozbuck kings of that realm, Meer Zulnoon Beg had declared his independence with impunity. His son, however, bowed before the over-whelming power of the Moghuls.

quered Seeweestan, Kutch Gundava, and Sinde. At first he continued Jam Feerooz in charge of the latter province, fixing his own residence at Seewee, the principal town of the former; but discovering that he was intriguing to subvert his authority, he appointed Abdool Allee Khan Toorkhan, to supersede him, and Jam Feerooz fled to Guzeratte, where he died of a broken heart. The irresistible arms of Baber soon forced Shah Beg to take refuge in the most southern part of his newly acquired dominions; but being a prince of great ambition and valour, his spirit could not brook the reverse he had met with, and he committed suicide, on board a boat, on his passage between Bhukor and Tattah, the former of which forts he had just evacuated to escape from the Moghul troops. His only son, Shah Hussun Beg, was endowed with all his father's noble qualities, and retrieved his fortunes so far as to retake Bhukor, and even plunder the rich city of Mooltan; but all his aspiring projects were suddenly quelled, by the seizure of Tattah and its dependant territory, by Meerza Eesa, the eldest son of Abdool Allee Toorkhan, who it will be recollected was appointed governor in the time of Shah Beg. The young prince immediately turned his steps to chastise the rebel, but after a very long negotiation, he was unwillingly forced to cede all that part of Sinde lying to the southward of the fort of Sehwan, to be held as a feudatory possession by the chiefs of the family of Toorkhan. He did not, however, long survive this division of his territories, as his death happened at the fortress of Bhukor, towards the end of the same year in which it was made; and the remainder of his dominions were then seized by different generals of his army; but though they lay principally within the present boundaries of Sinde, it would be quite useless to enter into any discussion regarding them.

During the period that the events I have just detailed were transacting in Sinde, the empire of Hindoostan had passed from a Puttan to the present Moghul dynasty, and Humayoon, the successor of Baber, was on the throne, after his return from exile into Persia; when Meerza Eesa first assumed the title of Nuwwab of the Sirkar (or government) of Tattah, and in common with all his predecessors since the last of the Sumuh family, disavowed his allegiance to that monarch *. The state of affairs did not, however, authorize the Emperor to direct his attention to so distant a province as Sinde, therefore, Meerza Eesa left his possessions uncontrouled to his sons; the eldest of whom, being a violent madman, was put aside by the unanimous voice of the people, and his second child Meerza Mohummud Bakee proclaimed Nuwwab; he soon, however, shewed symptoms of the same insanity, and put an end to his life, by stabbing himself with a dagger, in the public mosque at Tattah, in the year of the Hijree, 993, (A. D. 1578). On this event his son, Meerza Janee Beg, took charge of the government; and three years after the troops of the renowned Emperor Akbar subjugated the whole of Sinde, since which, its rulers have never ventured to avow their independence, although they have not unfrequently evaded the payment of the tribute that was then fixed, and have likewise repeatedly appeared in arms against their lord paramount.

In A. H. 1014, (A. D. 1599,) Juhangeer succeeded his father, Akbar, as Emperor of Hindoostan, and throughout his reign and the two following, of Shah Jehan and Alumgeer (usually known by the title of Aurungzebe), the princes of the province of Sinde were kept in the utmost subjection, although on the death of the latter monarch, the unsettled aspect of affairs in India, encouraged them to withhold the payment of the tribute. The population had within the period I allude to, undergone a great change, by the introduction of vast tribes of Belooches, as mercenaries; and the rule of the family of Toorkhan had long given place to that of the chiefs of a tribe called Kulora, which originally came from Persia, but the exact period, or cause, of this change in the government I have

* A very interesting account of the flight of the Emperor Humayoon, will be found in Dow's Hindoostan. The birth of Prince Akbar, which took place at Omarkote, and the sufferings of the Queen and her infant, are very pathetically described in the History of Sinde, but the story would be too long to insert here.

hitherto unsuccessfully tried to discover. The Persians had, in this interval, possessed themselves of Kandahar, and it is probable that the Kuloras may have been a tribe of adventurers, sprung from their army, who usurped the supreme authority in Sinde, and at the same time professed fealty to the Emperors of Hindoostan; who were always less scrupulous about the justice of the claims of those governors, who were not appointed from court, provided the tribute was paid with its accustomed regularity.*

It would only be repeating what I have already for my present purpose sufficiently explained †, were I to enlarge on the invasion of Hindoostan by Nadir Shah. That great event in the annals of India occurred in 1739, and one of the results of it was, the cession of Sinde and all the provinces lying west of the river Indus to the crown of Persia. Nadir visited Tattah on his return homewards, where, according to oral accounts, he was most magnificently entertained ‡, and did not remove the governor. The murder of that conqueror was perpetrated in 1747, and on the dismemberment of the vast empire he had founded, arose the monarchy of Kabool, of which Sinde is now a dependent province. The Nuwwabs of it do not, however, seem to have at once acknowledged the title of this

* Since I wrote the above I find that the Kuloras were originally sprung from a religious sect, and claimed descent from the Abbaside dynasty. About the year 1580, they began, under the cloak of religion, to levy contributions in Sinde, which they extended until the natives became so much exasperated that they rose against them, and notwithstanding the sanctity of his character, put their chief to death, driving all his disciples to Kelat in Beloochistan. They afterwards returned, with the permission of the Emperor of Hindoostan, and gradually advanced themselves until their chief got possession of the government of Tattah.

† See historical account of Beloochistan, Chapter III. Part II. also remarks on Tattah, Chapter IX. Part II.

‡ In Sir William Jones's French translation of the history of Nadir Shah, Meean Noor Mohummud, the then Nuwwab of Tattah, is spoken of as Khodayar Khan, which was a title bestowed upon him by Mohummud, Emperor of Hindoostan. He fled to Omarkote on the approach of the Persian army, but having been made prisoner, and brought back to Tattah; it was there that he gave such satisfaction to the conqueror, and that the events happened that I have mentioned in a preceding Chapter.

new dynasty, but, rather to have reverted to their allegiance to the Kings of Delhi, as in 1756 we find Alumgeer the Second, then on that throne, bestowing the Punjab and Sinde on the Prince Tymoor, the eldest son of Ahmed Shah Douranee, as a dowry with one of the princesses whom he had espoused. The Mahrattas had just at this epocha, overrun Hindoostan; and in 1757 they drove Tymoor across the Attock, and afforded the Uffghans so much employment, that they found it impracticable to interfere with the Sindians, who gladly availed themselves of this confusion, to refuse to transmit the tribute to the royal treasury. This posture of affairs, did not, however, long exempt them from that burthen; for after the battle of Panniput *, they were glad to compromise their failure in that point, by paying a considerable sum of the arrears due; and advancing the amount of two years' tribute, to assist Ahmed Shah in carrying on a war against the Persians, who were then invading Khorasan.

Ahmed Shah died in 1773, and Tymoor then ascended the throne of Kabool. In the month of June 1779, a tribe of Belooche origin, called the Talpoories, headed by the present Umeers, and their elder brother, rebelled against the existing authority of the Kulora Nuwwab of Sinde, and forced him to fly towards Kandahar, after some hundred of his adherents had been put to the sword. Tymoor Shah immediately dispatched an army under Mudud Khan, to reinstate the Nuwwab in his right, which was accomplished without striking a blow, as the Talpoories fled to the desert the moment the royal forces entered the province; they were, however, equally expeditious in returning, and the Kulora prince was deposed a second time without a struggle, for the people seeing that the good fortune of his enemies was certain to prevail, left him to his fate. In 1786 another army came from Kabool to adjust the disputes in Sinde; but the Talpooree chiefs had then been some length of time in quiet

* This battle was fought in 1761. Vide Chapter III. Part II. (Note).

possession of the government and revenues, which latter enabled them to collect a force very superior in number to the Uffghans, whom they totally defeated at the village of Jeeund, twenty kos south-west of the city of Shikarpoor, to which the discomfited troops fled. A negociation was then set on foot, and the Talpoories proposing to discharge all arrears of tribute, as well as to be most punctual in the payment of it thenceforward, the matter was amicably adjusted between them and the King, by the latter issuing a furman, appointing Meer Futtuh Allee, the eldest of four brothers, to the government, and declaring all subjects of Sinde free from their allegiance to the Kulora family, of whom there now remains one chief, who escaped to Guzeratte, where he was, within these few years, a soldier of fortune in the service of one of the native princes.

A little more than three years subsequent to this arrangement, the Talpooree Umeers positively declined paying a single rupee of tribute, and Tymoor Shah could not then spare troops to awe them into obedience; his son Zeman Shah, who succeeded him in 1793, advanced to their frontier the following year, but not being willing to lose time in a protracted warfare, he accepted twenty-four lacs of rupees *, which was not one-fourth of the amount due; and marched back to his own dominions. This impolitic compromise opened the eyes of the Sindians to their own strength and importance, and they have never since spoken of the tribute as any thing more than nominal, though in 1805, when Shah Shooja Ool Moolk, moved to enforce it, they deputed Wulee Mohummud Khan to meet him on the confines of their territories, and he had sufficient address to prevail on the King to return, contrary to the strenuous advice of one of his ministers, Futtuh Khan, on receiving twenty-seven lacs of rupees in lieu of seventy-one†, that were then unpaid.

* 300,000l. sterling.

† 337,500l. sterling, instead of 887,500l. sterling.

On the nomination, by Tymoor Shah, of Meer Futtuh Allee to the supreme authority in Sinde, that chief made over large tracts of country to different branches of his own family, who had aided him in usurping the government; among these Meer Sohrab and Meer Thara shared on the largest scale; and as they were vested with uncontrouled powers within their respective territories, beside not being bound by any feudatory agreement, they may now in reality be considered independent. The country of the former lies in the north-east quarter of Sinde, commencing on the southern frontier of Buhawul Khan's dominions, and extending to the town of Khyrpoor, which is his capital; his revenues amount to seven lacs of rupees, and he can muster between four and five thousand troops. Meer Thara's districts adjoin those of Meer Sohrab to the southward; his annual receipts are above four lacs of rupees, and his standing army amounts to four thousand men.

After the decease of Meer Futtuh Allee, his three brothers divided the revenues of their branch of the family into four quarters, two of which were allotted to Meer Gholam Allee, as the principal Umeer, and one to each of his younger brothers. The sum thus disposed of then amounted to thirty-four lacs, and thirteen thousand rupees, but it is greatly increased since that period; and in consideration of the extra allowance granted to Meer Gholam Allee, he was bound to defray the permanent civil and military expences, which are, however, very trifling, beside providing a double share of the tribute due to the King of Kabool, in the event of payment being enforced.

At the same time that these regulations were framed, with the concurrence of the three brothers, they entered into the most extraordinary compact, of governing the province conjointly; under the designation of the Umeers or rulers of Sinde, and on the death of Meer Gholam Allee *, the senior of the three that were on the

* Meer Gholam Allee was killed by the charge of a buck when hunting deer in 1812.

Musnud when the mission was at their court, his eldest son took the lowest seat in the triumvirate, while his two brothers each ascended a step. It is impossible to conjecture how long this curious system will be preserved; it seems at present very firmly established, but its basis is in such direct opposition to every idea that the experience of ages has taught us to form of Asiatic governments, that we may justly presume it cannot be of long endurance; and in all human probability it will eventually terminate in the ambitious projects of one of its members, who may be tempted to usurp the unconditional supremacy by the imbecility of his colleagues in power.

The total amount of the revenues of Sinde, including those of all the collateral branches of the reigning family, are stated to be sixty-one lacs of rupees yearly, which, if correct, proves an increase in them of above eighteen lacs since the year 1809, as they then only netted forty-two lacs and seventy-eight thousand *. The tribute to Kabool is thirteen lacs per annum, but probably, since it was arranged, the sum actually paid would not average one-sixth that amount. The vast accumulation of treasures, together with the unusually long cessation from any internal commotion in Sinde, has lately enabled the Umeers to take advantage of the demise of Meer Sohrab to annex his extensive territories to their possessions, thereby utterly ruining his children, who have taken refuge with Muhmood Shah, the King of Kabool †. The latter end of 1816 they also sent a large force to reduce the fort of Omarkote ‡, that had been for

* Sixty-one lacs of rupees are 767,500*l.* sterling. Eighteen lacs, 125,000*l.* sterling. Forty-two lacs and seventy-eight thousand, 534,750*l.* sterling.

† I have just learned (November 1814) that the King of Kabool meditates an attack on the Umeers of Sinde, not only with a view to restore Meer Sohrab's territory to his family, but to demand the payment of the accumulated arrears of tribute, that are supposed to exceed one crore and a half of rupees (1,500,000*l.* sterling). If the attempt is made, I trust it will prove prosperous, both on account of the justice of the cause and the absolute necessity of curbing the increasing power of the Sindians.

‡ The fort of Omarkote is celebrated in the East as the birth-place of the Emperor Akbar. It is a place of some strength, and considered so inaccessible, from the desert

some generations in the hands of the Rajahs of Joudpoor. In that expedition they were completely successful, and such now are the insolence and resources of those usurpers, that they have more than once made preparations for invading the country of Kutch Booje, lying on the south-eastern frontier of their dominions, in which they would, ere this, have assuredly succeeded, had not the British government of India, announced to them its firm determination to resist any attempt that might be contemplated on that kingdom, in an equal degree, as if it were directed to the possessions of the Honourable East India Company, or its allies. A native agent on the part of the supreme government was left in Sinde, when the mission quitted it in 1809, and still remains at Hyderabad. That country has now attained the foremost rank among those states that border immediately on the province of Guzeratte, and as its rulers are only restrained by dread of our power from crossing the boundary that nature seems to have fixed for their territories, any future pretence, however unimportant, to encroach in that quarter, will evince a diminution of that respect and awe towards us which it is decidedly our interest to inculcate; and therefore should, in my opinion, be resisted by the most decisive measures. Had the Umeers, on the expulsion of the Honourable Company's commercial resident from Sinde, and the seizure of a vast quantity of public property, been then * made to feel the force of our arms within their dominions, their conduct would doubtless have been of a very different nature towards the late missions to their court.

that surrounds it, that the Umeers of Sinde have now allotted it as a place of security to deposit a part of their treasures.

* This happened in 1801-2. The Honourable East India Company lost above one lac of rupees worth of property, and the Sindians even made an attempt to have the gentleman who was resident murdered.

APPENDIX.

ABSTRACT OF CAPTAIN CHRISTIE'S JOURNAL,

AFTER HIS SEPARATION FROM LIEUT. POTTINGER, AT NOOSHKY.

MARCH 22d. I left Nooshky on the *22d of March*, and crossing small sand hills, stopped for Jooma Khan at a small pool of rain water, which although dirty was fresh; we waited about one hour, until Jooma Khan (whose camel was soon found) came up, and then we moved on. He and his associates told me to be at ease in their company, as we were all brothers. After crossing a flat salt tract, which from the top of the Lukh or Pass appeared to be water, at fourteen miles we halted to dine under some hills. The water was brackish, but there was grazing for the camels. Having made a hasty meal of bread and dates, we moved on westerly, crossing the Salt Desert. Our guide urged us to be expeditious, to avoid our enemies, who, so soon as we departed from the Toomun, he said, would also start by another road, and meet us in the desert. About ten at night we espied a light, and soon came to a shepherd's hut fenced round by bushes to keep in his sheep; he brought out a carpet, and after the usual salutation told us, that thirty Uffghans had been there inquiring for us, and had gone to occupy a pass in the hills. He then produced sour milk, and we bought a goat, which my men slew in an instant and devoured; we then advanced a few miles, and striking out of the path, lay down to rest in a small patch of barley cultivation.

23d March. Rising before day light we marched westerly, and crossed what was once a fine tract, but now, from drought, a waste. We halted to breakfast at the ruins of Gholam Shah: part of the town still remains; we found here a small tank of rain water, and after two hours rest continued our route: sand hills very near us on the right; the tract to the right is called Dhak, and is very bare: we passed a Belooche Toomun and flocks, but could not venture to go near them on account of the party looking out for us. It came on to rain with thunder and lightning and a high wind, which raised the sand in our faces, so as to compel us to take refuge for some hours under the lee of a bank, with our backs to the wind; on clearing up we advanced a little farther and halted to sleep.

24th March. After supper and a few hours rest we rose and mounted; the air was cold with slight rain and fog; we halted for breakfast at seven in the morning, a range of mountains in front, and a curious looking hill on the left about ten miles distant, in the shape of a cone, called Mekhé Roostum. We had then got on a hard flat sand, without a trace of vegetation; we resumed our route after breakfast, the range a-head approaching, and a fine heath appeared at its base, so putting my camel into a smart trot, we soon reached it and halted among some low bushes and trees, sending two or three Belooches to look for water: they were indefatigable in their search, and soon returned telling us that they had found a Toomun, with plenty of good rain water, two miles off; they also brought a goat with them as a present to Jooma Khan, who, they had affirmed, was going on pilgrimage. This jungle is called Chaguy, there is a fine pasture in it; and within one day's journey to the southward are salt water pools very narrow but deep.

25th March. We halted until mid-day for the sake of grazing the cattle; the sleep refreshed us all, although we lay in our cloaths and arms, to be prepared for attack, and about one *p. m.* we mounted, and soon got to the range in front. It comes round in a circle from Kharan, and terminates at no great distance to the northward of where I passed it. The whole country on the right is a desert up to Kandahar; over the range (I afterwards found) are two passes, the northern one in our line was said to be occupied by the Uffghans, to avoid whom we took a circuitous route to the left, and doubling these hills got into a route parallel, and arrived at Koochen the third day, (*27th March*). Here fine water is abundant. Each day's march I saw flocks of sheep throughout the district called Pooshtc Koh, or back of the mountains. We met on the *27th* a party of Belooches coming from the northward, and carrying their women, children, tents, and flocks, towards the mountains of Mukran; they told us that they were flying from Gurmsyl, having heard that Futteh Khan, the minister of the King of Kabool, was on his way there from Kandahar.

28th March. We marched before day-light, and travelled a little northward of west, over shifting sand hills, stopping to breakfast at Mummoo; this place derives its name from being the spot where the Peer, or saint, Mulick Mummoo was buried, and the Belooches demanded charity for good luck. They exacted flour and dates from Jooma Khan and myself, in proportion to the number of our camels, and having made bread, it was equally dealt out to every one; they were all punctual at prayers at the shrine, excepting Jooma Khan and another who were excused on account of their youth. At Mummoo we had bad water, but advancing in the afternoon, westerly seven miles, we came to Kulchee, also celebrated as being the seat of a Peer, who produced a small well of excellent water, by striking his spear through the rock: we quitted this spot after dinner, and when it became dusk halted at the end of four miles north-west to sleep.

29th March. We encountered the sand-hills again, and moved twelve miles to breakfast among them and Guz * bushes. Here we met unloaded camels returning to Gurmsyl. After breakfast we had a tedious march over uneven ground with sand and gravel. At fifteen miles we dismounted under cover of some low sand-hills, after the most fatiguing march I ever experienced, of which forty-five miles had no water; however, the Helmind river was near, and I knew that it would amply repay us for our sufferings.

30th March. This morning we started early, and descending the sand hills in a north-westerly direction, soon got upon a hard gravelly desert, and at eleven miles arrived at the bank of the Helmind: we descended by ravines and entered a valley, about one and a half or two miles across, the river Helmind flowing down between fine tamarisk jungle. Here we halted, and forgetting all our past troubles, sat down and began to cook our bread and prepare for breakfast.

From Nooshky to the Helmind river is, by my estimation, a hundred and ninety-one miles, which we made in nine marches; the three first are rather long (twenty-five miles each), and fresh rain water is to be had on the second day: the route is mostly over hard sand. The fourth march is short: the fifth and sixth rather long; however, there is a good supply of water, and the road, though hilly, is not difficult or tedious. The seventh march, to Kulchee, is very long, tedious, and difficult, from the sand-hills, and likewise has bad water. The eighth march has no water, and is tedious. The last is a short march of eleven miles. We ought to have compressed the three last into two, which would only have made them thirty-two miles each. There is forage for camels the whole way, and at Dhak, Chaguy, and Booloo sheep are to be had.

* The tamarisk.

The Helmind river runs from Kandahar south-west and westerly into Seistan, where it takes a circuit round the hills about four days' journey from Dooshak, and forms a lake. At Pullaluk it is about four hundred yards wide, very deep, with uncommonly fine water. About half a mile of the country on each side is cultivated by irrigation, and the desert then rises in perpendicular cliffs. The banks abound with the tamarisk, and also afford grazing for cattle. Kandahar was seven Munzils or stages from our halting place to day; the intermediate country is much infested by robbers, and is very barren. During the day we continued our march along the banks of the river, passing ruins of villages and fortlets. At night we halted in the jungle near an Uffghan village, the people of which, perceiving the smoke arising from the fire we were cooking our bread with, came down in hopes to surprize us. We had mostly gone to sleep, but one of our men, observing the thieves, gave the alarm, and after some argument, they came to terms.

31st March. We arrived this day at Rodbar, and put up at the Toomun of Lunyar Khan, the head of the Towkee tribe of Belooches. He is a fine looking young man, and his men superior to those Belooches whom I had seen at Nooshky, of whom they are a subdivision. I passed here for a Hajee or pilgrim, though I believe the chief took me for a Persian in disguise.

1st April. This day we entered Seistan, having forded the river (after two unsuccessful attempts) near Rodbar. At night we slept in the ruins of a very large city called Poolkee; here a few men who reside in the ruins made an attempt to steal my camels, but luckily they fixed on one belonging to my guide, Jooma Khan, which they carried off.

2d April. I mounted very early this morning in hope of getting to Illumdar before dark, but about five *p.m.* coming to the Toomun of one of Khan Juhan Khan's Sirdars, my people declared they would not go further that evening, and I was obliged to submit; I, however, threatened to return to Nooshky, which had such an effect that they only loitered for a few hours, and the next morning at day-light we found ourselves within half a mile of Illumdar. By my guide's advice I here halted and sent over for Thalldass, the Hindoo to whom I was recommended. He soon appeared, riding on a poney, when I took him aside, and told him that I was a servant of Soondurjee, and had a bill on him for two hundred rupees, and a letter of recommendation, which last I delivered. After perusing the letter, he told me the money I spoke of was ready, and offered his services in any other way, "but," said he, "the people here are all robbers: you must get rid of these "Belooches and assume the character of a Hadjee, and I will see that, as "such, you shall be furnished with a guide.". I instantly returned to my party and gave them a trifling present, then taking leave of Jooma Khan, I mounted my camel, and rode over to the small town of Ilumdar accompanied by Thalldass, who lodged me in his own house for the night.

3d April. This morning I walked over to see the chief, (called Khan Juhan Khan) who, on being told I was a Hadjee, received me most politely. He was very elegantly dressed, and attended by five or six servants. This chief is quite the terror of all the circumjacent countries, and subsists almost entirely by plunder, having very little territory.

4th April. In the course of the day I settled accounts with Thalldass, who had been so fortunate as to get me the best guide in this country. I made him a present for the trouble I had given him, and prepared every thing for starting as soon as possible.

Seistan is a very small province on the banks of the Helmind, comprising not more than five hundred square miles, bounded on the north and north-east by Khorasan, on the west by Persia, and on the south and south-east it is separated from Mukran by an uninhabited desert. The only parts of Seistan now inhabited are the banks of the Helmind river, the bed of which annually sinks, and the desert on either side has been making proportional encroachments.

We entered Seistan at the town of Rodbar; there the banks of the river are well cultivated and fruitful, having a fine rich soil, irrigated by the stream, but the utmost breadth of this fertile stripe does not exceed two miles, whence the desert rises in lofty cliffs, and extends over an uninterrupted tract, without water or vegetation, to the great road from Heerat to Kandahar on the one side, and on the other, down towards the route pursued by Lieutenant Pottinger from Nooshky to Dizuk and Bunpoor. The country, although now only inhabited by Uffghans and Belooches in felt tents, still bears the marks of former civilization and opulence; and there are ruins of villages, forts, and windmills along the whole route from Rodbar to Dooshak, the capital, which is now called Julallabad, in honour of the chief's eldest son.

The first place which excites attention is Kykobad, about five miles from Rodbar. This was formerly the residence of Shah Kai Khoosroo; nothing, however remains, but the parapets and towers of a small square fort, and the mud walls of buildings adjacent, formerly inhabited by his mother. On crossing the river we came to Synabad, on the north-west bank of it, which is, however, of modern date, and said to have been inhabited by Arabs; hence, by mistake of my guide, I crossed the desert to Poolkee, twenty-five miles, whereby I lost an opportunity of seeing the city of Kuleaput on the river; the palace there, they say, is still in good preservation, but of the size of the city or time of its foundation I could get no intelligence. Poolkee exhibits the remains of a once large and flourishing city; the ruins of its walls, houses, and gardens, cover at least a space of sixteen square miles; the banks of the Helmind are here extremely luxuriant, and afford fine pasturage for sheep, of which I observed large flocks. The river is about two hundred yards broad, not fordable, and extremely picturesque. We staid at this place with a Toomun of hospitable Nousherwanee Beloochees, who, however, would not be answerable for the safety of our camels, as we had now, they said, got into the midst of the robbers, and we were consequently obliged to have a portion of our party always on the alert.

Ilumdar was built and peopled by Khan Juhan Khan, the most noted robber in this country, and the terror of all the Karwans that travel between Heerat and Kandahar. The country here assumes a new feature; instead of the cultivation being confined to the narrow stripe on each side of the river, large channels have been cut, and the water well distributed over the face of the country, and thus much must be said in justice to Khan Juhan Khan, that although he is a greater robber than his neighbours, his country is in a far better state of cultivation.

I staid at Ilumdar on the 6th, and on the 7th, accompanied by Thalldass, I rode over four miles to the city of Julallabad, also called Dooshak. The ruins of the ancient city cover at least as much ground as the city of Isfahan: it has been built in the same way as the other towns in Seistan, of half burnt brick, the houses with vaulted roofs, and two stories high. The modern city of Julallabad is neat and in a state of improvement, it contains about two thousand houses, and has a tolerable Bazar; it is governed by Behram Khan Kyanee, of a very ancient and independent family; but his revenues do not amount to more than thirty thousand rupees, and he has not power to restrain the depredations of Khan Juhan Khan. From Dooshak to Kirman in Persia is twenty days journey for a horseman, and the same to Yezd, over a desert with little water; this road leads past Ghaen, (famous for its manufacture of carpets,) and Khubees, of which I obtained no information.

8*th of April.* Having taken leave of my attentive friend, Thalldas, I left Dooshak this day about eight *a. m.*, my guide, whose name was Moolla Gunnee, was an Uffghan of the Ghiljee tribe from Joaeen, a man of information, which he was ready to communicate, good tempered and cheerful, and he was, (what I prized much,) well mounted; it was so great a contrast to the slow movements of the Belooches, that I went off in high spirits, and after passing the small villages of Akbar and Doulatabad, we quitted Seistan about twenty five miles north of Dooshak, and entered Khorasan, travelling on over a bare hard desert, with a gentle ascent. Throughout the forenoon we made, at an easy trot, twenty-five miles; when we arrived at the ruins of the city of Peshawuroon, which are of immense extent, we rode directly through them for upwards of five miles. A little farther on we came to the tomb of Syud Ikbal: here is a well of sulphurous water. It is the usual halting place for a strong party, but as we were not such in point of number, our guide deemed it proper to move on; we therefore did so, and at thirty-four miles halted in the ruins of the old town of Joaeen in the Zillah of Oke. We had our cattle in the ruins, and lay down to sleep supperless, being afraid to light a fire, lest the smoke should point out our situation to the straggling bands of robbers who infest this country.

9*th of April.* This morning we went over to the fort and inhabited village, and alighted at the house of my guide. Uffghans flocked to visit me, and I was introduced by the Moollah as a Syyud going on pilgrimage. They were pleased to see me, and paid me great attention, asking me what description of Syud I was, I told them Korreshee. My guide had now killed a sheep, and soon after we sat down, together with my camel drivers and a visitor, to a large bowl of soup and bouillé. When breakfast was over I was glad to get rid of my visitors, by lying down, and pretending to be much fatigued by my ride. I passed the next day much in the same way, waiting until my guide had procured a forged letter of recommendation from Mohummud Khan Ghiljee to an Uffghan at the town of Furrah.

Joaeen is a fertile little spot in the district of Oke, nearly encompassed by hills, whence a stream issues and supplies the whole valley; here they have horizontal windmills to raise the water, as well as for grinding corn. The fort is, (like all Persian-built forts,) lofty, with thin, weak walls, surrounded by a small ditch, flanked by circular towers. The people of

Joaeen are under Mohummud Khan, chief of a tribe of the Ghiljees; he lives at Durg, a fort within two miles of Joaeen; he maintains four hundred horse, and is dreaded all over the country. Having procured the letter, and got Mohummud Khan's seal to it, we slept outside at night, and the next morning marched a little eastward of north; at fifteen miles we came to a spring of excellent water, where we halted two or three hours, and then proceeded on ten miles further, and stopped at sun-set in a water-course. No forage procurable, though contiguous to Eliasabad, a small village.

10th of April. This day we got to Furrah, and rode straight to the house of Ibrahim Khan, for whom I had the forged letter. He came out, and having read it, ordered carpets to be spread, and received us hospitably. I spent the heat of the day in his garden, unmolested; our host and his brother joined us at dinner, which consisted of the standing Uffghan dish of mutton soup and bouillé.

In the evening a Moollah came down to see me, and being troublesome, I pretended to be sleepy, and went to rest; however, he was not to be put off by this artifice. He found I had been breathing upon necklaces and into children's mouths, that they might derive all the benefit a Syyud could bestow, and being fond of argument, he said he had come down to converse with me. He had a large book under his arm, and was questioned by my guide about some property acquired in a certain way, whether it was lawful or not. The Moollah began to expound the law, adding, that he spoke with diffidence in presence of the Syyud, and then appealed to me to know whether he was right or not. I unthinkingly nodded assent, and when that point was discussed, he commenced his attack on me by asking whether I was a Sheea or a Soonnee *. I answered him the latter, on which he repeated my words, observing, it was not a proper reply for a Syyud. I was at a loss, and took that opportunity to talk to some other persons, who had addressed themselves to me, hoping to get rid of this question, but the persevering Moollah would not be quieted so easily; after a short interval, he said with the greatest placidity imaginable, "You have not, perhaps, heard "the question I put to you, if you please, I will repeat it," which he did. I replied in Hindoostanee, that I did not comprehend him sufficiently to

* The Sheeas and Soonnees are the two great classes of Moosulmans. The Persians are all Sheeas, and I fancy I was taken for one.

hazard an opinion on the subject; he then called Gunnee, my guide, to interpret, supposing I did not understand Persian. Gunnee kindly explained and got me out of the scrape. When the Moollah went away, Gunnee said, you must observe, that one hundred negatives are better than one affirmative when you wish to avoid entering into an argument, for then no one can catch at your words or expressions. This advice I strictly followed afterwards, and made a point of denying knowledge of the Hudees *, Koran, &c., by which I avoided much trouble and altercation, perhaps, discovery, during the four days I halted here.

Furrah is a large walled town, situated in a fertile valley, half way nearly and on the high road from Kandahar to Heerat †. It is said to have a good Bazar, but as it is easy to enter a town, and extremely difficult to get out of it again, I would not venture into it, and staid entirely in the gardens, about a mile off. The valley is well watered by a stream from the mountains, and the gardens are extensive. The Uffghans pay no land tax here, and the Bazar duties are trifling.

From Dooshak to Furrah is about sixty-five miles, or three easy marches for a horseman. The first march is twenty-five miles without fuel or water: the two last have both, and are short, but the whole country is a barren, open desert.

14*th April*. This day a Karwan was to have set off for Heerat, and I was to join them, however, for six rupees worth of chintz, my Dooshak guide offered to accompany me half-way to the former city. I agreed, and mounted his brother-in-law on one of my camels, as an additional security. We marched north-westerly, on a good hard road, over flats surrounded by barren low hills and no cultivation; we passed the Karwan about sun-set, and determined to push on without them. At twenty-one miles we came to a range of hills, and entering a "Rood Khanu," or river bed, arrived at Unardurru, the most beautiful and romantic spot possible to be conceived. Unardurru is a small town built on a rivulet, in a valley half a mile in width, between lofty bare rocks. At the base of these rocks, on one side, are the houses, and on the opposite side are gardens full of apricot, mulberry, peach, apple, pear, and other fruit trees.

* The law, or word of God.

† There is another road over the hills by Subzwar.

15*th April.* We passed on between the gardens this morning at day-light, and at two miles arrived at the extremity of the valley: here we put up in a mosque, and in the evening marched again, northerly and east of north, between hills; no cultivation. At seventeen miles we left the road, and striking to the right of it, halted about thirty-two miles from Unardurru, in a dry water-course near the village of Okul. This evening, as my guide was riding on the camel with me, he observed that the people of the country would call out Hyyu Toubah, alas!! alas!! if I neglected my prayers. I excused myself on the plea of no water to wash; "take sand," said he; and at even-tide, being a little in front, he stopped to go to prayers. I could not decline joining him, and therefore watching his motions, I went through the forms; however, I did not repeat this afterwards, for having come on thus far in safety, I considered that the most likely way to lose the divine protection would be treating devotion with levity.

16*th April.* We moved six miles to an unfrequented Zearutgah, or seat of a saint, in the desert; and after bidding adieu to my guide, who went over to the village of Okul, I started for Heerat at three *p.m.*, trusting to Providence for safety on the road. Okul is a small place in the south-east corner of an immense valley, which lies between two high ridges running east and west. Parts of this valley, in the centre, are cultivated, and near the village there is plenty of water.

On quitting the Zearutgah, we travelled north-east until we gained the extreme end of the mountains, at that corner of the valley. We then entered on a fine road, the hills still continuing on our left, though diminished in size and immense mountains on the right running off to the east-north-east. At twenty miles came to a well of brackish water. This is the regular stage for Karwans, but we kept on west-north-west, good road and low hills on either side. At thirty miles we halted to sleep among the hillocks to the east of the path.

17*th April.* At day-light I moved again north-north-west, winding over the hills. We had hardly gone six miles ere we espied six armed Uffghans coming after us all well mounted; my guide blew his matchlock, I primed all the pistols; and moving our party to the left of the road, took up an elevated station within musket-shot of it. Here we alighted, and the guide, who alone had a matchlock, knelt down. The Uffghans advanced along the road until they came opposite to us, and then asked who we were. The guide replied that I was a Peerzadu, or devotee, of Mohummud Khan Ghiljee, and going on pilgrimage to Mushid in Khorasan. The last horseman turned his horse towards us, on which my guide, waving his hand, told him if he advanced a step farther he would fire at him. The Uffghan, on this, asked, "What will you do with one matchlock against six of us who are "well armed?" "Very true," said the guide, "but take away the old "man at the head of you, who goes for nothing, and we are five as good as you." "Put up your arms," said the old man, "and do not let the Peer-"zadu suppose we are robbers or murderers;" on which they turned their horses and rode off.

We now resumed our journey, well satisfied with having got rid of the Uffghans so peaceably, and at eight miles we came to a well called Plessy. This is also a halting-place for Karwans, having good water and forage. Here we opened on a spacious plain between two ridges of hills running east and west, intersected by deep ravines. We turned out of the direct road and went to the right across the country to avoid meeting any more Uffghans. At noon we halted at the foot of the northern range of mountains, in a hollow where there was a well of brackish water. After we had breakfasted, we marched on round the base of the mountain, and crossing successive deep ravines, between which we had a good road, at twenty-one miles arrived at the top of a pass, short and not difficult. At night we halted in the Dushté Ham, or desert of Ham, on the top of the mountains bounding the valley of Heerat.

18th April. We mounted early and marched twenty-five miles before we breakfasted at a small Zearutgah, after which eight miles more brought us to the city of Heerat, the intermediate country bare except in the vicinity of the different villages.

The road from Furrah to Unardurru being good, and not hilly, it is an easy stage of twenty-one miles although no water intermediate. From Unardurru to Okul is one long and very tedious march, and usually made by Karwans in two; the road is rough and lies between hills, and though Okul is out of the way, by going that route we had less to fear from robbers. From Okul the road is tolerable, but the water very brackish at the first stage, and none farther on till you come to Plessy; thence to Heerat you have no water except a little salt well at six miles; this last is a long stage, being thirty miles to the Zearutgah, and eight from thence to the city.

The city of Heerat is situated in a valley, surrounded by lofty mountains, and contiguous to the northern ridge, which separates it from the country of

Bokhara. The valley extends at least thirty miles, from east to west, and is about fifteen broad, watered by a river rising in the mountains and running through the centre; it is highly cultivated, and the whole face of it is covered with villages and gardens. The approach to Heerat from the Zearutgah, lies four miles between orchards, with a capital road; at the end of this road we came to the river, over which there is a very ancient bridge, four hundred yards in length, built of burnt brick, and said to have been erected by an oil woman at her own private expence; it is now, however, miserably decayed, and will soon tumble to pieces unless the government repair it. Previous to the building of this bridge the communication between the city and country was yearly cut off, on the melting of the snow in the mountains, and the consequent swell of the river. When we had passed the bridge, we rode four miles through the suburbs along a good road, to the city gate.

The city covers an area of four square miles, and is fortified by a lofty mud wall, with towers and a wet ditch; in the northern face is a citadel elevated on a mound above the wall; this is a small square castle with towers at the angles, built of burnt brick, the whole in line with the wall, and encompassed by a wet ditch, over which is a draw-bridge. Beyond this, there is also a recently constructed outer wall and dry ditch.* The city has a gate in each face, and two in the northern one; but on the whole it is very contemptible as a fortification.

From each gate Bazars lead to the "Char Soobh," or market-place, in the centre of the town, which are spacious and well lined with shops; the principal one extends from the south gate to the Gunje Bazar, or cattle-market, in front of the citadel, and is covered in with a vaulted roof the whole length. These streets and the Char Soobh are so filled with the crowd of people on Thursday (the Bazar day), as to be almost impassable. On either side as you go along are large spacious Suraés, where the merchants have their Kothees, or factories; the city is well supplied with water, every Suraé having a Houz, or cistern, independant of the public ones on either side the Bazar streets. The meanest building in appearance, is the residence of the prince, of which you see no more than a common-gate way, over which is a wretched building, and in front an open square, with galleries in the centre, for the Nukurah Khana, or kettle-drums.

The Musjidé Jooma, or Friday's Mosque, was once a grand building, comprising an area eight hundred yards square, but this is fast going to decay. The private buildings in Heerat are by no means in this state, for no city has less ground unoccupied, and none, for its extent, can boast of a greater population. Heerat and its suburbs are computed to contain above one hundred thousand inhabitants, of whom ten thousand are Uffghans, the rest are Moghuls, a few Jews, and six hundred Hindoos. The Hindoos are here highly respected, and alone possess capital. The government is sensible of their value, and they have in consequence much influence. They live in the best Suraés, and have gardens outside, but do not venture to bring their families with them to this city.

Heerat is a city of more trade than perhaps any other in Asia under a native government; it is called by distinction the Bunder, or port, and is the emporium between Kabool, Kandahar, Hindoostan, Kashmeer, and Persia, Bagdad, &c. From the four former it receives shawls, indigo, sugar, chintz, muslin, bafta, kincob, hides, and leather, which are exported to Mushid, Yezd, Tehraun, Bagdad, and Kirman; receiving in return, dollars, tea, sugar-candy, china ware, broad-cloth, chintz, silk, copper, pepper, and all kinds of spices, dates, shawls, numuds, and carpets. The hides which are imported from Hindoostan return a profit of one hundred per cent. nett; indeed, the whole trade is uncommonly advantageous to any one possessing capital. The currency here is that of Muhmood Shahee rupees, but accounts are kept in Kureem Khanee, at one hundred and twenty-five per hundred Muhmood Shahees.

The staples of Heerat are silk, saffron, and assafœtida, which are exported to Hindoostan; the silk cloths are not equal to the manufacture of Persia. The gardens are full of mulberry trees reared solely for the sake of the silk worm, and all the plains and hills round Heerat, particularly to the westward, produce assafœtida. It grows to the height of two or three feet, the stem two inches in diameter, and the head, when ripe, is yellow and resembles a cauliflower; the Hindoos and the Belooches are fond of it, they eat it by roasting the stem in the ashes, and stewing the head of it like other greens. It still, however, preserves its fœtid taste and smell.

The gardens of Heerat are extensive; the Oordooé Bagh, belonging to the Prince and Baghé Shahee, planted by Tymoor Shah (this being his favourite seat,) are the only public ones, and now only attended to for their annual produce, which is sold in the Bazar. Leading to the latter is an avenue one mile in length, between fir trees; and adjoining are four minarets of a mosque that was intended for the tomb of the Imam Moosa Allee

Reza, who, however, was disappointed of his visit to Heerat by dying at Mushid.

The villages in the neighbourhood of Heerat are numerous, and nothing can exeeed the fertility of this valley; wheat and barley are most abundant, and fruit of all kinds amazingly cheap. When I was at Heerat, the horses were all at Bagh, up a place one stage over the mountains, for the benefit of the fine grass procurable there. They are generally half bred, but the merchants from Bokhara bring Toorkumanee horses, that sell in proportion to their height. The most celebrated breeder in this country is Booniad Beg of the tribe of Huzaree; he resides in the mountains towards Mushid, and has large herds of horses and mares: his colts are highly prized, and are often sold for from one to four thousand rupees * each. The tolls at Heerat are two rupees on every camel load going out of the city, and one anna, or sixteenth of a rupee on every twenty rupees' worth of merchandize sold in it. This is levied from the purchaser by the Suraédar or tax-gatherer, who farms the tolls from government. Although, the toll on camels appears so very trivial, it is avoided by every means, to a large extent, of which I had an opportunity of knowing two or three instances. The revenues are estimated at four and a half lacs of rupees, and are levied on the Suraes, shops and gardens; a part is taken in kind, or grain and cattle; and from the total amount the prince pays fifty thousand rupees annually to the King of Persia.

The government of Heerat is in the hands of the Shahzadah Hadjee Fejroozoodeen Khan, third son of the late Tymoor Shah, and full brother to the present Muhmood Shah. He is about fifty years of age, appears to take little active participation in public affairs, but leaves every thing to Hadjee Aga Khan, his minister. In the present distracted state of Khorasan, he endeavours to remain neutral, without incurring the displeasure of either of the contending parties. The prince has two wives, the one a Moghul lady, the other a daughter of Shakoor Khan Douranee, by each of whom he has two sons. Kasim Khan, the eldest, is a good looking young man, about twenty-two years of age. The reins of government being in the hands of a Moghul excites a great degree of jealousy in the minds of the Uffghans, but the prince gives the former a decided preference over his

* 125l. to 500l.

own tribe, as he finds that the rapacious exactions of the former from the subject, are more enforced to enrich his coffers, than they could possibly be through his countrymen, who being accustomed to free and independent tenure of the land, are not so likely to assist in that system of plunder for which the Moghuls are proverbial.

The police of Heerat is strict, not so much for the sake of morality, as for the fines which come into government; and no one can appear in the streets after dark. This city is, of all others in Khorasan, celebrated for cheats, who allure the unsuspecting stranger into their houses to partake of an entertainment, and then lay him by the heels on a false charge of seduction of their female relatives, and breach of hospitality, for which the accused person may consider himself fortunate to escape with a mulct of five hundred rupees. On these occasions they previously inform themselves of the state and condition of the person, and levy accordingly; half of this fine goes to the informer as a reward for his ingenuity, and the other half to the minister and government.

I remained at Heerat nearly a month in my assumed character of a horse-dealer, and declared I should go to Mushid on pilgrimage, a common circumstance among people of that class, who visit this country. I deemed it expedient to announce this as my intention, being thereby furnished with an excuse for leaving Heerat at any time; and what was to me of great moment, without encumbering myself with a number of horses, which I naturally said I could purchase on my return; by this means I only found it necessary to buy two during my sojourn there.

18th and 19th May. Having procured a guide from my Hindoo agent, I left Heerat on the *18th of May* at five *p. m.*; we passed westerly between gardens for about five miles, when the path opened out to cultivated ground, which by degrees diminished, as we left the city and drew near the mountains. At twelve miles we picketted our horses, and lay down to sleep. We moved on again before day-light westerly, passed the large village of Sekhwan at twenty-two miles, and going one mile through it, stopped at a small dervishes' village: the road was good the whole way, but it blew a gale of wind, and the clouds of sand were very troublesome. I had now the satisfaction of knowing that we had passed the Uffghan frontier, and had entered the dominions of the King of Persia, in which, after my numerous escapes, I felt a comparative degree of security to what I had enjoyed for some months. We halted for two hours, and advanced in the afternoon twelve miles, to Ghoorian, a large town abounding with water, grain, and forage, thirty-five miles from Heerat.

20th May. We marched this morning before day-light, westerly. At ten miles, leaving the tilled ground, we entered on a tract covered with the assafœtida bush, a range of hills in front running north and south, and joining the ridge of mountains which had continued from Heerat upon our right. Having crossed these hills by an easy ascent and tolerable road, at twenty miles we came to a well of good water, where we halted. We marched again at one *p.m.*, crossing a fine plain, on which there are ruins of different villages, formerly destroyed by the Oozbucks, in one of which we put up for the night: no water or forage.

21st, 22d, and 23d May. The former day we got to Kelaté Nadir, where there is plenty of water and forage. Thence we made a march through a very hilly country, and on the third day, after passing a very extensive bare plain, arrived at Khaff.

Khaff is a small town situated immediately under a range of hills well supplied with grain and water, and having much cultivation and many gardens in its vicinity. During the four summer months it blows here a gale of wind day and night, by which the wind-mills are turned. Ghiljee Khan is the governor, and always resides here. We put up in a field of stubble near the town, and proceeded on the next morning.

24th May. We this day altered the direction of our course to north-west, and skirting the hills on the left of the road, crossed a fine cultivated plain. We passed several villages, and halted at Sherawan, thirty-four miles. This march there is water and forage the whole way, with large flocks of sheep. At Sherawan the wind decreased, which had annoyed us so much at Khaff.

25th, 26th, and 27th May. Our march on the *25th* was north-westerly only twelve miles, as I was obliged to halt, on account of a fever which I had had for several days, at a fine village called Skar, that is famous for the almonds it produces. My intention otherwise was to have gone on eight miles farther to Sungoon, where I arrived on the *26th.* At Sungoon the water is brackish and the country hilly. We moved on the *27th,* north-west and westerly, and at sixteen miles arrived at Tujurrood, a compact village among hills. These three stages, from Sherawan to Tujurrood, may be performed by a horseman in one day with great ease. From Tujurrood we crossed two or three small hills; and travelling south-west, halted at night at a miserable village called Chilsar twelve miles from it.

28th May. We marched very early in the morning, and leaving the hills, (the mountainous ridge on our right running off to the north-west,) crossed a fine flat, but no water. At sixteen miles arrived at a large village called Nasuray, water brackish. Here we halted and had something to eat, after which we advanced in the evening twelve miles to Oonshy. At eight of these twelve miles the road from Mushid to Heerat joins. This is a large village with a little cultivation, and plenty of good water and flocks of sheep. A Karwansuraé here also gave us the first idea of approaching civilization.

29th May. From Oonshy we crossed over five miles this morning to an old ruined Suraé on the edge of the desert; plenty of water, but no supplies. We marched again at three *p.m.*, keeping close to mountains on our left, first going west and then south. The road to Tubbus lies over the hills to the left, but is only inhabited for eight fursukhs *, and being stony is not so good for camels as that of the desert, which I therefore adopted. We came to wells at three miles, at seven, and also at eleven; at which last I stopped to refresh for four hours, and then continued on south-westerly for thirty-seven miles We found dry wells every fursukh, and at the twenty-fifth mile, one with water in it.

30th May. Marching this morning before day-light, we altered our course more westerly. At twelve miles obtained water at a well where the Karwans halt. We proceeded on seven miles to the village of Ispuk. It is a small place and abounds with grain, fruit, water, forage, and sheep. From Oonshy it is four easy marches for laden camels. We continued our route the same day between hills until we came to Dehi Mahomed, at fifteen miles. Here is a capital Suraé, a Hindoo shopkeeper, good water, grain, and forage.

31st May. From Dehi Mahomed to Chardih: first twelve miles loose gravel, descending gradually; then wind round a peak on the left, good road over a desert, and along the base of a ridge of mountains. At twenty-four miles arrived at Chardih. Eight miles south-east of this place is the city of Tubbus.

---

* A Fursukh or Parasang is three miles and seven-eighths.

Chardih is composed of four small villages, and well supplied with water, grain, and forage; there is a Suraé a little out of repair. Thence to Khaff is performed in thirteen stages, by Karwans, but a horseman will do it in eight with great ease, one march of thirty-seven miles being alone tedious, the road is tolerably good the whole way.

1st and 2d June. We marched from Chardih, eleven miles westerly, on the *1st*, and slept in a dry water course; whence the following day, ascending between hills, we came to Kulbut, ten miles; there is no cultivation here, and only a Hindoo shopkeeper, who supplies a Suraé with bread and barley; water brackish.

3d June. We marched southerly over a hilly rough road, with ravines, and halted at eighteen miles, at Shootooran. Here we procured bread and barley for the horses; but the water is bad.

4th June. We moved at five *a. m.* descending sand hills south-westerly; at first the road lay through deep sand, afterwards over a hard flat; no water; at twenty-four miles Pooshté Baddam, a large village, at which supplies of every kind are abundant.

5th June. Our march this day was southerly, with a gentle ascent; at five miles a stream of water. In the evening we halted at Illahabad, fourteen miles from Pooshté Baddam; this village is situated in the desert, has a new Suraé, and supplies are procurable.

6th June. From Illahabad to Sahganna, a short stage of ten miles; there is no Suraé here, but grain, and good water are plentiful.

7th June. From Sahganna to Rezab, along a narrow road winding over small hills, mountains close on our right, and to the left distant five miles; at eight miles we arrived at Rezab, a good Suraé, with grain and forage; water bad.

8th June. March south-west; at fourteen miles entered a dry river bed, winding between hills, that spring from an immense range of mountains, which runs east and west; at fourteen miles we found water; we then ascended a steep intricate path, among and over rocks, to Kharanee, which is twenty miles from Sahganna: here is a good Suraé, bread, grain, and forage abundant, the water the same, but brackish.

9th June. We marched from Kharanee southerly between rocky mountains, about a mile distant on each side; at six miles the route tends south-east over a little plain; at twelve miles there is a cistern of good water. Here the mountains diverge on the right; at seventeen miles the road is stony and bad; at twenty miles enter a sandy desert, range of mountains on the left running off across the sandy plain; at twenty six miles the city of Yezd.

From Chardih to Kulbut, Karwans go in two stages; the second is tedious and no water; thence it is eighteen miles to Shootooran, with plenty of water; the fourth stage to Pooshté Baddam is a very long one, whence to Yezd is five easy marches, well supplied with water and forage. A horseman well mounted, will, however, travel from Kulbut to Yezd in six days. The road all the way from Heerat to Yezd has suffered from the former incursions of the Oozbucks, who ravaged the country, and destroyed the reservoirs for containing rain water. The distances are:

Khaff	117 miles.
Chardih	210
Yezd	151
	478 miles.

Yezd is a very large and populous city, situated on the edge of a sandy desert, contiguous to a range of mountains running east and west. It is called the Dar-ool Ibadut, or seat of worship, but with more propriety might be termed the Dar-ool Amanut, or seat of safety, which is applied to Kirman; as it is celebrated by all merchants, for the protection afforded to speculators, and the security of its inhabitants and their property. It is the grand mart between Hindoostan, Khorasan, Bagdad, and Persia, and is said to be a place of greater trade than any other in the latter empire; the Bazar is extensive and well supplied: the city contains twenty thousand houses, besides those of the Guebres, or ancient Persians, who are reckoned at four thousand; they are an industrious race, though sadly oppressed, being taxed at twenty-five rupees a head, besides various other means of extortion, which the Persian government possesses; the revenue paid to the king from Yezd, is three lacs of rupees yearly.

Yezd being situated in a sandy plain, it produces little of itself, and that too with infinite labour; a tract of gardens and orchards has been cultivated near the base of the hills, where very fine apricots and melons are grown. The manufactures of Kusb and Aluhee (two sorts of silk cloth) are superior to any of the kind in Persia; the Guebres also make excellent candied sugar, and the Numuds, or felts, from Tuft, (a small village within eight miles,) are equal to the best made at Kirman. Sheep they bring to this place from Sheeraz, and grain from Isfahan. There are at least fifty thousand camels in the city; and a jackass will here sell as high as fifteen tomans, or fifteeen pounds sterling; the city has a mean appearance, and has once had a wall, part of which still remains.

24th June. Leaving Yezd this day, I marched westerly along the base of the hills over a deep sandy road. The gardens on either side extend for six miles. At fourteen miles I passed through a large village called Eshkidur, and winding over sand-hills, altered my course more northerly. At twenty-four miles arrived at Yezdawah, a small town, the country around well cultivated, and affording plenty of water.

25th June. Twelve miles to the small village of Myboot, contiguous to a range of hills on the left; to the right the country is well cultivated. Eight miles hence is Ardakoo, a large village; and ten further, the village of Tafta. At thirty miles I arrived at Oogda.

Oogda is a small village of about one hundred and sixty houses, with a good Suraé, situated on the edge of a desert between two ranges of mountains, running north-west and south-east. Here the authority of the governor of Yezd terminates.

26th June. Moved west and west by south, over the desert. At twenty-seven miles, the village of Charbashee. There is a small Suraé here; the water bad, but forage cheap.

27th June. Crossing the hills on the left of the road, at six miles, we got good water and fine grazing, where we halted two hours: thence the country hilly and tolerably cultivated. At twenty-seven miles halted at Gutchkoo, a large village with a Suraé and abundance of every thing.

28th June. From Gutchkoo moved on three miles between hills, then opened out on a plain, a ridge of mountains in front, about twenty-five miles, good road, due west; at six miles the village of Mooshkynoon, and three miles in advance from it is a Houz or cistern of good water. Thence it is nine miles to Koopah, where I halted: a good Suraé here, built by Shah Abbass the Great.

29th June. Marched over the plain. A well at every fursukh; road west-south-west. At fifteen miles passed the village of Nadir Shool, and at thirty miles halted at Nooshkynoon, where there is a good Suraé; it is a small village close to a range of mountains, and we had grain and forage in abundance.

30th June. From Nooshkynoon I travelled west thirty miles; mountains at west-south-west, distant ten or fifteen leagues. Here the road enters among gardens, and nine miles farther I arrived at the palace of the Umeen Ood Doulu in Isfahan. The aggregate distance from Yezd to Isfahan I computed to be a hundred and seventy-seven miles. The course principally west, and the road good. I had the pleasure of joining Lieutenant Pottinger at Isfahan, that officer being then on his way to join General Malcolm at Muragha, where we arrived on the 1*st of August*, just seven months after our departure from Bombay.

FINIS.